MW01092087

# Literary Cosmopolitanism in the English *Fin de Siècle*

# Literary Cosmopolitanism in the English *Fin de Siècle*

## *Citizens of Nowhere*

STEFANO EVANGELISTA

# OXFORD
## UNIVERSITY PRESS

Great Clarendon Street, Oxford, OX2 6DP,
United Kingdom

Oxford University Press is a department of the University of Oxford.
It furthers the University's objective of excellence in research, scholarship,
and education by publishing worldwide. Oxford is a registered trade mark of
Oxford University Press in the UK and in certain other countries

© Stefano Evangelista 2021

The moral rights of the author have been asserted

First Edition published in 2021

Impression: 1

All rights reserved. No part of this publication may be reproduced, stored in
a retrieval system, or transmitted, in any form or by any means, without the
prior permission in writing of Oxford University Press, or as expressly permitted
by law, by licence or under terms agreed with the appropriate reprographics
rights organization. Enquiries concerning reproduction outside the scope of the
above should be sent to the Rights Department, Oxford University Press, at the
address above

You must not circulate this work in any other form
and you must impose this same condition on any acquirer

Published in the United States of America by Oxford University Press
198 Madison Avenue, New York, NY 10016, United States of America

British Library Cataloguing in Publication Data
Data available

Library of Congress Control Number: 2021941215

ISBN 978-0-19-886424-0

DOI: 10.1093/oso/9780198864240.001.0001

Printed and bound by
CPI Group (UK) Ltd, Croydon, CR0 4YY

Links to third party websites are provided by Oxford in good faith and
for information only. Oxford disclaims any responsibility for the materials
contained in any third party website referenced in this work.

*For Philip*

# Acknowledgements

My first thanks go to the Arts and Humanities Research Council and the British Academy for generously funding periods of research leave without which this book could not have been written. The Sasakawa Fund enabled an eye-opening visit to archives and museums in Japan. I am extremely grateful to Trinity College and the Faculty of English Language and Literature at Oxford, and would like to acknowledge in particular Ros Ballaster, Elleke Boehmer, Seamus Perry, and Helen Small. Also in the English Faculty, David Dwan, Laura Marcus, and David Russell have provided a bracing mixture of intellectual stimulus and camaraderie. In Trinity College, my special thanks go to my colleagues Kantik Ghosh and Beatrice Groves for their support and friendship.

The ideas discussed in this book have taken shape over a long period of time, evolving in the course of many conversations and travels. During my AHRC fellowship I was fortunate to work side by side Clément Dessy, who shared with me his knowledge of literary cosmopolitanism, periodicals, the Belgian and French *fin de siècle*, and much else besides. Philip Ross Bullock, Clément Dessy, Michiko Kanetake, Catherine Maxwell, Josephine McDonagh, and Valerie Worth all read and commented on one or more draft chapters. I have profited enormously from their insights. Several more colleagues and friends have given advice, criticism, and practical help, or collaborated on activities connected to the research of this book. Among those, I would like to express my gratitude to Emily Apter, Rebecca Beasley, Laurel Brake, Luisa Calè, Denis Eckert, Emily Eells, Hilary Fraser, Regenia Gagnier, Analía Gerbaudo, Katharina Herold, Richard Hibbitt (with whom I shared my first foray into literary cosmopolitanism in our joint issue of *Comparative Critical Studies*), Daichi Ishikawa, Bon Koizumi, Kristin Mahoney, Sandra Mayer, Alex Murray, Ayako Nasuno, Tina O'Toole, Tim Owen, Ana Parejo Vadillo, Matthew Potolsky, Lloyd Pratt, Fraser Riddell, Gisèle Sapiro, and Akiko Yamanaka-Binns. Special thanks are due to Joseph Bristow, Tore Rem, Margaret D. Stetz, and Birgit Van Puymbroeck for their extreme generosity in sharing research and historical sources with me.

Writing about cosmopolitanism teaches one to appreciate the gift of hospitality. For this reason, I would like to offer special thanks to Gesa Stedman and the staff of the Centre for British Studies of the Humboldt-Universität zu Berlin, which has been a home for me for many years. A considerable part of this book was written during various stays in Berlin. The chapter on Lafcadio Hearn was written largely in Paris, during my tenure as visiting professor in the Sorbonne, for which I am extremely thankful to Charlotte Ribeyrol. Other institutions that have invited me to present work in progress include the universities of Amsterdam, Bard College Berlin, Birkbeck, Birmingham, Bologna, Bordeaux, Bristol, Chicago, Copenhagen, Exeter, Georgia (Athens, USA), Glasgow, Lille 3, Paris Sorbonne, Pisa, Royal Holloway, Milan, Stockholm, Sussex, UCLA, and Vienna. My gratitude goes to my hosts in all these places, who have made me welcome and provided me with invaluable opportunities to receive feedback from engaged audiences: Joseph Bristow, Grace Brockington, Matthew Creasy, Roxanne Eberle, Carlotta Farese, Hannah Field, Holly Fling, Laura Giovannelli, Rudolph Glitz, Béatrice Laurent, Ruth Livesey, Ronan Ludot-Vlasak, Josephine McDonagh, Sandra Mayer, Rebecca N. Mitchell, Alex Murray, Francesca Orestano, Lene Østermark-Johansen, Caroline Patey, Charlotte Ribeyrol, Gino Scatasta, Laura Scuriatti, Giles Whiteley. Heartfelt thanks are also due to Leire Barrera-Medrano, Alexander Bubb, Katharina Herold, and Sara Thornton for inviting me to present material from the book at their conferences. I feel particularly lucky to have been able to share my research in the seminar on 'The Politics of Aesthetics' at the Fondation des Treilles, for which I thank Bénédicte Coste, Catherine Delyfer, and Christine Reynier; and in the Institute for World Literature at Harvard, for which my thanks go to David Damrosch and Delia Ungureanu. I also owe a huge debt of gratitude to the members of the Writing1900 group and the AHRC-funded Decadence and Translation Network for many stimulating conversations through the years.

Significant portions of the research for this book have taken place in the Bodleian Library, the British Library, the Butler Library, the Department of Planned Languages of the Österreichische Nationalbibliothek, the Harry Ransom Center, the Howard-Tilton Memorial Library of Tulane University (New Orleans), the New York Public Library, the National Library of Norway, Toyama University Library, and The William Andrews Clark Memorial Library, University of California, Los Angeles. Among the librarians and archivists who have helped me in these places, I would like to thank in particular Elizabeth Adams, Sarah Cox, Sharon Cure, Scott Jacobs, Viv O'Dunne, Emma Sillett, and Bernhard Tuider.

For the provision of images and permission to reproduce them, I would like to acknowledge Punch Cartoon Library/TopFoto; the Master and Fellows of University College, Oxford; Tate; the Sammlung für Plansprachen of the Österreichische Nationalbibliothek; and the Esperanto Association of Britain. The *Imperial Federation Map of the World* has been reproduced from Cornell University Library Digital Collections, and the cover image, Oda Krohg's *Japansk lykt* (Japanese Lantern, 1886) from the National Museum, Norway. I thank the William Andrews Clark Memorial Library, University of California, Los Angeles, for permission to quote from the Oscar Wilde MSS and George Egerton's correspondence; the Harry Ransom Center, The University of Texas at Austin, to quote from the John Lane Company Records and the Lafcadio Hearn Collection; the Henry W. and Albert A. Berg Collection of English and American Literature, the

New York Public Library, Astor, Lenox and Tilden Foundations to quote from the Lafcadio Hearn papers; the National Library of Ireland to quote material from Ola Hansson's letters to George Egerton; and the Manuscripts Division, Special Collections, Princeton University Library to quote from Selected Papers of Mary Chavelita Bright (C0105). Some of the material in Chapter 1 has previously appeared in an essay titled 'Cosmopolitan Classicism: Wilde between Greece and France', in *Oscar Wilde and Classical Antiquity* (OUP, 2017). My thanks to Kathleen Riley and the other editors of that volume for allowing me to use it again here.

Finally, my heartfelt thanks go to Jacqueline Norton, who has been an ideal editor, and to Aimee Wright, who has guided me through the process of production at OUP.

# Contents

# List of Illustrations

# Note on Translations

I have provided originals for all sources originally written in languages other than English where these attract substantial discussion. English translations are given in the main body of the text, with the original provided in footnotes and occasionally, for very short quotations, in parenthesis. Unless specified, translations of foreign-language material into English are my own. For Japanese names, I have followed the standard Japanese practice of giving surnames followed by first names (e.g. Koizumi Yakumo), unless they appear as part of Western-style bibliographies.

# Introduction

## The Small World of the *Fin de Siècle*

What does it mean to live in a cosmopolitan age? In an essay from 1892, Walter
Pater succinctly defined the late nineteenth century as 'sympathetic, eclectic,
cosmopolitan, full of curiosity and abounding in the "historic sense"'.[1] It is
impossible not to be struck by Pater's inclusion of cosmopolitanism alongside
such keywords of Victorian liberal humanism as sympathy and curiosity. Pater,
who was nearing the end of his career as one of Britain's foremost critics and
stylists, had never used this word before in print. He now associated cosmopolitanism with habits of discrimination and comparison that characterized good
criticism: it denoted a type of intellectual distinction that combined power of
observation with the capacity to situate one's point of view always in a longer
historical perspective and in relation to the wider world. In Pater's specific
context, this meant looking beyond and maybe against the grain of English culture
for new ideas and outlooks—which explains the link to eclecticism and, later in
the same essay, to the act of 'removing prejudice'.[2] Given how notoriously
painstaking Pater was in his choice of words, his prominent reference to cosmopolitanism as an attribute of the 'genius of the nineteenth century' should give
us pause.[3]

Derived from the ancient Greek for 'world citizenship', cosmopolitanism asks
individuals to imagine themselves as part of a community that reaches beyond the
geographical, political, and linguistic boundaries of the nation. For the Greek
cynic philosopher Diogenes, who is credited as having coined the term, cosmopolitanism was a category of resistance and non-belonging. When asked where he
came from, Diogenes memorably retorted that he was 'a citizen of the world'
(κοσμοπολίτης), implying that his outlook and loyalties would not be bound by
the limits of any one *polis* or state.[4] Closer to Pater's time, Immanuel Kant posited
the desirability of 'a universal *cosmopolitan existence*' that would enable people
from all nations to join together in a 'great federation', where the rights and

---

[1] Walter Pater, 'Introduction', in *The Purgatory of Dante Alighieri: An Experiment in Literal Verse
Translation*, tr. C. L. Shadwell (London and New York: Macmillan, 1892), pp. xiii–xxviii (p. xv).
[2] Ibid., p. xvi.    [3] Ibid., p. xiv.
[4] Diogenes Laertius, *Diogenis Laertii Vitae Philosophorum*, ed. Miroslav Marcovich, 3 vols (Stuttgart
and Leipzig: Teubner, 1999–2002), i, 414 (6.63).

*Literary Cosmopolitanism in the English* Fin de Siècle: *Citizens of Nowhere*. Stefano Evangelista,
Oxford University Press. © Stefano Evangelista 2021. DOI: 10.1093/oso/9780198864240.003.0001

security of all would be safeguarded.[5] Kant, who also developed the idea of universal human rights, saw cosmopolitanism as a great political and ethical project, integral to the realization of the civilizing mission of the Enlightenment. But while for Kant cosmopolitanism was a utopian vision or, at best, 'a feeling [that] is beginning to stir',[6] for Pater it was part of the material and historical reality of the present. Crucially, it was also intimately associated with literature. It is significant that Pater's remarks occur in the introduction to a new translation of Dante. The concept of cosmopolitanism enables Pater to explain the universal appeal of Dante, that is, the qualities that make his work readily intelligible and attractive to different ages and nations, even through the distancing medium of translation. At the same time, cosmopolitanism refers to a distinctive literary orientation of the present that, more and more, removes 'certain barriers to a right appreciation' of foreign authors, such as Dante, and, in so doing, makes readers less insular in their tastes, more open-minded, and readier to value 'strangeness' as a positive quality.[7] In fact, Pater openly contrasts the cosmopolitanism of his time with the failure of the eighteenth century to appreciate Dante: 'If the characteristic minds of the last century, for instance, were apt to undervalue him, that was because they were themselves of an age not of cosmopolitan genius, but of singularly limited gifts, gifts temporary and local.'[8] Counterintuitively, the lofty abstract ideals of the eighteenth century led to a type of narrowness, according to Pater, whereas the nineteenth century is when cosmopolitanism becomes a true constituent of the modernity of the age.

Pater's attempt to reclaim cosmopolitanism was symptomatic of a period in which this concept came under increasing pressure from writers. Some three decades earlier, Charles Baudelaire—whose writings were foundational for Pater and his English contemporaries—had laid out the cosmopolitan tendencies of artistic modernity in his essay 'The Painter of Modern Life' ('Le Peintre de la vie moderne', 1863). Baudelaire defined cosmopolitanism as the ability to inhabit multiple points of view—what he called being 'of the entire world'—and, at the same time, the desire 'to know, understand and appreciate everything that happens on the surface of our globe'.[9] This clearly impossible ambition was the product of a world where advances in transport, media, and communication technologies compressed geographical space and accelerated the international

---

[5] Immanuel Kant, 'Idea for a Universal History with a Cosmopolitan Purpose' ['Idee zu einer allgemeinen Geschichte in weltbürgerlicher Absicht'], in *Kant's Political Writings*, ed. Hans Reiss, tr. H. B. Nisbet, 2nd edn (Cambridge: Cambridge University Press, 1990), 41–53 (51, 47).

[6] Ibid. 51.    [7] Pater, 'Introduction', in *The Purgatory of Dante Alighieri*, pp. xv, xvii.

[8] Ibid., p. xxiii.

[9] Charles Baudelaire, 'The Painter of Modern Life', in *The Painter of Modern Life and Other Essays*, tr. Jonathan Mayne (New York: Da Capo, 1986), 1–40 (7). The quotations in the main body of the text are taken from this English translation; the French original in the footnotes is from Baudelaire, 'Le Peintre de la vie moderne', in *Critique d'art, suivi de Critique musicale*, ed. Claude Pichois (Paris: Gallimard, 1992), 343–384 ('*Homme du monde*, c'est-à-dire homme du monde entier [. . .] il veut savoir, comprendre, apprécier tout ce qui se passe à la surface de notre sphéroïde', 349).

circulation of ideas. In this new, small world of the later nineteenth century, especially as viewed from Baudelaire's vantage point in metropolitan Paris, individuals were more intellectually mobile than ever before and, crucially, readier to appreciate what came from different parts of the globe. As a consequence, cosmopolitanism also meant a heightened state of receptivity towards impressions and sensual stimuli. In Baudelaire's gloss on Diogenes' famous definition, this combination of worldliness and hypersensitivity made the cosmopolitan subject 'the spiritual citizen of the universe',[10] where the spiritual citizenship of cosmopolitanism represented a radical alternative to Johann Gottfried Herder's notion of *Volkesgeist*, or 'spirit of the people' (to which we shall return shortly), and ideas of citizenship espoused by the modern nation states. Indeed, although neither of them said so explicitly, both Pater and Baudelaire celebrated cosmopolitanism as a spiritual force that challenged and corrected the cultural nationalism of large nations such as Britain and France, imaginatively driving the individual towards strangers and foreign space in search of new identities and new ideas. For Baudelaire, whose version of cosmopolitan modernity was altogether grittier than Pater's liberal and rather bookish ideal, this search could lead to dangerous places: 'a kind of cult of the self' and other types of antisocial desires infamously associated with decadence.[11]

The dialogue between Pater and Baudelaire brings to light two key ideas this book sets out to explore. The first is that, in the years around the turn of the twentieth century, literature became an important medium for simultaneously promoting and interrogating cosmopolitanism—a topic that had previously been largely confined to philosophical discussion. In the literature of the *fin de siècle*, cosmopolitanism took shape not as an abstract ideal but as something that informed the actual, living practices of authors and readers as they experimented with new ways of relating local and global identities in a world that they experienced as increasingly interconnected. The second is that cosmopolitanism was then, as it is now, a contested concept that generated debate and disagreement. Pater and Baudelaire both embraced the cosmopolitan ideal, but their interventions occurred within a largely hostile culture that denounced cosmopolitanism as politically and morally suspect, and stressed instead the responsibilities of literature towards the nation. My subtitle, *Citizens of Nowhere*, emphasizes this sense of controversy by adopting a distortion of Diogenes' formula ('I am a citizen of the world') that has been repeatedly used to stifle cosmopolitan sentiment and fuel nationalism. Baudelaire himself hinted at this discourse of alienation and non-belonging when he characterized cosmopolitanism as the ability to be simultaneously 'away from home and yet to feel oneself everywhere at home'.[12] Baudelaire

---

[10] Ibid. ('citoyen spirituel de l'univers', 349).
[11] Ibid. 27 ('une espèce de culte de soi-même', 370).
[12] Ibid. 9 ('Être hors de chez soi, et pourtant se sentir partout chez soi', 352).

viewed this condition in a positive light, as a strategy of radical defamiliarization that presented attractive advantages in the artistic and social spheres. However, the same attitude that potentially enables the cosmopolitan subject to belong in different spaces and contexts also places him or her at risk of becoming a stranger anywhere, that is, of weakening the social, linguistic, cultural, and affective ties that make individuals 'at home' in a community. In the *fin de siècle*, this paradoxical nature of cosmopolitanism started to emerge clearly: it was simultaneously a position of strength and vulnerability; a generalized condition of modernity and a form of exceptionalism that set some individuals apart from the rest of society.

In a series of definitions that, like Pater's, hark back to the core values of liberal societies, Kwame Anthony Appiah has linked cosmopolitanism to the celebration of 'the variety of human forms of social and cultural life', the cherishing of 'local differences', and the respect for minorities (national, ethnic, sexual, etc.) that facilitate a long-term process of 'cultural hybridization' of humanity.[13] Appiah's work belongs to a growing body of scholarship in the humanities and social sciences that has focused on cosmopolitanism since the 1990s. This includes important interventions by Homi K. Bhabha, Pheng Cheah, Jacques Derrida, Paul Gilroy, Julia Kristeva, Martha Nussbaum, and Bruce Robbins.[14] In different ways, these critics have all interrogated cosmopolitanism because they believe it capable of providing answers to some of the most pressing geopolitical challenges that we face in the present: globalization, diasporas, displacement, mass migration, multiculturalism, and integration, and, one must now add, the resurgence of xenophobic nationalisms and white supremacy in the West. The trend over the years has been to expand the concept of cosmopolitanism in order to emphasize its plurality—Pheng Cheah emphatically speaks of the 'new cosmopolitanisms'— and to make it as culturally inclusive as possible, in an attempt to correct the Eurocentric bias of its classic formulations (e.g. Kant's) and, sometimes, the American bias of much of the current debate.[15] In the twenty-first century as in

---

[13] Kwame Anthony Appiah, 'Cosmopolitan Patriots', *Critical Inquiry*, 23.3 (1997), 617–639 (621, 619, and *passim*). See also Appiah, *Cosmopolitanism: Ethics in a World of Strangers* (London: Allen Lane, 2006).

[14] Homi K. Bhabha, 'Unsatisfied: Notes on Vernacular Cosmopolitanism', in Laura García-Moreno and Peter C. Pfeiffer, eds, *Text and Nation: Cross-Disciplinary Essays on Cultural and National Identities* (Columbia, SC: Camden House, 1996), 191–207; Carol A. Breckenridge et al., *Cosmopolitanism* (Durham, NC, and London: Duke University Press, 2002); Jacques Derrida, *On Cosmopolitanism and Forgiveness*, tr. Mark Dooley and Michael Hughes (London: Routledge, 2001); Paul Gilroy, *Postcolonial Melancholia* (New York: Columbia University Press, 2005); Julia Kristeva, *Strangers to Ourselves*, tr. Leon S. Roudiez (New York: Columbia University Press, 1991); Bruce Robbins and Pheng Cheah, eds, *Cosmopolitics: Thinking and Feeling beyond the Nation* (Minneapolis and London: University of Minnesota Press, 1998); Martha Nussbaum, 'Patriotism and Cosmopolitanism', *Boston Review*, 19.5 (1994), 1–6. Nussbaum's provocative essay was crucial in triggering a wave of awareness and controversy around cosmopolitanism in the late twentieth century; a series of responses are collected in Joshua Cohen, ed., *For Love of Country: Debating the Limits of Patriotism* (Boston: Beacon Press, 1996).

[15] Pheng Cheah, *Inhuman Conditions: On Cosmopolitanism and Human Rights* (Cambridge, MA: Harvard University Press, 2006), 19. See also David A. Hollinger, 'Not Universalists, Not Pluralists: The New Cosmopolitans Find their Own Way', *Constellations*, 8.2 (2001), 236–248; Robert J. Holton,

the nineteenth, cosmopolitanism has of course also been criticized both from the right and the left, whether for its role in providing ways of undermining national loyalty or for being complicit with colonial mentality and neoliberal politics.[16] I shall come back to some of these criticisms in the course of the chapters. For now, it is enough to note that this book aims to show that the debate on cosmopolitanism that took place in the *fin de siècle* laid the foundations for our own understanding of this concept in the twenty-first century. While not engaging explicitly with the political situation of the present, this book argues that literature written over one hundred years ago is full of tensions and insights which are still surprisingly relevant to key issues that preoccupy us today: the cultural and emotional challenges of migration and uprooting, the tolerance of cultural diversity in a liberal state, the uneasy balance between patriotism and nationalism, the limits of universalism, and the pressure of ethical obligations towards strangers in a global society. Before delving further into how literature dealt with these issues, it is important to consider the complex history of the relation between nationalism and cosmopolitanism in the nineteenth century and the latter's rise as a distinctive social identity.

## Cosmopolitanism and Nationalism

We now tend to think of cosmopolitanism and nationalism as irreconcilable opposites but this has not always been the case. In the late eighteenth century the German philosopher Johann Gottfried Herder established a link between language and nationhood that would form the backbone of future theories of nationalism. However, Herder was also, at once and without experiencing this as a contradiction, a cosmopolitan and an internationalist. He believed that the variety of human languages was an undisputable proof of the difference between one nation and another; he argued that each nation had its own spiritual essence or soul (*Volkesgeist*); but he did not think that any one nation or its culture should be seen as superior to others. Herder celebrated diversity, noting that '[i]n almost all small nations of all parts of the world, however little cultivated (*gebildet*) they may be, ballads of their fathers, songs of the deeds of their ancestors, are the treasure of their language and history and poetic art, [they are] their wisdom and their

---

*Cosmopolitanisms: New Thinking and New Directions* (Basingstoke and New York: Palgrave Macmillan, 2009); Bruce Robbins and Paulo Lemos Horta, eds, *Cosmopolitanisms* (New York: New York University Press, 2017); Sheldon Pollock et al., 'Cosmopolitanisms', *Public Culture*, 12.3 (2000), 577–589.

[16] For examples of the latter see Timothy Brennan, *At Home in the World: Cosmopolitanism Now* (Cambridge, MA: Harvard University Press, 1997); and Hala Halim, *Alexandrian Cosmopolitanism: An Archive* (New York: Fordham University Press, 2013).

encouragement'.[17] His nationalism was based on the principle that all nations had equal dignity, even—one could almost say, especially—the politically oppressed ones. Herder warned against the dangers of nations turning inward on themselves and closing their borders to foreign influences, and reminded his German compatriots of all they had learned from foreign cultures.[18] He held that the transmission of culture from nation to nation was 'the finest *bond of further formation that nature has chosen*'.[19] For most of the nineteenth century, Kant's Enlightenment model of universalist cosmopolitanism and Herder's romantic particularism, with its emphasis on the uniqueness of national character, could exist alongside one another.[20] The Italian patriot Giuseppe Mazzini, for instance, was both a theorist of Italian nationalism and a committed cosmopolitan who campaigned for a united Europe.

Some time in the late nineteenth century, however, a shift occurred that caused the two to bifurcate. In 1893, the historian C. B. Roylance-Kent observed that it would have been natural to suppose that the increased contact between people from different nations would by then have caused 'a corresponding advance in cosmopolitan spirit and latitude of sympathy'.[21] However, quite the opposite seemed to be the case: everywhere, nationalist sentiment was 'running to excess' and taking the form of an 'exuberant patriotism' that manifested itself as a hostility towards foreigners.[22] This recent phenomenon, which Roylance-Kent deplored for having taken the world back to 'the ruder habits of an earlier age', was part of the paradoxical condition of modernity.[23] Corroborating Roylance-Kent's perception, historians of nationalism now see the *fin de siècle* as a turning point that marked the emergence of a new type of nationalism, which, in the words of E. J. Hobsbawm, 'had no fundamental similarity to state-patriotism, even when it attached itself to it. Its basic loyalty was, paradoxically, not to "the country", but only to its particular version of that country: to an ideological construct.'[24] In Britain and all over Europe, the birth of this 'domestic nationalism'

---

[17] Johann Gottfried Herder, 'Treatise on the Origin of Language' [1772], in *Philosophical Writings*, tr. and ed. Michael N. Forster (Cambridge and New York: Cambridge University Press, 2002), 65–164 (147). The quotations in the main body of the text are taken from this English translation; the German original in the footnotes is from Johann Gottfried Herder, 'Abhandlung über den Ursprung der Sprache', in *Werke in zehn Bänden*, ed. Martin Bollacher et al. (Frankfurt a.M.: Suhrkampf, 1985–2000), i: *Frühe Schriften 1764–1772*, ed. Ulrich Gaier (1985), 695–810 ('Fast in allen kleinen Nationen aller Weltteile, so wenig gebildet sie auch sein mögen, sind Lieder von ihren Vätern, Gesänge von den Taten ihrer Vorfahren der Schatz ihrer Sprache und Geschichte, und Dichtkunst; ihre Weisheit und ihre Aufmunterung', 791).

[18] Ibid. 160.

[19] Ibid., italics in the original ('das feinste *Band der Fortbildung, was die Natur gewählet*', 806).

[20] See Esther Wohlgemut, *Romantic Cosmopolitanism* (Basingstoke: Palgrave Macmillan, 2009).

[21] C. B. Roylance-Kent, 'The Growth of National Sentiment', *Macmillan's Magazine*, 69 (Nov. 1893), 340–347 (340).

[22] Ibid. 344.      [23] Ibid.

[24] E. J. Hobsbawm, *Nations and Nationalism since 1870: Programme, Myth, Reality* (Cambridge and New York: Cambridge University Press, 1990), 93.

fostered the growth of 'right-wing movements for which the term "nationalism" was in fact coined in this period, or, more generally, of the political xenophobia which found its most deplorable, but not its only, expression, in anti-Semitism'.[25] This 'fulfilment' of nationalism was effectively a betrayal of the ideals espoused by Herder and the romantics.[26] From being associated with liberalism and the left, nationalism turned to being, in Hobsbawm's words, 'a chauvinist, imperialist and xenophobic movement of the right, or more precisely, the radical right'.[27] While governments manipulated this new nationalism to their own ends (Roylance-Kent, for instance, reviewed a whole series of xenophobic laws that had recently come into force in various countries around the world), it is important to notice that it was not simply a phenomenon imposed from above in the form of political propaganda: it was at the same time an ideology and the expression of a popular sentiment that gave rise to extremely successful grassroot movements. The radicalized nationalism of the turn of the century fed on national feeling in complex, sometimes deliberate ways, seeking—albeit, obviously, not always successfully—to reorient patriotism towards an illiberal position, hostile to international cooperation and friendship.

Cosmopolitanism, with its millennial history that stretched all the way back to ancient Greece, long predated the birth of the nation as a political let alone ideological entity. In the second half of the nineteenth century, its abstract principles formulated by Kant were given more concrete shape through the proliferation of new, organized forms of internationalism. From the founding of the International Working Men's Association, or First International, in 1864 to the establishment of the International League for Peace and Freedom (1867), the Second, or Socialist, International (1889), and The Hague Conventions of 1899 and 1907, internationalism was as prominent a feature of this historical period as the nationalism described by Hobsbawm. These landmark events, and the many international congresses and initiatives for standardization that took place in these years, give the impression of a growing consensus that the nation no longer reflected the actual conditions of an interconnected modern world, in which people, goods, and ideas moved across borders. However, Raymond Williams, who draws a helpful distinction between nationalism and national feeling, cautions us against seeing a stark opposition between the concepts of nationalism and internationalism: internationalism 'is only the opposite of selfish and competitive

---

[25] Ibid. 105.

[26] Hans Kohn, *The Age of Nationalism: The First Era of Global History* (New York and Evanston, IL: Harper, 1968), 9–10. Kohn and Hobsbawm agree in dating this paradigm shift to the years from the 1880s to the First World War. See also Paul Lawrence, who dates to this period the birth of a process of cultural inquiry into the pros and cons of nationalism; Lawrence, *Nationalism: History and Theory* (Harlow and London: Longman, 2005), 17 ff.

[27] Hobsbawm, *Nation and Nationalism*, 121.

policies between existing political nations';[28] it does not necessarily question the fundamental principles of the nation as a political and social entity or its spiritual function described by Herder. Williams's insight is borne out, in this period, by the rise of movements of pan-Germanism, pan-Slavism, and pan-Latinism, which all built bridges between existing nations only in order to erect new barriers around them, and reassert highly exclusive forms of ethnic, cultural, and social identity. Indeed, looking specifically at the turn of the twentieth century, the historian Glenda Sluga has challenged the engrained position of narratives of nationalism in our understanding of history, speaking instead of a long symbiotic relationship between nationalism and internationalism as 'entangled ways of thinking about modernity, progress, and politics'.[29]

Within this complex and fluid field, cosmopolitanism provided philosophical, emotional, and ethical arguments that intellectuals and activists could use to curb the spread of an aggressive nationalism. In a 1900 pamphlet issued by the International Arbitration and Peace Association, the journalist George Herbert Perris described the present as a moment of unprecedented awareness about global interconnectedness: as it became increasingly difficult and indeed meaningless to separate domestic and foreign affairs, international relations assumed paramount importance, in the political as well as the ethical and cultural spheres. For Perris, not only was the nation showing signs of decline as a type of social organization, but the very 'spirit of nationality' was finally being revealed for what it was—a 'myth': 'it is in part a superstition of more or less ignorant sentimentalists, and in part a pretence of certain classes of persons who are in various ways interested in the maintenance of the superstition'.[30] Perris saw the 'new internationalism' of the turn of the twentieth century as part of a long history of cosmopolitanism in which the birth and collapse of the nation was only a short chapter. For that reason, he recommended that the present must study closely the 'cosmopolitan heritage' of the past (by which he meant the classical and Judaeo-Christian traditions), whose resources were still untapped.[31] Perris believed that, only by learning to see through the sentimental appeal of nationalism, could his contemporaries lay the foundations for new ethical and social structures suited to the material conditions of the modern age. While the Enlightenment cosmopolitanism of Kant, Goethe, and Goldsmith was still a valid model, it was also, for Perris, 'a vague sentiment', too 'academic and artificial'; the challenge for cosmopolitanism was that it must

---

[28] Raymond Williams, *Keywords: A Vocabulary of Culture and Society*, rev. edn (New York: Oxford University Press, 1983), 214.
[29] Glenda Sluga, *Internationalism in the Age of Nationalism* (Philadelphia: University of Pennsylvania Press, 2013), 3.
[30] G. H. Perris, *The New Internationalism* (London: International Arbitration Association, [1900]), 35. On Perris's involvement in the International Arbitration and Peace Association, see Paul Laity, *The British Peace Movement, 1870–1914* (Oxford: Clarendon, 2001), 133–138.
[31] Perris, *New Internationalism*, 32.

now grow into a 'popular and organic ideal'—its philosophical ideal, that is, must be built into the transactions of everyday life in a world where travel, commercial relations, and scientific and cultural cooperation were all happening on an international scale.[32] Perry's pamphlet shows how, in tandem with the transformation of nationalism, cosmopolitanism also took on a new identity in this period: it assumed an oppositional character, became radicalized. This change drew contributions from a wide social pool that went from internationalist activists, like Perris himself, to bourgeois liberals and intellectuals, socialist internationalists, anarchists, migrant groups, feminists, homosexuals, theosophists, and proponents of universal language movements. Unlike the nationalists, these scattered social and political entities did not unite under a single banner but their variety gave a special cultural energy to the culture of cosmopolitanism that this book seeks to reconstruct.

If, in Benedict Anderson's famous argument, the nation derived its coherence as an imagined community from print technology, which 'made it possible for rapidly growing numbers of people to think about themselves, and to relate themselves to others, in profoundly new ways', the print medium could now also be appropriated for the cosmopolitan cause.[33] Even when it did not criticize nationalism explicitly, the ever more effective and far-reaching print industry of the late nineteenth century made readers more international by orienting them outwards, beyond the horizons of expectations set by national borders. Within Europe at least, by circulating translations and foreign news (including, crucially, cultural items) with unprecedented speed and in unprecedented quantities, the press created international communities that shared tastes, interests, and cultural codes: readers in London, Copenhagen, and Milan engaged in very similar cultural debates (e.g. the controversies over decadence and naturalism) virtually at the same time, developing in this process new bonds of identity that transcended native customs. Unsurprisingly, one of the most contested issues among the enlarged, denationalized community of readers of the *fin de siècle* was the very nature and meaning of cosmopolitanism. Should individual and communal identities be rooted in Herder's ideas of the *Volkesgeist*? Was a world-map divided into small parcels of linguistic and cultural uniqueness something to regret or celebrate? And, in the case of Britain, what was the relationship between the multinational culture of the empire and cosmopolitan ideology?

[32] Ibid. 39.
[33] Benedict Anderson, *Imagined Communities: Reflections on the Origin and Spread of Nationalism* (London and New York: Verso, 1991), 36. For critiques of Anderson's model, with special relevance for literary studies, see Pheng Cheah, 'Grounds of Comparison', *Diacritics*, 29.4 (1999), 2–18; and Jonathan Culler, 'Anderson and the Novel', *Diacritics*, 29.4 (1999), 19–39. This journal issue is entirely dedicated to responses to Anderson's work.

We must imagine the confrontation between nationalism and cosmopolitanism as a slow game of pressures, frictions, and ironies, only occasionally enlivened by a visible conflagration. Take, for instance, a cartoon that appeared in *Punch's Almanack* in 1895, titled 'Britannia à la Beardsley' (illustration 0.1). The drawing shows a national symbol refashioned through the cosmopolitan sensibility of Aubrey Beardsley, an English artist then at the height of his fame: an armoured androgynous figure—it could be a woman or a man in drag—holding Britannia's iconic trident and shield is floating on the sea in the company of an anthropomorphic lion that looks a bit like a poodle and other grotesque figures. The White Cliffs of Dover are visible in the background and, in the foreground, an English patriotic bulldog in top hat and ruffles stares proudly ahead, resting on a pile of lavishly bound volumes. The caricaturist (Edward T. Reed) has skilfully reproduced signature features of Beardsley's style: the framing of the picture through theatrical curtains, allusions to eighteenth-century aesthetics, the mixture of classicism and the grotesque, the association with the art-book trade, and the self-referential joke (the tome on the top of the pile is a volume of *Punch*). He has even managed to capture something of the essence of Beardsley's droll humour. And what is funny is precisely to see that humour trumped by the caricaturist, following a tradition of avant-garde bashing that *Punch* had been peddling for decades. Here the cosmopolitan sympathies of progressive metropolitan types are exaggerated and made to clash with nationalist sentiment in front of the readers' eyes. A cosmopolitan artist like Beardsley is shown to be clearly unfit to represent the nation. His distorted vision of Britannia suggests at best non-belonging and, at worst, calculated disloyalty. The cartoon graphically demonstrates that patriotic and cosmopolitan sentiments cannot thrive on shared ground. We only need to remember that 1895 was also the year of the Oscar Wilde trials, and that Beardsley was closely associated with Wilde through his drawings of the 1894 English translation of *Salomé* (to which the physiognomy of the androgynous Britannia alludes) to realize how insidiously this caricature leverages the anti-Wilde sentiment that dominated press reports, compounding it with nationalism, as a highly toxic warning to Beardsley and his kind.

Nationalist sentiment was everywhere in late nineteenth-century Britain: it was institutionalized in schools and Baden-Powell's boy scouts, it was turned into spectacle and entertainment in monuments and military parades, it was endlessly broadcast by the popular press. Nationalism was given literary currency in jingoistic poems and popular appeal in music-hall songs. In many of these institutions and cultural products, patriotic and national feelings became exclusive and confrontational, often turning into aggressive weapons. Moreover, as the iconography of Britannia in the *Punch* cartoon reminds us, the oppositional relationship between nationalism and cosmopolitanism was further complicated by the presence of the empire. It is obvious that nationalism provided an

BRITANNIA À LA BEARDSLEY.
(*By Our " Yellow " Decadent.*)

**Illustration 0.1** 'Britannia à la Beardsley', *Punch's Almanack* (1895). Punch Cartoon Library/TopFoto

ideological justification for some of the worst forms of political abuse, violence, and cultural aggression committed in the name of the British Empire. But, at the same time, the empire created the conditions for an unprecedented global movement of people, goods, ideas, and, crucially, writers and texts, from and to the European metropolis; as Leela Gandhi has shown, this aided the formation of networks of sympathy and anti-colonial resistance that played a key role in shaping the new cosmopolitan self-awareness of this period.[34] In a similar vein, studying the testimonies of Indians travelling to Britain, Elleke Boehmer has suggested that it would be more accurate to conceive of the empire as simultaneously facilitating and thwarting forms of cosmopolitanism.[35] By the end of the century, this fraught relationship between empire, cosmopolitanism, and British nationalism was further complicated by the presence of different nationalisms that had flared up in various 'peripheral' territories. Among these, Ireland constituted an especially visible case because it was the one that was geographically and culturally closest to the imperial centre. Increasingly, therefore, the empire provided a global stage in which the new radicalized and chauvinistic English nationalism described by Hobsbawm clashed with other forms of progressive nationalism, such as the Irish. In these peripheral or semi-peripheral zones, nationalists invoked Herder's *Volkesgeist* as a means of political emancipation and to reclaim the dignity of native traditions, including language and literature, that were oppressed from outside. In this confusing scenario cosmopolitanism was sometimes even appropriated by imperialist ideologues. In his pamphlet G. H. Perris noted that the 'vogue of Imperialism represents in part [ ... ] a crude but genuine popular perception of the unreality of the ancient national barriers'; but he warned against the mistake of associating imperialism and anti-nationalist struggle.[36] The short-lived *Anglo-Saxon Review* (1899–1901) was founded precisely on such a misleading association: published by Beardsley's and Wilde's former publisher John Lane, the journal described its political sympathies as 'Imperial—one may say cosmopolitan—rather than insular', co-opting cosmopolitanism for a decidedly aggressive-sounding programme of 'extension of "Anglo-Saxon" influence in the waste places of the earth'.[37]

Another image can shed some light on this complex dynamic. The *Imperial Federation Map*, illustrated by Walter Crane, was issued as a supplement to the weekly newspaper, *The Graphic*, in July 1886 (illustration 0.2). The publication coincided with the Colonial and Indian Exhibition, which opened in South Kensington in May 1886, the year before Victoria's Golden Jubilee. The map, which circulated widely at the time and has attracted the attention of modern

---

[34] Leela Gandhi, *Affective Communities: Anticolonial Thought, Fin-de-Siècle Radicalism, and the Politics of Friendship* (Durham, NC, and London: Duke University Press, 2006).

[35] Elleke Boehmer, *Indian Arrivals, 1870–1915: Networks of British Empire* (Oxford and New York: Oxford University Press, 2015), 8 and *passim*. The twentieth- and twenty-first-century legacy of this phenomenon is explored in Gurminder K. Bhambra and John Narayan, eds, *European Cosmopolitanism: Colonial Histories and Postcolonial Societies* (London: Routledge, 2016).

[36] Perris, *New Internationalism*, 36.

[37] [Anon.], 'Impressions and Opinions', *Anglo-Saxon Review*, 1 (June 1899), 243–254 (247). The author is likely to be the journal's editor, Lady Randolph Spencer Churchill, Winston Churchill's mother.

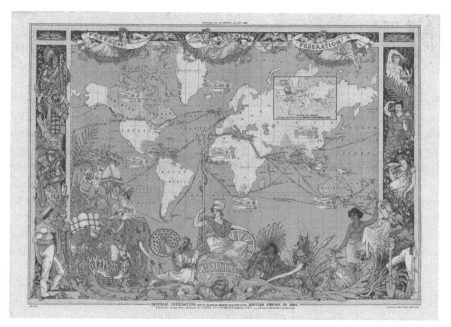

**Illustration 0.2**  *Imperial Federation Map of the World* (1886). Cornell University —PJ Mode Collection of Persuasive Cartography

geographers,[38] reflected the view of the recently formed Imperial Federation League (1884) that the introduction of a federal system that gave political representation to the colonies would strengthen democracy and, at the same time, increase the stability of the empire as a whole. With its clever nudging of Britain towards the middle of the field, following the Mercator projection, and the prominent marking of trade routes that connect the metropolis to the rest of the world, the map is an effective representation of the empire as a well-managed cosmopolitan space, politically and ethnically dominated by the British nation. The same message is attractively reiterated in the lush illustrations on the frame, where two processions of exotically attired individuals bearing the gifts and attributes of colonial diversity converge towards the figure of Britannia, sitting on the globe and thus leaving no doubt as to Britain's role as 'all-powerful civilising force'.[39] Yet, if we probe more closely into the iconography of this

[38] J. Brian Harley, 'Maps, Knowledge and Power', in Denis Cosgrove and Stephen Daniels, eds, *The Iconography of Landscape* (Cambridge: Cambridge University Press, 1988), 277–312; and Pippa Biltcliffe, 'Walter Crane and the *Imperial Federation Map showing the Extent of the British Empire* (1886)', *Imago Mundi*, 57.1 (2005), 63–69, who helpfully analyses Crane's ambivalent position towards empire. For a discussion of the Imperial Federation League, see John Kendle, *Federal Britain: A History* (London: Routledge, 1997), 48–53.

[39] Biltcliffe, 'Walter Crane', 64.

Britannia *à la* Crane, we notice a series of elements that muddle this appeal to sentimental notions of nation and race that were so pervasive in arguments in favour of a federal empire.[40] The globe at the bottom of the map rests on the shoulders of an Atlas figure (borrowed from Greek myth) who holds a barely visible banner that reads 'human labour'; in a similar vein, the top frame makes a surprising allusion to the French Revolution in the three allegorical female figures bearing banners inscribed 'freedom', 'fraternity', and 'federation', interspersed with peace-bearing doves. The socialist, internationalist, and pacifist messages in the map thus conjure a different version of world citizenship that, via Herder and Marx, infiltrates and disturbs the vision of the empire as a cosmopolitan space that is ostensibly being presented, questioning the very capitalist and nationalist foundations on which imperial politics was built. The iconographic tensions in the *Imperial Federation Map* show us just how unsettled and disputed the idea of cosmopolitanism was in the period covered by this book. To unpack the complex cultural representations of this idea is to unlock new ways of understanding the relationship between literature and national identity.

## At Home in the World

An important aspect of the new cosmopolitanism was that it became attached to a distinctive social identity. According to Baudelaire, the cosmopolitan subject was characterized by city-living and by a 'blasé' attitude to life. This calculated practice of detachment brought the cosmopolitan close to that other emblematic figure of late nineteenth-century urban modernity: the dandy.[41] In the early twentieth century, the German sociologist Georg Simmel seized on Baudelaire's notion of 'the blasé attitude' in order to argue for a deeper affinity between the metropolitan and cosmopolitan types.[42] In his influential essay 'The Metropolis and Mental Life' ('Die Großstädte und das Geistesleben', 1903), Simmel contrasted the modern metropolis to the ancient Greek *polis*, where citizens were subjected to strict mechanisms of supervision and de-individuation aimed at cementing a local, communal identity. By contrast, the new economic world order caused the urban metropolis to become 'the seat of cosmopolitanism': as the operations of modern capitalism shifted more and more to the international field, the social identities of city dwellers were determined by economic factors played out well

---

[40] Kendle, *Federal Britain*, 55–56.    [41] Baudelaire, 'The Painter of Modern Life', 9.
[42] Georg Simmel, 'The Metropolis and Mental Life', in Richard Sennett, ed., *Classic Essays on the Culture of Cities* (Englewood Cliffs, NJ: Prentice-Hall, 1969), 47–60 (51). The German original in the footnotes is taken from Georg Simmel, 'Die Großstädte und das Geistesleben', in *Gesamtausgabe*, 27 vols (Frankfurt a.M.: Suhrkamp, 1989–2015), vii: *Aufsätze und Abhandlungen, 1901–1908*, ed. Rüdiger Kramme, Angela Rammstedt, and Otthein Rammstedt (1995), 116–131 ('die Blasiertheit', 121).

beyond the city's, and indeed the nation's, geographical boundaries.[43] Simmel painted a less poetic picture of cosmopolitan individualism than Baudelaire: he spoke of 'extravagances of mannerism, caprice, and preciousness' and linked the blasé attitude to a 'boundless pursuit of pleasure' that caused an overstimulation of the nerves and eventually led to the inability to process new impressions.[44] Devoid of philosophical or political high-mindedness, Simmel's modern cosmopolite was little more than a creature of desires and incipient neuroses produced by the international capitalist money economy.

In the *fin de siècle* writers no less than sociologists attempted to capture the new cosmopolitan social identity. In *The Princess Casamassima* (1886), Henry James used it to characterize the geographically and socially mobile Captain Sholto, an upper-class radical who provides the crucial connection between the titular character and the novel's protagonist, the working-class aesthete Hyacinth Robinson. When Hyacinth awkwardly explains that he cannot formulate an opinion on the Captain because he has 'never seen him at home', he triggers the Princess's sarcastic retort: 'At home? Oh, he is never at home; he is all over the world. To-night he was as likely to have been in Paraguay, for instance. He is what they call a cosmopolite. I don't know whether you know that species; very modern, more and more frequent, and exceedingly tiresome. I prefer the Chinese!'[45] Always alert to the subtleties of social change, James records the birth of the cosmopolite as a new 'species' associated with modernity, mobility, and social privilege. The naïve Hyacinth mistakenly believes that he can rely on the concept of 'home' to frame the Captain within legible social structures. But, as he will learn, the cosmopolitan identity defamiliarizes and ultimately invalidates traditional categories of perception rooted in the idea of belonging. It is significant that this exchange takes place in a London theatre, where cosmopolitanism is on display as part of the vast array of social performances available to the metropolitan crowd.

Although James used the words 'cosmopolite' and 'cosmopolitan' sparingly, his works played a key role in crystallizing the new social type for readers of English, especially in the novels that deal with the so-called international theme. In *The Ambassadors* (1903), for instance, he described the transformation of the American Chad Newsome into 'a man of the world' in plastic terms, as a change from rough to smooth: 'for that he *was* smooth was as marked as in the taste of a sauce or in the rub of a hand'.[46] The effect of Europe—and, specifically, Paris—on Chad is to rub away the coarse or too pronounced elements of his American background, substituting for them a polish—'a form and a surface' as James says— that is the result of a process of standardization that affects his voice, accent, and

[43] Ibid. 56 ('die Sitze des Kosmopolitanismus', 126).

[44] Ibid. 57, 51 ('Extravaganzen des Apartseins, der Kaprice, des Pretiösentums', 'ein maßloses Genußleben', 128, 121).

[45] Henry James, *The Princess Casamassima* (London and New York: Penguin, 1987), 195–196.

[46] Henry James, *The Ambassadors* (London and New York: Penguin, 2008), 128.

his very physical features no less than his social presence: 'It was as if in short he had really, copious perhaps but shapeless, been put into a firm mould and turned successfully out.'[47] The culinary metaphors of sauces and moulds are an apt way of capturing the effort of elaboration that goes into becoming a man of the world.

However, the most interesting feature in James's observation of cosmopolitan identities in *The Ambassadors* is that it brings to light a gendered difference which escaped the notice of Simmel and Baudelaire.[48] With an obvious eye to character symmetry, James later characterizes Chad's counterpart, his French lover Madame de Vionnet, as a *femme du monde*. But, while the man of the world is defined by an abstract elegance, the *femme du monde* is an altogether more embodied, sexualized, and ambivalent being that James describes, with reference to Shakespeare's Cleopatra, as 'various and multifold': '[s]he had aspects, characters, days, nights'.[49] The distancing effect of the French expression *femme du monde* adds a further note of mystery to this feminine ideal that, by virtue of its somewhat overemphasized experience and individualism, is clearly a far cry from nineteenth-century bourgeois standards of female propriety. James uses this gendered difference for dramatic effect in the plot of *The Ambassadors*. Other writers, as we shall see when we turn to George Egerton, contested it and attempted to reclaim a more progressive model of female cosmopolitanism. Indeed, Vernon Lee responded directly to James's gendering of cosmopolitan identities in a short story pointedly titled 'A Worldly Woman' (1890), where the main characters embark on an extended discussion of *The Princess Casamassima*. Here Lee loaded the term 'worldly' with a bitter irony, using it to describe her female protagonist's abandonment of her inquisitiveness, independence, and queer identity in order to embrace a life of social conformity which went against her natural inclinations.[50]

These examples from James's fiction show how, in this period of transition, cosmopolitanism acquired the connotations of worldliness and material privilege that we have come to associate with it. As the citizen of the world became a man or woman of the world, cosmopolitanism became a byword for an international code of manners determined by the cosmopolitanism of capital noted by Simmel and of course earlier theorized by Karl Marx in the *Communist Manifesto* (1848). The increasingly globally oriented capitalist economy generated more specialized and elaborate habits of consumption that provided the middle classes of industrialized nations with new, international forms of sociability, behavioural codes, and shared spaces. If, in James's formulation, the cosmopolite was now a 'species', it could be distinguished by its ability to speak several languages (often the result

---

[47] Ibid. 129.

[48] But not of their modern critics, e.g. Janet Wolff, 'The Feminine in Modern Art: Benjamin, Simmel, and the Gender of Modernity', *Theory, Culture, and Society*, 17.6 (2000), 33–53.

[49] James, *The Ambassadors*, 216.

[50] Vernon Lee, 'A Worldly Woman', *Contemporary Review*, 58 (Oct. 1890), 520–541, and (Nov. 1890), 693–711.

of an international education, especially for women), recherché taste in food and clothes, constant travel, artistic connoisseurship, a distinctive type of elegance that worked by erasing traces of the local or provincial, and often a more relaxed sexual morality that stemmed from the self-conscious distancing from an older small-town bourgeoisie obsessed with the narrow moral horizon of the 'home'. Before the era of visas complicated the logistics of international travel, and aided by ever faster and more comfortable means of transportation, *fin-de-siècle* cosmopolites moved between European capitals and fashionable spa towns and seaside resorts where new international hotels catered specifically for their needs. These establishments, like the international exhibitions that became a regular feature of the second half of the nineteenth century, made a commodity of the 'ethics of hospitality' that philosophers have recognized as one of the key principles of cosmopolitanism, from Kant to Derrida.[51] Indeed, cosmopolitan worldliness could be completely detached from the old philosophical idealism: we just need to turn to Proust's *Le Côté de Guermantes* (1920–1), set in the 1890s at the time of the Dreyfus affair, to find a perfect alliance between the 'worldly' set of Parisian high society and anti-Semitic nationalism.

Today, these associations of cosmopolitanism with high society prove uncomfortable to many critics, especially on the left, because they undercut the radical potential of cosmopolitanism as expressing an identity that extends beyond white and middle-class privilege, and as offering a useful tool for world-political critique.[52] Indeed, it would be possible to view the rise of cosmopolitanism as a social identity in an entirely negative way, as a betrayal both of Kant's universal law and Herder's particularism. It is telling that the socialist internationalism that was also sharply on the rise at the time preferred to abandon cosmopolitan as a term of self-definition precisely due to its elitist connotations. When the Austrian writer Stefan Zweig happily describes turn-of-the-century Vienna as a city where everyone became a 'cosmopolitan citizen of the world', twenty-first-century readers are likely to be struck by his blindness to class and imperial geopolitics.[53] However, the liberal compromise between cosmopolitanism and the (upper) bourgeoisie was not as stable or cosy as it might appear at first glance. If we go back to James's *Princess Casamassima*, for instance, it is important to note that the modern cosmopolite comes into the world within a (for James highly unusual) plot of

[51] Jacques Derrida, *Of Hospitality*, tr. Rachel Bowlby (Stanford, CA: Stanford University Press, 2000), 65. In this essay, Derrida is partly responding to Kant's 'Perpetual Peace: A Philosophical Sketch' ('Zum ewigen Frieden: Ein philosophischer Entwurf', 1795), his other major pronouncement on cosmopolitanism alongside the 'Idea for a Universal History with a Cosmopolitan Purpose'.

[52] Bruce Robbins, 'Comparative Cosmopolitanism', *Social Text*, 31/32 (1992), 169–186 (171 and *passim*).

[53] Stefan Zweig, *The World of Yesterday: Memoirs of a European*, tr. Anthea Bell (London: Pushkin Press, 2011), 34. The German original in the footnotes is from Stefan Zweig, *Die Welt von Gestern: Erinnerungen eines Europäers* (Frankfurt a.M.: Fischer, 2010) ('unbewußt wurde jeder Bürger dieser Stadt zum Übernationalen, zum Kosmopolitischen, zum Weltbürger erzogen', 28).

conspiracy and revolution. The 'cosmopolite' and upper-class Captain Sholto has anarchist leanings, in common with the Princess and Hyacinth, James's working-class protagonist. Likewise, the latter's social elevation that eventually enables him to pass as 'one of the cosmopolites' bred in the poshest part of town does not turn him away from the revolutionary cause.[54] *The Princess Casamassima* shows that the ascent of the cosmopolite as a social type in *fin-de-siècle* London cannot be easily separated from other very politicized offshoots of modern cosmopolitanism, ranging from anarchist terrorism to a utopian socialism that looks forward to the day when 'all the nations of the earth would abolish their frontiers and armies and custom-houses, and embrace on both cheeks'.[55] James significantly attributes this last doctrine to the character of Eustache Poupin—a French refugee who had arrived in England after the Commune of 1871, and who is very distant from English middle-class ideals.

The association between cosmopolitanism and revolutionary anarchism in particular was one that reverberated through the literature of this period. In Joseph Conrad's novel of anarchist terrorism *The Secret Agent* (1906), the protagonist Mr Verloc is described as 'cosmopolitan enough' to navigate the labyrinthine urban geography of London and, at the same time, to pass unnoticed by policemen when he is out on his shady errands.[56] Conrad's novel shows that the ability 'to remain hidden from the world' observed by Baudelaire imaginatively associated the figure of the cosmopolite with underground networks of intrigue that posed a very concrete threat to established social and political orders. Following Conrad's lead, it is legitimate to speculate whether the patina of social elitism that attached itself to cosmopolitanism at this point might in fact be a function of prevalent social anxieties about displacement: whether its purpose was to create a way of distinguishing between the urbane foreignness of the Chad Newsomes on the one side, and the more threatening foreignness of the Mr Verlocs and M. Poupins on the other. From an historicist perspective, therefore, it is just as important to examine the mechanisms by which cosmopolitanism came to be associated with leisure and class privilege, as to unearth its less visible associations with grittier forms of cultural dislocation such as migration and subversive activism.

Nowhere were the new men and women of the world dissected more systematically and acerbically, their habits investigated, and their pretentions unmasked, than in the French writer Paul Bourget's 'romance of international life', *Cosmopolis* (1892). Bourget—a close associate of Henry James—is now a largely forgotten figure but at the turn of the century he enjoyed a huge international reputation. In the dedication to *Cosmopolis* (addressed to the Italian aristocratic

---

[54] James, *Princess Casamassima*, 427.     [55] Ibid. 116.
[56] Joseph Conrad, *The Secret Agent*, ed. Tanya Aghathocleous (Peterborough, Ont.: Broadview, 2009), 47.

*salonnier* Giuseppe Primoli), Bourget presented cosmopolitanism negatively as a 'mode of life, which is the most modern, and also the most arbitrary and most momentary'. Bourget believed that the social performance of the cosmopolite was always ultimately undermined by what he called 'the permanence of the race': 'the more one is familiar with Cosmopolites, the more we are assured that the most irreducible *datum* in them is that special force of heredity which slumbers under the uniform monotony of superficial relations'.[57] Bourget's criticism is pernicious because it relies on a radicalized nationalism propped up by spurious scientific theories of race and compounded with anti-Semitism—the main target of Bourget's satire in *Cosmopolis* is a wealthy Jewish family. In the twentieth century, Zweig was to experience the violence of that noxious compound at first hand when the takeover of Austria by the Nazis forced him into exile. In the foreword to his autobiography *The World of Yesterday* (*Die Welt von Gestern*, 1942), he movingly describes the feeling of 'belong[ing] nowhere' and having been made 'a stranger or at the most a guest everywhere' that Baudelaire had conjured in 'The Painter of Modern Life'.[58] In doing so he stumbles, like James's Hyacinth, on the idea of home: 'I find myself saying that "at home" we do this or that, by "we" meaning Austrians, and remember, with a shock, that for some time I have been no more of an Austrian than I am an Englishman or an American; I am no longer organically bound to my native land and I never really fit into any other.'[59] Zweig struggles to find a connection between the liberal cosmopolitanism of his young adulthood in the *fin de siècle* and the homelessness of exile. The latter only conveys abjection and loss: loss of identity, language, dignity, material belongings. The very hotel room in which he writes his memoirs becomes a grotesque spectre of the well-appointed hotel rooms of the *belle époque* that he had depicted extensively in his fiction. Zweig's tragic circumstances represent an extreme case of the transformation from cosmopolite to citizen of nowhere. But, as we shall see, the spectres of loss and abjection, fuelled by nationalism, already haunted the literature of the *fin de siècle*, where cosmopolitan privilege and exile existed in an uncomfortable state of symbiosis.

---

[57] Paul Bourget, *Cosmopolis*, [tr. anon.] (New York: Tait, Sons, & Co., 1893), p. viii. The French original is from Paul Bourget, *Cosmopolis* (Paris: Lemerre, 1894) ('genre d'existence le plus moderne, et aussi le plus arbitraire et le plus momentane [. . .] la permanence de la race [. . .] plus on fréquente les Cosmopolites, plus on constate que la donnée la plus irréducible en eux est cette force spéciale de l'hérédité qui sommeille sous l'uniforme monotonie des rapports superficiels', pp. ii, iii).

[58] Zweig, *World of Yesterday*, 18 ('So gehöre ich nirgends mehr hin, überall Fremder und bestenfalls Gast', 8).

[59] Ibid. 18–19 ('Oder daß ich "bei uns" sage und erschrocken mich erinnern muß, daß ich für die Menschen meiner Heimat längst ebensowenig dazugehöre wie für die Engländer oder für die Amerikaner, dort nicht mehr organisch verbunden und hier wiederum niemals ganz eingegliedert', 9). The idea of home brought out by the English translator fuses the concept of 'Heimat' in this sentence with the previous sentence, where Zweig talks about his 'Haus'.

## Literary Cosmopolitanism

This book aims to show that literature offers an exceptionally rich archive for the study of cosmopolitanism. In literary texts and periodicals national feeling and social identities are embedded in complex ways that reveal the textures and ambiguities of this concept. At the same time, the book shows that the literary medium not only reflects but *creates* specific conditions to reach beyond the social, cultural, linguistic, affective, and ethical boundaries of national cultures. At first sight literature's claim to cosmopolitanism might appear counterintuitive: unlike other artistic mediums such as music and the visual arts, literature seems to resist universality by virtue of its fundamental link with language, which fragments it into pockets of particularity enclosed within national borders. In other words, literary texts can easily be construed as the heritage or property of a specific people because language puts an indelible, individual national stamp on them, excluding or at least disadvantaging 'non-native' readers. In the nineteenth century, the alignment of literature, national language, and the idea of the mother tongue, to which we shall return especially in Chapters 1 and 5, did provide support for nationalist readings of literary texts based on Herder. Indeed, in this period, in Britain as in other European countries, literature was used to isolate and define the characteristics of a unique or native genius, which was then used to reinforce a sense of national identity. In other words, as English literature was mined to find the supposedly distinctive characteristics of Englishness, that very quest for Englishness provided a justification for why literature mattered, and why it should be studied in schools and universities. The last few decades of the nineteenth century, as Stefan Collini has observed, witnessed a noticeable intensification of this process through the production of primers, anthologies, and biographies, and the establishment of new English courses in various universities, all of which aimed to create a 'celebratory and consensual' view of the Englishness of English literature, which in turn provided fuel for English cultural nationalism.[60] In the *fin de siècle*, writers and critics who shared a cosmopolitan orientation wanted to challenge the cultural consensus identified by Collini. In order to do so, they had to find new ways of reading and writing capable of undoing the link between Herder's legacy and the radicalized nationalism that increasingly asserted its presence in society and in the press. How could they reclaim literature from the destructive forces of nationalism? Could literature simultaneously embody a distinctive, English national character *and* transcend its particularity? Could literature foster international exchange and hybridity rather than localism and exclusion of foreign elements?

---

[60] Stefan Collini, *Public Moralists: Political Thought and Intellectual Life in Britain 1850–1930* (Oxford and New York: Clarendon Press, 1991), 347.

At the turn of the twentieth century, the greater international mobility of authors, readers, and texts enabled the formation of a widespread countercultural movement that consciously sought to question and undermine what by then seemed an obvious link between literature and the nation. This cosmopolitan reorientation reached across the spectrum, from popular literature to the most cutting-edge literary criticism. In the pamphlet for the International Arbitration Association cited earlier, Perris lamented the fact that, while jingoism and imperialism had their poets (he cited Tennyson's 'The Golden Year' as an example), there was no such thing as a literature of cosmopolitanism.[61] As we will see, cosmopolitanism did have its bards, so to speak—writers, like Pater, who sought to enlarge the cultural and ethical sympathies of their readers by showing them how to relate to the wider world. But a cosmopolitan turn required more radical interventions than could be possible for single individuals; it necessitated new approaches to literature that seized both on the new imaginative orientation and the new opportunities that arose from global interconnectivity.

It is telling, therefore, that this is also the period that saw the birth of comparative literature as a distinctive discipline of literary studies, following the experimental application of the comparative method in various branches of the nineteenth-century humanities and in reaction to the national focus that was fast becoming the norm in university departments. In his foundational book of 1886 that introduced the idea of comparative literature into English, the Irish classical scholar H. M. Posnett drew on evolutionary theory to justify why the modern study of literature necessitated a broader perspective than that of a single nation. Comparative literature was, according to him, the logical outcome of the historical process of 'gradual expansion of social life, from clan to city, from city to nation, from both of these to cosmopolitan humanity'.[62] In an interesting retrospective article on the genesis of his book, Posnett later added that Britain ought to be the ideal ground for the development of comparative literature because the British Empire, with its multinational fabric, was the world's most diverse social body and therefore the most advanced stage in the historical chain of progress towards ever higher complexity. Posnett also warned, however, that the 'cosmopolitan spirit' should look beyond the boundaries of empire: 'while the making of our empire's literature is going on before our eyes, our best writers are every day expressing more deeply that cosmopolitan and world-wide spirit which is the servant of no one social group but the sympathetic friend of all'.[63] Posnett, to whom we shall return in Chapter 1, repeatedly leaned on ideas of cosmopolitanism and world citizenship. His critical writings show how in this period

[61] Perris, *New Internationalism*, 49.
[62] H. M. Posnett, *Comparative Literature* (London: Kegan Paul, Trench, & Co., 1886), 86.
[63] H. M. Posnett, 'The Science of Comparative Literature', *Contemporary Review*, 79 (Jan. 1901), 855–872 (860).

cosmopolitanism entered the vocabulary of literary discourse, where it became attached to a particular literary sensibility and ushered new creative practices.

However, in literature as in the political and social spheres, 'cosmopolitan' was far from a consensual term: it could be associated with progressive ideas and technical innovation but it could also (and this was more often the case) be synonymous with disloyalty, pretentiousness, and failure. Vernon Lee, for instance, berated her friend, the Italian writer Carlo Placci, in the following terms:

> You cannot yet be a good or tolerable novelist because you still look upon life as so much material, as something for you to employ, as distinguished from something to employ you, to fill your heart and mind with problems. [. . .] Now you seem to me never to let yourself go to life. You find it interesting, but not absorbing. [. . .] your cosmopolitanism, your constant moving about, your constantly seeking and surrendering to new impressions and influences, all that makes you intelligent and lively, is a great danger for you. Your greatest danger is a tendency to say *this or that bores me*. It is when you have rooted out of yourself the last traces of *dilettantism* that you will become a true novelist, a novelist for people who live and feel, not for dilettantes.[64]

Lee's words closely echo Baudelaire's characterization of the blasé attitude but, in her view, Baudelairean cosmopolitanism places the writer in a position of weakness. The detached and sensation-hungry habits of the cosmopolite and what is required to be 'a true novelist' are incompatible with each other. As a form of alienation and disengagement, cosmopolitanism has negative aesthetic as well as ethical consequences for Lee. To paraphrase her somewhat crudely, the cosmopolitan writer feels badly and therefore writes badly. This statement is the more surprising because it comes from a writer who is now often held as quintessentially cosmopolitan:[65] Lee read and wrote fluently in four languages, spent her entire life moving around Europe, and was a prominent pacifist and internationalist. Her censure of her friend's 'constant moving about' should therefore not be interpreted as an attack on cosmopolitanism per se, but rather as an effort to distinguish between bad and good forms of cosmopolitan literary practice: between—to adapt Lee's metaphor—an 'absorbent' attitude that constantly challenges and modifies, and therefore enriches, the self, and a superficial aestheticism that skims the surface of experience, collapsing into dilettantism.

---

[64] Vernon Lee to Carlo Placci, 3 Jan. [1893?], Biblioteca Marucelliana, Florence, Carte Placci, 690.5; cited in Francèsca Billiani and Stefano Evangelista, 'Carlo Placci and Vernon Lee: The Aesthetics and Ethics of Cosmopolitanism in Florence', *Comparative Critical Studies*, 10.2 (2013), 141–161 (152–153).

[65] See, for instance, Hilary Fraser, 'Vernon Lee: England, Italy and Identity Politics', in Carol M. Richardson and Graham Smith, eds, *Britannia, Italia, Germania: Taste and Travel in the Nineteenth Century* (Edinburgh: VARIE, 2001), 175–191; and Christa Zorn, 'Cosmopolitan Shaw and the Transformation of the Public Sphere', *Shaw*, 28 (2008), 188–208.

Another case in point is the popular sensation novelist 'Ouida', who in an essay for the *Fortnightly Review* criticized the Italian decadent Gabriele D'Annunzio—then at the height of his international fame—for allowing himself to be 'absorbed and assimilated by foreign influences' to the detriment of his 'Italian individuality' and of his literary use of the Italian language.[66] She provocatively added that D'Annunzio 'would have been a greater Italian writer if he had known no language save Italian and, of course, Latin and Greek'.[67] Again, this seems highly contradictory, coming from a writer who moved in international society, publicly boasted of 'prefer[ring] the literature of other countries' over English literature,[68] and was, in fact, routinely attacked by English-speaking critics for betraying 'Anglo-Saxon ideas of society and of human life'.[69] But Ouida was not advocating that literature should be bound by the cultural horizon of the nation. On the contrary, her point is that D'Annunzio, for all his foreign reading, 'never really becomes what is implied by the word cosmopolitan':[70] that is, that he falls short of a higher ideal.

It is significant that both Lee's and Ouida's anti-cosmopolitan jibes were aimed at Italian writers: it is as though they wanted to bring the wider British experience of cosmopolitan literary modernity to bear on Italy, a recently unified country peripheral to global literary networks, where the tensions between nationalists and cosmopolitans were particularly acute. Lee and Ouida wanted to lay down the rules for a good practice of literary cosmopolitanism because their own careers and individual identities were so heavily invested in the fight against a chauvinistic cultural nationalism. As Ouida knew from experience, nationalist sentiment could be a vicious weapon. The reviewer who accused her of letting down 'Anglo-Saxon ideas', for instance, defined English literature, in a post-Herderian vein, as a truthful reflection of 'the social life, the character, and the manners of the people whose blood is English' and, on the basis of this definition, punished her by symbolically stripping her of literary citizenship: Ouida was 'a much-traveled adventuress of no nationality' who had 'no claim to the title of English-woman'.[71] Such attacks stigmatized individual writers by placing them outside the national consensus described by Collini. Lee would be subjected to even more extreme forms of censure for her pacifist writings during the First World War. In many ways, Lee and Ouida could not be more different from each other: the former was a rigorous and ethically committed thinker; the latter was inconsistent and histrionic, and keen to associate herself with international networks of social

---

[66] Ouida, 'The Genius of D'Annunzio', *Fortnightly Review*, 61 (Mar. 1897), 349–373 (353–354).
[67] Ibid. 353.
[68] Ouida, 'Unwritten Literary Laws', in *Critical Studies* (London: Fisher Unwin, 1900), 180–200 (183).
[69] A. K. Fiske, 'Profligacy in Fiction', *North American Review*, 131 (July 1880), 79–88 (86). This phobic attack is a double review of Ouida's romance of international life, *Moths* (1880), and Zola's *Nana* (1880).
[70] Ouida, 'Genius of D'Annunzio', 353.     [71] Fiske, 'Profligacy in Fiction', 86, 87.

privilege like those satirized by Bourget in *Cosmopolis*. Their remarks show us that cosmopolitanism created a new shared ground in the literature of the turn of the century, making possible new alliances that cut across genres and engrained distinctions between high and popular culture. An historically informed understanding of cosmopolitanism therefore enables us, in the twenty-first century, to see new relations between categories such as aestheticism, decadence, sensation, and naturalism, that critics have traditionally used to frame this period. In particular, by recognizing the cosmopolitanism endorsed by Lee and Ouida (and of course Pater and James) as a response to the very concrete threat posed by xenophobic nationalism, we can start to revise the charge of apoliticized formalism that critics on the left have long directed at aestheticism and decadence, following Theodor Adorno's seminal critique.

For some years now, scholars have been increasingly aware of the need to pay attention to the international reach of literature written in English, as part of a renewed effort to connect authors and texts across cultures and thus release them from the artificially sealed—and, as we have seen, ideologically inflected—disciplinary category of 'English literature'. In particular, within the nineteenth century, Regenia Gagnier has called on Victorian studies to adopt a much wider perspective that takes account of movements of global circulation and moments of 'cross-cultural contact', while respecting the particularity of the local.[72] As Gangier acknowledges, the majority of this work so far has gone into investigating imperial networks, driven by postcolonial scholarship. A number of critics, however, have focused on cosmopolitanism explicitly. Amanda Anderson was the first to trace the influence of cosmopolitanism on a line of canonical writers going from Charlotte Brontë to Wilde. For Anderson, Victorian cosmopolitanism is synonymous with a practice of detachment (the keyword of her study) reflected in the main literary forms of the era, such as the realist novel and the dramatic monologue, but also in its scientific culture and in the cultivation of disinterestedness in criticism.[73] While for Anderson cosmopolitanism is a philosophical

---

[72] Regenia Gagnier, *Literatures of Liberalization: Global Circulation and the Long Nineteenth Century* (Basingstoke and New York: Palgrave Macmillan, 2018), 9. Gagnier approaches the intertwined fields of literature and commodity history through the notion of 'transculturation', borrowed from the anthropologist Fernando Ortiz. See also Lauren M. E. Goodlad, *The Victorian Geopolitical Aesthetic: Realism, Sovereignty, and Transnational Experience* (Oxford and New York: Oxford University Press, 2015); Sharon Marcus, 'Same Difference? Transnationalism, Comparative Literature, and Victorian Studies', *Victorian Studies*, 45.4 (2003), 677–686; Pablo Mukherjee, 'Introduction: Victorian World Literatures', *Yearbook of English Studies*, 41.2 (2011), 1–19.

[73] Amanda Anderson, *The Powers of Distance: Cosmopolitanism and the Cultivation of Detachment* (Princeton and Oxford: Princeton University Press, 2001), 30–31, for the relationship between cosmopolitanism and detachment. Critics of twentieth-century literature have employed the perspective of cosmopolitanism more extensively, mostly in relation to canonical modernist writers; see, for instance, Jessica Berman, *Modernist Fiction, Cosmopolitanism, and the Politics of Community* (Cambridge and New York: Cambridge University Press, 2001); Jed Esty, *A Shrinking Island: Modernism and National Culture in England* (Princeton and Oxford: Princeton University Press, 2004); Pericles Lewis, *Modernism, Nationalism, and the Novel* (Cambridge and New York: Cambridge University Press,

(ethical) concern, for Tanya Agathocleous it is mainly a 'representational challenge' faced by novelists who responded to the changing social fabric of the nineteenth-century city.[74] A similar interest in the impact of cosmopolitanism on literary form drives Ana Parejo Vadillo's approach to the poetry of A. Mary F. Robinson and Amy Levy.[75] With specific reference to the period covered by this book, if Parejo Vadillo speaks of a 'cosmopolitan aestheticism' that is particularly hospitable to women poets, Gagnier again and Matthew Potolsky have used cosmopolitanism to put forward revisionary critiques of literary decadence that rescue it from accusations of solipsism and affirm it as philosophically and politically progressive.[76] For both Gagnier and Potolsky the main problem posed by cosmopolitanism is how to square its conflicting impulses towards individualism (the radical detachment explored by Anderson) and intersubjectivity (the desire to be connected to strangers and people far away). Thus Potolsky argues that the widespread practices of international borrowing and citation adopted by the decadents aided the creation of a 'cosmopolitan community' modelled on the Enlightenment Republic of Letters.[77] The legacy of these progressive cosmopolitan cultures of decadence and aestheticism vividly comes to life in the work of Kristin Mahoney and Robert Stilling, who have traced their links to anti-colonial struggle in the early twentieth century and in contemporary literature and art.[78]

The present book builds on the important work of these critics, while it also aims to bridge the gap between English studies and new developments in comparative and world literature. In the twenty-first century, the desire to push comparative literature beyond its traditional European (or Euro-American) focus has led scholars to interrogate again the foundations laid by Posnett and his nineteenth-century contemporaries. The categories of global and world literature have emerged in an attempt to meet the challenges of providing truly

2000); and Rebecca L. Walkowitz, *Cosmopolitan Style: Modernism beyond the Nation* (New York: Columbia University Press, 2006). While focused on the twentieth century, these studies all recognize the importance of the *fin de siècle* as a key turning point.

[74] Tanya Agathocleous, *Urban Realism and the Cosmopolitan Imagination in the Nineteenth Century: Visible City, Invisible World* (Cambridge and New York: Cambridge University Press, 2011), 13.

[75] Ana Parejo Vadillo, 'Cosmopolitan Aestheticism: The Affective Italian Ethics of A. Mary F. Robinson', *Comparative Critical Studies*, 10.2 (2013), 163–182; and Vadillo, 'Cosmopolitan Disturbances: Amy Levy in Dresden', *Forum for Modern Language Studies*, 53.3 (2017), 325–337.

[76] Regenia Gagnier, *Individualism, Decadence, Globalization: On the Relationship of Part to Whole, 1859–1920* (Basingstoke and New York: Palgrave Macmillan, 2010); Matthew Potolsky, *The Decadent Republic of Letters: Taste, Politics, and Cosmopolitan Community from Baudelaire to Beardsley* (Philadelphia: University of Pennsylvania Press, 2013).

[77] Potolsky, *Decadent Republic*, 5.

[78] Kristin Mahoney, 'On the *Ceylon National Review*, 1906–1911', *BRANCH: Britain, Representation, and Nineteenth-Century History* (2018) <http://www.branchcollective.org/?ps_articles=kristin-mahoney-on-the-ceylon-national-review-1906-1911#_ftn1.end> [accessed 28 July 2020]; Robert Stilling, *Beginning at the End: Decadence, Modernism, and Postcolonial Poetry* (Cambridge, MA: Harvard University Press, 2018).

multicultural perspectives. Looking back explicitly to the nineteenth century, David Damrosch has rescued the internationalist ambition encapsulated in Goethe's notion of *Weltliteratur*, or world literature, as still capable of creating a framework for respecting the diversity of a discontinuous and global canon.[79] By contrast, Emily Apter has insisted that 'untranslatability' rather than familiarity and universality should be the focus of critics' approach to comparative literary studies.[80] Both Damrosch and Apter have come under criticism from the Warwick Research Collective, who have drawn on the notion of combined and uneven development borrowed from Marxist sociology and political theory in order to argue that studies of world literary encounters must focus, first and foremost, on the material conditions of inequality in which such encounters inevitably take place. For the Warwick Research Collective, world literature should be understood as the literature 'of the modern capitalist world-system', not as a free space of circulation and comparison.[81] The disagreement among contemporary critics reflects tensions around the concept of world literature that, as we will see in the course of the chapters, were already at work in the *fin de siècle*. Unlike these critics, my engagement with world literature does not aim to provide a totalizing model, but to open up a wider perspective on linguistic and geographical entanglements, actual engagements, and aspirations that cannot be framed within a narrow focus on Britain or the English language. For similar reasons, in setting the geographical parameters in my title, I have preferred English over British as designating a common field where language, as a material condition, provides a wider and more meaningful shared literary identity than the geographical space of the British nation.

Another very productive approach to questions of international literary relations builds on Pierre Bourdieu's notion of the literary field, which, as Gisèle Sapiro has demonstrated, can be read from a transnational no less than national perspective.[82] In her widely cited *World Republic of Letters*, Pascale Casanova describes the post-Herderian international literary space as a field of struggle, and identifies the nineteenth century as marking a crucial stage in the history of its

---

[79] David Damrosch, *What is World Literature?* (Princeton and Oxford: Princeton University Press, 2003), 2 and *passim*.

[80] Emily Apter, *Against World Literature: On the Politics of Untranslatability* (London and New York: Verso, 2013), esp. 3–4. See also Apter, *The Translation Zone: A New Comparative Literature* (Princeton and Oxford: Princeton University Press, 2006).

[81] WReC [Warwick Research Collective], *Combined and Uneven Development: Towards a New Theory of World-Literature* (Liverpool: Liverpool University Press, 2015), 8, 22, and *passim*. Their work is heavily indebted to another crucial intervention: Franco Moretti, 'Conjectures on World Literature', *New Left Review*, 1 (Jan.–Feb. 2000), 54–68. The model of world literature proposed by the Warwick Collective is criticized in Karima Laachir, Sara Marzagora, and Francesca Orsini, 'Significant Geographies: In Lieu of World Literature', *Journal of World Literature*, 3 (2018), 290–310 (291–292).

[82] Gisèle Sapiro, 'Field Theory from a Transnational Perspective', in Thomas Medvetz and Jeffrey J. Sallaz, eds, *The Oxford Handbook of Pierre Bourdieu* (New York: Oxford University Press, 2018), 161–182.

formation.[83] Reading the geopolitics of literature through a sociological interpretative prism inspired by Bourdieu, Casanova frames her argument in the language of economics, speaking of the import and export of literature, the accumulation and circulation of literary capital, and the 'bourse of literary values'.[84] In this vision of the world's literature informed by competition and hierarchy, Paris was, according to Casanova, 'the world capital of literature in the nineteenth century' or, in a well-known metaphor, 'the Greenwich meridian of literature' against which other literary cultures around the world measured their own modernity.[85] It is easy to see why some have criticized Casanova's book for its openly hierarchical and Francocentric views. Nonetheless, her work is an important reminder that, in the period covered by this book, while English was already challenging the prestige of French as a world literary language and despite the vast economic and political power that Britain commanded by means of its empire, France and Paris remained the main centres of international literary 'consecration'—at least as far as European literatures are concerned.

This particular state of Anglo-French literary relations explains the symbolic, polarizing role that French literature played in the English-speaking world: while cosmopolitans, such as Pater and James, gravitated towards France, not only for its own sake but as a window onto the international field, in nationalists French literature unleashed particularly pernicious phobias of cultural contamination and foreign invasion. It is telling that the reviewer who accused Ouida of letting down 'Anglo-Saxon ideas' compared her novels to Emile Zola's, or that the caricaturist of 'Britannia à la Beardsley' blamed the French perspective for generating a distorted view of Britain. Casanova's French angle is thus extremely helpful in enabling us to place the British *fin de siècle* within a more truly global set of interactions between literary centres and peripheries than the familiar one played out within the British Empire, to which most Anglophone scholarship confines itself. The relative marginality that English literature occupied vis-à-vis France must not be understood as a disadvantage: it made English literary culture more outward-looking and permeable before English and the London–New York axis inherited the burden of global cultural dominance from Paris, much as that is difficult to imagine from our twenty-first-century perspective.

This book starts with detailed studies of three authors who bring to light different ways of embodying the cosmopolitan mission of the writer: Oscar Wilde, Lafcadio Hearn, and George Egerton (Mary Chavelita Dunne). Several other major writers could have deserved a chapter of their own: Mathilde Blind, Joseph Conrad, Henry James, Vernon Lee, Ouida, George Bernard Shaw, Robert Louis Stevenson, Arthur Symons, Israel Zangwill, Helen Zimmern . . . The fact that

[83] Pascale Casanova, *The World Republic of Letters*, tr. M. B. DeBevoise (Cambridge, MA, and London: Harvard University Press, 2004), esp. 82–125.
[84] Ibid. 12–34.   [85] Ibid. 87–103.

the list is potentially very long testifies to the pervasiveness of cosmopolitan practices in the literature of this period. My three writers offer the advantage of covering different geographical and linguistic areas—Germany and France for Wilde; America, France, and Japan for Hearn; Scandinavia for Egerton—while sharing a number of important similarities: they all had biographical experiences of uprooting that made them simultaneously culturally authoritative and socially vulnerable; they used literature to open international channels of communication that worked against English insularity and cultural nationalism; they were all interested in translation and in reaching out to readers outside the boundaries of English. Significantly, moreover, all three were of Irish descent. However, while Ireland deeply influenced their interactions with English culture, they all had an uneasy relationship with Irishness, questioning the affect and politics of national identity from a cosmopolitan perspective. From our point of view, reconstructing this perspective enables us to see how their works operate in a wider and more plural space—a world literary space, as Casanova would put it—than that delimited by the Dublin–London axis.

For all their common traits, however, Wilde, Hearn, and Egerton also exemplify my overarching claim about the contested nature of *fin-de-siècle* literary cosmopolitanism: Wilde and Hearn took opposite stances over the legacy of Herder, as they discussed whether borders shut down or in fact multiplied opportunities for cross-cultural dialogue; while Egerton, unlike her male contemporaries, drew attention to the overwhelming importance of gender in the construction of cosmopolitan identities and in determining women's access to international mobility. It is also important that today these writers enjoy quite different statuses within English literary studies: while Wilde is now recognized as a key figure and Egerton is certainly a familiar name, Hearn still awaits a full rehabilitation in the English-speaking world (by contrast, as we shall see, he is a literary celebrity in Japan). One of the interests of this book is precisely to determine how cosmopolitan practices affect literary reputations and the formation of a national canon.

Two further chapters shift the focus away from individual authors by examining how literary cosmopolitanism played out in the periodical press and in movements for the promotion of universal languages—a phenomenon that boomed in these years. The first three chapters already emphasize the importance of understanding literature as an international network; the final two, however, foreground the network itself as an object of study. A comparative analysis of the multilingual *Cosmopolis* (1896–8), printed simultaneously in various European capitals, and the American *Cosmopolitan* (1886–), which has enjoyed a long afterlife as a fashion magazine, highlights the important role played by the periodical medium in the creation of literary cosmopolitanism as a discursive phenomenon. In particular, the periodical press enables us to observe more closely the social transformations of cosmopolitanism discussed in this introduction, charting the tensions between philosophical idealism and an increasingly prominent understanding of cosmopolitan identities linked to fashion and consumer culture. Cosmopolitanism was also widely discussed in the many journals written in artificial languages, mainly Volapük and its more successful follower, Esperanto. The literal meaning of the word Esperanto as 'one who hopes' directly connects this linguistic experiment with the ideas of international cooperation and universal peace harboured by Kant's Enlightenment philosophy. While many authors dismissed artificial languages as inherently anti-literary, Esperanto in particular was profoundly invested in literature, as is reflected in the extensive activity of literary translation undertaken by the early British Esperanto movement. Indeed, the eccentric perspective of the artificial language generated creative and provocative contributions to questions of translation and world literature.

As we shall see, several of the figures and key concepts encountered in the first three chapters return in different contexts and guises in the final two, which use the plural structure of the network to reveal mechanisms of identity formation and dissemination of knowledge that an exclusive focus on the category of the author would otherwise occlude. The final chapters of the book therefore move progressively further away from concerns of genre and literary form in order to examine what literary cosmopolitanism meant for communities of readers who existed at the margins of conventional literary histories.

Throughout my analysis of this diverse body of writings, I seek to combine the creative and textured historicism that, within English literary studies, has generated much of the best scholarship on the *fin de siècle,* with the belief that, in order to gain a proper understanding of English literature, we cannot stop at the geographical and linguistic boundaries of English. While it is important to acknowledge the ethical dimension of cosmopolitanism, a philosophical focus, such as Anderson's, risks abstracting and disembodying the presence of the foreign other and, at its worst, reducing it to a potentiality, erasing its actual presence in and around the literary text.[86] Following Pater in his introduction to Dante, I view literary cosmopolitanism primarily as a materially embodied set of practices and aesthetic encounters that came into being as authors and readers studied foreign languages, read foreign authors in the original or in English translation, travelled, translated, and worked hard to forge international connections and keep up with what was being written in other countries. At the same time and inseparably from the material dimension, literary cosmopolitanism was also a special way of relating to the world—the acute awareness of being 'of the entire world', to go back to Baudelaire, often expressed as a form of idealism or spiritual orientation, that marked out certain writers or communities of readers

---

[86] For arguments in favour of the recuperation of 'actually existing cosmopolitanisms', see Scott L. Malcomson, 'The Varieties of Cosmopolitan Experience', in Robbins and Cheah, *Cosmopolitics*, 233–245 (238); Robbins's introduction to the same volume, 1–19; and Lauren M. E. Goodlad, 'Cosmopolitanism's Actually Existing Beyond; Toward a Victorian Geopolitical Aesthetic', *Victorian Literature and Culture*, 38 (2010), 399–411 (400–401).

and bound them closer together. I am interested in when, why, and how this desire to be a literary cosmopolitan took on a political dimension, translating into a desire to challenge and undo the alliance between literature and nationalism, questioning the identities, emotions, and cultural practices on which this alliance relied. It is because of this very importance of affect and identity politics that the term cosmopolitan offers attractive advantages for literary historians over the more objective-sounding (and, when it comes to the nineteenth century, anachronistic) 'transnational', which is widely used in the social sciences.[87]

The question of translation recurs in all of the chapters. Mostly ignored by English critics or ascribed a distinctly lesser value than even minor genres of domestic literature, translations are a crucial constituent of the literary culture of any period. In the *fin de siècle*, the much advertised prosecution of Zola's English translator, Henry Vizetelly, on grounds of obscenity led to a particularly acute awareness of the fact that translation was not a secondary or safe branch of literary trade but rather that it was capable of pushing cultural boundaries in sometimes spectacular ways.[88] The media controversy that surrounded the Zola/Vizetelly events, technically about naturalism, was, in fact, primarily a controversy about the free international circulation of literature and the role of literary censorship for the 'protection' of the English nation. In this respect, it is important to remember that the definitions of cosmopolitanism by Pater and Baudelaire which were discussed at the start of this introduction came to light in contexts that were directly informed by translation: Pater's essay was the preface to a new translation of Dante, while Baudelaire built on his own experience of translating Edgar Allan Poe. Like Baudelaire, several of the internationally minded authors studied here (including Hearn and Egerton, as well as Ludwik Zamenhof, the creator of Esperanto) were also active translators who set great store by this aspect of their work and often pursued it idealistically, out of a genuine commitment to the international circulation of ideas. A cosmopolitan perspective recognizes that translations should be considered alongside authors' other forms of creative work—in other words that there is a constant productive exchange between literary and 'translational' aesthetics—and that the material circumstances relating to the marketing and circulation of translations are intertwined with the mechanisms that regulate domestic literary culture.

---

[87] See Tanya Agathocleous and Jason R. Rudy, 'Victorian Cosmopolitanisms: An Introduction', *Victorian Literature and Culture*, 38.2 (2010), 389–397, 390. For the literary application of transnationalism see Peter Morgan, 'Literary Transnationalism: A Europeanist's Perspective', *Journal of European Studies*, 47.1 (2017), 3–20. Within literary criticism, the transnational has provided a particularly productive framework for American studies; see Paul Giles, *Transnationalism in Practice: Essays on American Studies, Literature and Religion* (Edinburgh: Edinburgh University Press, 2010), esp. the introduction, 1–15.

[88] Vizetelly was tried for obscenity twice, in 1888 and 1889, on the instigation of the National Vigilance Association, and finally sentenced to three months' imprisonment.

To literary critics, the historical study of cosmopolitanism should provide an opportunity to reflect critically on the national bias that affects their approach to fundamental categories such as author, canon, and text. It should suggest a radical epistemology of literature as a dynamic space of exchange and mediation, respecting the cultural and linguistic particularities of its international engagements. To adapt what Franco Moretti has said in relation to world and comparative literature, cosmopolitanism was and is 'a thorn in the side, a permanent intellectual challenge to national literatures'.[89] For when it comes to critical practice, the twenty-first century still operates in the shadow of the nineteenth-century nationalization of literary history. The very notion of 'Victorian literature', which critics rarely dispute, uses the local and highly arbitrary circumstances of a British monarch's reign as a tool to give historical coherence to a body of literature and, at the same time, to assert its separateness from the literary cultures of other nations. Likewise, within the academy, the international connections of literature still tend to be the object of specialized interest groups such as comparatists, as though the national and transnational literary fields were mutually independent and could be kept apart. As Elinor Shaffer explains, however, '[o]ur knowledge of the writers of the British Isles is simply incomplete and inadequate' if we ignore how their works were received and criticized by different national audiences or, in other words, how they simultaneously live(d) within and without their native context.[90] At the same time, one can add, a true historical knowledge of literature in English, in the *fin de siècle* or any period, cannot ignore that the circulation of foreign literatures—books and periodicals imported from abroad, translations, criticism of foreign literatures in the media, etc.—is inextricably entangled with the production and understanding of domestic literature. To study the literary cosmopolitanism of the *fin de siècle* means to deconstruct this deceptive dichotomy between the national and the foreign by looking for the traces of non-native traditions that are written out of national literary histories.

---

[89] Moretti, 'Conjectures on World Literature', 68.
[90] Elinor Shaffer, 'Series Editor's Preface', in Stefano Evangelista, ed., *The Reception of Oscar Wilde in Europe* (London and New York: Continuum, 2010), pp. vii–xii (p. viii). Shaffer explains that this is a fundamental principle of the series on 'The Reception of British and Irish Authors in Europe', of which this volume forms part.

# 1

# Oscar Wilde's World Literature

It is criticism that makes us cosmopolitan.

(Oscar Wilde, 'The Critic as Artist')

Is Wilde's *Salomé* in bad French?

(Richard Strauss to Romain Rolland)

When he was subjected to routine questioning by an American customs officer at the start of his 1882 lecture tour, Oscar Wilde came back with a *bon mot* that has since become famous: 'I have nothing to declare except my genius.'[1] Whether authentic or—as often with Wilde—posthumously fabricated, this anecdote captures the importance of the border as a symbolic space in Wilde's career. Wilde understood that international literary relations are subject to rules similar to those that regulate the movement of people and material goods. He played with those rules—ironizing them, as in the American anecdote, but also studying them closely in order to learn how to mediate between different cultures, and between national and transnational perspectives. From his early experiences in America to the self-imposed exile that followed his release from Reading Gaol, Wilde would often speak and write from the other side of the border: he proselytized for English aestheticism in America; he satirized English bourgeois habits through Irish eyes; he was a staunch Francophile in London; and, in Paris, he acted as an ambassador of English letters, associating with French authors who were keen to learn about the new trends from across the Channel.

This book starts with a study of Wilde because this central figure in the literary culture of the English *fin de siècle* was also a key theorist and promoter of the new literary cosmopolitanism of that era. As Julia Prewitt-Brown has shown, Wilde was deeply aware of cosmopolitanism as a distinctive philosophical tradition with a history spanning from antiquity to the German Enlightenment to his own day.[2]

---

[1] In his recent biography of Wilde, Matthew Sturgis reviews the sources for this story, which has been around at least since Arthur Ransome's *Oscar Wilde: A Critical Study* (1912), and concludes that there is no firm evidence that it did, in fact, take place; it may have been a later fabrication by Wilde himself. Sturgis, *Oscar: A Life* (London: Head of Zeus, 2018), 201.

[2] Julia Prewitt-Brown, *Cosmopolitan Criticism: Oscar Wilde's Philosophy of Art* (Charlottesville, VA, and London: University Press of Virginia, 1997). This book, written before the recent kindling of interest in cosmopolitanism in the humanities, remains to this day the fullest study of this subject, focused on the philosophical tradition. Wilde's engagement with philosophy is also the focus of Bruce Bashford, *Oscar Wilde: The Critic as Humanist* (Madison, NJ: Fairleigh Dickinson University Press, 1999); and Giles Whiteley, *Oscar Wilde and the Simulacrum: The Truth of Masks* (Oxford: Legenda,

*Literary Cosmopolitanism in the English* Fin de Siècle: *Citizens of Nowhere.* Stefano Evangelista,
Oxford University Press. © Stefano Evangelista 2021. DOI: 10.1093/oso/9780198864240.003.0002

He also knew that in the modern world the old philosophical ideal was being remoulded by the capitalist economy. But this is not something he necessarily regretted. He himself used the word 'cosmopolitan' with the new inflection of worldly or chic, without giving it a pejorative meaning,[3] for he knew that his success depended in no small measure on what Robert H. Sherard referred to as his 'gloire de salon'.[4] Most importantly, though, Wilde had a profound understanding of the mechanisms that bound literature with the space of the nation and, as the American anecdote shows, he was determined to test those mechanisms.

Wilde constantly reminded his English contemporaries that, in order to gain a proper critical understanding of their national literature, they needed to see it on a global scale. He fought English cultural chauvinism by urging readers to become more international in their taste. Wilde's cosmopolitan outlook was already in evidence in his work as a paid journalist in the 1880s, when he reviewed foreign literature extensively and left his mark as an early enthusiast of Russian fiction—a literary trend that came to Britain via France. He even tried his hand at translating a short story by Turgenev, 'A Fire at Sea', from a French version of the original Russian.[5] He partly modelled his critical voice on Matthew Arnold, one of the prominent Francophiles of the previous generation. In particular, Wilde continued Arnold's campaign against British philistinism and its appropriation by the popular press for a nationalist agenda. Like Arnold, he used cultural nationalism as a negative entity against which he defined his positive identity as a cosmopolitan writer. Unlike Arnold, though, Wilde tempered his tendency to slip into a haughty tone with a characteristic brand of self-irony. So, for instance, when he called Mrs Humphry Ward's hugely successful novel Robert Elsmere (1888) 'a masterpiece of the "genre ennuyeux," the one form of literature that the English people seem to thoroughly enjoy', the droll humour enabled him to give the impression that he was laughing with the public rather than berating it from on high.[6] For Wilde, accusing English readers of provincialism meant more than

2015). Amanda Anderson's analysis of Wilde in her book on cosmopolitan detachment focuses on his use of the epigraph; Anderson, Powers of Distance, 147–176.

[3] See for instance his praise for American women as 'wonderfully cosmopolitan'. Oscar Wilde, 'The American Invasion', in The Complete Works of Oscar Wilde, ed. Ian Small (Oxford and New York: Oxford University Press, 2000–), vi: Journalism, ed. John Stokes and Mark W. Turner (2013), 131–132.

[4] Robert H. Sherard, Oscar Wilde: The Story of an Unhappy Friendship (London: Privately Printed at the Hermes Press, 1902), 39. Sherard (1861–1943) was a close friend of Wilde who specialized in writing about French literature for the British and American presses. In this book, which is Wilde's first biography, he stresses Wilde's natural propensity for being at home among French artists and writers, maybe in order to create a reassuring feeling of distance between the disgraced author and the English readers of his book.

[5] 'A Fire at Sea' was published in Macmillan's Magazine in May 1886. His review of Crime and Punishment appeared in the Pall Mall Gazette on 28 May 1886. Wilde also toyed with the idea of translating Flaubert's La Tentation de saint Antoine (1874), a task that was eventually accomplished by Lafcadio Hearn, as we shall see in Chapter 2.

[6] Wilde, 'The Decay of Lying', in The Complete Works of Oscar Wilde, iv: Criticism: Historical Criticism, Intentions, The Soul of Man, ed. Josephine M. Guy (2007), 72–103 (78).

asserting his own cosmopolitan authority: he wanted to impress on his contemporaries—especially those who were seduced into thinking that the military and economic successes of the British Empire had made it the centre of the world—that being conscious of one's relative position in a larger world system carries with it a special sense of freedom that promotes openness, curiosity, and receptivity. Anticipating the argument made by Milan Kundera in his essay 'Die Weltliteratur' (2005), Wilde intuited that large nations, especially what we now call world powers, are prone to a special form of provincialism that makes them less receptive to what comes from the outside, impoverishing their literary cultures.[7]

Wilde also brings to light the uneasy and often misunderstood relationship between cosmopolitanism and national identity. In the early twentieth century George Bernard Shaw asserted that, 'though by culture Wilde was a citizen of all civilized capitals, he was at root a very Irish Irishman, and, as such, a foreigner everywhere but in Ireland'.[8] Shaw set up a tension between cultural cosmopolitanism and national identity, and chose the essential category of ethnos as the best key to Wilde's works: Irishness, following this reading, was what best revealed Wilde's true self to the reader; it was the innermost essence of his writings, the ultimate meaning that they somehow sought to obfuscate. Shaw's use of the powerful but hackneyed symbol of the root was meant to quash Wilde's perceived intellectual pretensions, that is, his efforts to hide his 'provincial' identity from the metropolitan social circles in which he moved. Following Shaw's lead, Wilde's Irish identity has provided an effective prism for revisionary readings, although modern critics usually posit an inclusive, less ethnocentric conception of what constitutes Irish literature.[9] Wilde, who declared himself 'a most recalcitrant patriot' on the issue of Irish Home Rule,[10] was himself capable of expressing patriotic sentiments, not least in his own exchanges with Shaw, to whom he declared, 'we are both Celtic', adding that 'England is the land of intellectual fogs, but you have done much to clear the air'.[11] To see an Irish Wilde, however, ought not to prevent us from also seeing his fundamentally cosmopolitan allegiances. Wilde shows that it is possible to be a cosmopolitan patriot, in Appiah's

---

[7] Milan Kundera, 'Die Weltliteratur', in Theo D'haen, César Domínguez, and Mads Rosendahl Thomsen, eds, *World Literature: A Reader* (London and New York: Routledge, 2013), 290–300; the essay was originally published in *Le Rideau* (2005). Martin Puchner discusses 'the provincialism of the centre' in relation to Ibsen in 'Goethe, Marx, Ibsen, and the Creation of a World Literature', *Ibsen Studies*, 13.1 (2013), 28–46.

[8] George Bernard Shaw, 'Preface', in Frank Harris, *Oscar Wilde: His Life and Confessions* (London: Constable: 1938), pp. ix–lii (p. xlviii).

[9] For instance Davis Coakley, *Oscar Wilde: The Importance of Being Irish* (Dublin: Town House, 1994); and Jerusha McCormack, ed., *Wilde the Irishman* (New Haven and London: Yale University Press, 1998).

[10] Wilde to James Nicol Dunn, managing editor of the *Scots Observer* (Nov.–Dec. 1888), in *The Complete Letters of Oscar Wilde*, ed. Merlin Holland and Rupert Hart-Davis (London: Fourth Estate, 2000), 371.

[11] Wilde to Shaw [23 Feb. 1893], ibid. 554.

sense of the term: as Appiah has argued, a liberal cosmopolitan ideal easily accommodates patriotism and, at the same time, prevents it from becoming a radicalized sentiment of exclusion that leads to cultural nationalism and xenophobia.[12] As an expatriate Irishman in Britain (and America and France), Wilde was particularly alert to the ideological trappings of nationalism and keen to expose and oppose their negative effects on literature.

Wilde encapsulated his cosmopolitan identity in a letter to the French writer Edmond de Goncourt: 'Français de sympatie, je suis Irlandais de race, et les Anglais m'ont condamné à parler le langage de Shakespeare.'[13] Juxtaposing nature and nurture, Wilde upset an easy dichotomy between these categories. On a superficial level the letter seems to say that the Irish Wilde chose France as his adopted home. But for the writer the tie of language is paramount, so Wilde, who did not speak Gaelic, had to grapple with Englishness as an inescapable source of identity.[14] In this respect, the choice of the word 'condamné' to describe his relationship with Britain was clearly ironic, but it also embodied the trauma of dislocation typical of the colonial author: it captured an enforced cosmopolitan identity that had to navigate a sense of privilege for having been assimilated into a culturally prestigious metropolitan tradition and resentment for having been uprooted. If English was the language of enforcement and obedience, French represented personal, political, and artistic freedom because, by embracing its foreignness, Wilde could turn his uprootedness into a means of empowerment: French was the language that allowed Wilde to forge a free and new identity, setting affect and desire against race and nationality. Here and throughout his writings, Wilde's cosmopolitanism carries an anti-colonial message: by distancing himself from English as the language of empire, Wilde unmasks literature as a political tool capable of propagating racism and exploitation as part of its alleged civilizing mission ('le langage de Shakespeare') in Ireland as well as Africa and Asia. At the same time, however, Wilde's anti-colonial stance was somewhat undercut by his professed allegiance with France—a country with its own history of colonial violence of which Wilde was of course perfectly aware, seductive though Paris was to him. So where did his real loyalties lie? Wilde refused to clarify this point because, as he implied, being cosmopolitan meant rejecting the stark oppositional terms of this question. There were many who found this self-fashioning suspect, even before the disastrous trials of 1895 when, as we shall see, the revelations about his sexuality were compounded with hostility towards his perceived foreignness within English society that had been accumulating for years.

---

[12] Kwame Anthony Appiah, 'Cosmopolitan Patriots', 618 and *passim*.

[13] 'French by sympathy, I am Irish by race, and the English have condemned me to speak the language of Shakespeare.' Wilde to Edmond de Goncourt, 17 Dec. 1891, in *Complete Letters*, 505.

[14] On the role of Irishness in Wilde's subversive attitude to the English language see Declan Kiberd, 'Oscar Wilde: The Resurgence of Lying', in Peter Raby, ed., *The Cambridge Companion to Oscar Wilde* (Cambridge: Cambridge University Press, 1997), 276–294.

In this chapter, I examine Wilde's literary cosmopolitanism through the prism of world literature. First articulated by Goethe in the 1820s, the idea of world literature has provided a powerful model for thinking of literature outside and indeed against national frameworks from the nineteenth century to the present. Wilde lived in the time when Goethe's idea of world literature first gained widespread currency in the English-speaking world, thanks to H. M. Posnett's theories of comparative literature, discussed in the Introduction, and the work of the internationally oriented English Goethe Society. Launched in the same year as Posnett's book (1886), the English Goethe Society was inaugurated by Wilde's former Oxford tutor, Max Müller, with a lecture about world literature. Wilde's most important theorization of literary cosmopolitanism in 'The Critic as Artist' (1891) explicitly looked back to Goethe's ideal of world literature, as mediated by Müller. However, as 'The Critic as Artist' also shows, Wilde's exploration of the philosophical and literary heritage of cosmopolitanism went together with a keen awareness of its social dimension. His French-language Symbolist play, *Salomé* (1893), encapsulates Wilde's social and cultural mobility between France and England in this crucial period of his career. Wilde's switch to French should not trick us into regarding the play as eccentric to his oeuvre:[15] *Salomé* represents the culmination of his desire to cross and disrupt national borders, providing at the same time a practical outlet for the theory of world literature elaborated in his critical writings. Wilde's different identities as theorist and practitioner of literary cosmopolitanism call for different approaches: his criticism requires a deep reading, aimed at recovering the multiple layers of Wilde's philosophical engagement and his dense literary intertextuality, which ranged from Goethe to Müller and Matthew Arnold; while *Salomé* is best examined by means of a phenomenological reading that concentrates on the intervention of the play in the discursive formation of cosmopolitan literary identities at the time, focusing especially on the Parisian scene. First of all, though, in order to provide a context for Wilde, it is necessary to provide some background on Goethe's concept of world literature and its English reception.

## World Literature, the English Goethe Society, and Max Müller

The problem with *Weltliteratur* or world literature is that Goethe formulated this concept relatively late in life and did not leave a systematic discussion. His followers and critics were therefore left to reconstruct what he meant from fragments—about twenty of them in total, according to the Swiss critic Fritz

---

[15] Even in his important positive reassessment, Holbrook Jackson argued that *Salomé* 'missed fire' and noted the 'suspicion among English and American critics' still current in the 1930s. Holbrook Jackson, 'Introduction', in Oscar Wilde, *Salome* (London: Limited Editions Club, 1938), 11–27 (11, 13).

Strich—distributed across published sources, diaries, and private correspondence.[16] Some of these are so brief that they have an almost epigrammatic character, which lends a high degree of flexibility to the concept of world literature, enabling its many returns in later criticism, but which also creates an amount of ambiguity. The first substantive public statement about world literature occurs in the pages of *Über Kunst und Altertum* (1827), the journal for which Goethe worked as editor and chief contributor over the last two decades of his life:

> We hear and read everywhere of the progress of the human race, of the wider prospects in world relationships between men. How far this is the case it is not within my province to examine or to determine: for my part I seek only to point out to my friends my conviction that a universal world literature is in process of formation in which we Germans are called to play an honourable part.[17]

This brief definition lays bare some of the most important characteristics of world literature as Goethe conceived it. First and foremost it shows Goethe's belief that modern literary culture arises from international relations rather within the sealed space of the nation and that, as a result, literature facilitates not only cultural, but also spiritual connections between different peoples. This is the sense in which world literature is 'universal' (*allgemeine*): it provides a common ground that transcends differences in language and habit that make literatures and people foreign to each other. The principle of universality has proved the greatest stumbling block in the reception of world literature, triggering fears of homologation and (Western) cultural hegemony.[18] In a later issue of the same journal, though, Goethe made it clear that he did not think that nations should ever come to think alike,[19] suggesting that world literature should acknowledge and indeed safeguard the local and foster cultural difference within the universal. This is why he thought that Germany would not only benefit from world literature by absorbing influences from abroad, but that it would be of benefit to it by contributing its particular intellectual temper to the shared patrimony of

---

[16] They are listed in a useful appendix to Fritz Strich, *Goethe and World Literature*, tr. C. A. Sym (London: Routledge & Kegan Paul, 1949), 349–351. Strich's book, written in German and published in Switzerland in 1946, tried to relaunch world literature as an ideal of international collaboration after the Second World War. The quotations in the main body of the text are taken from the English translation; the German original in the footnotes is from Strich's first German edition, *Goethe und die Weltliteratur* (Bern: Francke, 1946).

[17] Strich, *Goethe and World Literature*, 349 ('Überall hört und liest man von dem Vorschreiten des Menschengeschlechts, von den weiteren Aussichten der Welt- und Menschenverhältnisse. Wie es auch im Ganzen hiemit beschaffen sein mag [ . . . ], will ich doch von meiner Seite meine Freunde aufmerksam machen, daß ich überzeugt sei, es bilde sich eine allgemeine Weltliteratur, worin uns Deutschen eine ehrenvolle Rolle vorbehalten ist', 397).

[18] See, for instance, Emily Apter, *Against World Literature: On the Politics of Untranslatability* (London and New York: Verso, 2013).

[19] See Strich, *Goethe and World Literature*, 350: 'there can be no question of the nations thinking alike' ('daß nicht die Rede sein könne, die Nationen sollen überein denken', 399).

humanity. For Goethe, therefore, world literature would aid international understanding and, at the same time, promote a liberal ideal of tolerance, as more and more people would gradually come to assimilate foreign ways of thinking.

The political dimension is paramount in Goethe's introduction to the German translation (1830) of Carlyle's life of Schiller (1825), where world literature is explicitly associated with peace and prosperity:

> There has for some time been talk of a Universal World Literature, and indeed not without reason: for all the nations that had been flung together by frightful wars and had then settled down again became aware of having imbibed much that was foreign, and conscious of spiritual needs hitherto unknown. Hence arose a sense of their relationship as neighbours, and, instead of shutting themselves up as heretofore, the desire gradually awoke within them to become associated in a more or less free commerce.[20]

As former enemies become peaceful neighbours they wake up to different 'spiritual needs' (*geistliche Bedürfnisse*). An earlier draft of this passage clearly spelled out how this process of spiritual reorientation was part and parcel of the coming of modernity. Here Goethe pronounced world literature to be an inevitable result of the 'ever-quickening speed of intercourse' between nations created by the increased international movement of individuals and the development of new media technologies, such as journals, which multiplied the amount of information that it was possible to share with people far away.[21]

As part of the historical 'progress of the human race', as he says in *Über Kunst und Altertum*, world literature was therefore an inevitable fact of the future for Goethe. The repeated emphasis on the future is important. For, crucially, Goethe always spoke about world literature as a potential rather than an actual state, realizable but unrealized, linked to desire and projection. In the twentieth century, Goethe's concept of world literature would be criticized as a model of value-judgement that promotes exclusion, whereby only a tiny portion of what is written can become universal: in this view world literature is made up of a series of classics or selected high points of local traditions—or, to adopt Matthew Arnold's famous formula, 'the best that has been thought and said [and written in this case] in the world'.[22] But for Goethe world literature was not so much a body of already

---

[20] Ibid. 351 ('Es ist schon einige Zeit von einer allgemeinen Weltliteratur die Rede, und zwar nicht mit Unrecht: denn die sämtlichen Nationen, in den fürchterlichsten Kriegen durcheinander geschüttelt, sodann wieder auf sich selbst einzeln zurückgeführt, hatten zu bemerken, daß sie manches Fremdes gewahr worden, in sich aufgenommen, bisher unbekannte geistige Bedürfnisse hie und da empfunden', 399–400).

[21] Ibid. 351 ('der sich immer vermehrenden Schnelligkeit des Verkehrs', 400).

[22] Matthew Arnold, 'Preface' (1869) to *Culture and Anarchy*, in *Culture and Anarchy*, ed. R. H. Super (Ann Arbor: University of Michigan Press, 1965), 231–256 (233). Here Arnold is defining the object of culture.

existing works as, in David Damrosch's words, 'a mode of circulation and of reading'[23]—that is, a process of reception by means of which works transform themselves as they move beyond their linguistic and national points of origin, generating new meanings and fulfilling new potentialities as they reach new, foreign audiences.

Despite the fact that Carlyle—Goethe's main British mediator—played an important role in contributing to Goethe's ongoing definition of world literature, the concept itself attracted little attention in Britain for much of the nineteenth century. It is striking that George Henry Lewes, in his canonical mid-Victorian biography of Goethe (1855), made no mention at all of world literature. Goethe for Lewes was universal inasmuch as he exemplified the syncretic identity of the modern man of letters as a freethinker, a student of the natural sciences as well as the arts, and a religious sceptic. The last two decades of the century, however, saw a first kindling of interest in the concept of world literature. This new trend may have been triggered in part by the increased circulation of John Oxenford's English translation of the *Conversations of Goethe with Eckermann and Soret*, originally published in 1850, which went into several reprints from the mid-1870s, attracting more interest than on its first publication. It is in this posthumous work that Goethe gave some of his most detailed definitions of world literature.

In 1886, Posnett's *Comparative Literature* contained the first extensive treatment of the concept of world literature in English. Posnett tactfully respected the Herderian view of literature as a binding agent for national feeling and patriotism but he also urged that, 'in this time of international literature', English critics must look abroad more and more, as no national literature could exist in isolation from a larger world-system of exchanges.[24] Posnett followed Goethe in linking world literature with modernity and the future, seeing it as the telos or last stage in the evolution of humanity from local to cosmopolitan forms of social organization. Posnett was adamant that the new comparative literature should be seen as a science and its internationalism as a reflection of the international orientation of nineteenth-century scientific culture. However, his championing of world literature as the expression of a 'universal ideal of humanity' belied the tendency, also shared with Goethe, to politicize literature as a weapon against nationalism.[25] Strangely, for all his borrowings and despite the fact that Goethe featured largely among his examples, Posnett did not explicitly attribute the idea of world literature to Goethe. He would only make the connection explicit fifteen years later in a retrospective article, where he glossed world literature as the 'cosmopolitan spirit' of the 'best writers' of today, and took his revenge on English critics who attacked

---

[23] Damrosch, *What is World Literature?*, 5. Cf. Franco Moretti, 'Evolution, World-Systems, *Weltliteratur*', in Gunilla Lindberg-Wada, ed., *Studying Transcultural Literary Theory* (Berlin: de Gruyter, 2006), 113–121; and Christopher Prendergast, 'Negotiating World Literature', *New Left Review*, 8 (2001), 100–121.

[24] H. M. Posnett, *Comparative Literature*, 79.      [25] Ibid. 238.

his use of this 'ugly term' in 1886, unaware that he had in fact taken it from Goethe.[26]

The real turning point in the delayed English reception of world literature, however, came with the foundation of the English Goethe Society just a few months after the publication of Posnett's book. The aim of the society was to promote the knowledge of Goethe in England while also providing a gathering point for the 'large and growing number of persons whose interest in foreign literature is not precisely that of amateurs; [. . . ] the time appears to have come when they should unite, as the Anglicists have long ago united, to undertake a more systematic study of their department than has hitherto in England been possible'.[27] The English Goethe Society was one of the many national branches of the Weimar Goethe Society, which, from its foundation in 1885, vigorously promoted Goethe's works internationally and, by so doing, provided a de facto network and platform for the transnational ideal of world literature. In fact, the *Goethe Jahrbuch* published by the Weimar society included regular updates on the English branch and members of the latter were entitled to purchase the publications of the German Goethe Society at discounted prices. In 1887, the Weimar Goethe Society was reported in the British press to number nearly 3,000 members distributed around the world (a considerable figure, especially when compared to a global membership of 2,500 quoted by the Society's website today), stemming from various European countries but also Turkey, India, and China.[28]

Given this internationalist ambition, it is not surprising that the opening address to the English Goethe Society, delivered by its first president, Max Müller, on 28 May 1886, should have been on the subject of world literature. Müller, a German expatriate who held the chair of comparative philology at Oxford, was not so much a Goethe expert as a prominent *comparatist* who had worked all his life to promote the study of foreign cultures and intercultural understanding.[29] In particular, his work on comparative mythology, for which he became famous, was based on a study of the similarities between ancient Greek and Sanskrit aimed at demonstrating the existence of a common linguistic root

---

[26] H. M. Posnett, 'The Science of Comparative Literature', 860.

[27] C. H. Herford, 'An English Goethe Society', *The Academy*, 26 (1884), 324. Herford was one of the founders of the Society and later, following an internal split in the 1890s, of the independent Manchester Goethe Society. For a historical overview, see Günter Hollenberg, 'Die English Goethe Society und die deutsch-englischen kulturellen Beziehungen im 19. Jahrhundert', *Zeitschrift für Religions- und Geistesgeschichte*, 30 (1978), 36–45.

[28] Horatio S. White, 'The Meeting of the Weimar Goethe Society and the New "Faust" MS.', *The Academy*, 31 (1887), 395. On membership figures, see <http://www.goethe-gesellschaft.de/netzwerk.html> [accessed 29 July 2020].

[29] Müller's multiple disciplinary interests are examined in the special issue of the *Publications of the English Goethe Society*, 85.2 and 3 (2016). John R. Davis and Angus Nicholls stress Müller's role as part of the Society's diplomatic mission of promoting closer peaceful ties between Britain and Germany at a time of mounting political tension; Davis and Nicholls, 'Friedrich Max Müller: The Career and Intellectual Trajectory of a German Philologist in Victorian Britain', *Publications of the English Goethe Society*, 85.2 and 3 (2016), 67–97 (79–84).

but also of common myths that linked European and Asian classical civilizations. Müller was both an international authority on European and Asian languages, mythology, and religions, and a recognizable public figure. His books achieved global circulation not only in English, but also in Bengali, Marathi, Guajarati, and Japanese translations, as he reminded his audience, and he collected honorary doctorates and memberships of learned societies from all over the world.[30] He was moreover himself an active translator of German literature and philosophy (including Kant) into English. In other words, Müller was an ideal candidate for the presidency inasmuch as he could be seen as a sort of 'English' Goethe even though, as Angus Nicholls has pointed out, the differences between their comparative methods were substantial.[31]

In his lecture Müller drew on his philological expertise in order to argue that we can already see 'the rudiments of a world-literature' (p. 775) in ancient Egyptian and Babylonian inscriptions, as well as more familiar classical works from Greece and Rome. These works, he claimed, were carved or written with the whole of humanity, present and future, as their intended audience, rather than addressing a narrow national group as was the norm in modern times. Therefore, while world literature was Goethe's 'modern dream' according to Müller, it was also, at the same time, 'one of the most ancient historical realities' (p. 778):

> I believe it was the same awakening spirit of human sympathy which Goethe preached, the same reverence for a past which was no more, the same faith in a future which was not yet, which led the great historical nations of the world to lay the first foundations of what we now call literature, and what to them was world-literature, so far as they could realize it.   (p. 775)

For Müller, philology held the key to world literature: the study of the ancient languages revealed that world literature actually preceded national literature rather than being its ideal future form—an argument that we can relate to Müller's famous theories of the degeneration of a primitive 'Aryan' idiom into a multiplicity of local or, as he would have it, 'diseased' linguistic branches that constituted the origin of mythology.

Müller painted a bleak picture of the present as an age of mounting nationalisms, which harmed literature and literary criticism by erecting artificial borders that blocked the international flow of ideas and promoted hostility towards

---

[30] Max Müller, 'Goethe and Carlyle', *Contemporary Review*, 49 (1886), 772–793 (790). All quotations are from the periodical reprint of Müller's lecture and are made parenthetically in the main body of the text.

[31] 'Whereas Goethe tended to valorize difference and particularity over similarity, Müller undertook comparison in order to argue for a primordial unity between all peoples, languages and religions'; Angus Nicholls, 'Max Müller and the Comparative Method', *Comparative Critical Studies*, 12.2 (2015), 213–234 (217).

foreign influences. In this depressing scenario, Müller argued, Goethe was more important than ever because he reminded intellectuals today that 'the true poet, the true philosopher, the true historian belongs not to one country only, but to the world at large' (p. 774). Goethe showed that the cosmopolitan mission of the writer carried with it a sense of 'universal responsibility' (p. 775). Lewes and other Victorian critics had struggled with Goethe's cosmopolitanism, preferring to see it as an intermediate step towards a healthy cultural nationalism: in this view, the mature Goethe grew out of what one Victorian critic called the 'cosmopolitan characterlessness' of his early years in order to become a fully fledged German author, providing his country with a truly national culture at last.[32] Müller, by contrast, was completely unapologetic about Goethe's '*cosmopolitan sympathies*' (p. 774) as providing his greatest legacy for posterity.

At the core of Müller's lecture was a small literary coup: he revealed he had found several letters from Goethe to Carlyle that were thought to have been lost. Müller was therefore able to disclose original pronouncements on world literature that had not been seen before. At the same time, he drew an intimate picture of the epistolary exchanges between Goethe and Carlyle as displaying the type of collaboration and international friendship that world literature promoted in the abstract.

Yet, for all Müller's efforts to put forward an optimistic vision of the present and of the work that lay ahead for the society, it is impossible not to sense his feelings of scepticism and anxiety. Looking back on the progress of world literature from the 1820s to the present, Müller saw that many of its conditions had now been realized: the growing internationalization of the press, the proliferation of international exhibitions, the development of new media, and the increase in translations of science as well as literature—all of these meant that writers were now more and more frequently writing for an audience that far exceeded the linguistic and political boundaries of their nation. But, Müller noted, the ideals of universal sympathy and 'love between nation and nation' (p. 791), that is, the ethical or spiritual mission of world literature on which Goethe was very keen, remained unrealized. He therefore concluded by setting an explicitly political task for the members of the Society: to work within their powers in order to promote good relations with foreign countries, especially with Bismarck's Germany, where 'ill-feeling against England [. . .] has been artificially stirred up' by nationalist propaganda (p. 792). What Müller could not of course say was that the same was true of the way in which Germany was represented in Britain. The German émigré, naturalized British citizen in 1855, was himself in a delicate position of having to strike a balance between his national and cosmopolitan loyalties.

---

[32] J. R. Seeley, *Goethe, Reviewed After Sixty Years* (London: Seeley & Co., 1894), 102. The articles that make up this book were originally published in the *Contemporary Review* in 1884, two years before Müller's lecture.

When he explicitly turned to the question of empire, Müller launched a cautious attack on patriotism, suggesting that the very vastness of the British Empire risked discouraging the British from looking beyond its boundaries, preventing them from cultivating 'larger sympathies' (p. 789). In Müller's ambivalent assessment, imperial patriotism was both a 'duty' and a less desirable form of 'enthusiasm'; in any case, it should be only one in a series of 'steps leading higher and higher till we repeat with some of the greatest men the words of Terence, "I count nothing strange to me that is human."' (p. 790) The argument that world literature and imperial mentality were at odds with each other exposed, as Posnett had also done in his book, the fallacy of thinking that the empire was intrinsically cosmopolitan because of its supranational social structure. However, Müller undercut his progressive argument against imperialism by urging the British to look for intellectual partners within Europe and of course especially in Germany, on the grounds that the British and the Germans shared the same religion and 'the same Aryan, nay the same Teutonic, blood' (p. 790). Even though in other contexts Müller cautioned against conflating linguistic kinship with 'blood-relationship',[33] his appeal to the racial unity that supposedly linked the British and the Germans as Aryans undermined the universalist foundations of his cosmopolitanism, as did his racist remark that 'the international relations between the leading countries of Europe have become worse than among savages in Africa' (p. 772).

Despite these obvious limitations, Müller's lecture marked an important symbolic moment in which one of Britain's foremost academic authorities spoke publicly about literature as a tool to question and reject nationalism. It is striking how thoroughly Müller now revised his earlier opinion in *The German Classics* (1858) that 'as long as there are different languages and different nations, let each poet think, and work, and write for his own people, without caring for the applause of other countries. Science and philosophy are cosmopolitan; poetry and art are national.'[34] In this earlier work he had also linked Goethe's idea of world literature, which he then saw realized in the ever closer ties between Britain and Germany, with 'the supremacy of the Teutonic race, not only in Europe but all over the world'.[35] Nearly thirty years later, the gradual drifting apart of Britain and Germany, which in a sense deepened a rift within his own individual identity, turned Müller into a more reflective critic of literary nationalism.

The opening address achieved a wide resonance as the lecture was quickly published both in the first volume of the *Publications of the English Goethe Society* and in the prestigious *Contemporary Review*, and eventually found its way into an

---

[33] See Léon Poliakov, *The Aryan Myth: A History of Racist and Nationalist Ideas in Europe*, tr. Edmund Howard (London: Chatto, Heinemann, 1974), 214.
[34] Müller, *The German Classics from the Fourth to the Nineteenth Century: A German Reading-Book* (London: Longman, 1858), p. xxxix.
[35] Ibid., p. vi.

enlarged new edition (1894) of Müller's collected essays, *Chips from a German Workshop*. The political message was picked up by the International Arbitration Association, which published extracts of Müller's lecture in its monthly journal and in a specially issued pamphlet, where they highlighted the effectiveness of Goethe's idea of world literature in counteracting narrow forms of patriotism.[36] As it reverberated in the public sphere, Müller's essay helped to naturalize world literature into English. It is therefore no coincidence that, when Charles Eliot Norton brought out his bilingual edition of the *Correspondence between Goethe and Carlyle* the year after Müller's lecture, he singled out the idea of world literature—glossed as 'the establishment of an exchange between different countries of their highest mental products'—as one of the keystones of Goethe's thought.[37]

## Wilde, Goethe, and the Cosmopolitanism of the Future

When Müller delivered his lecture on Goethe and Carlyle, Wilde was about to embark on the most productive phase of his career. His own lecturing days of the early 1880s were over. Now, he set out to write a small number of highly crafted critical essays, published in quality periodicals, later collected in book form in *Intentions* (1891). Of these works, 'The Critic as Artist' in particular bears the imprint of the new interest in world literature and comparative literature. Wilde's well-known argument that criticism should be seen as an art form develops within a quintessentially philological and comparative framework: Wilde presents all texts, and all forms of cultural production, as fundamentally unstable and only loosely connected to their points of origin, including their geographical or national origin. It follows that their meaning is best sought in a long history of development and variations that displaces them in space, across linguistic and cultural borders, no less than in time. In 'The Critic as Artist', Wilde approaches cosmopolitanism through a philosophical tradition that reaches back to Kant via Goethe and his most recent Anglo-German interpreter, Müller. Pater and Matthew Arnold also remained, as ever, crucial sources of inspiration, in associating cosmopolitanism with the analytical power, intellectual openness, and liberal humanism that characterize the best work of the literary critic: 'It is criticism that makes us cosmopolitan', Wilde declares in a climactic passage that

---

[36] [Anon.], *The Unity of Man* (London: [privately printed for the International Arbitration Association], 1886), 1. The pamphlet is a reprint of an article that originally appeared in the *Monthly Journal of the International Arbitration Association* (June 1886).

[37] *Correspondence between Goethe and Carlyle*, ed. Charles Eliot Norton (London: Macmillan, 1887), p. xvi.

introduces his reading of Goethe.[38] At the same time, however, Wilde's creative use of the dialogue form deliberately takes criticism out of the dusty settings of libraries and lecture halls, underscoring the social dimension and the feeling of worldliness that mark the new understanding of cosmopolitanism that James explores in *The Ambassadors*.[39] The dandified speakers of Wilde's critical dialogues are men of the world who perform philosophy and criticism in the form of brilliant conversation and *savoir faire*.

Wilde's defence of criticism as an art form in its own right leads to two intertwined areas of revision: an *historical* one, in that it enables us to see new patterns and relations across texts; and an *aesthetic* one, in that it undoes what Wilde regards as a false dichotomy between creative and critical practices. At the same time, it allows Wilde to reclaim status for the profession of criticism that, as scholars have pointed out, was being redefined due to the expansion of Victorian journalism.[40] In order to make his point Wilde went all the way back to the ancient Greeks, challenging the received view of Greece as the origin of European art and culture. In doing so, he took issue with one of the most influential theories on the relationship between classical and modern literature, Friedrich Schiller's 'On Naïve and Sentimental Poetry' ('Über naïve und sentimentalische Dichtung', 1795). Schiller had suggested that Greek literature sprang from an unmediated or naïve relationship with nature that enabled their poetry to be 'the completest possible *imitation of actuality*'.[41] By contrast, he believed that modern forms of writing were characterized by a 'sentimental' approach rooted in the consciousness of belatedness. Wilde corrected Schiller by arguing that the Greeks were in fact 'a nation of art critics' (p. 135), whose greatest legacy to posterity was not in their original artistic creations but in the critical spirit itself. He thus rejected the dichotomy between naïve and sentimental poetry and indeed dismissed the aesthetic value of naïve art and originality *tout court*, maintaining instead that 'the work that seems to us to be the most natural and simple product of its time is always the result of the most self-conscious effort' (p. 143). By tactically emphasizing self-consciousness and artificiality, Wilde argued that all literature was in fact 'sentimental' in Schiller's sense, and that creative and critical forms of art have evolved in close partnership with each other since ancient Greek days.

---

[38] Wilde, 'The Critic as Artist', in *The Complete Works of Oscar Wilde*, iv. 123–206 (202). Subsequent references in the text.

[39] Cf. Chapter 4.

[40] Laurel Brake, *Subjugated Knowledges: Journalism, Gender, and Literature in the Nineteenth Century* (Basingstoke: Macmillan, 1994); Josephine M. Guy and Ian Small, *Oscar Wilde's Profession: Writing and the Culture Industry in the Late Nineteenth Century* (Oxford: Oxford University Press, 2000).

[41] Friedrich Schiller, 'On Naïve and Sentimental Poetry', tr. Julius A. Elias, in H. B. Nisbet, ed., *German Aesthetic and Literary Criticism: Winckelmann, Lessing, Hamann, Herder, Schiller, Goethe* (Cambridge: Cambridge University Press, 1985), 180–232 (194).

This realignment enabled Wilde to claim that Alexandria, and not classical Athens, should be seen as the intellectual centre of the ancient world: it was there that 'the Greek spirit became most self-conscious' (p. 144) and criticism acquired the same intellectual freedom and aesthetic autonomy as art. With its famous library and academy which were for centuries the home of textual criticism and philology, Alexandria was attractive to Wilde because it was a culture that committed itself to preservation, transition, and transmission. As Wilde put it, Alexandria guaranteed the 'survival' (p. 144) of ideas and art forms from Greek to Roman antiquity and from Rome to the Renaissance and, ultimately, the present. This view went against standard accounts by classicists who usually associated Alexandria with, in the words of John Addington Symonds, 'parasitic *littérateurs*' and the decay of classical Greek culture.[42] More broadly, in the late nineteenth century, the epithet 'Alexandrian' was used pejoratively to stigmatize the perceived 'mannerism and affectation' of contemporary literature, with a clear swipe at decadent writers, and to express a feeling of nostalgia for a mythicized past in which English literature was the straightforward expression of English national character, untroubled by foreign contaminations.[43] Wilde overturned this negative discourse and its nationalistic associations following the revisionary line that Posnett had taken in his pioneering *Comparative Literature*, which celebrated the strategic importance of Alexandria in the history of world literature as 'the city in which the cosmopolitan Greek spirit was [...] to find a more congenial home than in any of the old city commonwealths'.[44] In a series of passages that Wilde echoed in 'The Critic as Artist', Posnett had related how the 'world culture' of Alexandria created the conditions for world literature by rising 'above old restrictions of place and time'; and how the imitation of early models should be understood in close connection with the 'reflective and critical spirit, which is another striking characteristic of world-literature'.[45] Similarly, for Wilde the cosmopolitan Hellenistic metropolis, poised between East and West and home to different ethnicities and religious communities, suggested an alternative model of cultural history which is not identified with the birth and development of the nation, but rather with migration, contamination, and the constant uprooting of ideas and art forms from their native soil.

Could the cosmopolitan spirit of ancient Alexandria be rekindled in the present? Wilde broached this question in a key passage dense with allusions to Goethe that is worth reproducing in full:

---

[42] John Addington Symonds, *Studies of the Greek Poets* (London: Smith, Elder, & Co., 1873), 32.
[43] [Anon.], 'An Alexandrian Age', *Macmillan's Magazine*, 55 (1 Nov.1886), 27–35 (29). It is worth noting that this article was published in the same year as Müller's inaugural lecture and Posnett's book.
[44] Posnett, *Comparative Literature*, 253.     [45] Ibid. 236.

No: the emotions will not make us cosmopolitan, any more than the greed for gain could do so. It is only by the cultivation of the habit of intellectual criticism that we shall be able to rise superior to race prejudices. Goethe—you will not misunderstand what I say—was a German of the Germans. He loved his country—no man more so. Its people were dear to him; and he led them. Yet, when the iron hoof of Napoleon trampled upon vineyard and cornfield, his lips were silent. 'How can one write songs of hatred without hating?' he said to Eckermann, 'and how could I, to whom culture and barbarism are alone of importance, hate a nation which is among the most cultivated of the earth, and to which I owe so great a part of my own cultivation.' This note, sounded in the modern world by Goethe first, will become, I think, the starting point for the cosmopolitanism of the future. Criticism will annihilate race prejudices, by insisting upon the unity of the human mind in the variety of its forms. If we are tempted to make war upon another nation, we shall remember that we are seeking to destroy an element of our own culture, and possibly its most import- ant element. [ ... ] Intellectual criticism will bind Europe together in bonds far closer than those that can be forged by shopman or sentimentalist. It will give us the peace that springs from understanding.   (pp. 202–203)

Goethe was, for Wilde, the founding figure of literary cosmopolitanism, and his idea of world literature the corner stone for what he calls the 'cosmopolitanism of the future'. The passage cited by Wilde, which has been called 'the classical expression of [Goethe's] cosmopolitanism',[46] comes from Oxenford's English translation of the *Conversations of Goethe with Eckermann and Soret*—the work that contains most of the widely quoted passages on world literature. It occurs in the entry for 14 March 1830, in which Goethe explains his revulsion for war and denounces 'national hatred' as being 'strongest and most violent where there is the lowest degree of culture. But [Goethe goes on to explain] there is a degree where it vanishes altogether, and where one stands to a certain extent *above* nations, and feels the weal or woe of a neighbouring people, as if it had happened to one's own'.[47] In 'The Critic as Artist', Wilde channelled Goethe's belief that literature could undo nationalist feeling by promoting a utopian ideal of world citizenship founded on a liberal principle of unity within difference ('the unity of the human mind in the variety of its forms'). Like Müller in his inaugural address to the Goethe Society, Wilde wanted to show the renewed urgency of Goethe's political message for the present: in the time of the Napoleonic wars as in the different

[46] W. H. Bruford, *Germany in the Eighteenth Century: The Social Background of the Literary Revival* (Cambridge: Cambridge University Press, 1935), 305.
[47] Johann Wolfgang von Goethe, *Conversations of Goethe with Eckermann and Soret*, tr. John Oxenford, 2 vols (London: Smith, Elder, & Co., 1850), ii. 259.

geo-political landscape of the *fin de siècle*—an era that Wilde sees as marked by parochial theological disputes, fanaticism, and hostility towards 'the free play of the mind' (p. 204)—cosmopolitanism can save English society from the dangers of radicalized nationalism or what he calls 'race prejudices' by promoting tolerance instead of hatred and by educating people into valuing cultural differences, glossed here as the 'variety of [...] forms' of the human mind. And, like Müller, Wilde wanted to make cosmopolitanism attractive to English readers by reassuring them that it need not entail the loss of national character or a sense of disloyalty. This is why he stressed that Goethe was 'a German of the Germans', suggesting that the 'real love between nation and nation' that Müller had seen as 'the greatest blessing which Goethe hoped for from the spreading of a world-literature' can coexist with the love of one's country.[48]

Still, attentive readers could not fail to notice that Wilde's description of the cosmopolitanism of the future was dominated by the negative presence of Goethe's silence, which introduced elements of absence, conflict, and self-censorship. The collapse of speech that seized the great oracle at the upsurge of wartime nationalism highlights a fundamental conflict between the claims of culture, with its broad humanist ethical outlook, and the narrow duties of state citizenship. Indeed, in the same conversation with Eckermann, Goethe confessed to having often felt alienated from the German public, complaining of its hostility and comparing himself to Byron being 'driven from England by evil tongues'.[49] Goethe's feeling of distance from his domestic readership spoke directly to Wilde's own self-perception. Responding to negative reviews of *The Picture of Dorian Gray* around this time, for instance, he repeatedly claimed that French critics understood him much better than their English counterparts, and portrayed himself as a victim of English puritanism and philistinism.[50] For Wilde as for Goethe, the image of the cosmopolitan author who is misunderstood and marginalized at home lends force to the idea that literature should teach us how to *feel* together with a foreign people as if its emotions were our own. Both emphasize that literature is by no means a field of national consensus, but a space where national identities collapse: foreignness, in Wilde's arresting paradox, becomes the 'most important element' of a national culture.

Wilde never credited the idea of world literature explicitly, but he had been playing with it since the very start of his career. In his American lecture 'The English Renaissance of Art' (1882), which is thick with references to Goethe, he had somewhat cryptically referred to Goethe's prediction about 'the dawn of a new literature which all people may claim as their own, for all have contributed to its

---

[48]   Müller, 'Goethe and Carlyle', 791.
[49]   Goethe, *Conversations with Eckermann and Soret*, ii. 258.
[50]   Wilde, letter to the editor of the *St James's Gazette*, 27 June [1890], in *Complete Letters*, 432.

foundation'.[51] Wilde's aim was to encourage his American audiences to borrow liberally from foreign cultures—notably, of course, English aestheticism—in their own literature and art. Echoes of Goethe can also be heard in his assertion, in the same lecture, that in literature 'noble work is not national merely, but universal'; and in his warning that, in matters of politics, the 'independence of a nation must not be confused with any intellectual isolation'.[52] In the more coherent edifice of 'The Critic as Artist', Wilde went back to those early ideas. Now, however, he shifted the emphasis onto criticism as the prime medium of world literature. In so doing, Wilde aligned his argument with the new method of comparative literature laid out by fellow Irishman H. M. Posnett, but he also stayed close to what Goethe outlined in another conversation with Eckermann, this time of 15 July 1827:

> It is pleasant to see that intercourse is now so close between the French, English, and Germans, that we shall be able to correct one another. This is the greatest use of a world-literature, which will show itself more and more. Carlyle has written a life of Schiller, and judged him as it would be difficult for a German to judge him. On the other hand, we are clear about Shakespeare and Byron, and can, perhaps, appreciate their merits better than the English themselves.[53]

Here Goethe described world literature as an international critical dialogue in which authors and works acquired different meanings when viewed from abroad or in a global perspective—meanings that Goethe found more valuable than those generated within enclosed national traditions (Goethe's remarks were prompted by Eckermann's surprise at the perceptiveness of Carlyle's criticism of the then popular German romantic writer Friedrich de La Motte Fouqué). Cultural distance and linguistic difference, far from being disadvantages, sharpened the critic's judgement. Once again Goethe projected world literature into a future of increased international communication in which nations would be able to 'correct one another', as he said. This time, however, critics, not writers, were the true protagonists of the cosmopolitan turn.

The ability to inhabit the supranational space described by Goethe is also part of what makes Wilde's critic a better artist than the writer. But Wilde's repurposing of world literature as cosmopolitan criticism is also where he comes closest to his main English source: Matthew Arnold's 'The Function of Criticism at the Present Time' (1864). The playful intertextuality with Arnold was made plain in the first, periodical version (1890) of 'The Critic as Artist', which bore the unmistakably Arnoldian title 'The True Function and Value of Criticism'.

---

[51] Wilde, 'The English Renaissance of Art', in *Essays and Lectures*, ed. Robert Ross (London: Methuen & Co., 1909), 109–155 (141). Characteristically for Wilde, this creative 'quotation' comes close to, but does not exactly match, any of Goethe's surviving definitions of world literature.
[52] Ibid. 143.    [53] Goethe, *Conversations with Eckermann and Soret*, i. 432.

Arnold had also argued that criticism should question and broaden the limits of national cultures, providing incentives to learn from foreign ideas. While characteristically despairing of English provincialism, Arnold had nonetheless seen the present moment (he was writing in the 1860s) as ripe with opportunity for a cosmopolitan turn: he observed that 'an epoch of expansion seems to be opening in this country', aided both by a long period of peace, which meant that 'the ideas of Europe steal gradually and amicably in, and mingle, though in infinitesimally small quantities at a time, with our own notions', and by technological and social changes, so that 'our railways, our business, and our fortune-making' are promoting travel and freedom as never before.[54] Wilde followed Arnold in defining criticism as the exercise of curiosity and in detecting a quintessentially English prejudice against curiosity as having an intellectual value in its own right; he also embraced Arnold's injunction that the 'English critic of literature' should 'dwell much on foreign thought', as well as Arnold's notion of the critical spirit as an internationalist force 'which regards Europe as being, for intellectual and spiritual purposes, one great confederation, bound to a joint action and working to a common result'.[55] However, he made a number of important revisions. First of all he rejected, as we have seen, Arnold's argument that '[t]he critical power is of lower rank than the creative'.[56] But Wilde also discarded Arnold's emphasis on objectivity ('The man who sees both sides of a question, is a man who sees absolutely nothing at all', p. 188) and rationality ('There are two ways of disliking art, Ernest. One is to dislike it. The other, to like it rationally', p. 188) in favour of a critical method guided by what he called 'a temperament exquisitely susceptible to beauty' (p. 190).

Wilde's most distinctive departure from Arnold was on the role of economics and global free trade in facilitating international literary relations. In the *Communist Manifesto* (1848), Marx had invoked Goethe's idea of world literature to describe the evolution of global capitalism, which replaced 'the old local and national seclusion' with 'intercourse in every direction'.[57] Following the same logic, Arnold had linked the cosmopolitan opening of nineteenth-century Britain to its rise as a commercial world power, which brought the country into increased contact with other nations. Müller, in his inaugural lecture, had also drawn readers' attention to the fact that Goethe had described world literature as 'free commerce' and, in his own account, multiplied metaphors of reading as buying, translation as trading, literary conversation as exchange of commodities. By contrast, Wilde urged readers to be sceptical of collapsing the networks of international capitalism with those of world literature. This is the meaning of his

---

[54] Matthew Arnold, 'The Function of Criticism at the Present Time', in *Lectures and Essays in Criticism*, ed. R. H. Super (Ann Arbor: University of Michigan Press, 1962), 258–285 (269).
[55] Ibid. 282–283 and 284, respectively.    [56] Ibid. 260.
[57] Karl Marx, *The Communist Manifesto*, ed. Frederic L. Bender (New York and London: Norton, 1988), 59.

assertion that '[i]intellectual criticism will bind Europe together in bonds far closer than those that can be forged by shopman or sentimentalist'. Wilde's sentimentalists were those people who busied themselves with philanthropic enterprises such as the societies for peace and international arbitration that, as we have seen, gathered momentum in those years. Despite the fact that his wife Constance was a public supporter of International Arbitration,[58] Wilde dismissed these efforts as driven by 'mere emotional sympathy' (p. 202). To illustrate what he meant by the cosmopolitanism of the shopman, Wilde spoke of the failure of the Manchester school of economic liberalism, a mid-Victorian movement which argued that global peace would come naturally out of free trade, as all nations would in time realize the commercial advantages of peace. Wilde ridiculed economic liberalism as an attempt 'to degrade the wonderful world into a common market-place for the buyer and the seller' (p. 202), that is, he warned against compromising cultural diversity by subjecting it to the laws of global capitalism. While Arnold had also been critical of the Manchester school in other writings, in 'The Function of Criticism at the Present Time' his faith in 'our business, and our fortune-making' bespoke his support for British global trade and, indirectly, for the empire in effecting the cosmopolitan opening he yearned for. Even his metaphor of 'expansion' to talk of the rise of the critical spirit acquires on close inspection a sinister colonialist ring. The result is that Arnold could only imagine a system in which a liberal ideal of culture, rooted in the values of 'disinterestedness' and 'curiosity' on which he was so keen, was inseparable from economic liberalism. In 'The Critic as Artist', Wilde launched an ironic attack on the collusion between liberal values and imperial politics: 'England will never be civilized till she has added Utopia to her dominions. There is more than one of her colonies that she might with advantage surrender for so fair a land' (p. 181). Playing on the notion of the 'civilizing mission' of the British Empire, Wilde inverted the hierarchy between citizens and barbarians and turned the language of imperial conquest back towards the centre, as he showed Britain awaiting civilization by the hand of foreigners.

Wilde's divergence from Arnold can best be seen in the two writers' different ways of mapping the spatio-temporal boundaries of world literature. Arnold's take on what the 'world' should include was fundamentally conservative. In 'The Function of Criticism at the Present Time' his criterion for inclusion into the network of world literature was to be part of the *'best in the world'*, where 'world' was the function of competition and exclusion and temporally oriented towards the past. By contrast, when Wilde talked about the world he tended to conjure a

---

[58] Mrs Oscar Wilde is listed among the people who attended the annual meeting of the International Arbitration and Peace Association at the Westminster Palace Hotel in 1890, and again in following years. See *The Concord: Journal of the International Arbitration and Peace Association*, 5 (19 May 1890), 55. The role of this association is explored more fully in Chapter 5.

place of fluid boundaries and to look to the future rather than the past. This statement is characteristic: 'it is the function of Literature to create, from the rough material of actual existence, a new world that will be more marvellous, more enduring, and more true than the world that common eyes look upon, and through which common natures seek to realize their perfection' (p. 152). The radical mission of world literature as Wilde conceived it was to rewrite existing geographies and hierarchies of power in order to set new shared spiritual horizons for humankind.

## The Love of Strangers

Wilde's discovery of a politically radical Goethe was part of a broader turn-of-the-century attempt to free the German author's reputation from the patina of puritanism left by Carlyle, who had dominated the early years of the English-language reception. Havelock Ellis, for instance, remembered that the Fellowship of the New Life chose a quotation from Goethe as its early motto, to capture its ethos of social reform.[59] Wilde's intervention in 'The Critic as Artist' was caught between this left-leaning politicization of Goethe and a different but equally influential strand of reception represented by Pater and John Addington Symonds, who both read Goethe as a proto-aesthete. These authors, whose works Wilde knew as intimately as he knew Arnold's, valued Goethe as the modern precursor of their ideas of intellectual freedom and artistic autonomy, which they otherwise associated primarily with ancient Greece and the Renaissance. It is in this guise that Goethe featured in Symonds's *Studies of the Greek Poets* (1873) and in Pater's essay on Winckelmann, in *Studies in the History of the Renaissance* (1873), both works that Wilde studied very closely when he was an undergraduate at Oxford.[60] Wilde followed clearly in their path in the early American lecture; but traces of the aesthetic Goethe persist in 'The Critic as Artist', when Wilde argues that Goethe should be regarded as pre-eminent among the moderns because, like the Greeks, he understood that 'self-culture is the true ideal of man' (p. 182). Wilde identified this liberal ideal of 'self-culture' or *Bildung* with the 'contemplative life' and inaction (another Arnoldian move: Wilde co-opted Arnold's idea of disinterestedness), but also with the readiness to confront and embrace otherness: 'To know about oneself, one must know all

---

[59] Havelock Ellis, *My Life* (Boston: Houghton Mifflin, 1939), 203. The quotation in question, also used by Symonds as an epigraph to *Studies of the Greek Poets*, comes from the poem 'Generalbeichte' and runs as follows: 'Im Ganzen, Guten, Schönen, Resolut zu Leben.' I trace the afterlife of these lines in the context of a radical Victorian reception of Goethe in '"Life in the Whole": Goethe and English Aestheticism', *Publications of the English Goethe Society*, 82.3 (2013), 180–192.

[60] Wilde, *Oscar Wilde's Oxford Notebooks: A Portrait of Mind in the Making*, ed. Michael S. Helfand and Philip E. Smith (New York and Oxford: Oxford University Press, 1989), 22.

about others. There must be no mood with which one cannot sympathize, no dead mode of life that one cannot make alive' (pp. 176–177).

Goethe's intellectual openness towards strangers was part of the great author's reputation. His habit of sociability was symbolically captured by the word 'salve' inscribed on the door of his study in Weimar, which Eckermann noticed at the beginning of the *Conversations*. Reflecting on the same inscription, the French critic Sainte-Beuve saw it as exemplifying the intimate connection between Goethe's constant desire to enlarge his taste in matters of literature and culture and his hospitality towards strangers.[61] When he defined his critic as artist as someone 'to whom no form of thought is alien, no emotional impulse obscure' (p. 178), Wilde glossed Goethe's 'salve' by way of an echo of the famous quotation from the Roman playwright Terence: 'homo sum, humani nihil a me alienum puto'—I am a human being, and do not regard anything human as foreign to me. These words, written by an African man who was born a slave, have been repeatedly cited in the course of history, from Cicero and Seneca to eighteenth-century anti-slavery activists, to argue for universal human rights.[62] Closer to Wilde's time, as we have seen, Müller redeployed Terence's quotation in his critique of imperial patriotism as but one in a series of 'steps leading higher and higher' to the cosmopolitan ideal.[63] Like Goethe's 'salve', Müller's and Wilde's references to Terence describe a process whereby the sympathetic encounter with the foreign constantly enlarges the boundaries of the self, making it grow ethically; while the self constantly absorbs the foreign without domesticating it fully, because that would mean to neutralize its potentially unsettling otherness. By placing his critic in this tradition, Wilde seemingly fell into the nineteenth-century tradition of liberal humanism exemplified by Arnold. But, on closer inspection, it is possible to see that Wilde's notion of encounters with the foreign was not policed like Arnold's, who only welcomed the 'best' of what came from abroad, but disarmingly open and unpredetermined. Following Baudelaire's analysis of the cosmopolitanism of modernity in 'The Painter of Modern Life', Wilde's ideal of intellectual freedom—in 'The Critic as Artist' and throughout his work—welcomed temptation, transgression, and even perversion, as revealed in the ambiguous statement that the true critic will find 'no emotional impulse obscure'.

With its gentle nod towards psychopathology, this last remark suggests that Wilde understood a truly cosmopolitan liberal humanism as simultaneously celebrating cultural variety and promoting social tolerance for different modes

---

[61] '*Salve*, il exerçait l'hospitalité envers les étrangers, les recevant indistinctement, causant avec eux dans leurs langue, faisant servir chacun de sujet à son etude, à sa connaissance, n'ayant d'autre but en toute chose que *l'aggrandissement de son goût*.' Charles Augustin Sainte-Beuve, 'Introduction', in Johann Wolfgang von Goethe, *Conversations de Goethe pendant les dernières annés de sa vie*, tr. Émile Délerot (Paris: Charpentier, 1863), pp. i–xxii (p. xiii).
[62] Terence's famous quotation comes from his play *The Self-Tormentor* (*Heauton Timorumenos*).
[63] Cf. Müller, 'Goethe and Carlyle', 790.

of affect, including, obviously, same-sex love. Goethe himself had been interested in the subject of homosexuality. W. Daniel Wilson has connected Goethe's 'salve' and his display in his home of homoerotic art as related parts of a public gesture against the rise of homophobic feeling in Germany.[64] Nineteenth-century English critics also intuited that Goethe's 'manysidedness'—the word they routinely employed to refer to his openness to all opinions and influences—would or at least could stretch to include a sympathetic attitude towards same-sex desire.[65] Symonds's and Pater's enthusiastic championing of the classical or Olympian Goethe, for example, encouraged readers to admire his ethos of sexual tolerance, placing him in a tradition of 'queer' liberal humanism that went from the Greeks to Winckelmann—Goethe's major influence in classical matters—to the nineteenth century. In a more scientific key, Havelock Ellis would interpret Eckermann's relationship with Goethe—the relationship recorded in the *Conversations*, in the course of which his reflections on world literature came into being—in terms of perverse sexuality, as 'a transformation of the lover's attitude', i.e. as a displaced erotic attachment that recalled those described by Plato in his transcriptions of Socrates's philosophical conversations with the male youths of Athens.[66] Although Wilde did not push the homoerotic interpretation in 'The Critic as Artist', his use of the dialogue form, by referring back to Plato via Eckermann, implicitly located Goethe's cosmopolitan hospitality in a long history of philosophy arising out of erotic male friendship. The type of sociability that Wilde's speakers perform in the course of the dialogue—based on openness to ideas, love of paradox, humour, and flirtation—updated this philosophical tradition to the English *fin de siècle*, adding to it the aura of sophisticated worldliness that was now also associated with cosmopolitanism.

What Wilde certainly did want to emphasize was the important role that individualism had to play in his understanding of cosmopolitanism. In 'The Soul of Man under Socialism' (1891)—an essay written also at this time, and with which 'The Critic as Artist' shared some of its main ideas—he famously argued that individualism was only apparently incompatible with the aims of socialism; rather, the abolishment of private property would lead to the flourishing of a new individualism, free from materialistic desires.[67] In 'The Critic as Artist', individualism becomes a weapon against cultural chauvinism: 'just as it is only by contact with the art of foreign nations that the art of a country gains that individual and separate life that we call nationality, so, by curious inversion, it is

---

[64] W. Daniel Wilson, *Goethe, Männer, Knaben: Ansichten zur 'Homosexualität'* (Berlin: Insel, 2012), 312.

[65] George Henry Lewes defines 'manysidedness' as Goethe's ability to keep 'a mind open to all influences, swayed by every gust, and yet, while thus swayed as to the direction of his activity, master over that activity'. Lewes, *The Life and Works of Goethe* (London: Smith, Elder, & Co., 1864), 34.

[66] Havelock Ellis, 'Introduction', in Johann Wolfgang von Goethe, *Conversations of Goethe with Eckermann*, tr. John Oxenford (London and Toronto: Dent & Sons, 1930), pp. vii–xix (p. x).

[67] Wilde, 'The Soul of Man under Socialism', in *Complete Works*, iv. 231–268 (248 and *passim*).

only by intensifying his own personality that the critic can interpret the personality and work of others, and the more strongly this personality enters into the interpretation the more real the interpretation becomes, the more satisfying, the more convincing, the more true' (p. 164). Wilde was right to see a paradox (a 'curious inversion', as he calls it) in aligning cosmopolitanism and individualism. Here, he harked back to a classical philosophical argument on the tension between individualism and cosmopolitan universalism. In 'Idea for a Universal History with a Cosmopolitan Intent', Kant had spoken, in similar paradoxical terms, of an *'unsocial sociabilty'* in humans, arguing that, while humans could only develop their capacities to the highest possible degree *within* society, the individual's opposition towards his/her environment and wish to stand out from the others, manifested in the arts, was the necessary first step towards the attainment of what he called 'a perfect civil union of mankind'.[68] Kant's example was a forest in which each tree grows straight by virtue of having to fight for space with other trees; in contrast, trees that grow in isolation, and do not have to contend for air and sun, tend to sprawl and grow crooked. He concluded: 'All the culture and art which adorn mankind and the finest social order man creates are fruits of his unsociability. For it is compelled by its own nature to discipline itself, and thus, by enforced art, to develop completely the germs which nature implanted.'[69] Wilde did not see the need to 'discipline' unsociable impulses, which for him provided a crucial incentive for literature and the arts ('in literature mere egotism is delightful', p. 124). By the same token, literature and the arts had a key role to play in the attainment of 'the cosmopolitanism of the future' because they preserved 'the unity of the human mind in the variety of its forms', that is, the vital element of diversity, with its sometimes conflicting forces, within the universal. Unlike Kant's well-ordered world federation, Wilde's vision of the cosmopolitanism of the future shared elements with the anarchist utopianism of 'The Soul of Man', especially the antipathy for structures of social regulation imposed from above. More fundamentally, in stressing the role of the aesthetic in his theory of cosmopolitanism, Wilde revised Kant's emphasis on ethics, which in 'The Critic as Artist' he attacked as distracting for the critic and as having been hijacked by the respectable middle classes for their hypocritical ends.

In 'The Critic as Artist', Wilde used the medium of criticism to attempt a fusion between theories of world literature and philosophical approaches to cosmopolitanism. However, if we shift from theory to practice, a different set of questions starts to arise. How can literature embody the cosmopolitan individualism of the critic as artist? Can writers break the bond between literature, national language,

---

[68] Kant, 'Idea for a Universal History with a Cosmopolitan Purpose', in *Kant's Political Writings*, ed. Hans Reiss, tr. H. B. Nisbet, 2nd edn (Cambridge: Cambridge University Press, 1990), respectively 44 and 51, italics in the original.
[69] Ibid. 46.

and national identity? Can literature, in other words, be written as world litera- ture? Wilde's bold answer to these questions was *Salomé*.

## *Salomé* and the 'Querelle des Nationalistes et des Cosmopolites'

The story of how Wilde came to write *Salomé* is well-known. In the autumn of 1891 he drafted the play in French, during an extended stay in Paris. The original manuscript was then reviewed by some of Wilde's French literary friends includ- ing, notably, the Symbolist author Pierre Louÿs but also Stuart Merrill, Adolphe Retté, and possibly Marcel Schwob, who helped Wilde with questions of linguistic accuracy without however modifying the content of the play.[70] The premiere of *Salomé* was scheduled to take place in London in 1892, with celebrated French diva Sarah Bernhardt in the title role. However, the plan fell through when the Lord Chamberlain denied a licence for the production by appealing to an English law that banned the representation of biblical characters on stage. The play was eventually premiered in Paris in 1896, when Wilde was in prison; and, in Britain, the ban on public performances was not officially lifted until 1931. *Salomé* thus circulated in the first instance in book form: the first edition of the original French text came out simultaneously in London and Paris in 1893; this was followed, one year later, by an exquisite edition of its English translation—the product of a troubled collaboration between Alfred Douglas and Wilde—with drawings by Aubrey Beardsley that, as we have seen in the Introduction, became iconic of the cosmopolitan orientation of the literary milieu that gravitated around deca- dence and the *Yellow Book*.

Even such a bare-bones history gives us a clear idea that *Salomé*—a work that flaunts its own foreignness and sense of non-belonging—was the product of Wilde's cultural and physical mobility between France and Britain. Wilde's attempt to fuse literary, dramatic, and artistic influences has encouraged critics to mine the text of *Salomé* for sources, especially within French literature and art. It is undeniable that unpicking the rich intertextual fabric of the play brings to light the extraordinary breadth of Wilde's references and borrowings, which ranged from the Gospels to Gustave Flaubert, Joris-Karl Huysmans, and Maurice Maeterlinck.[71] Rewarding though they can be, however, philological readings tend to portray Wilde as a fundamentally derivative writer. In so

[70] The most complete and reliable reconstruction of the play's composition to date is Joseph Donohue's introduction to his edition of *Salomé* in *The Complete Works of Oscar Wilde*, v: *Plays I*, ed. Joseph Donohue (2013), 334–347. Since that volume went to press one further manuscript of *Salomé* has been found in the Free Library of Philadelphia. This appears to be a rehearsal copy, printed before the first book publication of the play for use by the actors of the aborted 1892 production.

[71] See the foundational Mario Praz, *The Romantic Agony*, tr. Angus Davidson (Oxford and London: Oxford University Press, 1970); and Wilde, *Salomé*, ed. Pascal Aquien (Paris: Flammarion, 1993), 180–204. For a comprehensive survey of *Salomé*'s sources see Donohue, 'Introduction', 351–391.

doing, they contribute to a negative image of the author as plagiarist—an image that has been comprehensively debunked by Joseph Bristow and Rebecca N. Mitchell.[72] A related branch of inquiry is the question of Wilde's competence in French, which has brought some critics to dismiss the play as poorly written and even to argue that the text unintentionally slips into parody because of Wilde's awkward handling of literary French.[73] Issues of imitation and competency are of course relevant to the present argument, if nothing else because they show that *Salomé* emerged out of the discussion of contamination and rewriting undertaken in 'The Critic as Artist', embodying the Alexandrian principle of the text as cosmopolitan network.[74] However, instead of concentrating on *what* Wilde imitated, by means of close-reading and source-finding, we should ask *how* the tropes of imitation and foreignness were deployed by both the author and early British and French critics of *Salomé*, in order to see how this work sparked debates about literature and national identity on both sides of the Channel.

The ban on British performances of *Salomé* triggered a series of public pronouncements in which Wilde relaunched his plea for a cosmopolitanism of the future, urging readers to think of literature not in terms of national heritage and genetic inheritance but rather as promoting international mobility and free choice of individual identity. In an interview reported in the French newspaper *Le Gaulois*, Wilde presented the censorship of *Salomé* as a crisis in international relations, dramatically declaring his intention to become a naturalized French citizen:

> Since it is impossible to have a work of art performed in England, I shall take myself to another homeland, which I have loved for a long time. There is only one Paris, you see, and Paris is in France; it is the city of artists, I should readily say: it is the city . . . as artist. I adore Paris. [ . . . ] Here [in England], people are essentially anti-artistic in spirit and there are, unfortunately, too many examples of their narrow-mindedness.[75]

---

[72] Joseph Bristow and Rebecca N. Mitchell, *Oscar Wilde's Chatterton: Literary History, Romanticism, and the Art of Forgery* (New Haven: Yale University Press, 2015).

[73] Again Praz, in *Romantic Agony*, is a classic exponent of the theory that the play is a parody (312). Like other decadent works (e.g. Huysmans's *Against Nature*) *Salomé* disorientates audiences by deliberately treading the line between seriousness and self-irony.

[74] Lawrence Danson expressed the connection between the essay and the play in a disparaging but amusing way: 'Wilde's critic-as-artist reads (*inter alia*) Flaubert, Baudelaire, and Mallarmé, and in response writes an essay called *Salomé*.' Danson, *Wilde's Intentions: The Artist in his Criticism* (Oxford: Clarendon, 1997), 142.

[75] Maurice Sisley, 'La *Salomé* de M. Oscar Wilde', *Le Gaulois*, 29 June 1892, 1 ('Puisque, en Angleterre, il est impossible de faire jouer une oeuvre d'art, je vais entrer dans une nouvelle patrie que j'aime déjà depuis longtemps. Il n'y a qu'un Paris, voyez-vous, et Paris est en France; c'est la ville des artistes, je dirais volontiers: c'est la ville . . . artiste. J'adore Paris. [ . . . ] Ici, on a l'esprit essentiellement anti-artistique et d'une étroitesse dont les examples sont malheureusement trop nombreux').

And in reply to the interviewer's pressing on whether he really had such a low opinion of his countrymen ('compatriotes'):

> they possess certain practical qualities, I won't deny it; but, as an artist, these qualities are not the qualities that I admire most—far from it. Moreover, I am not at present an Englishman; I am still an *Irishman*, which is by no means the same thing. No doubt, I have English friends whom I love very much. But I do not love the *English people*.[76]

Wilde's answers are interesting for the way in which he manipulated the language of citizenship and national loyalty. His declaration of his love of France adopted the rhetoric of patriotism by setting philistine (materialistic) Britain against liberal (idealistic) France: in actual fact, however, he rejected patriotism by arguing that the sentiments of belonging and love of nation are matters of individual choice. Following the example of Goethe discussed in 'The Critic as Artist', he intimated that art and literature should encompass a broader cultural and emotive horizon than the nation. This argument put the author in a privileged but, as we shall see, precarious position of extraterritoriality. In this context, Wilde's reference to his Irishness resonated with the remarks he had made privately to Edmond de Goncourt only a few months previously about being 'Français de sympathie' and 'Irlandais de race'. As in that instance, Irishness, just as it seemed to provide the ultimate key to Wilde's identity, in fact destabilized it further, rendering it even more multi-faceted and provisional.

It is significant that, when speaking of love and loyalty in the interview for *Le Gaulois*, Wilde first mentioned Paris, extending his remarks more broadly to France almost as an afterthought. Conforming to the cosmopolitan typology traced by Baudelaire and Simmel, Wilde identified much more readily with the urban space of the modern metropolis—imaginatively characterized by social openness and multiple identities—than with the nation, which is defined by closed and exclusive discourses of ethnos and borders (Wilde's amusing jibes at provincialism are well known). And, like many writers from all over the world, Wilde believed that the French capital would provide him with the best cultural and social opportunities to help him forge his cosmopolitan identity as an author. As early as 1883, fresh from his American tour, he started to frequent Paris in a professional capacity, contacting prominent figures in the literary world, making himself visible in society, and eventually attracting notice in the press.[77] When he

---

[76] Ibid. ('ils ont des qualités... practiques, je ne le nie pas; mais, en ma qualité d'artiste, ce n'est pas celles—loin de là—que j'admire le plus. Je ne suis pas d'ailleurs, à l'heure où je vous parle, Anglais, je suis encore *Irlandais*, ce qui n'est pas du tout la même chose. Certes, j'ai des amis anglais que j'aime beaucoup. Mais je n'aime pas la *race anglaise*').

[77] Richard Hibbitt, 'The Artist as Aesthete: The French Creation of Wilde', in Evangelista, ed., *The Reception of Oscar Wilde in Europe*, 65–79; Rebecca N. Mitchell, 'Oscar Wilde and the French Press,

went back in 1891, he intensified his social contacts and tried to embed himself more deeply within the fabric of Parisian literary life. Now, Wilde's engagement with Paris was transformed by the rise of Symbolism, which, in the second half of the 1880s, contributed to a cosmopolitan opening of the city's literary culture that made it particularly hospitable to foreigners: among prominent members of Symbolist circles, Jean Moréas, the author of the 'Symbolist Manifesto' (1886), was Greek by birth;[78] Téodor de Wyzewa and the poet Marie Krysinska were of Polish origins; Francis Vielé-Griffin and Stuart Merrill came from North America. These authors perfected the art of mediating between national and cosmopolitan identities, using Parisian networks in order to pursue their interests outside the normative expectations of their domestic cultures.[79] Symbolism, in other words, created a space where authors like Wilde could turn their foreignness and real or presumed marginality to French culture into a position of authority. Therefore, by writing *Salomé* as a Symbolist play, Wilde was not simply co-opting a model for which there was no real equivalent in English. He was engaging with the Symbolists' xenophilia and, at the same time, laying claim to the valuable cultural capital that French Symbolism enjoyed internationally. From its first drafting to an aborted first performance at the Théâtre d'Art in February 1892 and eventual premiere in the Théâtre de l'Oeuvre,[80] *Salomé* was shaped by the spaces, artistic networks, and forms of sociability of cosmopolitan Symbolist Paris, which left a deeper imprint on the text than the linguistic corrections to the manuscript made by Wilde's French friends.

In fact, however, the myth of cosmopolitan Paris that Wilde rehearsed for the interviewer of *Le Gaulois* was a fragile one. In the months leading to the composition of *Salomé*, the Parisian press became the stage for a heated debate between critics who welcomed literary cosmopolitanism and a gathering reactionary movement that aimed to protect French literature against foreign influences. The former tended to share Symbolist leanings; while the latter eventually

1880–91', *Victorian Periodicals Review*, 49.1 (2016), 123–148; Sturgis, *Oscar*, 272–285 and *passim*. David Charles Rose provides a detailed account of the influence of Parisian society on Wilde's work and self-construction in *Oscar Wilde's Elegant Republic: Transformation, Dislocation, and Fantasy in* Fin-de-Siècle *Paris* (Newcastle upon Tyne: Cambridge Scholars Publishing, 2015).

[78] In Oct. 1886 Moréas (Joannes Papadiamantopoulos) launched, together with Gustave Kahn, a small magazine called *Le Symboliste*.

[79] Blaise Wilfert identifies the Symbolists and the academics ('les académiques') as the two key groups responsible for literary imports into late nineteenth-century France; Wilfert, 'Cosmopolis et l'homme invisible: Les importateurs de literature étrangère en France, 1885–1914', *Actes de la recherche en sciences sociales*, 144 (2002), 33–46 (42). For an overview of Symbolism, see Anna Balakian, ed., *The Symbolist Movement in the Literatures of the European Languages* (Budapest: Akadémiai Kiadó, 1982); the introduction and several essays address the relationship between French and international Symbolism. For the Belgian context, relevant to the present argument, see Daniel Laqua and Christophe Verbruggen, 'Beyond the Metropolis: French and Belgian Symbolists between the Region and the Republic of Letters', *Comparative Critical Studies*, 10.2 (2013), 241–258.

[80] The aborted performance of *Salomé* in the Théâtre d'art was advertised in *L'Ermitage*, 5 (Jan. 1892), 60. Donohue gives a full account of the 1896 Parisian premiere in his introduction to *Salomé*, 473–482.

coalesced around the so-called *école romane*, launched in September 1891 by Jean Moréas only days before Wilde started working on the play. Moréas, who had formerly been at the head of the Symbolist avant-garde, now declared Symbolism dead and advocated instead a return to the classical roots of French literature and to nationalistically connoted ideals of 'purity and dignity' ('pureté et dignité'). He urged the renewal of what he called a 'Gallic chain' ('chaine gallique')—an idealized continuum of national culture that had allegedly been broken by the introduction of foreign models by romantic and post-romantic movements.[81]

The clash took a critical turn between the composition and the first print edition of *Salomé*, when the novelist Maurice Barrès published a provocative article titled 'La Querelle des nationalistes et des cosmopolites', which appeared on the front page of *Le Figaro* on 4 July 1892. *Le Figaro* was a loaded venue, as it had previously published both Jean Moréas's Symbolist manifesto and his foundational articles on the *école romane*. Barrès described French literary culture as a fractured field. He argued that the prevalent Anglophilia and the increasing popularity of Russian novels, Scandinavian drama, and Nietzsche's philosophy were all responsible for a cosmopolitan turn in French literature, which he saw as an inevitable trend for the future. He also noted, however, that this openness to foreign literatures was offset by a corresponding increase in nationalism, represented by Moréas's *école romane*. Whether or not the internationalization diagnosed by Barrès was an actual feature of the French 1890s or only the reflection of minority interests,[82] the importance of his article lay in identifying cosmopolitanism as a major *literary* trend of the end of the century and in giving it extreme visibility on the front page of a big daily paper. At the same time, Barrès also helped to crystallize the concept of literary nationalism as a tool of self-definition for those who wanted to defend the uniqueness of French literature in representing the shared heritage and values of the French people, and to preserve its purity against foreign influences. In Barrès's astute analysis, cosmopolitanism and nationalism were thus opposing yet intertwined tendencies, and the conflict between the two camps was a momentous event in modern literature, which he implicitly compared to the famous *querelle* between the ancients and the moderns that had bedevilled French intellectuals in the seventeenth century.

---

[81] Jean Moréas, [letter to the editor], *Le Figaro*, 14 Sept. 1891, 1. Patrick McGuinness provides an analysis of the nationalist politics of the *école romane* in *Poetry and Radical Politics in* Fin-de-Siècle *France: From Anarchism to the Action française* (Oxford and New York: Oxford University Press, 2015), 182–232.

[82] Blaise Wilfert, for instance, disputes that there was an effective increase in the circulation of foreign literature in France in this period. He argues instead that the literary cosmopolitanism diagnosed by Barrès reflected a minority culture partly promoted by small Symbolist magazines. Wilfert, 'La Place de la littérature étrangère dans le champ littéraire français autour de 1900', *Histoire et Mesure*, 23.2 (2008), 69–101 (esp. 94–95).

In 1892, the conservative Barrès, who would become ever closer to cultural nationalism in years to come, strove to present as balanced a case as possible, putting forward the views of both *nationalistes* and *cosmopolites* in an unbiased fashion. Yet, paradoxically enough, his arguments *against* literary nationalism were particularly persuasive even when they were formulated from a conservative perspective: this was the case for his point that Zola's stylistic exaggerations and 'gros méridionalisme' might well be more foreign to most French readers than Dostoevsky.[83] Moreover, by associating cosmopolitanism with the young and with the future of literature, Barrès made it palatable to progressive readers who were keen to embrace new trends. What was at stake in the new literary cosmopolitanism was not only the diffusion of different tastes and reading habits but a far-reaching political reorientation of readers and writers who were now asked to substitute their 'French soul' for a 'European soul'.[84]

Wilde moved in the heart of the cosmopolitan Parisian milieu described by Barrès. Among his prominent *cosmopolites*, Barrès singled out Stuart Merrill and Marcel Schwob, who were at that very moment busy helping Wilde with the revisions to *Salomé*. Indeed, 'La Querelle des nationalistes et des cosmopolites' appeared less than a week after Wilde's interview in *Le Gaulois* in which he declared his love of France and his intention to become a naturalized French citizen. Seen through the prism of Barrès, *Salomé* is therefore not so much the product of Wilde's love of France as of the Anglophilia of Symbolist and cosmopolitan Paris, which welcomed Wilde as part of its de-nationalizing agenda.[85] The play's association with the aesthetic and political aims of the *cosmopolites* would be sealed by its world premiere in 1896 in the Théâtre de l'Oeuvre, home to the controversial Symbolist productions of Ibsen by Aurélien Lugné-Poe that had enthralled cosmopolitan Paris.[86] But this French play by a foreign author also did something different: if, to adopt Barrès's somewhat baroque gastronomic metaphor, Wilde's English writings could be seen as 'sauces anglaises' which fashionable Parisians used to dress their 'table nationale trop bien servie', *Salomé* was at once too domestic and not French enough to suit the palates of cosmopolitan gourmands. In other words, it upset the neat distinction between national and foreign literature sketched out by Barrès.

---

[83] Maurice Barrès, 'La Querelle des nationalistes et des cosmopolites', *Le Figaro*, 4 July 1892, 1.

[84] Ibid. ('à l'âme française substituer l'âme européenne').

[85] Cf. also Téodor de Wyzewa, 'M. Oscar Wilde et les jeunes littérateurs anglais', *La Revue bleue*, 49 (2 Apr.1892), 423–429.

[86] See Pascale Casanova, 'The Ibsen Battle: A Comparative Analysis of the Introduction of Henrik Ibsen in France, England and Ireland', in Christophe Charle, Julien Vincent, and Jay Winter, eds, *Anglo-French Attitudes: Comparisons and Transfers between English and French Intellectuals since the Eighteenth Century* (Manchester: Manchester University Press, 2007), 214–232 (220–221). Lugné-Poe started staging the Norwegian dramatist in a symbolist style in Dec. 1892, the year in which the aborted production of *Salomé* was rehearsing in London.

From a French perspective, therefore, Wilde's public performances of his love of France in the French press could be seen as rejecting the nationalizing agenda of the newly founded *école romane* with its leanings towards reactionary politics and xenophobia. Instead, Wilde reaffirmed hospitality as a fundamental value of French literary culture: the interview in *Le Gaulois* pointedly concluded with the French journalist expressing his hope that the applause of the audience at the Parisian premiere of *Salomé* would be Wilde's 'best letter of naturalization' ('la meilleure lettre de naturalisation').[87] The same discourse of hospitality resurfaced in the French reviews of the first book version of the play, now in a negative key. The critic Bernard Lazare, for instance, compared Wilde to 'a guest who, having been left alone in a room decorated with precious objects and antique jewels, has adorned himself, not without some gaucheness, with enamels and gems'.[88] While a notice in the *Mercure de France* cattily praised Wilde for having skilfully captured all the best export wares of French decadent literature, playfully urging Sarah Bernhardt, after the fiasco of the aborted London premiere, to take *Salomé* on tour to America.[89] As Emily Eells has shown, accusations of excessive or awkward use of French sources would again punctuate the reviews of the play's Parisian premiere in 1896, now embittered by the open knowledge of Wilde's homosexuality.[90] These French reviews show that, with *Salomé*, Wilde tested the ethics of hospitality of *fin-de-siècle* literary Paris: he became a visible emblem of the city's success at welcoming foreign writers; but, at the same time, to nationalistic critics, he also highlighted the need to protect the 'Frenchness' of French literature in a system of global free commerce, to go back to Goethe's definition of world literature, in which the domestic decadent/Symbolist brand carried a particularly high market value. In other words, Wilde's work on the border between France and Britain simultaneously built bridges between the two literatures and created a perceived need to make that border more secure. As Wilde exported the French-accented cosmopolitanism of the Parisian 1890s across the Channel, there were those in France who feared that French literature would lose its particularity, and consequently its prestige, in a world economy of imitations; just as in Britain there were critics who, for similar protectionist reasons, wanted to keep foreign influences at bay. In this way, *Salomé* exported to Britain not only French Symbolism, but the literary controversy between nationalists and cosmopolitans, of which Wilde became the public symbol.

---

[87] Sisley, 'La *Salomé* de M. Oscar Wilde', 1.

[88] Bernard Lazare, '*Salomé* par Oscar Wilde', *Entretiens politiques et littéraires*, 41 (25 Apr. 1893), 382–384 (384) ('Il est peu comme un hôte qu'on aurait laissé seul dans une salle ornée de patrimoniaux et antiques bijoux, et qui se serait paré, non sans maladresse, des émaux et des pierreries').

[89] [Anon.], '*Salomé* par Oscar Wilde', *Mercure de France*, 8 (July 1893), 279–280.

[90] Emily Eells, 'Naturalizing Oscar Wilde as an *homme de lettres*: The French Reception of *Dorian Gray* and *Salomé* (1895–1922)', in Evangelista, ed., *Reception of Oscar Wilde*, 80–95 (86–87). Eells also shows that the accusations of abusing French sources provoked by *Salomé* resurfaced in the reception of the first French translation of *Dorian Gray* in 1895.

## Against the Mother Tongue

News travelled fast in the 1890s. The same interview in which Wilde threatened to become a naturalized French citizen also appeared in Britain, on the same day, in the pages of the *Pall Mall Gazette*. In fact, Wilde had been speaking simultaneously to a French and an English journalist, impressing both with his ability to switch comfortably between the two languages. The English version contained an extended explanation of his motivations for writing *Salomé* in French:

> My idea of writing the play was simply this: I have one instrument that I know I can command, and that is the English language. There was another instrument to which I had listened all my life, and I wanted once to touch this new instrument to see whether I could make any beautiful thing out of it. The play was written in Paris some six months ago, where I read it to some young poets, who admired it immensely. Of course there are modes of expression that a French man of letters would not have used, but they give a certain relief or colour to the play. A great deal of the curious effect Maeterlinck produces comes from the fact that he, a Flamand by race, writes in an alien language. The same thing is true of Rossetti, who, though he wrote in English, was essentially Latin in temperament.[91]

Wilde's point is that national literatures are enriched by the addition of foreign elements brought in by non-native writers. His comparison with Dante Gabriel Rossetti and Maurice Maeterlinck was somewhat disingenuous, though, because neither of them wrote in a language that was as foreign to them as French was to Wilde: Rossetti, who was born in England of Italian parents, was bilingual; while the Belgian Maeterlinck was brought up and educated entirely in French. Yet, the comparison with Maeterlinck in particular is apt in a different way. Maeterlinck, who moved in the cosmopolitan milieu of Symbolist Paris and was of course widely recognized as the main inspiration for Wilde's poetic style in *Salomé*, was often mocked in the French press for foreignizing the French language—a habit that was ascribed to his Belgian identity. Maeterlinck learnt to turn this discourse of marginalization into a strength, strategically using his ambiguous position in order to criticize the stagnation of modern French as literary language:

> Among Latin races, words—the debris of dead languages and without any direct expressive power—are like a cold and eternal shadow between things and the

---

[91] [Anon.], 'The Censure and *Salome*: An Interview with Mr. Oscar Wilde', *Pall Mall Gazette*, 29 June 1892, 1–2 (2).

soul, and even those who have turned words around, and seen their meaning on the other side of language, still cannot wash away the stench of dead flesh.[92]

Maeterlinck set up this decadent scenario in which the French language was envisaged as a putrefying corpse in order to prepare the conditions for a reinvigorating barbarian invasion into modern French literature. This, as Patrick McGuinness has argued, Maeterlinck believed himself ideally placed to carry out because of the 'Germanic soul' of his native Flanders.[93] In *Salomé*, Wilde aspired to a similar type of cultural authority: writing in French, he tried to get to what Maeterlinck evocatively called the 'meaning on the other side of language', or what Arthur Symons, in the most important study of French Symbolism in English, described as 'that seeming artificiality which comes from using words as if they had never been used before, that chimerical search after the virginity of language'.[94] The literary author writing in an 'alien language', as Wilde said of Maeterlinck (and, by implication, himself), re-enacts a primordial encounter with language that renews its freshness and mystery as s/he stumbles and pauses over words unhindered by familiarity and habit. As Emily Eells has noted, the 'distancing effect' produced by this encounter simultaneously made Wilde exceptionally sensitive to the musicality of the French language and lent him a special freedom to attempt to 'articulate the unspeakable' in *Salomé*.[95]

To critics who were less easily seduced by Symbolist theories of language, the image of the literary author writing as a foreign speaker readily lent itself to caricature. Beardsley's cartoon 'Oscar Wilde at Work', which refers to the composition of *Salomé*, showed Wilde busy reading a book by Gautier, surrounded by a number of well-thumbed volumes that include a Bible, a French dictionary, Flaubert's *Trois Contes*, an unidentified work by Swinburne, and Wilde's own *Picture of Dorian Gray* (illustration 1.1). The joke was that, in the privacy of his study, Wilde was at 'work' copying the works of other writers, turning what should be the creative labour of the writer into a too easy commerce in imitation, plagiarism, and self-plagiarism. Beardsley debunked Wilde's authority by exposing the possible sources for *Salomé*, including the first-century historian Flavius Josephus and Flaubert's *Hérodias* (one of the *Trois Contes*). His satire, however,

---

[92] Maurice Maeterlinck, *Le Cahier bleu*, ed. Joanne Wieland-Burston, *Annales de la Fondation Maurice Maeterlinck*, 22 (1976), 7–184 (139); quoted in Patrick McGuinness, *Maurice Maeterlinck and the Making of Modern Theatre* (Oxford and New York: Oxford University Press, 2000), 36 ('chez les peuples de races latines, les mot débris de langues mortes et sans expression directe, sont comme une ombre froid et éternelle entre les choses et l'âme et la pluspart et même seux qui ont tourné les mots, et ont vu leur signification de l'autre côté de la langue, ne peuvent cependant pas laver l'odeur de cadavre').

[93] McGuinness, *Maurice Maeterlinck*, 18.

[94] Arthur Symons, *The Symbolist Movement in Literature*, ed. Matthew Creasy (Manchester: Carcanet, 2014), 68. Symons makes these remarks with reference to Mallarmé.

[95] Emily Eells, 'Wilde's French *Salomé*', *Cahiers victoriens et édouardiens*, 72 (Autumn 2020) <https://journals.openedition.org/cve/2729> [accessed 10 Jan. 2019].

**Illustration 1.1** Aubrey Beardsley, 'Oscar Wilde at Work', University College Oxford, Ross Env d.5.ii

had a wider aim than *Salomé*: it questioned the very ethics of Wilde's cosmopolitan mediation between France and Britain, asking what happens to the liberal ideology of the 'free' international circulation of literature—the ideal of world literature that Wilde had espoused in 'The Critic as Artist'—when it becomes a means of profit, in a modern world literary system driven by market values. In short, Beardsley caricatured Wilde's literary cosmopolitanism as, at best, a form of clever dilettantism and, at worst, an act of opportunism and dishonesty. In order to do so, he outed Wilde's French as a gauche performance as the author is seen brushing up on French verbs and turning to language instruction books.

'Oscar Wilde at Work' visually encapsulated a set of critiques that dominated the early British reactions to *Salomé*. Beardsley's humour took on a darker shade in an unsigned review of the 1893 book edition of the French version of the play in the *Pall Mall Gazette*, in which the anonymous journalist also complained of the excessive imitation of French models and, in a crucial passage, attacked *Salomé* by describing it as 'the daughter of too many fathers'. The review went on: 'She is a victim of heredity. Her bones want strength, her flesh wants vitality, her blood is polluted. There is no pulse of passion on her.'[96] Repeating the slippage between cultural criticism and pseudoscience of Max Nordau's *Degeneration*, which had been published in German only the previous year, this critic diagnosed the cause of the alleged weakness (moral and aesthetic) of the work in the degeneracy of its author, here envisaged as the perverse commerce with too many French writers. The metaphors of blood and inheritance conjured a nationalist agenda by unleashing fears that the healthy body of national literature was being corrupted by the foreign elements imported by Wilde. His use of a foreign language in particular harmed, in almost vampiric fashion, the 'strength' and 'vitality' of his work.

We would be wrong to underestimate the power of the nationalist and xenophobic rhetoric unleashed against Wilde by the appearance of *Salomé*. Humorous or sensationalist though they sometimes were, these criticisms spread a hostile nationalist feeling that would later burst into the open during the trials. Now the Irish and Francophile Wilde could finally be exposed as foreign other, traitor, and public danger for the nation in the most virulent terms. Wilde's homosexual and cosmopolitan identities bled into each other and, in a sense, reinforced each other as modes of deviance and deceit that were finally out into the open. An editorial published in the *Daily Telegraph* at the time of the trials was characteristic in claiming that 'every honest and wholesome-minded Englishman must grieve to notice how largely this French and Pagan plague has filtered into the healthy fields of British life'.[97] According to this anonymous journalist, the Wilde trials called for tighter policing of the borders of British culture aimed at safeguarding a sentimental vision of a national community built on 'the natural affections, the domestic joys, the sanctity and sweetness of the home'. This was not, however, simply a clash of worlds between wholesome Britain and corrupted France—the author had to admit that in France 'also, as here, the vast body of social and civil life is no doubt sound and sober' (the *école romane*'s commitment to 'purity and

---

[96] Unsigned review, *Pall Mall Gazette*, 27 Feb. 1893, 3; reprinted in Karl Beckson, ed., *Oscar Wilde: The Critical Heritage* (London: Routledge & Kegan Paul, 1970), 135–137.

[97] [Anon.], *Daily Telegraph*, 6 Apr. 1895, reprinted in Jonathan Goodman, *The Oscar Wilde File* (London: Allen & Co., 1988), 75–77 (76). All quotations in this paragraph are from this same page.

dignity' comes to mind). Rather, as in France, British literary culture was split by an internecine war between a dangerous new international 'aestheticism', represented by Wilde, and the guardians of the nation, which, as the journalist pointed out, 'prospers and profits by precisely those national qualities which these innovators deride and abjure'. In this scenario, in which the unity and ethical backbone of the nation were allegedly being threatened by subversive elements *inside* it, literary cosmopolitanism constituted a threat to public morality. These sentiments were mirrored in the French press, where the coverage of the Wilde trials triggered a similar compound of chauvinism and homophobia, which denounced Wilde's sexual behaviour as foreign to French national character.[98] In this way English literary nationalism joined in a symbolic, if highly paradoxical transnational alliance with the French *école romane*, with which it shared the desire to restore a conservative ideal of national culture unpolluted by foreign influences. The Wilde trials thus interacted not only with the international backlash against 'degeneration' launched by Max Nordau, but also with prominent episodes of xenophobic nationalism that marked the end of the century, such as the Dreyfus affair and the founding of the Action française.[99]

Going back to *Salomé*, it is now easier to see why Wilde's decision to adopt a foreign language should be so provocative. Abandoning his native English in favour of French, Wilde not only made a deliberate gesture to distance himself from his domestic readership, deepening the feeling of deceit and betrayal described by the *Daily Telegraph*, but he also deliberately subverted the alliance between literature, national language, and national feeling that was such a pillar of cultural nationalism. In the 'Treatise on the Origin of Language' ('Abhandlung über den Ursprung der Sprache', 1772), Herder had identified the possession of a common language as a key element of the idea of nationality or *Volk*. According to Herder, the spontaneous development of individual identity through language took place harmoniously alongside the creation of a communal, national identity through shared language, effecting a complete blending together of self and nation that was in fact a *natural* process. The inextricable entanglement of language, culture, and community found its ultimate expression in the notion of the 'mother tongue':

---

[98] Nancy Erber, 'The French Trials of Oscar Wilde', *Journal of the History of Sexuality*, 6.4 (1996), 549–588 (565 and *passim*). Erber quotes Jacques St.-Cère, 'A l'Étranger, Scandales partout!', *Le Figaro*, 6 Apr. 1895, 2. See also Erin Williams Hyman, '*Salomé* as Bombshell, or How Oscar Wilde Became an Anarchist', in Joseph Bristow, ed., *Oscar Wilde and Modern Culture: The Making of a Legend* (Athens, OH: Ohio University Press, 2008), 96–109 (104).

[99] Several critics have explored the connection between Wilde and Nordau's *Degeneration*, which appeared in English translation exactly during the Wilde trials; for a focus on strategies of resistance, see esp. Richard Dellamora, 'Productive Decadence: "The Queer Comradeship of Outlawed Thought": Vernon Lee, Max Nordau, and Oscar Wilde', *New Literary History*, 35.4 (2004), 529–546. Robert Maguire gives a lucid historical account of Wilde's involvement in the Dreyfus affair in 'Oscar Wilde and the Dreyfus Affair', *Victorian Studies*, 41.1 (1997), 1–29.

The infant who stammers his first words, stammers a repetition of the feelings of his parents, and swears with each early stammering, in accordance with which his tongue and soul forms itself, that he will make these feelings endure eternally, as truly as he calls them father- or mother-tongue. For his whole life these first impressions from his childhood, these images from the soul and the heart of his parents, will live and take effect within him; with the word will come back the whole feeling that then, early on, flowed over his soul [ ... ].[100]

Herder associated the mother tongue with the subtlest fibres of the emotional fabric of the self. The mother tongue transformed the biological and affective link between generations into a process of national identity formation forged through language. It followed that the mother tongue, inasmuch as it was bound to the special 'spiritual richness' of the family and, by extension, the nation, perpetuated modes of thinking that bound together a people, providing it with a distinctive identity that differentiated it from other peoples.[101] Reflecting on Herder's powerful legacy on nationalist ideology, Etienne Balibar has explained how the peculiar 'love of the language' mobilized by the idea of the mother tongue, which transcends learning processes and specialized forms of usage, becomes, by that very fact, 'the metaphor for the love fellow nationals feel for one another'.[102]

Nationalist critiques of Wilde invoked the essentialist ideology of the mother tongue to stigmatize the author as unpatriotic. Particularly telling, in this sense, is the recurrence of satirical references to language textbooks in the early reception of *Salomé*. I have already noted the French grammar aids in Beardsley's drawing. In a similar vein, a review in *The Times* compared the opening of *Salomé* to 'a page from one of Ollendorff's exercises',[103] dismissing Wilde's pared down and repetitive poetic language as reminiscent of a then popular method of foreign-language learning that involved the extensive use of declining and conjugating foreign words aloud.[104] The satirical evocation of language textbooks drew attention to a fundamental transgression of Herder's ideas that Wilde deliberately undertook

---

[100] J. G. Herder, 'Treatise on the Origin of Language', 142 ('Der Säugling, der die ersten Worte stammlet, stammelt die Gefühle seiner Eltern wieder, und schwört mit jedem frühen Stammeln, nachdem sich seine Zunge und Seele bildet, diese Gefühle zu verewigen, so wahr er sie Vater- oder Muttersprache nennet. Lebenslang werden diese ersten Eindrücke seiner Kindheit, diese Bilder aus der Seele und dem Herzen seiner Eltern in ihm leben und würken: mit dem Wort wird das ganze Gefühl wiederkommen, was damals frühe seine Seele überströmte, mit der Idee des Worts alle Nebenideen, die ihm damals bei diesem, neuen frühen Morgenausblick in das Reich der Schöpfung vorlagen', 786).
[101] Ibid. 141 ('Reichtum [des] Geistes', 785).
[102] Etienne Balibar, 'The Nation Form: History and Ideology', in Balibar and Immanuel Maurice Wallerstein, *Race, Nation, Class: Ambiguous Identities* (London and New York: Verso, 1991), 86–106 (98).
[103] [Anon.], unsigned notice, *The Times*, 23 Feb. 1893, 8; reprinted in Beckson, *Wilde: Critical Heritage*,133.
[104] William Archer, 'A Pessimist Playwright', *Fortnightly Review*, 50 (Sept. 1891), 346–354 (349). H. G. Ollendorff (1803–65) was a German grammarian. His language-learning manuals were translated into various European languages including French and English.

in *Salomé*. The dictionary and the grammar book, where language is abstracted, codified, and turned into series of lists represented, in the eyes of hostile critics, Wilde's futile attempt to learn to *feel* in a foreign language. They were intended to remind readers of the unbridgeable gap that separates the native from the foreigner. They denounced as impossible the desire to replace the 'natural' affective heritage that comes with the mother tongue, which cannot be assimilated through education and bookish learning. For Herder, as we have seen, the mother tongue projected onto a national scale feelings that had their roots in individual childhood impressions and experiences. Literature's role was to stir those deep-seated emotions back into life and, by doing so, transform language into the nation's 'treasure' (*Schatz*), the source of its unique spirit and collective identity.[105] By writing *Salomé* in French, Wilde deliberately set out to break the supposedly 'natural' link between individual and national community forged by the mother tongue. No matter that, as William A. Cohen has rightly argued, Wilde's use of French in *Salomé* was not, or not so much, a strategy to identify with France as the expression of 'a fantasy of an alternative *to* national belonging'.[106] Wilde's statements about his love of the French language only exacerbated the sense that he had betrayed something natural and fundamental in the unwritten contract between writer and nation. In the *Pall Mall Gazette*, for instance, the lampooning of *Salomé* as 'the daughter of too many fathers' plainly conjured English as the absent mother of the cosmopolitan text.[107] Paraphrasing the words of this critic in the light of Balibar, we could say that, with *Salomé*, Wilde substituted the proper love of the mother tongue, which should at once be the origin and purpose of literature, for a form of perverse love—with the homophobic implication that this criticism carries with it.

English critics were not alone in detecting something unsettling in Wilde's use of French. In his biographical portrait of Wilde (1901), André Gide remembered being struck by Wilde's mastery of spoken French on making his first acquaintance around the time of *Salomé*:

> [Wilde] narrated gently, slowly; his very voice was wonderful. He knew French admirably, but he pretended to hunt about a bit for the words which he wanted to keep waiting. He had almost no accent, or at least only such as it pleased him to retain and which might give the words a sometimes new and strange aspect. He was fond of pronouncing *skepticisme* for 'scepticisme'...[108]

---

[105] Herder, 'Treatise on the Origin of Language', 147.

[106] William A. Cohen, 'Wilde's French', in Joseph Bristow, ed., *Wilde Discoveries: Traditions, Histories, Archives* (Toronto: Toronto University Press, 2013), 233–259 (241).

[107] For readings of the concept of 'mother tongue' from gendered and psychoanalytic perspectives, see Yasemin Yildiz, *Beyond the Mother Tongue: The Postmonolingual Condition* (New York: Fordham University Press, 2012), 10–14.

[108] André Gide, 'In Memoriam', in *Oscar Wilde*, tr. Bernard Frechtman (London: Kimber, 1951), 11–45 (16). The original appeared as André Gide, 'Oscar Wilde', *L'Ermitage*, 13.6 (June 1902), 401–29

In Gide's account Wilde comes across as being able to manipulate his own foreignness to the French language, affecting an incorrect pronunciation and creating pauses for dramatic effect. To Gide, there was something uncanny in the way in which Wilde transfigured French into an arresting and highly individual idiom in which words became 'new and strange', acquiring unusual sounds and revealing meanings and associations that were otherwise hidden to him as a native speaker. But the most striking part of the reminiscence is the image of Wilde's pretence to hunt for words which he in fact knew very well. Wilde's deliberate distance towards language rendered his position between cultures— what we could call his cosmopolitan voice—as ambiguous and almost suspicious to Gide as it was to many English critics. Gide reacted to the way in which Wilde played with foreignness as an epistemological category, blurring the stark line that separates French and non-French. For Gide, Wilde's linguistic pretence was inextricably bound with what he called Wilde's 'showy mask'—the studied artificiality of his social performance that he linked to Wilde's artful negotiation of his homosexual identity.[109]

A suspiciousness about Wilde's French haunts the critical reception of *Salomé*, a work that frustrates readers' desire to slot literature into stable national categories. 'Is Wilde's *Salomé* in bad French?', the German composer Richard Strauss asked French author Romain Rolland, who was helping Strauss to set Wilde's original French version of *Salomé* to music.[110] Strauss was not confident in his French and therefore enlisted Rolland to check that he had not 'done violence to the French language'.[111] Rolland returned Strauss's transcription with a palpable feeling of frustration, complaining that Wilde's French was unidiomatic, ambiguous, or, quite simply, repeatedly, 'not French'.[112] He explained to Strauss: 'However remarkable Wilde's knowledge of French may have been, it is nevertheless impossible to consider him a French poet.'[113] That *Salomé* simply would not conform to the rules of French prosody therefore did not surprise Rolland, who believed that it would be 'extremely difficult' for a foreigner to take note of 'the infinite number of shades in a language like the French language, which is the

('[Wilde] contait doucement, lentement: sa voix même était merveilleuse. Il savait admirablement le français, mais feignait de chercher un peu les mots qu'il voulait faire attendre. Il n'avait presque pas d'accent, ou du moins que ce qu'il lui plaisait d'en garder, et qui pouvait donner aux mots un aspect parfois neuf et étrange. Il prononçait volontiers *skepticisme*', p. 404).

[109] Ibid. ('masque de parade', p. 405). Several critics have analysed the complicated relationship between Gide and Wilde. For relevant passages see Jonathan Fryer, *André and Oscar: Gide, Wilde and the Gay Art of Living* (London: Constable, 1997), 49–62; and Victoria Reid, 'André Gide's "Hommage à Oscar Wilde" or "The Tale of Judas"', in Evangelista, *Reception of Oscar Wilde*, 96–107.

[110] Strauss to Romain Rolland, July 1905, *Richard Strauss and Romain Rolland: Correspondence, together with Fragments from the Diary of Romain Rolland and other Essays*, ed. Rollo Myers (London: Calder & Boyars, 1968), 40. The first and still more popular version of the opera uses a libretto based on a German translation by Hedwig Lachmann.

[111] Strauss to Rolland, 5 July 1905, ibid. 29.     [112] Rolland to Strauss, 5 Nov. 1905, ibid. 73.

[113] Rolland to Strauss, 12 Nov. 1905, ibid. 77.

product of centuries of art and of life, [and which] are the very shades of the soul of a great people'. He added: 'One has enough difficulty in mastering one's own mother-tongue in a lifetime.'[114] Even in a cosmopolitan thinker such as Rolland, *Salomé* sparks a desire to protect the mother tongue and reassert its sanctity in holding together what Herder called the 'spiritual richness' of the nation, using it as a means of distancing and exclusion. Like some of the early French reviewers of the play, Rolland was baffled and irritated by the international success of a work that looked flawed from a French domestic perspective. This irritation moved him to stand up for the uniqueness of French culture against its cosmopolitan artistic appropriations—in this case by both Wilde and Strauss.

Just as the 'original' of *Salomé* refuses to conform to the rules that make good literary French, its English translations—starting from the very first translation by Alfred Douglas in which Wilde played a still unspecified role—represent a paradox of domestication: they effect an impossible or uncanny return of the text to the native idiom of the author that haunts the text like an absent presence.[115] From the first manuscript corrected by Pierre Louÿs and others to the version set to music that went backwards and forwards between Strauss and Rolland, *Salomé* has provoked and frustrated the desire to clean and standardize the text, to make it fit into a stable language and national identity. Ironically, these very conversations helped to shape the delayed meaning of *Salomé* as a work that both affirmed and tested the principles of literary cosmopolitanism. Partly thanks to Strauss's 1905 opera, in the longer term this seemingly ill-fated Symbolist play outstripped the international success of Wilde's other works: according to Holbrook Jackson, in the early twentieth century *Salomé* was 'performed in all the capitals of the western world more constantly than any other modern English play'.[116] Born as Wilde's practical experiment to bring about the 'cosmopolitanism of the future', *Salomé* thus became a modern classic of world literature in Goethe's sense.[117] It is not by coincidence that the first manuscript of the play, with its undeleted traces of Wilde's foreignness, should have made its way to the Bibliotheca Bodmeriana in Geneva, a collection that was set up with the explicit mission of assembling a library of world literature as Goethe conceived it.

---

[114] Rolland to Strauss, 16 July 1905, ibid. 39.

[115] Holbrook Jackson noted this point in his early attempt to rehabilitate *Salomé* for English readers; Jackson, 'Introduction', in Wilde, *Salome*, 21.

[116] Ibid. 12.

[117] Accounts that emphasize the international perspective in the complex reception and performance history of *Salomé* include Petra Dierkes-Thrun, *Salome's Modernity: Oscar Wilde and the Aesthetics of Transgression* (Ann Arbor: University of Michigan Press, 2011); and William Tydeman and Steven Price, *Wilde: Salome* (Cambridge and New York: Cambridge University Press, 1996).

# 2

# Lafcadio Hearn and Global Aestheticism

> When Madame de Staël wrote *De l'Allemagne*, about 1810, she was
> doing for Germany something not unlike what Lafcadio Hearn did for
> Japan in our own memory.
>
> (Vernon Lee, 'Bismarck Towers')

> To be away from home and yet to feel oneself everywhere at home; to
> see the world, to be at the centre of the world, and yet to remain
> hidden from the world—such are a few of the slightest pleasures of
> those independent, passionate impartial natures which the tongue can
> but clumsily define.
>
> (Charles Baudelaire, 'The Painter of Modern Life')

In June 1882, in the middle of his lecture tour of North America, Wilde made a
proposal to his friend, the painter James McNeill Whistler: 'You dear good-for-
nothing old Dry-point [ ... ] when will you come to Japan? Fancy the book, I to
write it, you to illustrate it. We would be rich.'[1] Wilde was more serious than his
teasing tone implies. Letters of introduction had already been dispatched to
Tokyo on his behalf, including one to the noted art historian Ernest Fenollosa,
stating that Wilde intended to travel to Japan in order to make a study of 'the art
methods and products of the Japanese'.[2] He was also shortly to negotiate the
handsome sum of 500 dollars with the brand new American literary weekly, *Our
Continent*, for a series of four articles on Japanese traditional arts and crafts,
which the journal promised to 'illustrate [ ... ] profusely, in the best style of
wood-engraving'.[3] After touring the United States and Canada in order to
introduce American audiences to English aestheticism, Wilde now planned to
travel on to the Far East in order to bring back to Europe a commercially
valuable first-hand knowledge of a country that was then at the height of
fashion. Whistler, one of the most notable exponents of *japonisme*, was to be

---

[1] Oscar Wilde to James McNeill Whistler, [?] June 1882, in *Complete Letters*, 173–174.
[2] T. C. Mendenhall to E. F. Fenollosa, 21 May 1882, William Andrews Clark Memorial Library,
University of California, Los Angeles, ms. Wilde S625Z 1882. My thanks to Joseph Bristow for pointing
me to this material.
[3] H. W. B. Howard to Oscar Wilde, 2 Sept. 1882, William Andrews Clark Memorial Library,
University of California, Los Angeles, Wilde H849L W6721.

*Literary Cosmopolitanism in the English* Fin de Siècle: *Citizens of Nowhere*. Stefano Evangelista,
Oxford University Press. © Stefano Evangelista 2021. DOI: 10.1093/oso/9780198864240.003.0003

Wilde's business partner in this new international venture for the global circulation of aestheticism.[4]

In the event, neither Wilde nor Whistler ever made it to Japan. However, by the end of that decade, as he developed the ideas on cosmopolitanism and world literature analysed in the previous chapter, Wilde approached the cultural capital of Japan from a very different perspective. In 'The Decay of Lying: A Dialogue' (1889)—the companion piece to 'The Critic as Artist'—he argued that, in order to preserve its true significance for artists and writers in the West, Japan must remain a place of the imagination:

> I know that you are fond of Japanese things. Now, do you really imagine that the Japanese people, as they are presented to us in art, have any existence? If you do, you have never understood Japanese art at all. The Japanese people are the deliberate self-conscious creation of certain individual artists. If you set a picture by Hokusai, or Hokkei, or any of the great native painters, beside a real Japanese gentleman or lady, you will see that there is not the slightest resemblance between them. The actual people who live in Japan are not unlike the general run of English people; that is to say, they are extremely commonplace, and have nothing curious or extraordinary about them. In fact the whole of Japan is a pure invention. There is no such country, there are no such people. [ ... ] And so, if you desire to see a Japanese effect, you will not behave like a tourist and go to Tokio. On the contrary, you will stay at home and steep yourself in the work of certain Japanese artists, and then, when you have absorbed the spirit of their style, and caught their imaginative manner of vision, you will go some afternoon and sit in the Park or stroll down Piccadilly, and if you cannot see an absolutely Japanese effect there, you will not see it anywhere.[5]

Wilde's amusing paradox contains a serious reflection on how to attain a truly cosmopolitan point of view. He makes his point by comparing between the lines the different ways in which Japan inspired two contemporary artists. The reference to seeing 'Japanese effects' in the middle of London conjures up Whistler, who, in paintings like 'Nocturne: Blue and Gold—Old Battersea Bridge' (1872–5), had made familiar London views and landmarks look Japanese by borrowing compositional techniques and visual elements from woodblock-print artists like Hiroshige and Hokusai, also mentioned by Wilde (illustration 2.1). While the

---

[4] There is a large secondary literature on nineteenth-century *japonisme*. With specific reference to the figures treated here, see Lionel Lambourne, *Japonisme: Cultural Crossings between Japan and the West* (London: Phaidon, 2005); Ayako Ono, *Japonisme in Britain: Whistler, Menpes, Henry, Hornel, and Nineteenth-Century Japan* (London and New York: Routledge, 2003); and Linda Gertner Zatlin, *Beardsley, Japonisme, and the Perversion of the Victorian Ideal* (Cambridge and New York: Cambridge University Press, 1997).

[5] Wilde, 'The Decay of Lying', in *Complete Works*, iv. 97–98.

**Illustration 2.1** *Nocturne: Blue and Gold—Old Battersea Bridge, c.* 1872–5, James Abbott McNeill Whistler (1834–1903). Tate. Photo © Tate

figure of the naïve tourist is a caricature of the Australian painter Mortimer Menpes, a pupil of Whistler who had travelled to Japan in order to study art with Japanese masters. Menpes (who was incidentally godfather to Wilde's son Vyvyan, who gave his name to the character of Vivian, who speaks these lines in the dialogue) did win some popularity with his watercolours of Japanese life, which had been exhibited in the Dowdeswell Gallery in 1888, shortly before the first publication of 'The Decay of Lying'.[6] Nonetheless, Wilde's judgement was trenchant: by depicting Japan through the lens of European realism, Menpes domesticated its culture, erasing its particularity. In contrast to Menpes, who reduced transcontinental travel to a form of provincialism, Whistler drew inspiration from art, favouring representation over reality, and disregarding chimeric ideas of authenticity. To adapt what Christopher Reed has seen as the link between Victorian *japonisme* and modernism, Japan enabled Whistler to challenge 'fundamental Western ideas about the nature of representation'.[7] By so doing, following Wilde's logic, he produced formally accomplished works that, at the same time, revealed a deeper understanding and sympathy with Japan, even as he ostensibly depicted European cityscapes and fashionable interiors in Paris and London.

Wilde's argument on the power of the aesthetic to forge ties between different cultures resonates with his advocacy of the 'cosmopolitanism of the future' in 'The Critic as Artist'. But in 'The Decay of Lying' he casts doubts on what it really means to experience a foreign culture at first hand. As in J.-K. Huysmans's decadent novel *À Rebours* (1884), where Des Esseintes experiences his 'London of the imagination' ('ce Londres fictif') in the rue de Rivoli,[8] Vivian's urge to find Tokyo in the West End of London is a gesture of cosmopolitan disenchantment. In an age of mass tourism and global mobility, distance, desire, and projection are paradoxically the most meaningful ways of preserving cultural difference, while travel results in a form of universalism that actually impoverishes experience—the realization that the exotic inhabitants of Japan are in fact 'extremely commonplace'. With this, Wilde shelved his projected Japanese book of 1882 as a juvenile blunder.

In the 1890s, however, another uprooted Irishman was successfully to claim for himself the role of aesthetic discoverer of Japan coveted by Wilde: Lafcadio Hearn moved to Japan in 1890 and, over the next decade and into the twentieth century, he brought out a series of books that had an enormous international impact on Western perceptions of the country. In Vernon Lee's striking formulation, Hearn did for Japan what Madame de Staël had done for Germany almost one hundred years earlier, that is, he opened a whole new channel of communication and literary exchange.[9] Indeed, Hearn provided English-speaking readers with a still

---

[6] Grace E. Lavery reads the triangulation between Wilde, Whistler, and Menpes as bringing to light a controversy, within British aestheticism, around the figure of the craftsman, and also as introducing uses of Japan and *japonisme* as signifiers of effeminacy and queer affect. Lavery, *Quaint, Exquisite: Victorian Aesthetics and the Idea of Japan* (Princeton: Princeton University Press, 2019), 56–80.

[7] Christopher Reed, *Bachelor Japanists: Japanese Aesthetics and Western Masculinities* (New York: Columbia University Press, 2016), 10.

[8] Joris-Karl Huysmans, *Against Nature*, tr. Robert Baldick (London and New York: Penguin, 1959), 138.

[9] Vernon Lee, 'Bismarck Towers', *New Statesman*, 20 Feb. 1915, 481–483 (482). I am grateful to Fraser Riddell for bringing this essay to my attention.

rare first-hand knowledge of Japan, while at the same time striving to preserve the elements of exoticism, defamiliarization, and desire for the unknown that were so important for Wilde. After spending fourteen years in Japan, Hearn would still claim that the 'wonder and delight' of his first impressions had never passed away.[10] And in his last published book he came up with a systematic theory about the 'strangeness' of the Japanese that reads like a riposte to Wilde's cosmopolitan disenchantment in 'The Decay of Lying':

> The ideas of these people are not our ideas; their sentiments are not our sentiments; their ethical life represents for us regions of thought and emotion yet unexplored, or perhaps long forgotten. Any one of their ordinary phrases, translated into Western speech, makes hopeless nonsense; and the literal rendering into Japanese of the simplest English sentence would scarcely be comprehended by any Japanese who had never studied a European tongue. Could you learn all the words in a Japanese dictionary, your acquisition would not help you in the least to make yourself understood in speaking, unless you had learned also to think like a Japanese,—that is to say, to think backwards, to think upside-down and inside-out, to think in directions totally foreign to Aryan habit.[11]

For Hearn the difference between Japan and the West showed itself not only in language, traditions, and habits, but also in psychology, emotions, and what he habitually subsumed under the ambiguous term 'race'. Neither time nor familiarity with the country ever erased what Hearn calls the 'strangeness' of Japan—a concept saturated with positive meanings. Hearn found the aesthetic and ethical appeal of 'strangeness' in almost every aspect of Japanese culture but especially in its fine and applied arts, religious and social customs, and hospitality towards foreigners. His Japanese writings are punctuated with adjectives such as 'enigmatic', 'queer', 'fantastic', 'incomprehensible', 'unimaginable', which all point to the problem of representation and translatability: Japan forces Western writers to think 'backwards' and 'upside-down', that is, to go against the grain of their native tendencies and to inhabit new subject positions that are fundamentally unlike the metropolitan vantage points favoured by the aesthetic *flâneurs* of Wilde and Huysmans.

Both Wilde and Hearn were committed to opening English literature to a dialogue with foreign cultures but their styles of literary cosmopolitanism were profoundly different. While Wilde moved in the heart of international metropolitan networks, frequenting *salons* and trying to capture the latest literary trends, Hearn was in constant flight from the metropolis and, throughout his works,

---

[10] Lafcadio Hearn, 'Strangeness and Charm', in *Japan: An Attempt at Interpretation* (New York and London: Macmillan, 1904), 9–23 (9).
[11] Ibid. 13–14.

attempted to emphasize and preserve cultural diversity by paying attention to the minor and peripheral. Their fundamental difference is encapsulated in Hearn's profound investment, in the previous quotation, in the mother tongue, which makes a striking contrast to Wilde's attempt to shake off its burden. Hearn's Japanese writings show that, even at the turn of the twentieth century, Herderian cultural nationalism still could and did inspire an alternative model of literary cosmopolitanism from the one favoured by Wilde. For Hearn, Japan's unintelligibility merely revealed a condition of illegibility that was true of all encounters with a foreign culture. This did not mean that literature could not communicate across the gulf of linguistic and national differences, but rather that the ethical mission of literary cosmopolitanism was to respect those differences by making them visible. In other words, cosmopolitanism, as Hearn understood it, should not aim to erase borders but to put them in focus as sites of curiosity and productive contamination—as 'outward-facing' tropes, in the words of Kwame Anthony Appiah.[12]

Hearn was a popular and respected writer in his day—W. B. Yeats, for instance, is said to have credited him with the best definition of poetry he knew.[13] However, after his death in 1904 he was first marginalized as a middle-brow travel writer, then as a Japanophile at a time of anti-Japanese political sentiment, and finally, with the rise of postcolonial criticism, he was bracketed as an orientalist—a label that, however fitting in many respects, also underplays the complexity of his subject position.[14] In Japan, by contrast, where his works have never been out of print, his reputation has been phenomenal: under his adopted Japanese name of Koizumi Yakumo, Hearn has been familiar to generations of Japanese readers who have encountered his works in translation, in the original, as language primers for learners of English, or adapted into films and manga. Hearn is so recognizable that his name is attached to brands of commercial goods (coffee, tea, sake, etc.) and his face featured on a Japanese stamp, as a fitting tribute to his ability to forge transcultural connections. Among Japanese academics, Hearn has likewise attracted considerable attention for having contributed to the transmission of their culture on a global stage.[15] This split reputation is a function of the fact that his work resists single, stable national literary identities. Irish, Greek, English, American, Japanese: Hearn was all and none of these at the same time.

---

[12] Kwame Anthony Appiah, 'Boundaries of Culture', *PMLA*, 123.3 (2017), 513–525 (515). Appiah thus reminds us that Herder was foundational to Goethe's theory of *Weltliteratur*.

[13] Reginald Hine, *Confessions of an Un-Common Attorney* (1945), 152; cited in *The Collected Letters of W. B. Yeats*, ed. John Kelly (Oxford: Clarendon Press, 1986–), iii: *1901–04*, ed. John Kelly and Ronald Schuchard (1994), 101. The definition in question is 'There is something ghostly in all great art.'

[14] For a relevant argument on the need to nuance Edward Said's theories of Orientalism in relation to *japonisme*, see Reed, *Bachelor Japanists*, 19–26.

[15] The bibliography of Hearn's Japanese translations, adaptations, and criticism is vast. Among Japanese academic studies written in English it is worth signalling in particular the work of Hirakawa Sukehiro, e.g. Hirakawa, ed., *Rediscovering Lafcadio Hearn: Japanese Legends, Life and Culture* (Folkestone: Global Oriental, 1997).

However, the comparison with Wilde also helps us to see that, in fact, Hearn operated more closely to literary networks familiar to English scholars than his geographical distance might at first suggest. Like many writers of his generation, as a young man in the 1870s and 1880s, Hearn came under the influence of English aestheticism, especially Dante Gabriel Rossetti, A. C. Swinburne, and John Addington Symonds, for the last of whom he felt an almost religious reverence.[16] Reading Hearn within this literary context helps us not only to see his stylistic debt to aestheticism: for instance, the very concept of 'strangeness' that he employed so frequently resounds with echoes of Swinburne and Pater. It also shows us how the metropolitan aestheticism that developed within English and French literatures in the nineteenth century adapted to different geographies and, in particular, how it coped with the task of 'translating' the deeply alien context of Japan. A cosmopolitan perspective on Hearn therefore enables us both to recuperate his highly personal history of uprooting and global migration and to reconnect the different literary products of that migration—his American and Japanese works; journalism, translations, and essays; published and private writings.

## The Aesthetics of Transplantation

Patrick Lafcadio Hearn was the only son of an Anglo-Irish army surgeon and a Greek woman native to the island of Kythira. He received his unusual name from his birthplace on Lefkada, one of the Ionian islands, where his newly wed parents had stopped on their way to Dublin. Like the rest of his life, Hearn's childhood was not a straightforward affair: his parents broke up when he was 6 years old, his mother was sent back to Greece under dubious circumstances, and the young Paddy, as he was known in those days, was put into the care of one of his Irish aunts. In a series of letters to a half-sister whom he never met, written from Japan in the early 1890s, Hearn told the story of his life as a romantic adventure, full of sentimental vignettes and dramatic plot turns: the unhappy early years in Ireland, Britain, and France dominated by a repressive Catholic schooling and the loss of his left eye ('punched out at school') that left him permanently disfigured. Then, when he was 19 years old, came the enforced emigration to America, where he

---

[16] Hearn to Basil Hall Chamberlain, 14 June 1893, in *The Japanese Letters of Lafcadio Hearn*, ed. Elizabeth Bisland (London: Constable; Boston and New York: Houghton Mifflin, 1910), 112. In one of the rare studies of Hearn in the context of English aestheticism and decadence, Catherine Maxwell compares him to John Addington Symonds as 'cosmopolitan *flaireurs*'; Maxwell, *Scents and Sensibility: Perfume in Victorian Literary Culture* (Oxford and New York: Oxford University Press, 2017), 161–181. See also Daichi Ishikawa, 'For Curiosity's Sake: British Aestheticism and Cosmopolitan Notions of Curiosity in Walter Pater, John Addington Symonds, and Lafcadio Hearn, 1864–1904' (unpublished doctoral thesis, Queen Mary, University of London, 2018). Carl Dawson makes a brief comparison with Pater in *Lafcadio Hearn and the Vision of Japan* (Baltimore and London: Johns Hopkins University Press, 1992), 71.

broke loose from all family ties and the conventions of bourgeois respectability. As he put it: 'I was told to go to the devil, and take care of myself. I did both.'[17] Hearn spent nearly twenty years in America, where he started off from nothing, as most Irish emigrants did in those days. He lived first in Cincinnati, where he experienced extreme poverty, working as a boarding-house servant and an unpaid printing apprentice, and slowly making his way into journalism. While in Cincinnati, Hearn married an African American woman named Alethea ('Mattie') Foley, against local legislation, which prohibited mixed marriages. The two quickly became estranged, however, and Hearn seems to have avoided making reference to this episode in later life.[18] Eventually Hearn moved to New Orleans, where he achieved a degree of financial stability and built up a solid reputation as the literary editor of the city's chief newspaper, the *Times-Democrat*. Stimulated by the ethnic and cultural diversity that he encountered in the American South, Hearn then moved to the West Indies for two years. Hearn's nomadism was clearly the product of difficult family circumstances that alienated him from his home environment. Out of these grew a form of extreme individualism, compounded with a desire to experience different places and cultures and also, in the early days at least, a desire for adventure and sexual libertinism.[19]

In a striking vicarious realization of Wilde's never-to-be trip with Whistler, in 1890 Hearn travelled to Japan together with the artist C. W. Weldon, with whom he had been jointly commissioned to produce an illustrated article eventually published in *Harper's New Monthly Magazine*.[20] He would never leave the country again. Hearn was captivated by the natural beauty of Japan and by the arts, literature, folklore, and religion of the Japanese, whom he described, in a letter to his American friend Elizabeth Bisland, as 'the best people in the world to live among'.[21] In his Japanese years Hearn's main profession was as a teacher of English, first in provincial high schools in Matsue and Kumamoto and eventually at the Imperial University in Tokyo, where he was awarded the prestigious Chair

---

[17] Hearn to Minnie Atkinson, quoted in Nina H. Kennard, *Lafcadio Hearn: Containing Some Letters from Lafcadio Hearn to his Half-Sister, Mrs Atkinson* (New York: Appleton & Co., 1912), 32. Hearn's correspondence with his sister Minnie is preserved in the Lafcadio Hearn Collection of the Howard-Tilton Memorial Library, Tulane University, New Orleans. Biographical information about Hearn is drawn from Elizabeth Bisland, *Life and Letters of Lafcadio Hearn*, 2 vols (Boston and New York: Houghton Mifflin, 1911); Elizabeth Stevenson, *Lafcadio Hearn* (New York: Macmillan, 1961); and Paul Murray, *A Fantastic Journey: The Life and Literature of Lafcadio Hearn* (London and New York: Routledge Curzon, 1993).

[18] See Murray, *Fantastic Journey*, 40–44. Foley made their history public after Hearn's death, believing that she would be entitled to part of his inheritance.

[19] Hearn's sexual morality became a matter of controversy among his early biographers, following George M. Gould's vitriolic attack on Hearn in his *Concerning Lafcadio Hearn* (London: Fisher Unwin, 1908). Gould was a biologist and his approach bears the mark of degeneration theory. Much of the posthumous scandal hinged on Hearn's relationships with African American women in Cincinnati and is inflected by what, to modern eyes, appears as racist prejudice.

[20] Hearn, 'A Winter Journey to Japan', *Harper's New Monthly Magazine*, 81 (June 1890), 860–868.

[21] Hearn to Elizabeth Bisland, 27 Jan. 1894, in *Japanese Letters*, ed. Bisland, 232.

of English Language and Literature. At the same time, he kept up his collaborations with American periodicals and produced the many collections of Japanese essays—nearly one every year, from 1894 until his death in 1904—which earned him notoriety both in Japan and in the West. Hearn's international reputation reached its peak in the first decades of the twentieth century with the publication of biographies and collected letters, as well as multi-volume editions of his complete writings in America (1922) and Japan (1926–32). At this time Hearn's work had a truly global reach, extending beyond Japan and the English-speaking world thanks to numerous translations into several European languages including French, German, and Italian.

In Japan as in the United States and the Caribbean, Hearn was never a tourist in Wilde's belittling sense of the term. In a letter to his half-sister he spoke disparagingly of modern tourism, saying that nothing was to him 'more frightful than a fashionable sea-side resort—such as those of the Atlantic Coast. My happiest sojourns of this sort have been in little fishing-villages, and little queer old unknown towns, where there are no big vulgar hotels, and where one can dress and do exactly as one pleases.'[22] Hearn always shunned the worldly glamour of international society. Throughout his life he would be most comfortable when he felt most foreign, which helps to explain his great attraction towards Japan. Within Japan, he preferred small provincial centres to Tokyo and to open ports such as Yokohama and Kobe, with their noticeable presence of American and European nationals. As he moved around the world, Hearn cultivated this role of perpetual outsider and used it in his writings as a position of authority. Virtually all of Hearn's works are set in places that are assumed to be unfamiliar or exotic to his English-speaking readers. None of them could be straightforwardly classed as travel writing, though, because Hearn's engagement with the local went far beyond mere impression, although impressionism was a key element of his style: by means of careful research and by building local networks, Hearn always endeavoured to reach aspects of local culture that would not normally be accessible to travellers and foreign observers.

Adapting what Appiah and Homi Bhabha have argued in the postcolonial context, we could say that this was Hearn's way of 'rooting' his cosmopolitanism, that is, of anchoring his experience of living and writing across cultures in a specific space, in order to prevent it from collapsing into a form of untenable universalism or a globe-trotting mentality that is unable to penetrate beyond the outer surface of foreign space.[23] Appiah and Bhabha use the concept of 'rooted' or 'vernacular' cosmopolitanism to describe the efforts made by migrants from

---

[22] Hearn to Minnie Atkinson, 17 Sept. 1893, quoted in Kennard, *Lafcadio Hearn*, 213.
[23] Kwame Anthony Appiah, 'Rooted Cosmopolitanism', in *The Ethics of Identity* (Princeton and Oxford: Princeton University Press, 2005), 213–272; Homi K. Bhabha, 'The Vernacular Cosmopolitan', in Ferdinand Dennis and Naseem Khan, eds, *Voices of the Crossing: The Impact of Britain on Writers from Asia, the Caribbean, and Africa* (London: Serpent's Tail, 2000), 133–142.

economic peripheries to the metropolis (especially Africans and Asians living in Britain today) to preserve an attachment to their native culture while embracing a cosmopolitan identity that is forced upon them by the postcolonial world order. Hearn complicates this model in productive ways: coming from the Irish periphery, he still benefited (passively or actively) from the social and economic networks of the British Empire, especially while in Japan, much as he was often very critical of Britain and British imperialism. Hearn's cosmopolitanism consists precisely of this unsolved dialectic of uprooting and rootedness, of balancing contradictory positions of socio-cultural privilege and vulnerability. Politically and aesthetically, his literary cosmopolitanism compounds anti-imperialism with elements of orientalism, understood in Edward Said's influential terms as a field of knowledge that is complicit with a 'Western style for dominating, restructuring, and having authority over the Orient.'[24]

Hearn's deep engagement with foreign space enabled him to become an active agent in the production of the 'local' in the different cultures that hosted him. In New Orleans, for instance, he published a pioneering dictionary of Creole proverbs and a Creole cookbook, as well as contributing to a *Historical Sketch Book and Guide to New Orleans* (1885) in the guise of one of the foremost cultural authorities on the city. In these works of non-fiction just as in his stories, Hearn used his position as outsider/insider to project the local onto a larger, 'world' stage. At the same time, he also worked to transform the literatures of his adopted homelands by opening them to cosmopolitan influences. As we shall see, this would be one his most important legacies to Japan.

In the preface to a 1919 German selection of Hearn's works, Stefan Zweig underscored Hearn's world citizenship (*Weltbürgertum*), which he traced to his international parentage. This, according to Zweig, was the key to understanding Hearn's ambiguous position vis-à-vis Japan as, at the same time, a foreigner and assimilated citizen. Zweig described Hearn's cosmopolitan voice with a striking botanical metaphor: as Hearn spent more and more time in Japan, his writings became 'a wonder of transplantation, of artificial grafting: the works of a Westerner written by an Eastern author'.[25] The image of 'artificial grafting' repurposes the hackneyed essentializing symbolism of roots used in nationalist discourse in order to portray cosmopolitan authorship as an aesthetics of desirable artificiality. The exotic and decadent associations of the image of the grafted plant multiplied when Zweig further compared Hearn's act of becoming Japanese to the making of a cultivated pearl: Hearn

---

[24] Edward W. Said, *Orientalism* (London and Henley: Routledge & Kegan Paul, 1978), 3.
[25] Stefan Zweig, 'Lafcadio Hearn', in Hearn, *Das Japanbuch: Eine Auswhal aus den Werken von Lafcadio Hearn* (Frankfurt a.M.: Rütten & Loening, 1919), 1–12 (8) ('[Hearns Bücher] sind etwas ganz Eigenartiges in der Kunst, ein Wunder der Transplantation, der künstlichen Aufpropfung: Die Werke eines Abendländers, aber von einem Fernorientalen geschrieben').

was like the alien body that is artificially inserted into an oyster, which envelops it with 'its glistening slime' ('ihrem glitzernden Schleim') and eventually turns it into something rare and precious.[26] As we have seen, Zweig openly identified as a cosmopolitan, although, like Wilde, he had a taste for the seaside-resort cosmopolitanism that Hearn abhorred. He therefore wanted to offer a sympathetic reading of Hearn's hybrid identity and convey the richness of Hearn's work of cultural mediation, but his metaphors were nonetheless haunted by images of violence and loss—the perhaps inevitable loss of identity that beset Hearn as he drew closer to Japan.

Zweig admired Hearn but other critics used similar arguments in order to marginalize him, accusing him of excessive softness and passivity in his relation to Japan, which allegedly resulted in a form of weakness. The British critic and poet Edward Thomas, for instance, was troubled by the difficulty of distinguishing between what is 'Japanese' and what is 'really Hearn'.[27] For Thomas, who also wrote studies of other authors associated with aestheticism, Hearn's Japanese writings should be seen as 'choice translations'—a formula that undermined their originality and literary value just as it paid a bland homage to their style.[28] Thomas—sympathetic though he was to Hearn and aesthetic writing in many ways—reveals a bias that was prominent in Hearn's reception in Britain and America: critics tried to slot his work into essentialist categories and tended to be suspicious of the aesthetics of transplantation that fascinated Zweig. Inevitably, such approaches were deeply at odds with Hearn's belief that the function of literature lay precisely in imaginatively transporting readers beyond the experiential and moral boundaries of the nation.

There are multiple national and transnational perspectives, just as there are entangled cosmopolitan and rooted points of view, at work in Hearn's writings. Hearn translated French literature into English and mediated Japan to the West. At the same time, through his work as teacher and critic, he also spread knowledge of modern English literature in Japan, just as he made elements of Japanese folklore known to the Japanese themselves, mostly indirectly, through Japanese translations of his essays that redomesticated old Japanese tales and legends by way of their English retellings. The very categories of translation and mediation are far from stable in Hearn's writings. Only by working outside and against rigid national perspectives can we cause Hearn to become visible again in a redrawn map of the literature of the *fin de siècle* no longer divided into discrete national units.

---

[26] Ibid. 10.
[27] Edward Thomas, *Lafcadio Hearn* (London: Constable; Boston and New York: Houghton Mifflin, 1912), 91.
[28] Ibid. 90.

## Translating Aestheticism in New Orleans

Hearn's literary career started with his arrival in New Orleans in 1877. He quickly worked his way into the local daily press, building on his previous experience in Cincinnati as a sensational journalist who specialized in tales of the gruesome.[29] In New Orleans he worked first as a reporter and assistant editor for the *City Item*, introducing scholarly and literary content into what had essentially been a purely political publication, and then became literary editor for the more prominent newspaper *Times-Democrat*, where he brought out most of his more substantial work. By the early 1880s he had established himself as a firm reference point in the local literary culture. Hearn's American journalism is a large corpus of short pieces made up of literary reviews, critical items, editorials, translations, and fictional sketches. In his early days in the *Item* he even published over 150 cartoons.

In New Orleans, Hearn's work was shaped by and, at the same time, shaped the multi-layered fabric of the city, which had until recently been a prominent centre of the slave trade. As Mary Gallagher has noted, the legacy of the traumatic histories of enslavement and forced migration on folk cultures was one of the constant preoccupations of Hearn's American and Caribbean writings.[30] New Orleans was also characterized by the presence of a deeply rooted French culture, reflected in a number of prominent institutions such as the daily French-language newspaper, *L'Abeille*, still active in Hearn's time. Hearn was fascinated both by the descendants of enslaved people and by the local French- and Spanish-descended Creole population, describing in several articles how the latter had kept old European traditions and adapted them to the New World. He also wrote in favour of preserving the use of French in Louisiana, arguing against those who maintained that English should be the only official language in schools and public institutions.[31] This did not mean that Hearn was committed to the notion of a Parisian, European, or metropolitan purity—on the contrary, he was drawn precisely to the cultural and racial crossings that, according to him, made New Orleans a cosmopolitan city hospitable to migrants from different countries and of different ethnicities, as he emphasized repeatedly in his articles.[32] Hearn's writings

[29] These are collected in *Period of the Gruesome: Selected Cincinnati Journalism of Lafcadio Hearn*, ed. Jon Christopher Hughes (Lanham, MD, and New York: University Press of America, 1990). Hearn wrote more than 400 articles during his residence in Cincinnati.

[30] Mary Gallagher, 'Lafcadio Hearn's American Writings and the Creole Continuum', in *American Creoles: The Francophone Caribbean and the American South*, ed. Martin Munro and Celia Britton (Liverpool: Liverpool University Press, 2012), 19–39 (25 and *passim*).

[31] Hearn, 'The French in Louisiana', *Daily City Item*, 2 Mar. 1880, reprinted in *Editorials*, ed. Charles Woodward Hutson (Boston and New York: Houghton Mifflin, 1926), 81–83.

[32] See, for instance, Hearn, 'The Glamour of New Orleans', in *Daily City Item*, 26 Nov. 1878; reprinted in Hearn, *American Writings*, ed. Christopher Benfey (New York: Library of America, 2009), 709–710 (710).

on New Orleans are so invested in uncovering and celebrating the diversity of the city that one of his recent editors has credited Hearn with having *invented* cosmopolitan New Orleans as we now know it.[33] Indeed, when writing both for the local and national presses, he would often draw attention to the way in which the different foreign traditions brought by the modern inhabitants of the city were harmonized into a distinctive spectacle that unfolded before the eyes of residents and visitors, like a perennial version of the famous local carnival of which Hearn also wrote.

The prime symbol of New Orleans cosmopolitanism was, for Hearn, the local Creole language, with its mixing of different linguistic heritages. He compared it to the speech of Homer and Beowulf, collected poems and legends, and produced a carefully researched, annotated dictionary of Louisiana proverbs, *Gombo Zhèbes* (1885), in which he transcribed popular sayings in a variety of Creole dialects, providing his own French and English translations.[34] To him the language of the New Orleans Creoles embodied the attractive notion of a vernacular cosmopolitanism, the product of what Zweig, as we have seen, was to describe as 'transplantation' with reference to Hearn's own Japanese writings. Hearn called Louisiana Creole 'the offspring of linguistic miscegenation, an offspring which exhibits but a very faint shade of African color, and nevertheless possesses a strangely supple comeliness by virtue of the very intercrossing which created it, like a beautiful octoroon'.[35] The ethnographic simile connects the language of the city with the bodies that populate its streets, which Hearn was fond of describing in detail in his articles, lingering in particular on the varieties of tones of skin colour. His private writings reveal an element of erotic desire in this fascination with mixed-race bodies that was left out of the published essays: for instance, in a series of letters from the West Indies to the New Orleans doctor Rudolph Matas, Hearn spoke frankly about taking particular pleasure in experiencing different racial combinations in his dealings with local prostitutes.[36] Hearn, in other words, exoticized the

---

[33] S. Frederick Starr, 'Introduction', in Lafcadio Hearn, *Inventing New Orleans: Writings of Lafcadio Hearn* (Jackson, MS: University Press of Mississippi, 2001), pp. xi–xxvii.

[34] Hearn, 'The Creole Patois', *Harper's Weekly* (10 Jan. 1885), reprinted in Hearn, *American Writings*, 744–748 (746); Hearn, *Gombo Zhèbes: Little Dictionary of Creole Proverbs* (New York: Coleman, 1885).

[35] Hearn, 'The Creole Patois', 746. Hearn saw the same vernacular cosmopolitanism of New Orleans reflected in the local cuisine, which he studied in his cookbook, *La Cuisine Créole: A Collection of Culinary Recipes* (New Orleans: Hansell & Bro., 1885). On ethnographic interests in Hearn's journalism, see Simon J. Bronner, ed., *Lafcadio Hearn's America: Ethnographic Sketches and Editorials* (Lexington: University Press of Kentucky, 2002); and Gallagher, 'Lafcadio Hearn's American Writings'. When applied to individuals, the concept of Creole was somewhat ambiguous: it was originally used to designate Louisiana-born people (as opposed to those who had migrated there from elsewhere), but in Hearn's times it was also applied to people of mixed European and African or Caribbean blood, who were also sometimes called 'creoles of colour'. Hearn was drawn to the pliability of this concept, which spanned national, linguistic, and racial divides.

[36] Hearn's letters to his friend Rudolph Matas are held in the Howard-Tilton Memorial Library, Tulane University, New Orleans.

racialized body, in sometimes uncomfortable ways, in order to celebrate what he perceived as the city's hybridity, and to convey the appeal of a culture that was both exquisitely local (since it was unique to this part of the world) and global, in that it made visible the often violent histories of displacement and migration by virtue of which it existed.

Translation occupied a central position in Hearn's early work. His first published piece for the *Item* was the beginning of a serialized English version of Théophile Gautier's 'The Mummy's Foot' ('Le Pied de momie', 1840). Particularly noteworthy, however, is a series of translations that Hearn undertook for the *Times-Democrat* in the mid-1880s, which became a regular feature of the Sunday editions of the newspaper. Hearn gathered his material from Parisian reviews such as the *Supplement litteraire du Figaro, Le Gaulois* (the paper that published Wilde's interview after the British ban on *Salomé*), and the *Revue Politique et Litteraire*, which printed serialized new fiction by French authors. He would either translate the full serial (as with Guy de Maupassant's *L'Aventure de Walter Schnaffs*, 1883) or the finale only, prefacing it with a brief summary of the plot up to that point. In this way readers of the New Orleans *Times-Democrat* were among the first in the English-speaking world to become acquainted with modern French authors such as Villiers de l'Isle Adam, Maupassant, and Pierre Loti, whose works Hearn translated or summarized even before they were published in book form in France, and indeed well before they attracted attention in other British and American periodicals.[37] The case of Loti—an author with whom Hearn felt a strong affinity and who, as we shall see, exercised a lasting influence on his writings—is especially interesting: on one occasion Hearn managed to obtain a manuscript directly from Loti before its French publication, so that the translation came out before the original, putting readers in New Orleans ahead of their counterparts in Paris.[38] The American journalist Elizabeth Bisland, who founded the New Orleans Women's Club in 1884 and knew Hearn well in those early days, recognized Hearn's translations as an important cosmopolitan influence on American literature. In her introduction to the posthumous first edition (1910) of his translation of Flaubert's *La Tentation de saint Antoine* (1874), she remembered how American publishers would not contemplate issuing the translation in the nineteenth century, put off by the contents of the book. Bisland went on to describe Hearn's work as an attack on 'the stultifying influence of blind

---

[37] Other French authors Hearn translated either for the *Item* or the *Times-Democrat* include François Coppée, Alphonse Daudet, Flaubert, and Zola. For a comprehensive list of Hearn's unsigned American journalism, see P. D. Perkins and Ione Perkins, *Lafcadio Hearn: A Bibliography of his Writings* (Boston and New York: Houghton Mifflin, 1934).
[38] Albert Mordell, 'Introduction', in *Stories from Pierre Loti*, tr. Lafcadio Hearn (Tokyo: Hokuseido Press, 1933), pp. v–xi (p. v). The manuscript in question was published in the *Times-Democrat* on 28 Dec. 1884.

puritanism upon American literature'.[39] To her, the history of the composition and non-publication of this translation was emblematic of the struggle between the moral narrowness of American 'provincial propriety' and the progressive cosmopolitanism represented by Hearn.[40]

Bisland would play a very active role in curating Hearn's legacy after his death, editing his correspondence and writing an early biography. We will come back to her in Chapter 4, which examines her involvement in the *Cosmopolitan* magazine, to which Hearn also contributed. For now, though, it is worth noticing that Hearn suffered from the fact that translation was a tiring and ill-paid task. In an article ironically titled 'For the Sum of 25$', he complained that translators were paid less than physical labourers and were at the same time expected to turn out their work at great speed. However, in the same piece he also depicted the translator as first and foremost a fine literary critic who must be able to appreciate 'precise shades of meaning' and 'harmonies of tones and their relation to other tones, and their general interrelation with the music of the entire idea'. Modern French literature in particular demanded that the 'sense, forms, force, sonority, color of every word must be studied; the shape of every phrase chiselled out; the beauty of every naked sentence polished like statuary marble'.[41] The comparison with sculpture—taken from Gautier's characterization of Parnassian poetics in *Émaux et camées* (1852)—shows that Hearn regarded translation as a highly complex and specialized literary craft: translation brought the writer to feel the sound, texture, and architecture of language with an almost physical touch, and to absorb the influence of foreign authors more completely than any other process of close reading. In Hearn's early apology of translation as a fine art we can already see the practice of writing as a loss of individuality and merging with the other, which Zweig and Edward Thomas would seize on in their different ways. Hearn's ideas also resonate with Wilde's Alexandrian model of world literature as a space in which creation and reception blur. It is telling in this sense that, for his translations, Hearn focused on French authors who showed a marked affinity with his own style, such as Gautier, Flaubert, and Loti. Translation exercised a slow-burning but marked, transformative influence on Hearn's writing—both on the stories that he published in America and, as we shall see, in Japan.[42]

Hearn, who was physically remote from European literary networks, also used the Parisian press as a medium to discover foreign (that is, non-French) authors.

[39] Elizabeth Bisland, 'Introduction', in Gustave Flaubert, *The Temptation of Saint Anthony*, tr. Lafcadio Hearn (New York and Seattle: Alice Harriman, 1910), n. p.

[40] Ibid.

[41] Hearn, 'For the Sum of 25$', *Times-Democrat* (24 Sept. 1882); reprinted in *Editorials*, 183–186 (resp. 184 and 185–186).

[42] Cf. Bernadette Lemoine's remarks on translation as a form of 'literary apprenticeship' for Hearn; Lemoine, 'Lafcadio Hearn as an Ambassador for French Literature in the United States and Japan', *Revue de littérature comparée*, 319 (2006), 299–317 (315–316); see 306 for an overview of Hearn's French translation corpus.

This is how he found new Russian, Italian, and German writers, translating, via French, works by Dostoevsky, Matilde Serao, and Leopold von Sacher-Masoch among others. This practice of using French as a filter or transitional zone between world literature and English-speaking readers was not unusual. We have seen in the previous chapter that Wilde published an English translation of Turgenev out of a French text. Like Wilde and Hearn, many other translators in Britain (and other countries) relied on French books and periodicals as a way into foreign literatures in which they had no direct competence. In this way, according to Pascale Casanova, the French press exerted a special power to canonize foreign literary works internationally by 'impressing the stamp of *littérarité* upon texts that came from farflung lands, thereby denationalizing and departicularizing them'.[43] Tendentious though it is, Casanova's account of French 'literary dominance' helps us to see why writers like Wilde and Hearn looked to France as a source of desirable modernity they could import into the English-speaking world, benefiting at the same time from the social and cultural prestige conferred on them by the French connection. However, Hearn's work as translator, critic, and writer of imaginative fiction also brings to light more intricate patterns of global circulation than those described by Casanova: his translations did not simply transfer the literature of the centre to the periphery, from Paris to America, making it available to new readers. Rather, they deliberately activated new meanings that resulted from moving literary content across languages and geographical space.

Hearn's creative handling of translation is particularly evident in his versions of Gautier's fantastic tales, which he partly serialized in the *Item* in 1878–9. He later collected and published them in book form in 1882, with the New York publisher R. Worthington, under the title *One of Cleopatra's Nights and Other Fantastic Romances*. Hearn made a selection from Gautier's collections *Nouvelles* (1845) and *Romans et contes* (1863), choosing for inclusion six stories in which the artistic, archaeological, and erotic elements were most pronounced.[44] In general, Hearn thought that his early translations suffered from the restrictions imposed by journalistic work, which according to him 'emasculate[d] thought and style'; but he remained proud of his translation of Gautier's fantastic tales, believing that, despite its shortcomings, it was not 'castrated'.[45] Time proved him right, as *One of Cleopatra's Nights and Other Fantastic Romances* would be Hearn's most influential and long-lived translation, running into several reprints on both sides of the

---

[43] Casanova, *World Republic of Letters*, 87.
[44] Théophile Gautier, *One of Cleopatra's Nights and Other Fantastic Romances*, tr. Lafcadio Hearn (New York: Worthington, 1882). The volume contains 'One of Cleopatra's Nights', 'Clarimonde', 'Arria Marcella: A Souvenir of Pompeii', 'The Mummy's Foot', 'Omphale: A Rococo Story', and 'King Candaules'.
[45] Hearn to W. D. O'Connor, Aug. 1883, Howard-Tilton Memorial Library, Tulane University, New Orleans, typescript of an original held in the Harold B. Lee Library in Brigham Young University.

Atlantic, well into the twentieth century.[46] Gautier was different from Maupassant and the other contemporary authors that Hearn encountered in the pages of the Paris reviews because his stories had already been around for decades, in some cases since the 1830s, although they had never been translated into English before. Gautier died in 1872 and his reputation in France started to decline as the Parnassian movement with which he was associated gave way to new decadent, symbolist, and naturalist tendencies. Since the 1860s, however, he had increasingly gained popularity among English aesthetic writers: Swinburne and Pater, for instance, drew inspiration from Gautier's elaborately crafted prose style that infused art criticism with powerful visual sensations and an intensely emotive idiom. In particular, British aesthetes looked to Gautier as a precursor of their principles of art for art's sake and aesthetic autonomy, which Gautier laid out in the 'Preface' to his erotic novel *Mademoiselle de Maupin* (1835)—a work that attained an almost cultish semi-clandestine status in late nineteenth-century Britain. Here Gautier railed against the hypocrisy of the periodical press, especially in matters of sexuality, arguing that the beautiful and the useful should be seen as incongruous and fundamentally opposed quantities.

Hearn's preface to his translation of Gautier's supernatural tales was a mani-festo of aestheticism in miniature, addressed to 'lovers of physical beauty and artistic truth'.[47] He adopted Gautier's belief that art stood above morality and, harking back to ancient paganism as the natural religion of artists of all times, he praised Gautier's style and his descriptive power in sometimes extravagant terms ('a faint perfume of unknown balm seems to hover over the open pages').[48] Hearn also compared the French author to a Greek sculptor for his firm command over his medium and his inspired lack of prudery in dealing with erotic subjects. The short preface/manifesto shows that Hearn practised translation as simultaneously a form of advocacy and a way of entering into dialogue with what Matthew Potolsky calls a 'decadent community'—a cosmopolitan network of advanced authors who sought to challenge middle-class taste by pushing the boundary of the acceptable in literature.[49] He must have known he had succeeded when a reviewer complained that his translations 'reeked with the miasma of the brothel'.[50] That Hearn's work was perceived as partaking of the transgressive sexuality of the original was evidence that it was certainly not 'castrated', to use his own metaphor from the letter quoted.

[46] The first British edition came out in 1899 with Harper & Bros (London); notable later reprints include a 1908 edition titled *Stories by Théophile Gautier* with a preface by Arthur Ransome, and a 1927 one with a preface by George Saintsbury.

[47] Hearn, 'To the Reader', in Gautier, *One of Cleopatra's Nights and Other Fantastic Romances*, pp. v–ix (p. ix).

[48] Ibid., p. vi.

[49] For Gautier's role in the creation of decadent networks, see Potolsky, *The Decadent Republic of Letters* (Philadelphia: University of Pennsylvania Press, 2013), 48–56 and *passim*.

[50] Quoted in Bisland, *Life and Letters of Lafcadio Hearn*, i. 248.

Hearn further enforced his textual presence by inserting short but intrusive paratexts in the volume. An epigraph consisting of two stanzas from Swinburne's 'Memorial Verses on the death of Theophile Gautier' referred directly to the story that Hearn translated as 'One of Cleopatra's Nights' ('Une Nuit de Cléopatra'), highlighting the eros/thanatos dynamics in Gautier which is of course also a recognizably Swinburnean topos. In this way Hearn encouraged readers to see a link between Gautier and Swinburne, using Swinburne's voice and reputation as a stepping-stone into the French text and almost as a guide to its transgressive content. But just as he used Swinburne to introduce Gautier, Hearn used Gautier to enter into a dialogue with Swinburne, whose ideas on literature and public morality inform the argument of the preface. In this way Hearn wrote himself into a lineage of militant advocates of art for art's sake, complicating his role as translator by blurring the line between translation and criticism. More radically, by using Swinburne to open up the exclusive and hierarchical relationship between author and translator, Hearn presented translation as a creative act of textual networking involving multiple mediators and voices.

Similar interventions occur in a section of 'Addenda' at the end of the volume, in which Hearn provided extra contextual material (including his translation of Gautier's poem 'Les Tâches Jaunes') and possible sources for the tales, as well as a couple of technical clarifications of linguistic matters. One of these is striking for its apparent eccentricity:

> In the opening scene of 'One of Cleopatra's Nights,' the reader may be surprised at the expression 'the *chuckling* of the crocodiles.' Our own southern alligators often make a little noise which could not be better described—a low, guttural sound, bearing a sinister resemblance to a human chuckle or subdued, sneering laugh. A Creole friend who has lived much in those regions of Southern Louisiana intersected by bayous and haunted by alligators, comprehended at once the whole force of the term *rire étouffé* as applied to the sounds made by the crocodile. '*Je l'ai entendu souvent*,' he said, with a smile.[51]

If, with his epigraph from Swinburne, Hearn had projected his translation into a global dialogue between metropolitan voices, in this addendum he affixed to it the stamp of the periphery. Hearn's 'Creole friend' plays an important cameo role in the margin of the text as an unexpected but ideal reader of Gautier: the immediate communication between the Parisian French of the writer and the local idiom of the Louisiana Creole breaks down the barriers between metropolitan literary modernity and the vernacular aestheticism of New Orleans. This inconspicuous

---

[51] Hearn, 'Addenda', in Gautier, *One of Cleopatra's Nights and Other Fantastic Romances*, 317–321 (317).

endnote made it impossible for readers in London and New York to ignore the imprint of New Orleans, alerting them to the presence of another interpretative and spatial layer between them and the original text of Gautier that translation made at the same time visible and invisible.

## Hearn and Wilde: Crossing Paths

The New Orleans years were Hearn's apprenticeship in mediating between metropolitan Franco-English aestheticism and extra-European spaces and cultures. While he was there he crossed paths with Oscar Wilde, who was on his American lecture tour the year that Hearn's translation of Gautier came out, in 1882. The arrival of this fellow Irishman who styled himself as the standard-bearer of the English aesthetic movement caught Hearn's attention. In an article for the *Times-Democrat* titled 'The Apostle of Aestheticism', Hearn defended Wilde against the tide of American press reports that made fun of his mannerisms and that dismissed the principles of aestheticism which he was supposed to embody. Hearn exhorted readers to take Wilde seriously, speaking highly of his *Poems* (1881) and even of his sartorial affectations, which he compared to the eccentricities of the young Gautier. The strategic reference to Gautier was nothing short of a declaration of alliance: repeating his argument from the preface to *One of Cleopatra's Nights*, he now praised Wilde for reminding his contemporaries that 'the love of the beautiful is an important influence in civilization and progress' and that the 'influence of beauty purifies and moralizes'. Aestheticism, Hearn added, was particularly needed in America because of the general 'lack of taste' of the nation, even though in New Orleans this failing was somewhat lessened by the predominance of 'the naturally aesthetic Latin element'.[52] Fleshing out his titular figure of the 'apostle', Hearn upbraided the hostile American public for receiving Wilde 'much as early missionaries were first treated by the pagan ancestors of the Anglo-Saxon nations of to-day'. While the image of Wilde heading a civilizing mission against the 'modern paganism of bad taste' was meant to be an expression of praise, it also brought out an element of cultural imperialism in Wilde's commercially driven American lecture tour.

This feeling of scepticism intensified in a second article, in which Hearn still defended the 'deep philosophy' that hid behind the humorous façade, but exhorted Wilde that, in order to make his mission really worthwhile, he should

---

[52] [Hearn], 'The Apostle of Aestheticism', *Times-Democrat*, 16 Apr. 1882, 4. The article is, as was customary, unsigned, but it is attributed to Hearn in P. D. and Ione Perkins, *Lafcadio Hearn: A Bibliography*, 257. The style and position within the paper corroborate their attribution.

produce 'enduring books' and 'something more lasting and valuable to society than lectures and knee-breeches exhibitions'.[53] Hearn wanted to make the point that Wilde was not such a pioneer as he thought, since a sophisticated brand of vernacular aestheticism already existed in the American South, as he had already shown in his own work.

Wilde lectured in New Orleans twice in June 1882. The lectures were advertised in the pages of the *Times-Democrat* and attracted very large audiences of up to two thousand people.[54] Disappointingly, we have no record of whether Hearn attended Wilde's lectures or whether the two writers met in person. It may well be that Hearn was put off by Wilde's extravagancies and by the media hype and commercialism that accompanied his lecture tour. Yet, it seems inconceivable that Hearn should have missed the opportunity to see for himself the Irish celebrity aesthete about whom he had written two articles. Likewise, Wilde, whose busy schedule was always thick with social and literary engagements and who privately boasted of always carrying a copy of Gautier as he travelled around America,[55] would have naturally been curious about this young Irish translator of Gautier. Wilde's declared interests in artistic treatments of 'the Indian and the Negro' would also have pushed him in the direction of Hearn, who already had a reputation as an expert on the local Creole and Black cultures second only to the then extremely popular George Cable, whom Wilde praised in his interviews with the local press.[56] Whatever the case, the crossing of these two cosmopolitan writers in *fin-de-siècle* New Orleans shows us that the supposedly metropolitan 'English' aestheticism was in fact being negotiated and defined globally rather than domestically, in marginal spaces which still remain largely outside the map of scholars of English literature.

At the close of his second lecture in New Orleans, Wilde announced his intention to extend his tour to Japan, 'the art land of the East'.[57] As we know, this project would never come to fruition. But, if Hearn was one of those two thousand in the Spanish Fort that night or if he read the detailed report of the lecture in the press, it may well have been Wilde who planted in his head the seed for the ambitious plan that he was going to realize eight years later.

[53] [Hearn], 'Oscar Wilde as Fashion Designer', *Times-Democrat*, 14 May 1882, 4. Again, the article is unsigned but it is listed as Hearn's by P. D. and Ione Perkins; the style, arguments, and position within the paper point to Hearn as the anonymous author.

[54] [Anon.], 'Oscar Wilde. Lecture at Spanish Fort on Home Decorations. Practical Talk from an Apparently Unpractical Man', *Daily Picayune*, 27 June 1882, 3.

[55] Wilde to Julia Ward Howe, 6 July [1882], in *Complete Letters*, 175.

[56] Both from [anon.], 'Oscar Wilde: A Visit to the Apostle of Modern Art', *Daily Picayune*, afternoon edition, 16 June 1882, 1.

[57] [Anon.], 'Oscar Wilde. Lecture at Spanish Fort', 3.

## Hearn's Japan: The 'World of Strangeness'

There is another way of reading Wilde's jibe about seeing a 'Japanese effect' on Piccadilly: Wilde may have been humorously pointing out that, after years of overexposure, the country's exotic appeal had all but exhausted itself. Indeed, when Hearn got there in 1890, Japan had already been a popular subject for decades. Following the country's opening to foreign trade in the 1850s, Japanese arts and crafts flowed into Western markets, where they attracted the attention of artists such as Whistler, who collected Japanese woodblock prints and, as we have seen, used references to Japanese art to inject new life into European painting. His controversial 'Ten O'Clock' lecture (1885) ended with a flamboyant comparison between the Parthenon marbles and 'the fan of Hokusai', in which Whistler effectively hailed Japan as the new Greece—the source of a different classicism that could inspire artists in the West.[58] In the last quarter of the century the new interest in Japanese culture quickly generated a new European and American literature about Japan, made up of first-hand travel accounts, as well as a growing number of ethnographic, linguistic, historical, artistic, and religious studies.[59] In 1890, setting off for Japan from America, Hearn was aware that the ground was 'well-trodden' and that it would be difficult for him to discover new places or aspects of Japanese culture that were still unfamiliar in the West. In order to be original, he would therefore have to find a 'new way' to write about Japan: he would concentrate on reproducing the 'life and color' of the country, rather by means of 'vivid sensation given to the reader, than by any accounts or explanations such as may be found in other writers,—whether travellers or scholars'.[60]

Hearn was right: his first collection of Japanese writings, *Glimpses of Unfamiliar Japan* (1894), did provide something that did not exist in English so far. Looking back on it in 1910, Elizabeth Bisland called it the first book to describe Japan with 'intimate tenderness', that is, to approach the Japanese people 'from their own point of view'.[61] Bisland was hardly an impartial critic. Yet, it is undeniable that, after reading Hearn, a book like Isabella Bird's extremely popular *Unbeaten Tracks in Japan* (1880), published only a few years earlier, is bound to strike readers today as dry and frequently patronizing: writing in epistolary form and with 'accuracy'

---

[58] James McNeill Whistler, 'Mr Whistler's "Ten O'Clock"', in *The Gentle Art of Making Enemies* (London: Heinemann, 1890), 131–159 (159).

[59] Crucial in this respect were the writings of the British Basil Hall Chamberlain and Ernest Mason Satow, and of the American Percival Lowell, all of whom Hearn got to know in person. Lowell's work had a particularly strong influence on him.

[60] Hearn to N. W. Patten, undated [late 1880s], Harry Ransom Center, The University of Texas at Austin, Lafcadio Hearn Collection, 2.5. Hereafter Harry Ransom Center, Lafcadio Hearn Collection.

[61] Bisland, in Hearn, *Japanese Letters*, p. lii.

as her self-confessed main aim, Bird remained practically impermeable to Japan.[62] In fact, her letters were peppered with expressions of explicit or implicit patriotic pride that worked to discredit the Japanese. By contrast, Hearn set out to capture the 'invisible life' of Japan and, in order to do so, he cultivated a soft, pliable voice that was continuously modulated, enriched, and enlarged by the encounters with the unfamiliar.[63] His constant refrain that Britain and the West have much to learn from Japanese civilization is unthinkable in Bird as indeed in most works devoted to Japan at this point.

*Glimpses of Unfamiliar Japan* is a collection of generically hybrid sketches that mix reportage and learned discussions of topics such as philosophy, folklore, and religion. Most of Hearn's Japanese books would follow this successful model. The notion of the 'sketch'—Hearn's preferred term to describe his Japanese writings— is important because it conveys lack of premeditation and puts the emphasis on the fleeting and partial, as though to communicate the openness with which the author approached his different subjects. Hearn's favourite topics include the rituals of everyday life, art (especially domestic and applied art), the supernatural, religious customs and customs connected with death, gender, and the care of the body—the collection comprises essays on women's hair, for instance, and the Japanese smile. The autobiographical narrator typically starts by describing a specific place—usually an 'unfamiliar' location, ideally where Hearn could claim to have been the first Western visitor—but then the travel narrative is continuously delayed and complicated by anecdotes, snatches of translation, quotations from his students' English compositions, the retelling of tales and legends that Hearn learned from the people he encountered, and extended explanations of the function of specific objects, customs, and traditions. These digressions, often complete with learned footnotes that provide philological explanations or refer the reader to works of anthropology, comparative religion, and similar disciplines, serve to root Hearn's work within a more specialized form of knowledge, distinguishing it from standard travel literature. Meanwhile, the multiple digressive elements, ekphrases, and tales within tales combine to give a sense of aimlessness to the narrative, which shuttles backwards and forwards between the present and the past, material encounter and abstraction, direct and vicarious experience, so that the voices that Hearn records blend with the authorial voice, producing the effect of loosening of the boundaries of the self that troubled some of his early critics.

---

[62] Isabella L. Bird, 'Preface', in *Unbeaten Tracks in Japan: An Account of the Interior, Including Visits to the Aborigines of Yezo and the Shrines of Nikkō and Isé*, 2 vols (London: John Murray, 1880), i, pp. vii–x (p. ix).

[63] Lafcadio Hearn, *Glimpses of Unfamiliar Japan* (Rutland, VT, and Tokyo: Tuttle, 1997), p. xi. This is the most readily available modern reprint of the first edition. Subsequent references in the main body of the text. Hearn's ambition to record the 'invisible life' of Japan was formulated in response to A. B. Mitford's observation in *Tales of Old Japan* (1871) that the world was still completely ignorant about 'the inner life of the Japanese'. Mitford, *Tales of Old Japan*, 2 vols (London: Macmillan, 1871), i. 1.

The ethics of Hearn's cosmopolitan 'openness' should, however, rather be interrogated from a Japanese point of view. For, at a time in which Japanese literature remained largely undiscovered in the West due to lack of linguistic expertise, Hearn's versions of Japanese folk tales, gathered from second-hand accounts, represented an important form of translation, despite the fact that Hearn never mastered the Japanese language enough to read literary texts with confidence and thus produce literary translations in the recognizable meaning of the term. If we bring back to mind the virulence with which some French critics chastised Wilde for abusing the hospitality of French literary culture and turning it into a means of profit, we could question whether Hearn's use of Japanese sources, which were not always explicitly acknowledged, constitutes a form of appropriation that breaches the informal contract between foreign author and host culture. The answer lies in the fact that, in the late nineteenth century, France and Japan occupied very different positions in the global economy of circulation of literary texts: while French literature was extremely mobile, Japanese literature was mostly restricted to domestic consumption. Hearn was among the first to project Japanese literature—mostly, it should be remembered, in the form of folklore—onto the international stage, and therefore operated at a moment in time when the 'value' of Japanese literature was more volatile, the 'rules' of its ownership fuzzier.

Hearn liked to present the problem of translation in aesthetic rather than ethical terms, and in ways that transcended the question of language. In the preface to *Glimpses*, he described Japan as a 'world of strangeness' (p. xi) and, as we have seen, he would always cling on to this definition, upholding the strangeness of Japan, in strongly essentialist terms, as possessing a 'beauty' and distinctive 'ethical charm' of its own.[64] Throughout his Japanese writings Hearn used strangeness as a category of aesthetic perception that complicates easy binary distinctions between the familiar and the unfamiliar. In so doing, he went to the heart of the paradox of cosmopolitan identity politics captured by Baudelaire: the feeling of being 'at home' in being 'away from home'. Hearn was very clear that his uprooted point of view put him in a position of strength, for the 'strangeness' of Japan could be best appreciated through foreign eyes, just as non-native speakers were most capable of bringing out the 'strange aspect' of language, as Gide claimed in relation to Wilde's use of French.[65] In conveying the 'feeling' of Japan to Western readers, Hearn therefore confronted them with a paradox: how to communicate something that ultimately defied explanation. In the sketch titled 'A Pilgrimage to Enoshima', the question of translatability comes under scrutiny as Hearn attempts a general definition of the 'charm' of Japan:

---

[64] Hearn, 'Strangeness and Charm', 15.    [65] Cf. Chapter 1.

Not of strange sights alone is this charm made, but of numberless subtle sensations and ideas interwoven and interblended: the sweet sharp scents of grove and sea; the blood-brightening, vivifying touch of the free wind; the dumb appeal of ancient mystic mossy things; vague reverence evoked by knowledge of treading soil called holy for a thousand years; and a sense of sympathy, as a human duty, compelled by the vision of steps of rock worn down into shapelessness by the pilgrim feet of vanished generations.   (p. 95)

Readers of these descriptions are simultaneously encouraged to immerse themselves in the imaginative experience of a foreign culture *and* realize the ultimately impossibility of knowing that culture. The natural elements of landscape described by Hearn are universal and, as such, eminently accessible, on the imaginative plane, to foreigners who have no direct knowledge of Japan. Hearn therefore easily translates them into the highly crafted literary idiom of English metropolitan aestheticism (as practised by Swinburne, Pater, and Symonds) that relies on complex sensory impressions and synaesthetic effects. At the same time, though, Hearn also wanted to preserve the particularism of foreign space by ascribing to it a spiritual quality that defied domestication into literary English.

In the previous passage the reference to the 'sense of sympathy [being] a human duty' describes both a characteristic of traditional Japanese culture and a moral imperative that Hearn put at the heart of his work as a writer and that could be called an ethics of the unfamiliar. Hearn's ambition was to convey the smells, sounds, textures, and colours of Japanese life with the same mixture of faithfulness and artfulness that he admired in the exotic narratives of Pierre Loti, who, as he put it, 'perfum[ed] each scene with the strange exotic odours belonging to the original'.[66] However, unlike Loti in his famous Japanese novel *Madame Chrysanthème* (1885), he wanted to do so in a manner that would be sympathetic to the Japanese people.[67] Before sailing to Japan, Hearn laid out a plan for how to adopt a truly cosmopolitan point of view in the book of Japanese essays that would become *Glimpses*—a point of view that could claim for itself the advantages of both foreignness and acculturation:

A subject would be considered solely in the relation of personal experiences bearing upon it,—from which relation anything bordering upon commonplace narrative would be carefully excluded. The studied aim would be to create in the mind of the reader a vivid impression of <u>living</u> in Japan,—not simply as an

---

[66] Hearn, 'The Most Original of Modern Novelists: Pierre Loti', in *Essays in European and Oriental Literature*, ed. Albert Mordell (London: Heinemann, 1923), 133–140 (136).
[67] Hearn had admired Loti immensely but was sorely disappointed by the lack of sympathy in Loti's depiction of Japan, complaining to Osman Edwards that '[t]here is not much heart in Loti'. See Hearn, *Japanese Letters*, p. xlii. Ironically perhaps, both Loti and Hearn would later be classed as orientalists by postcolonial critics.

observer, but as one taking part in the daily existence of the common people, and thinking with their thoughts. Whenever possible, a narrative would be made at least as entertaining as a short story.[68]

As soon as he landed in Japan, Hearn went out hunting for suitable material, carrying around with him a small notebook in which he jotted down all manners of small impressions such as 'clapping of hands with prayer', 'blue hats', 'lotos flower of sugar', which he later used as the basis for 'My First Day in the Orient', the opening sketch in *Glimpses*.[69] The finished sketch, formed by a series of vignettes of the streets and temples of Yokohama that Hearn visited driven around in a rickshaw, reproduced the immediacy of his sensations, incorporating the raw elements of colour and sound from his notes but also adding artful touches and digressive elements. This process of revision resulted in highly self-conscious pieces of writing that investigate the workings of perception, memory, and affect as much as they are about the places, objects, and traditions they describe. A self-reflexive moment in 'My First Day in the Orient' is characteristic:

> And suddenly, a singular sensation comes upon me as I stand before this weirdly sculptured portal [of a Buddhist temple in Yokohama],—a sensation of dream and doubt. It seems to me that the steps, and the dragon-swarming gate, and the blue sky arching over the roofs of the town, and the ghostly beauty of Fuji, and the shadow of myself there stretching upon the gray masonry, must all vanish presently. Why such a feeling? Doubtless because the forms before me [ ... ] do not really appear to me as things new, but as things dreamed: the sight of them must have stirred to life forgotten memories of picture-books. A moment, and the delusion vanishes; the romance of reality returns, with freshened consciousness of all that which is truly and deliciously new; the magical transparencies of distance, the wondrous delicacy of the tones of the living picture, the enormous height of the summer blue, and the white soft witchery of the Japanese sun.
>
> (p. 13)

Hearn's 'doubt' about the truth of perception is a test of the representational limits of descriptive realism. As in this passage, in his writings on Japan, Hearn often blurred the dividing line between landscape and dreamscape, deliberately confusing the material reality of the object with its shadow or representation. As the sound merges with its echo, the narration dissolves the fixity of the subject and questions the authority of eyes and ears as organs of perception. Experienced,

---

[68] Hearn, fragment of a letter to an unidentified correspondent, 28 Nov. 1889, Harry Ransom Center, Lafcadio Hearn Collection, 2.1.

[69] The notebook is also held in the Harry Ransom Center, Lafcadio Hearn Collection, 1.8. The 'lotos flower of sugar' likely refers to traditional Buddhist offerings.

actual Japan and 'picture-book' Japan often shade into one another in the sketches, so that Hearn's Japan is both real and fantastic at the same time, fully embodied yet 'invisible' as he writes in the 'Preface', experienced but not fixed by a realist gaze, to return to the terms of Wilde's critique of cosmopolitan disenchantment in 'The Decay of Lying'.[70]

## 'A World Full of Ghosts'

Hearn's interest in the meeting of the familiar and the strange comes to life in the many ghost narratives that populate his Japanese books, some of which are devoted entirely to tales of the supernatural.[71] In *Glimpses*, Hearn wrote of spirits that lived inside trees and dead women who visited their former lovers in the night; he told of a certain cave by the sea where the ghosts of little children were said to congregate and of the ghost of a woman who was prematurely buried and gave birth to a child in her tomb. Hearn did not see the supernatural as a cause for fear or as the manifestation of a grotesque taste (he often spoke of the 'ghostly beauty' of places). Rather, he used the supernatural as a versatile category of perception that enabled him to access the unfamiliar worlds of Japanese myth, art, and eroticism. In a letter to the British philologist Basil Chamberlain, who had lived in Japan since 1873 and was widely held as one of the most distinguished scholars in the country, Hearn explicitly equated the belief in the supernatural with aesthetic refinement and power of perception:

> Now I believe in ghosts. Because I saw them? Not at all. I believe in ghosts, though I disbelieve in souls. I believe in ghosts because there are no ghosts now in the modern world. And the difference between a world full of ghosts and another kind of world, shows us what ghosts mean—and gods. [ ... ] What are our novelists doing? Crawford must write of Italy or India or ancient Persia;— Kipling of India;—Black of remote Scotch country life;—James lives only as a marvellous psychologist, and he has to live and make his characters live on the Continent [ ... ] No! those who write must seek their material in those parts of the world where ghosts still linger,—in Italy, in Spain, in Russia, in the old atmosphere of Catholicism. The Protestant world has become bald and cold as

---

[70] I provide a fuller analysis of Hearn's challenges to descriptive realism and his relation to Whistler's *japonisme*, in 'Symphonies in Haze and Blue: Lafcadio Hearn and the Colours of Japan', in Charlotte Ribeyrol, ed., *The Colours of the Past in Victorian England* (Oxford and Bern: Peter Lang, 2016), 71–94.

[71] See esp. the collections *In Ghostly Japan* (1899) and *Kwaidan: Stories and Studies of Strange Things* (1904). Carl Dawson suggests that 'all Hearn's Japanese books aspire to the condition of ghost stories'; Dawson, *Lafcadio Hearn*, 95.

a meeting-house. The ghosts are gone; and the results of their departure prove how real they were.[72]

For Hearn ghosts revealed the fragility of the past as it comes into contact with the destructive forces of modernization. They were the custodians of cultural memory, embodying the rich cultural diversity of humanity. Therefore, if Hearn's travel descriptions draw a geographical map of Japan, the inserted ghost stories break free of the two-dimensional perspective of the map or page, adding a third, spatial dimension that takes readers beyond the present moment and the physical reality of a place or object. The ghost narratives are, in other words, devices that Hearn used in order to add depth to his narratives and penetrate beneath the surface of Japan that presented itself to the foreign observer. In this sense Hearn's Japanese sketches closely resemble Vernon Lee's better-known Italian essays and short stories, which likewise blend learned disquisitions of cultural history with gothic and supernatural elements. In the 'Preface' to *Hauntings* (1890), Lee refused, like Hearn, to bracket the supernatural as pure superstition, understanding it instead as a subtle category of perception that uncovers forgotten histories: 'the Past, the more or less remote Past, of which the prose is clean obliterated by distance—that is the place to get our ghosts from'.[73] Like Hearn, Lee connected the supernatural with travel and uprootedness—'the weird places we have seen, the strange stories we have heard'.[74] Her work confirms Hearn's insight to Chamberlain about a class of modern British and American novelists that were gravitating away from domestic space physically as well as experientially.

We have already seen that Gautier exercised a formative influence on the young Hearn in New Orleans, and that his translation of Gautier's short stories attempted to situate aestheticism beyond the geographical space of Europe. In Japan, Hearn went back to Gautier's use of the fantastic in order to translate his experience of this 'world of strangeness' into a literary form that would preserve its unsettling aspects and its challenges to traditional categories of perception. In stories such as 'The Mummy's Foot' ('Le Pied de momie'), 'Omphale: A Rococo Story' ('Omphale: La Tapisserie amoureuse, histoire rococo'), and 'Arria Marcella: A Souvenir of Pompeii' ('Arria Marcella: Souvenir de Pompéi'), all translated by Hearn, ghosts disclose to Gautier's protagonists worlds that are at the same time uncanny and more desirable than the one they inhabit. Gautier compounds the supernatural with aesthetic theory and elements of the erotic tale in order to show that the past does not survive merely as the dry text of history books or as decrepit

---

[72] Hearn to Basil Chamberlain, 14 Dec. 1893, in *Japanese Letters*, 214–215. The inclusion of James alongside Crawford, Kipling, and Black shows that Hearn conceived of his works within a literary movement that was broader than the *fin-de-siècle* romance revival.

[73] Vernon Lee, 'Preface', in *Hauntings and Other Fantastic Tales*, ed. Catherine Maxwell and Patricia Pulham (Peterborough, Ont.: Broadview, 2006), 37–40 (39).

[74] Ibid.

monuments that only few people care about. Rather, the past exists as part of the present, hidden inside the deceivingly familiar and solid fabric of reality. Extraordinary individual acts of desire for the past—such as falling in love with a figure portrayed on an arras or the remains of an Egyptian mummy—can undo that fabric, revealing spectres that are in fact always there, in a parallel dimension that is spatially contiguous with what we experience as reality. In 'Arria Marcella', Gautier explains what he calls his theory of 'amorous invocation' ('évocation amoureuse'):

> In effect, nothing dies; all things are eternal: no power can annihilate that which once had being. Every action, every word, every thought which has fallen into the universal Ocean of being, therein creates circles which travel, and increase in travelling, even to the confines of Eternity. To vulgar eyes only do natural forms disappear; and the spectres which have thence detached themselves people Infinity:—Paris, in some unknown region of Space, continues to carry off Helen;—the galley of Cleopatra still floats down with swelling sails of silk upon the azure current of an ideal Cydnus;—a few passionate and powerful minds have been able to recall before them ages apparently long passed away, and to restore to life personages dead to all the world beside.[75]

In his Japanese writings, Hearn identified this questioning of normative Western ideas of linear time with Buddhist and Shinto beliefs about death and the afterlife. But his many references to Eastern spirituality should not blind us to the fact that Gautier's theories of the supernatural provided him with both an interpretative filter and a literary model for his experience of Japan as a place where ontological boundaries are fluid. As in Gautier, moreover, eroticism and exoticism are key elements of Hearn's narratives of haunting and time travel.

In Gautier's 'Arria Marcella', the subject of the 'amorous invocation' is a nineteenth-century French man named Octavian who, on a visit to Naples, is spellbound by a lava fragment recovered in Pompeii, which has preserved intact the imprint of a female body. That night Octavian is magically transported to ancient Pompeii for some hours, during which he meets and is seduced by that very woman—the Arria Marcella of the title—before returning to the present. Gautier recreates ancient Pompeii with lavish attention to details of topography,

---

[75] Gautier, 'Arria Marcella', in *One of Cleopatra's Nights and Other Fantastic Romances*, 173. The original French is taken from 'Arria Marcella: Souvenir de Pompei', in Gautier, *Contes fantastiques* (Paris: Corti, 1986), 215–251 ('En effet, rien ne meurt, tout existe toujours; nulle force ne peut anéantir ce qui fut une fois. Toute action, toute parole, toute forme, toute pensée tombée dans l'océan universel des choses y produit des cercles qui vont s'élargissant jusqu'aux confins de l'éternité. La figuration matérielle ne disparaît que pour les regards vulgaires, et les spectres qui s'en détachent peuplent l'infini. Pâris continue d'enlever Hélène dans une région inconnue de l'espace. La galère de Cléopâtre gonfle ses voiles de soie sur l'azur d'un Cydnus idéal. Quelques esprits passionnés et puissants ont pu amener à eux des siècles écoulés en apparence, et faire revivre des personnages morts pour tous', 245–246).

architecture, and costumes, which reproduce the feel of classical antiquity as fantastically experienced from the viewpoint of the modern protagonist. The story was a personal favourite of Hearn, who compared Gautier's archaeological accuracy to Alma-Tadema's 'fair magic of color-blending [which] evokes for us eidolons of ages vanished and civilizations passed away'.[76] He thought that Gautier's vivid pictorial style added actual scholarly value to the story by bringing to life 'all that fascinating lore gleaned by antiquarian research amid the ashes of the sepultured city'.[77]

In the early nineteenth century, Gautier's generation witnessed the concurrent rise of archaeological research and geographical exploration: Hellenism and orientalism provided two separate but intersecting paths that could take European readers to different worlds capable of offering idealized alternatives to the present reality.[78] At the end of the century, Hearn updated Gautier's archaeological fantastic in order to address the representational challenges that modern Japan posed to the Western writer. The material remains of the past scattered in the Japanese landscape constantly project Hearn's narrator, like the character of Octavian in 'Arria Marcella', to spectral worlds where desire is not frustrated by the reality of modernity, causing him to break the frame of descriptive realism. And like Gautier's 'universal ocean of being', Hearn's Japan is an experiential space where different temporalities coexist alongside one another.

Hearn explains this cognitive mechanism with explicit reference to romantic literature in 'A Pilgrimage to Enoshima' (another essay in *Glimpses*), where the encounter with some ancient statues connected with folk religion triggers an epiphanic realization:

> To have studied and loved an ancient faith only through the labors of palaeographers and archaeologists, and as something astronomically remote from one's own existence, and then suddenly in after years to find the same faith a part of one's human environment,—to feel that its mythology, though senescent, is *alive* around you,—is almost to realize the dream of the Romantics, to have the sensation of returning through twenty centuries into the life of a happier world. For these quaint Gods of Roads and Gods of Earth are really living still, though so worn and mossed and feebly worshipped. In this brief moment, at least, I am really in the Elder World—perhaps just at that epoch of it when the primal faith is growing a little old-fashioned, crumbling slowly before the

---

[76] Hearn, 'To the Reader', in Gautier, *One of Cleopatra's Nights and Other Fantastic Romances*, pp. v–vi.

[77] Ibid., p. vi.

[78] In his introduction to an early twentieth-century edition of Hearn's translation of Gautier's stories, Arthur Ransome draws attention to the 'magic' coming together of the East and Antiquity for Gautier's generation; 'Introductory Essay', in Théophile Gautier, *Stories by Théophile Gautier*, tr. Lafcadio Hearn (New York: Dutton & Co., 1908), pp. xiii–xxii (xv). Dawson has also noted Hearn's use of Greece as an integral component of his orientalism; *Lafcadio Hearn*, 19.

corrosive influence of a new philosophy; and I know myself a pagan still, loving these simple old gods, these gods of a people's childhood.    (pp. 102–103)

In a letter to his friend, the Japanese art historian Ernest Fenollosa, Hearn made the allusion to classical antiquity more explicit, retelling this same epiphanic moment in Enoshima (an island just off the coast of the ancient city of Kamakura) with reference to 'Elder Egypt', ancient Greece, and Pompeii. There he explained that 'the delicious ghostliness of it, is the sense of being in a world of mysteries and Gods all ALIVE, closer to you than neighbors, real, comprehensive, beautiful beyond description. After having lived ten or twelve years with archaeology, the effect on me is so queer that I sometimes think I am certainly dreaming it all.'[79] In these passages from his public and private writings, Hearn describes Japan as the fulfilment of an impossible archaeological fantasy, its presence like the miraculous return of someone we thought long dead. Again like Gautier's Octavian, Hearn pictures himself as a modern barbarian transported into a dazzling antique world for one night only, conscious that he has to make the most of his time there, drinking up impressions with all his senses. Indeed, like the resurrected Pompeii of Gautier's fantastic tale, Hearn's Japan often appears as an 'archaic phantasmagory', which leaves the narrator uncertain about the full reality of his perception.[80]

It is striking in this respect how often Hearn compares Japan to ancient Greece. At various points in *Glimpses*, the Japanese drawing of a fish makes him think of 'the dolphin of Greek art' (p. 47), a procession of traditional dancers recalls 'the dreams of shapes circling about certain antique vases' (p. 133), and Japanese folk tales about plants resemble 'the old Greek tales of metamorphoses' (p. 373). But the most recurring instances are those in which he builds a parallel between Japanese folk religion and Greek paganism, as in the extract quoted. In this Hearn drew on the work of the French historian Fustel de Coulanges, whose *La Cité antique* (1864) had pioneered the application of the new science of comparative mythography, headed in Britain by Max Müller, to the study of classical antiquity, comparing the religious customs of Greek, Roman, and Indian civilizations. As his heavily annotated copy of the book testifies, Hearn studied *La Cité antique* extremely closely, and he scattered references to it throughout his Japanese works.[81] His ethnographically oriented last book, *Japan: An Attempt at Interpretation* (1904), developed the comparison between modern Japan and European classical antiquity into a systematic theory: basing his observations, as Fustel had done, mainly on cults to do with death and ancestor worship, Hearn

[79] Hearn to Fenollosa, undated, Harry Ransom Center, Lafcadio Hearn Collection, 2.1.
[80] Gautier, *One of Cleopatra's Nights and Other Fantastic Romances*, 169.
[81] Hearn's copy of Fustel's *La Cité antique* is preserved as part of the Lafcadio Hearn Library, housed in Toyama University Library.

suggested that various Shinto religious practices he encountered in the course of his travels in rural Japan showed close similarities to those found in archaic Greek civilization. It followed that the well-preserved antiquity of Japan could offer Western readers a precious glimpse into their own classical past: 'to witness the revival of some perished Greek civilization,—to walk about the very Crotona of Pythagoras,—to wander through the Syracuse of Theocritus,—were not any more of a privilege than is the opportunity actually afforded us to study Japanese life'.[82] Indeed, as the 'spectacle' (a favourite word of Hearn's) of social customs and psychological conditions that predate the earliest recorded sources of Greek civilization, Japan is, according to Hearn, even more useful than Greece as a case study in evolutionary history.

Although well-read in archaeology, Hearn did not have a traditional classical education. But ever since childhood, when he was told off for reading an illustrated book on the Greek gods, he imagined Greek antiquity as a desirable but forbidden world.[83] His adult encounter with Japan repeated the emotional thrill and transgression of that childhood encounter with Greece, displacing to the Far East the desire for intellectual and social freedom that classically trained British aesthetes such as Pater and Symonds associated with Italy. Comparing Japan to ancient Greece, Hearn of course also made strategic use of the cultural prestige enjoyed by Greek antiquity among educated readers in the West in order to bestow a sense of classical dignity on Japanese customs and beliefs (especially to do with the Shinto gods) that unsympathetic commentators otherwise dismissed as primitive or barbaric.

If we go back to the epiphany at Enoshima one last time, we may be surprised to notice that Hearn experienced the spectacle of this world that he had always desired 'with a feeling of mingled melancholy and pleasure' (p. 102). Melancholia was a classic romantic response to the sight of classical ruins (remember that Hearn is contemplating ancient statues), which made the viewer aware of the passage of time and the inevitable obliteration that is the fate of all civilizations. The same note of pessimism haunts Hearn's depictions of Japanese places and objects, where the 'strangeness' of Japan queers the colonial optimism of much nineteenth-century English writing about Asia. By endowing Japan with what he called the 'charm of a vanished world',[84] Hearn portrayed Japan as a spectral world, which was both alive and dead at the same time. By a game of perspectival inversion, the archaeological fantasy projects the reader simultaneously into the remote past and into a future in which present-day Japan, with its art and immemorial customs, will have been obliterated by the forces of modernization coming from the West. The frequent comparisons with Egypt, Greece, and Pompeii therefore ultimately reveal that, for all his insistence on the longevity of

---

[82]  Hearn, *Japan: An Attempt at Interpretation*, 20.      [83]  Stevenson, *Lafcadio Hearn*, 17.
[84]  Hearn, *Japan: An Attempt at Interpretation*, 394.

Japan's ancient traditions, Hearn was painfully conscious of the fact that he was striving to capture a world in transition, evanescent, threatened, and, very possibly, on the brink of extinction.

## Nationalism in Japan

Hearn's romanticization of old Japan put him in a paradoxical relation to his adopted country. His very presence in Japan and his job as English language teacher were part of a process of cosmopolitan opening promoted in the Meiji period (1868–1912) that aimed to modernize the country and make it competitive in the international sphere. Hearn, however, resented the modernization of Japan and denounced it as a threat to its traditional culture. This ambiguity became more and more entrenched the longer he stayed, as he observed the growth of Japanese nationalism and saw the country go to war against China and build up for a military conflict with Russia (the Russo-Japanese war broke out only a few months before Hearn's death). The ideology of nationalism went against Hearn's liberal, cosmopolitan belief in celebrating human diversity and in peaceful relations between nations. Yet, he tried to understand and occasionally justified Japanese nationalist feeling and militarism as legitimate reactions to foreign pressures and commercial exploitation by the West.

In some of the essays in *Glimpses*, Hearn already noted with regret the passing away of old customs and the neglect for traditional ways of life. The ending of 'Kitsune', an essay on Japanese folk beliefs to do with foxes, is typical:

> Year by year, more shrines of Inari crumble down, never to be rebuilt. Year by year the statuaries make fewer images of foxes. Year by year fewer victims of fox-possession are taken to the hospitals to be treated according to the best scientific methods by Japanese physicians who speak German [ ... ]. There is no place for ghostly foxes in the beautiful nature-world revealed by new studies to the new generation.   (pp. 341–342)

Hearn blamed such unwelcome changes on the introduction of Western models of rationalism, competitive capitalism, and industrialization. He resented the adoption of modern scientific school curricula modelled on Britain, which meant that, as the new generations of Japanese schoolchildren learnt about Tyndall, Darwin, Huxley, and Herbert Spencer, they unlearnt another type of knowledge enshrined in immemorial customs for the respect of the community and the environment. He resented, above all, the way in which the discourse of modernity imported from Europe and America cast the Japanese as backward and primitive. He was particularly scathing towards Christian missionaries, repeatedly declaring, as in the preface to *Glimpses*, that 'Japan has nothing whatever to gain by conversion to Christianity, either morally or otherwise, but very much to lose' (p. xvi).

Other expatriate Western observers, such as Basil Chamberlain, were fascinated by the birth of a new hybrid culture in Japan. For Hearn, however, it was a case of a clear-cut opposition between two competing and incompatible models. He associated old Japan with the 'ethical charm' of the country made of simple living, hospitality, and equal dignity ascribed to all walks of life—all of which were reflected in its traditional arts and crafts, folklore, and Buddhist and Shinto beliefs. By contrast, new Japan connoted a loss of moral values due to Western-style individualism. Therefore, while he welcomed what he called 'a general infusion of barbarian blood' as a revitalizing influence on European literature,[85] he believed that Japan ought to resist Western influences in order to safeguard its particularity. As he wrote to his half-sister, in starkly essentialist terms:

> We are too conceitedly apt to think that what is good for Englishmen is good for all nations,—our ethics, our religion, our costumes; etc. The plain facts of the case are that all Eastern races lose, instead of gaining, by contact with us. They imitate our vices instead of our virtues, and learn all our weaknesses without getting any of our strengths.[86]

Hearn saw the struggle between Old and New Japan as a microcosmic incidence of a dialectics between East and West that was being played out on a global scale: to him, the transformation of Japan in the name of internationalization masked a new wave of colonial exploitation from the West that came in the form of global capitalism and technological progress. Hearn denounced the way in which the British Empire used the rhetoric of cosmopolitan universalism (the idea that 'what is good for Englishmen is good for all nations') to cloak its ambitions of geo-political domination. By contrast, his own cosmopolitan commitment consisted in fighting for the preservation of the local in Japan, in order to salvage the diversity of the margins against centripetal forces of cultural homologation coming from the West and also, indirectly, from the open ports and large metropolitan centres of New Japan. As his career as teacher, writer, and critic took him into larger cities (Kobe and Tokyo) and brought him to socialize with other foreigners and internationalized Japanese, Hearn continued to find his inspiration in the more remote parts of the country, where he sought an idealized notion of cultural purity.

The clash between a globally oriented, predatory West and the fragile ethnos of the East plays out in the pages of Hearn's sketches in the form of the dialogue between the cultivated, uprooted voice of the narrator and the local voices that

---

[85]   Hearn to Chamberlain, 5 Feb. 1893, in *Japanese Letters*, 55.
[86]   Hearn to Minnie Atkinson, 17 Sept. 93, quoted in Kennard, *Lafcadio Hearn*, 213–214.

Hearn wanted to preserve as untranslated as possible, as though they emanated directly from the Japanese landscape. Hearn often made his characters speak in transliterated Japanese and reproduced transliterations of Japanese proverbs, poems, and songs, usually providing translations and further philological explanations in the footnotes. His editors and friends warned him against this practice, arguing that it damaged the flow of the narrative and was potentially alienating to English-speaking readers who stumbled over the unfamiliar sounds of the Japanese language.[87] But this sense of defamiliarization was precisely what Hearn wanted to achieve: it is as though he wanted to make the English language speak Japanese. As he wrote to Chamberlain: 'For me words have colour, form, character [...]. That they are unintelligible makes no difference at all. Whether you are able to speak to a stranger or not, you can't help being impressed by his appearance sometimes,—by his dress,—by his air,—by his exotic look.'[88] The foreign words on the page embodied the mixture of curiosity and discomfort of a physical encounter with a stranger. Hearn's formative experience of translating French literature in America had made him acutely aware of the limits of translation. In the Japanese writings, his foreignizing techniques were more than ornamental elements of exoticism added to the metropolitan feel of Hearn's erudite and lyrical voice: they questioned the very effectiveness of that voice in conveying the experience of Japan, working against the fiction of order and mastery that syntax imposes upon the impressions of the unfamiliar and the strange. They protested against Western cultural assimilation of Japan by emphasizing elements of foreignness, dissonance, and difficulty. They exposed the limitations of the English language—of any language—in encompassing the diversity of human experience and emotions.

As his handling of language testifies, Hearn's approach to the particularism of Japan was shaped by Herder's theories of *Volkesgeist*, modified through nineteenth-century evolutionary science.[89] The work of Herbert Spencer in particular had a strong influence on Hearn. In *First Principles* (1862), Spencer had tried to explain the 'feelings characterizing a member of a given race' and the bond that citizens of a nation feel with each other by applying evolutionary theory to the disciplines of psychology and sociology.[90] Hearn used a similar evolutionary perspective in his observations of Japanese life. For instance, in *Glimpses*, witnessing the failure of a group of English children to be taught Japanese calligraphy,

[87] See for instance letters from Chamberlain dated 1 June 1893 and 25 Jan. 1894, in *More Letters from Basil Hall Chamberlain to Lafcadio Hearn*, ed. Kazuo Koizumi (Tokyo: Hokuseido Press, 1937), 67–68 and 120–121.

[88] Hearn to Chamberlain, 5 June 1893, in *Japanese Letters*, 105.

[89] Roy Starrs has suggested that Hearn's 'gentle' Herderian cultural nationalism of the American years was co-opted by the hard nationalist conservatism that was on the rise in late Meiji-era Japan; Starrs, 'Lafcadio Hearn as Japanese Nationalist', *Japan Review*, 18 (2006), 181–213 (185 and *passim*).

[90] Herbert Spencer, *First Principles*, ed. Michael Taylor (London: Routledge/Thoemmes, 1996), 477.

he concluded that their efforts were thwarted by the 'ancestral tendencies within them': '[i]t is not the Japanese boy alone who writes; the fingers of the dead move his brush, guide his stroke' (pp. 256–257). Hearn blended modern thinking on evolution and heredity with ancient Buddhist ideas of pre-existence, believing that there was a real equivalence between the two.[91] But he also made liberal use of a strongly essentialist language of race, also moulded by Spencer and nineteenth-century evolutionary philosophy. The sketches in *Glimpses* are dotted with references to the 'race-soul' or 'soul of the race' to refer to Japan's cultural specificity and its resistance to cosmopolitan universalism. Hearn tended to invoke race to designate positive qualities that the West was perceived to lack. For instance, the ethical spirit of Shinto is identified with 'the deepest and best emotions of the race' (p. 388), and it is 'the soul of the race' that enables the Japanese to comprehend the artistic beauty of stones (p. 346) and to master the elements of drawing that are necessary in order to write Chinese characters (p. 436).

Race is a powerful and unsettling presence in Hearn's Japanese writings. It gives them a dated orientalist and anthropological feel but, at the same time, it also enables the narrator to turn the tables on himself, scrutinizing his own ambiguous position as a foreigner in Japan and interrogating social attitudes towards hybrid identities (Hearn was highly self-conscious about the fact that his mixed Irish-Greek parentage also put him in a hybrid category). For instance, in 'Jizō', a sketch in *Glimpses* dedicated to this popular Buddhist divinity, Hearn recounts a troubling encounter during a visit to a cemetery in Yokohama:

All at once I become aware of a child standing before me, a very young girl who looks up wonderingly at my face; so light her approach that the joy of the birds and whispering of the leaves quite drowned the soft sound of her feet. Her ragged garb is Japanese; but her gaze, her loose fair hair, are not of Nippon only; the ghost of another race—perhaps my own—watches me through her flower-blue eyes. A strange playground surely is this for thee, my child; I wonder if all these shapes about thee do not seem very weird, very strange, to that little soul of thine. But no; 't is only I who seem strange to thee; thou hast forgotten the Other Birth, and thy father's world.

Half-caste, and poor, and pretty, in this foreign port! Better thou wert with the dead about thee, child! better than the splendor of this soft blue light the unknown darkness for thee.   (48–49)

---

[91] In *Glimpses* he makes this theory of equivalence explicit in 'The Household Shrine', 393–394. Hearn's synthesis of Buddhism and evolutionary psychology was noted in an early French article by the anti-colonial philosopher Félicien Challaye, 'Lafcadio Hearn: Un philosophe japonisant', *Revue de métaphysique et de morale*, 11 (1903), 338–351. Hearn's important role in the reception of Buddhism in the West is explored in Antony Goedhals, *The Neo-Buddhist Writings of Lafcadio Hearn: Light from the East* (Leiden and Boston: Brill, 2020).

The pessimism of this image is striking, especially when we set it aside Hearn's earlier writings on New Orleans and the Caribbean, where he associated the mix of different ethnicities with cultural and social vitality. Now, the ghostly appearance of the mixed-race girl among the graves conveys to Hearn the negative power of race to sever, as well as to connect, the individual to a place. The uncanny quality of the encounter is due to the fact that the girl in Yokohama appears to Hearn as a double of his own self: the product, like him, of mixed parentage, she embodies the trauma of exile and dislocation. She is the uncanny other of the cosmopolitan subject as citizen of nowhere. As the two regard each other with mutual suspicion across the racial divide, Hearn becomes conscious of his own uprootedness with a sudden surge of melancholia, which he displaces onto the girl: her in-between-ness appears to him as a state of death-in-life and an early death seems preferable to an inevitable future of social marginalization and sexual exploitation. The sexual theme is important. Hearn believes the dishevelled girl to be the likely offspring of the relationship between a Japanese prostitute and a Westerner, and he sees her prettiness as marking her out for an unhappy destiny in the sex industry. In this respect, too, the vision of the blue-eyed girl completely rewrites his former attitudes to sexuality in the American South and the Caribbean, where Hearn had treated the racialized female body as an object of sexual curiosity and had embraced sexual libertinism as part of his cosmopolitan identity. In fact, more generally, Hearn's commitment to the ideal of Old Japan caused him to turn towards a tamer and more conservative sexual politics, aimed at protecting the fragile traditional culture of the country.[92]

The ghostly image of the mixed-race girl provides a sharp contrast to the aesthetics and politics of sexuality and race projected by a studio photograph of Hearn taken in the mid-1890s with his wife Setsuko and his eldest son Kazuo (illustration 2.2). Here, Hearn's cosmopolitan love of Japan is subsumed into conjugal heterosexuality. In direct opposition to the girl in Yokohama, the well-cared-for child here is a symbol of cosmopolitan optimism, heralding a future in which, to paraphrase Wilde in 'The Critic as Artist', race prejudice will have been annihilated. This image has been extensively reproduced in editions of Hearn's works and biographical material as an illustration of the domesticated Hearn, who successfully made Japan into a home for himself. In fact, Hearn's Japanese writings are caught between the conflicting feelings embodied by the representations of these two mixed-race children.

---

[92] He set out his vision of the different sexual moralities of Japan and the West in the essay 'Of the Eternal Feminine', in *Out of the East: Reveries and Studies of New Japan* (Rutland, VT, and Tokyo: Tuttle, 1972), 85–125.

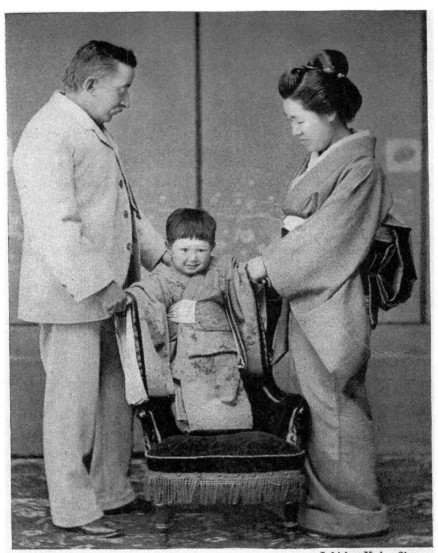

*Ichida, Kobe, Japan*

LAFCADIO HEARN WITH HIS WIFE AND SON KAZUO AT
KUMAMOTO, 1895

**Illustration 2.2** Studio photograph of Lafcadio Hearn, Koizumi Setsuko, and Koizumi Kazuo. From Koizumi Kazuo's *Father and I: Memories of Lafcadio Hearn* (1935), private collection

Racial theories could and did provide a spurious biological foundation for nationalism and colonial aggression. Hearn himself found in the race instinct an explanation for Japan's political decisions to limit Western influence on the domestic affairs of the country. In a later essay entitled 'Jiujutsu', after the ancient traditional martial art that teaches to manipulate the opponent's strength to one's own advantage, he accepted it as given that the race instinct should manifest itself as hostility towards foreigners. Here Hearn was open in his admiration of Japanese patriotism, praising the government-organized efforts to promote 'love of country' and even claiming that modern patriotic songs that were sung in schools revealed 'the fierce heart of Old Japan beating through every word'.[93] Hearn's endorsement of the sentimental appeal of nationalism is disquieting, and so is the way in which he sees a continuum stretching from the ethical core of Japanese traditional life, which he elsewhere associated with hospitality, to modern xenophobic nationalism. In an excised passage from an earlier draft of *Glimpses* he addressed the Japanese directly, exhorting them to defend themselves from 'foreign' intrusions even when this should involve violence:

Keep your beautiful manners, dear Japanese; and your beautiful costume: your most perfect footgear, your delightful little houses, your fairy food, your unapproachable and supremest art, your charming luminous nature-faith, your gods, your temples. Only for purposes of self-defence borrow foreign brutality, foreign knowledge of destructive appliances, foreign sciences which may enable you to face the perils of the future. There let the matter end: Keep foreigners out of your land, keep them forever from defiling your moral atmosphere with their thoughts and utterances.[94]

A few years later, the Bengali writer Rabindranath Tagore addressed the Japanese from the double perspective of a fellow Asian and a cosmopolitan. Tagore commended the way in which Japan had 'given heart to the rest of Asia', thanks to its rapid economic advancement that had put it on a par with Western countries.[95] But he was troubled by the growing feeling of nationalism that he saw there. He warned that '[w]hat is dangerous for Japan is, not the imitation of outer features of the West, but the acceptance of the motive force of the Western nationalism as her own'.[96] Tagore believed that the only way in which Asian cultures could profit from the tradition of humanism that came from colonizing

[93] Hearn, 'Jiujutsu', in *Out of the East*, 183–242 (225).
[94] Lafcadio Hearn, MS notebook, Holograph Notebooks 4, Lafcadio Hearn papers, The Henry W. and Albert A. Berg Collection of English and American Literature, The New York Public Library, Astor, Lenox and Tilden Foundations.
[95] Rabindranath Tagore, 'Nationalism in Japan', in *Nationalism* (New York: Macmillan, 1917), 63–114 (69).
[96] Ibid. 96.

European countries was by uncoupling that tradition from the selfishness and aggression that he associated with the Western construct of the nation.[97] This would be the starting point for a true emancipation of Asian societies on the world stage and, eventually, for the attainment of an Asian model of world citizenship that would be ethically superior to its Western counterpart.

Hearn—a European living in Japan in this period of transition—believed that his ethical mission was to encourage nationalist feelings. It was not his love of Old Japan that made Hearn an anti-cosmopolitan cosmopolitan but his readiness to compound that love with forms of prejudice and xenophobia or, in other words, his too easy conflation of patriotic and nationalist sentiments. In another letter to Chamberlain he commented on the mounting dislike of foreigners in Japan that he saw reflected in the writings of his students: 'I do not try to check their feeling about foreigners. I rather encourage it. I encourage it because it is patriotic, because it is just, because it indicates national recuperation. [ ... ] I teach them respect for their own faiths, for the beliefs of the common people, and for their own country. I am practically a traitor to England (eh?) and a renegade. But in the eternal order of things, I know I am right.'[98]

In 1896 Hearn took the highly unusual step of giving up his British citizenship in order to become a naturalized Japanese. This process involved adopting a Japanese name, so Hearn became Koizumi Yakumo, the identity under which he is known in Japan to this day. The strained negotiation of cosmopolitan and national, even nationalist identities, shows a tension at work between Lafcadio Hearn and Koizumi Yakumo, as the hard politics of citizenship infected the aesthetics of transplantation admired by Stefan Zweig. This precarious position is mostly underplayed in his published writings. But Hearn himself became vulnerable to the xenophobia that he had first witnessed among his students. In a letter to Chamberlain of January 1894, he claimed that he could feel 'the anti-foreign reaction', describing the 'sudden hiss of hatred with which [he was] greeted by passers-by sometimes, in unfamiliar districts'.[99] And, at the time of the first Sino-Japanese war, Hearn predicted that the conflict would be followed by 'a strong anti-foreign reaction [ ... ]. Life will be made wretched for Occidentals—in business—just as it is being made in the schools—by all sorts of little tricky plans which cannot be brought under law-provisions, or even so defined as to appear to justify resentment [ ... ]. The nation will show its ugly side to us—after a manner unexpected, but irresistible.'[100] In the light of these remarks, his change of citizenship, rather than marking the positive embracing of a new identity, can be seen as prompted by the fear that foreign citizens might be forced out of the

---

[97]  Tagore, 'Nationalism in the West', in *Nationalism*, 11–61 (31).
[98]  Hearn to Chamberlain, 15 June 1893, in *Japanese Letters*, 120–121.
[99]  Hearn to Chamberlain, [Jan. 1894], in *Japanese Letters*, 227.
[100] Hearn to Chamberlain, Jan. 1895, in Bisland, *Life and Letters of Lafcadio Hearn*, ii. 201–202.

country, together with the awareness that, if his wife and son were to become British, they would lose the right to hold property or live outside the open ports without a passport.[101] Nonetheless, Hearn was clear: he did not want to see Old Japan transformed into 'a sort of cosmopolitan industrial republic'.[102] Therefore, when faced with the threat that the cultural identity of traditional Japan could give way to a spurious ideal of world citizenship based on economic profit alone, Hearn was prepared to tolerate nationalism, even as he made himself vulnerable to its anti-liberal sentiments.

## Aestheticism in Japan

Hearn's uneasy and sometimes troubling relation with Japanese nationalism can be difficult to reconcile with a life's work driven by an incessant curiosity for foreign cultures and a desire to build bridges between different nations. Yet, in spite of that, he remains a powerful mediator whose work went in two directions: he shaped the knowledge of Japan in the West by broadcasting Japanese culture, refracted through the literary medium of a hybrid essayistic tradition favoured by metropolitan aesthetic writers; and, simultaneously, he left a lasting mark on the literary culture of his adopted country by promoting the preservation and appreciation of Japan's traditional folk tales. Hearn's success is attested by the fact that, over one hundred years after his death, Koizumi Yakumo is still a household name in Japan. In the early twentieth century Hearn's revitalizing influence on Japanese culture was already noted by Yone Noguchi. Noguchi wrote from the position of a cosmopolitan Japanese author transplanted in the West, which was, in a way, the mirror-image of Hearn's. By stressing Hearn's spiritual investment in the aesthetic, Noguchi also highlighted the link between Hearn's work and the so-called religion of art practised by the British aesthetes:

> We Japanese have been regenerated by his sudden magic, and baptized afresh under his transcendental rapture; in fact the old romances which we had forgotten ages ago were brought back again to quiver in the air, and the ancient beauty which we buried under the dust rose again with a strange yet new splendour.[103]

For Noguchi, Hearn's great achievement was to have alerted the Japanese to aspects of their own culture that they neglected through familiarity or as the result

---

[101] Cf. Stevenson, *Lafcadio Hearn*, 279; Murray, *Fantastic Journey*, 191.
[102] Hearn, 'Jiujutsu', 221.
[103] Yone Noguchi, *Lafcadio Hearn in Japan* (New York: Mitchell Kennerley; London: Elkin Mathews; Yokohama: Kelly & Walsh, 1911), 17.

of Westernization, revealing as precious and unique what they had otherwise grown used to dismissing as trivial. In this sense, his comparative ignorance of Japanese language and literature was a 'heavenly gift' according to Noguchi, because it preserved Hearn from pessimism and disenchantment, and what Noguchi calls the 'trivialism of our modern Japanese life'.[104] Wilde's praise of Whistler again comes to mind.

Like many commentators, Noguchi struggled to pin down Hearn's cosmopolitan voice: he stressed his distance from Japan but, at the same time, defended the accuracy of his descriptions. What is most noteworthy, though, is that he saw Hearn as 'a figure of protest', who imported into Japan different cultural values that worked against the prevailing ideology of modernization.[105] In Meiji-era Japan, intellectuals were encouraged to learn from the West (and in particular Britain, France, Germany, and America), and to admire the ideals of science and progress that formed the backbone of the hegemonic image that powerful Western countries projected around the world. Hearn went against this trend, teaching the Japanese that literature provided elements of dissent and chaos *within* the West to which they could turn in order to resist the forces of globalization and preserve their native traditions.

Hearn lectured extensively on English literature between 1896 and 1903, during his tenure as Professor of English at Tokyo Imperial University. After his death in 1904, a group of his former pupils gathered together their notes on Hearn's courses on the history of English literature and passed them on to his literary executor Mitchell McDonald. Noguchi had access to this material when he wrote his study of Hearn in Japan in 1911. The notes were eventually edited by the influential American educator John Erskine, who brought them out in three volumes from 1915 to 1917.[106] They would later be incorporated into the first multi-volume American and Japanese editions of Hearn's complete works that appeared in the 1920s, which marked the unofficial canonization of Hearn as 'interpreter' between Japan and the West.

Erskine rightly described the essays as a work of 'devotion' on the part of Hearn's Japanese students, who took down Hearn's lectures, slowly delivered on the basis of minimal notes, nearly word for word.[107] The lectures were thus literally the written records of Hearn's influence not only academically but also in personal, emotional terms: they embodied both his classroom presence and the affect of his students, who reconstructed the words of their teacher as an act of

---

[104] Ibid., p. vi.    [105] Ibid. 17.

[106] Hearn's lectures were originally published in America by Dodd, Mead, & Co., and were soon reprinted in Britain as *Interpretations of Literature*, ed. John Erskine, 2 vols (London: Heinemann, 1916); *Life and Literature*, ed. John Erskine (London: Heinemann, 1917); and *Appreciations of Poetry* (London: Heinemann, 1916). Erskine later brought out further selections titled *Books and Habits* (London: Heinemann, 1922) and *Pre-Raphaelite and Other Poets* (London: Heinemann, 1923).

[107] John Erskine, 'Introduction', in Hearn, *Pre-Raphaelite and Other Poets*, pp. v–ix (p. vi).

mourning after his death. Erskine recounted Hearn's investment in the scene of instruction not without a strong dose of Eurocentric bias:

> Day in and day out Hearn lectured at Tokyo before his boys with the same care and with the same elevation of spirit as though he had been addressing an audience at the Sorbonne or at Oxford—or better, as though he had been the official instead of the accidental spokesman of Western letters, and though the whole East, and not only his limited classroom, were hanging on his words.[108]

If we discount the patronizing tone, Erskine was right to compare Hearn's work in the classroom to an act of diplomacy. Hearn's pupils in the Imperial University were, it is worth stressing, the cultural elite of Japan. As they came to occupy positions of power in educational institutions across the country, Hearn's influence widened beyond his immediate circle, creating a network of cosmopolitan Anglophile Japanese while at the same time consolidating his role as 'official' canonizer of European literature recognized by Erskine.

The majority of Hearn's lectures were concerned with modern literature, with an emphasis on the Pre-Raphaelites, the aesthetes, and those authors towards whom he felt a greater affinity, such as Ruskin, D. G. Rossetti, and, especially, Swinburne. These were complemented by some eccentric choices, such as a lecture on William Johnson Cory's *Ionica* (1858), as well as lectures on English and French poems about insects, and one on the influence of Finnish poetry on English literature. When Hearn's lectures reached back to the English-speaking world in the form of critical essays, they went through several American and British editions. According to Albert Mordell, another of Hearn's early editors, they soon supplanted Hearn's other writings in popularity at a time in which the characteristically *fin-de-siècle* 'colourful style and exquisite diction' of the Japanese sketches had gone out of fashion.[109]

Hearn's deep engagement with aesthetic writers in the lectures marked the culmination of a life-long effort to create new cosmopolitan contexts for English aestheticism, starting with the translations of Gautier in New Orleans. Hearn criticized literary realism, praising D. G. Rossetti, Tennyson, and Swinburne for refusing to draw inspiration directly from their own life experiences, preferring instead to go back to the past and existing textual records. In *Appreciations* (1889), Pater had rendered the essence of aesthetic poetry as 'some strange second flowering after date', which seized on a 'transfigured world' and sublimated beyond it 'another still fainter and more spectral'.[110] In his Japanese lectures, Hearn also characterized

---

[108] Ibid., p. viii.
[109] Mordell finds it ironic that 'the works of Hearn that are being most read are not his polished, elaborate studies, but those which he wrote hastily in the form of letters or improvised as lectures'. Mordell, 'Preface', in Hearn, *Essays in European and Oriental Literature*, pp. v–xiii (p. vi).
[110] Walter Pater, 'Aesthetic Poetry', in *Appreciations* (London: Macmillan, 1889), 213–227 (213).

aesthetic poetry as an art of rebirth, but brought it closer to Japanese culture by referring to Buddhist ideas. Hearn developed an idiosyncratic theory of intertextuality as a form of reincarnation that fused English aestheticism and Japanese spirituality: he spoke of Rossetti as a man of the time of Dante 'reborn into the nineteenth century' and of Swinburne as 'Shelley in a new body'.[111] He also drew on Japanese Buddhism in order to explicate Rossetti's spirituality.

Despite these attempts to domesticate English literature within Japanese culture, Hearn was also acutely aware of cultural differences—indeed, the lectures are haunted by the same scepticism about translatability present in the Japanese essays. He therefore always encouraged students to approach literature through a prism of moral relativism, stressing for instance that gender is constructed through different social and literary codes in Japan and in the West.[112] In line with other aesthetic critics, he emphasized the importance of form as a prime site of meaning, arguing that criticism should disregard morality as a criterion of artistic value. Swinburne in particular was praised for pushing the boundaries of public decency in the name of intellectual freedom and for introducing into English an element of 'elegant immorality' that was otherwise characteristic of French literature.[113] Again and again, Hearn asked his students to appreciate acts of rebellion over and above the normative Western values that were officially promoted in Japan.

Hearn understood that his post at Tokyo Imperial University put him in a unique position of being able to present as canonical authors and works that would be viewed as eccentric from the domestic perspective. In a letter to Mitchell McDonald he portrayed his work as Japanese spokesman of art for art's sake with a mixture of pride and amusement:

> Fancy! I am lecturing now on Swinburne's poetry. They would not allow me to do this in a Western university perhaps—yet Swinburne, as to form, is the greatest 19th century poet of England. But he has offended the conventions; and they try to d-n him with silence. I believe you can trust me to do him justice here, when I get the chance.[114]

As these words show, Hearn was aware that being in Japan gave him the freedom to imagine a history of English literature that would not have been possible in British or American institutions, where the study of English at university level was then very unlikely to include authors like Swinburne and Cory. Hearn's Tokyo lectures were thus one of the first instances in which English Pre-Raphaelitism and

---

[111] Hearn, 'Studies in Rossetti' and 'Studies in Swinburne', in *Appreciations of Poetry*, 37–125 (37) and 126–171 (126).
[112] Hearn, 'On Love in English Poetry', in *Appreciations of Poetry*, 1–29; see also, 'The Insuperable Difficulty', in *Interpretations of Literature*, i. 1–6.
[113] Hearn, 'Studies in Swinburne', 132.
[114] Quoted in Bisland, *Life and Letters of Lafcadio Hearn*, ii. 427.

aestheticism were canonized, in a prestigious academic institution, as central to the literary history of the nineteenth century.

Most importantly, Hearn was adamant that his students should not view English literature solely as the property and mirror of the English nation. In this he went against the grain of how literature was institutionalized in British universities, promoting instead a comparative approach. In a lecture on the Norwegian novelist Bjørnstjerne Bjørnson (to whom we shall come back in Chapter 3)—a tellingly eccentric inclusion in an English literature curriculum— he opened by correcting the wrong notion that 'students of English literature ought to study in English only the books originally written in English'.[115] Instead, Hearn stressed the great importance of translations not only in creating the literacy of the British people, from their first childhood encounters with fairy tales onwards, but also in shaping the very category of English literature: 'if Englishmen had studied only English literature, English literature would never have become developed as it is now'.[116] It followed that, to the Japanese, the real use of studying English was as a key to a wider world literature; or, as he put it with an Arnoldian turn of phrase, 'not as the medium for expressing only the thought of one people, but as the medium through which you can obtain the best thought in the world'.[117] Likewise, he argued that 'if Japan is to produce an extensive new literature in the future, it will not be until after fresh ideas have become widely assimilated by the nation through thousands of translations'.[118] In this respect, Hearn's pedagogical work paralleled the work of literary mediation and translation undertaken in these years by Japanese writers such as Mori Ōgai and Natsume Sōseki, who assimilated Western classics in their Japanese writings, which have in turn become classics of modern Japanese literature. Nowhere is the direct legacy of this aspect of Hearn's teaching realized more fully than in the work of his pupil Ueda Bin, whose remarkable talent Hearn spotted, urging him to develop an individual, 'totally new style'.[119] Bin's celebrated anthology of translated European poetry, *Kaichōon* (The Sound of the Tide, 1905), was published the year after Hearn's death and dedicated to Ōgai. His selection, which was heavily shaped by Hearn's taste for the French Parnassians and the English Pre-Raphaelites, represented a milestone in the introduction of modern European poetry into Japan, and went on to become a classic in its own right, influencing generations of readers.[120]

Hearn believed that his role as professor of English in Japan did not consist in imparting knowledge of English literature for its own sake, but as a stimulus for

[115] Hearn, 'Björnson', in *Interpretations of Literature*, 71–82 (71).    [116] Ibid. 71.
[117] Ibid. 74.    [118] Ibid. 72.
[119] Matsumura Hisashi, 'Bin Ueda and Lafcadio Hearn on William Collins', *Otsuma Journal of Comparative Culture*, 5 (2004), 109–135 (135). I am extremely grateful to Kanetake Michiko for providing some of the references in this paragraph.
[120] On the translation strategies and impact of *Kaichōon*, see Isabelle Lavelle, '*Anywhere Out of the World*: Translating *Décadence* in Japanese Literature, 1885–1925', PhD thesis (Waseda University, 2018), 35–54.

the advancement of Japanese culture. In his concluding lecture in Tokyo, published as his 'Farewell Address', he told his students that the ultimate value of foreign literary studies was 'their effect upon your own capacity to make literature in your own tongue'.[121] He added: 'It is by such studies that all Western languages obtain—and obtain continually—new life and strength. English literature owns something to almost every other literature, not only in Europe, but even in the whole civilised world.'[122] The notion of a 'civilised world' is as vague as it is disappointingly exclusionary. For all that, these words aptly sum up Hearn's own ambition as a writer during his experiences of global migration, in the course of which he translated and transplanted the forms, themes, and practices of metropolitan Anglo-French aestheticism. Hearn's compromise with Japanese nationalism did not weaken his conviction that national literatures were best nurtured through an open-ended dialogue with world literature. Believing that Japanese literature at present mostly imitated Western models without assimilating them in the proper sense of the term, he incited his students to lead the way in a true cosmopolitan revolution of Japanese letters, which would start with the advent of 'a romantic movement in Japan'.[123] Such a movement would bring the Japanese cultural elite close to those folk legends and traditional popular culture that he had striven to preserve in his own writings.[124] His ultimate aim as a teacher was to contribute to the creation of a 'Japanese literature of the future' that would benefit from Western forms and ideas while remaining 'purely Japanese'.[125]

Anticipating what Zweig would write about him, Hearn expressed a good practice of cultural cosmopolitanism through a botanical metaphor: 'the original plant is not altered by the new sap; it is only made stronger and able to bear finer flowers'.[126] Throughout his writings and professional activity, Hearn believed that literary cosmopolitanism did not consist in reducing the differences between nations in order to achieve a universal culture, but rather in building networks that fostered difference through exchange. At a key moment in Japanese history that saw a clash between the outward-looking culture of Meiji-era cosmopolitanism and the escalation of an inward-looking cultural nationalism, Hearn carved for himself a unique position of authority in the debate on the preservation of Japanese cultural traditions, in Japan as well as on a global stage. His work stands as a complex, sometimes fraught, and always brave attempt to reclaim literature and literary studies as the field for the articulation of an ethical cosmopolitanism simultaneously in Japan and in the English-speaking world.

---

[121] Hearn, 'Farewell Address', in *Interpretations of Literature*, ii. 367–374 (369).     [122] Ibid.
[123] Ibid. 370.
[124] On Hearn's influence on the development of Japanese folklore studies, see Yoko Makino, 'Lafcadio Hearn and Yanagita Kunio: Who Initiated Folklore Studies in Japan?', in Sukehiro Hirakawa, ed., *Lafcadio Hearn in International Perspectives* (Folkestone: Global Oriental, 2007), 129–138.
[125] Hearn, 'Farewell Address', 370.     [126] Ibid. 369.

# 3

# George Egerton's Scandinavian Breakthrough

The world is small, we run in circles, perhaps we shall meet again...
(George Egerton, 'The Spell of the White Elf')

I think that it is unbelievable how my individuality rings straight out
of the English, which, however, must also be your personal, your own
most intimate property.

(Ola Hansson to George Egerton)

When George Egerton's *Keynotes* came out in 1893, this slim collection of eight
short stories divided English critics: there were, on one side, those who admired its
radical views on gender and experimental style; on the other, there were those who
condemned it as vulgar or, as the *Punch* caricaturists put it, 'smudgy'.[1] Either way, this
was a book that literary London found it impossible to ignore. Its author, a 34-year-
old woman with no previous experience as a writer, became a literary celebrity,
her book an icon of what people either loved or hated about the new writing of the
*fin de siècle*. Egerton's notoriety was relatively short-lived, though. With *Keynotes*
and its follow-up *Discords* (1894), she came to be strongly associated with the
cosmopolitan circle that gathered around her publisher John Lane, which prominently included Wilde and Beardsley. So, when the Wilde trials struck in 1895
and the tide started to turn, Egerton found it increasingly difficult to publish or,
when she did publish, to avoid having to make compromises that harmed her
creativity and self-esteem. Once the voice of transgression and literary innovation, Egerton spent the first four decades of the twentieth century feeling
increasingly redundant, failing in her repeated efforts to write successful plays.

Like Hearn (and, to a degree, Wilde) Egerton was overlooked for the best
part of the twentieth century, as new generations of readers favoured new
writing styles and new types of frankness in fiction that she had paradoxically
helped to take root. 'I came too soon', she complained in 1932 with a characteristic
tone of wounded pride, by which she meant that her early work anticipated

---

[1] Egerton was caricatured in *Punch* as 'Borgia Smudgiton', author of *She-Notes*. This name refers to
Egerton's allegedly 'smudging', or staining, women's reputation because of the sexual content of her
stories, but it applies equally to the perceived lack of clarity of her lyric, experimental style. The parodies
appeared in *Punch* as 'She-Notes Part I' and 'She-Notes Part II', respectively on 10 and 17 Mar. 1894.

*Literary Cosmopolitanism in the English* Fin de Siècle: *Citizens of Nowhere*. Stefano Evangelista,
Oxford University Press. © Stefano Evangelista 2021. DOI: 10.1093/oso/9780198864240.003.0004

psychoanalysis before she or anyone in Britain had ever heard of Freud.[2] Pouring scorn on *Ulysses* and what now passed as advanced literature, she called Joyce 'a head-hunter in the realm of words' and compared his work to putting 'a square of lavatory paper on each plate' at a cocktail party in a wild attempt to make the sandwiches more palatable.[3] Unlike Hearn, though, Egerton has by now undergone a thorough rehabilitation thanks to the efforts of feminist scholars such as Sally Ledger, Margaret D. Stetz, and Martha Vicinus, who have demonstrated her significance both in the debate on female emancipation and in literary history more broadly. However, the feminist take on Egerton has been so persuasive— even in pointing out how fraught with contradictions Egerton's feminism actually was—that critics have tended to overlook another aspect of her identity: how much Egerton positioned herself at the margins of English literary culture, writing from the point of view of strangers and outsiders, translating foreign literatures, and adopting cosmopolitanism as a discourse of cultural authority.

Biographically, her story of travel and migration is similar to Hearn's. Born as Mary Chavelita Dunne in Australia (1859), she was, like Hearn, the child of an Irishman serving in the British Army, while her mother was a Welsh woman who followed her husband around the British Empire.[4] She was brought up in Ireland, where the family returned when she was 11 years old, and was partly educated in a German convent school before emigrating to America in 1884. Disappointed by her experience there, she returned to London the following year. The turning point in Egerton's life came in 1887, when she fled to Norway with an older lover. During two years there she learnt Norwegian and experienced first-hand the thriving literary scene of the country at the time of the so-called modern breakthrough. Like Hearn, Egerton came to maturity as a writer when she was away from 'home' and for her, too, writing and reading would always be bound with the love of foreign places and a strong desire to be mobile. *Keynotes* was written during a spell in Ireland, where she returned in 1892. After the book's publication the following year, however, Egerton settled in London, where she would remain—uneasily, as we shall see—until her death in 1945, apart from short periods spent travelling abroad, notably in Norway.

Like Hearn and Wilde, Egerton's closest emotional ties, in terms of national identity, were with Ireland, her father's native country, towards which she nonetheless had a complex attitude, characterized by what Tina O'Toole calls 'anxious self-positioning'.[5] Using an essentialist language to which she was strongly drawn

---

[2] George Egerton, 'A Keynote to *Keynotes*', in John Gawsworthy, *Ten Contemporaries* (London: Ernest Benn, 1932), 57–60 (58).

[3] Egerton to Terence de Vere White, 8 Mar. 1934, in *A Leaf from the Yellow Book: The Correspondence of George Egerton*, ed. Terence de Vere White (London: Richard Press, 1958), 154.

[4] Biographical information on Egerton comes from Margaret Diane Stetz, '"George Egerton": Woman and Writer of the Eighteen-Nineties' (unpublished doctoral thesis, Harvard University, 1982). I would like to thank Margaret D. Stetz for generously providing me with a copy of this work.

[5] Tina O'Toole, *The Irish New Woman* (Basingstoke and New York: Palgrave Macmillan, 2013), 7.

(mostly, though, to define people other than herself), she was capable of describing herself as 'intensely Irish', especially later in life, when she followed Irish politics, learnt Gaelic, and tended to romanticize her Irish roots; and yet she was also keen to stress her distance from Ireland, dissociating herself from its culture and attacking its provincialism, which, she argued, would have made it impossible for her to 'pass the censor' there.[6] Her autobiographical novel, *The Wheel of God* (1898) conveys her sense of frustration with what she perceived as the moral and cultural narrowness of Ireland. Metropolitan London, imperial capital and thriving publishing centre, is where Egerton achieved her success. Even so, she never felt at home in London either, repeatedly complaining to her correspondents that England made her feel 'dull and down',[7] fantasizing of leaving the country for good,[8] and refusing to partake of the rituals of sociability that came with literary life. Like Wilde, she could be scathing towards English literary institutions, speaking openly to John Lane about her 'contempt' for English criticism and dismissing the obsession with morality as nothing more than 'so much rot', which made the English 'incapable of judging art or literature'.[9] And again as in Wilde's case, this conviction that her ideal readers were somehow geographically and experientially remote from Britain played an important role in the way that Egerton understood her mission as a writer. In 'A Keynote to *Keynotes*', a retrospective essay on the genesis of her major work, she gives a striking image of her life in England as a 'premature burial':

> As for myself, the Trappist monk digs a spadeful of clay a day towards his own grave. One does not need to do that in London, it digs itself. There are no 'Fairy Forts' to whisper music from the otherwhere to Souls in Exile.[10]

Egerton's bitterness is the emotion of someone who believes she has been consigned to the past and memory too soon. But her feeling of exile in twentieth-century literary London, in which she became all but invisible, also recalls Wilde's experience during his post-prison life in France and Hearn's growing unease in his last years in Japan, when rising nationalism was making his life there increasingly

---

[6] Letters from Egerton to Terence de Vere White, 27 Mar. 1926 and 13 Nov. 1929, in Egerton, *A Leaf from the Yellow Book*, 14, 126.

[7] Egerton to John Lane, 21 Mar. 1894, The William Andrews Clark Memorial Library, University of California, Los Angeles, George Egerton Correspondence, Oscar Wilde MSS, B855IL L265, box 7, folder 20. Hereafter Egerton Correspondence, Clark Library.

[8] E.g. Egerton to Lane, 8 July 1894: 'I have made up my mind to leave England as soon as it is feasible. I do not fit in with the folk or their whimsies and I do not think I ever shall.' Egerton, *A Leaf from the Yellow Book*, 39–40.

[9] Egerton to John Lane, St Stephen's day [1894], in Egerton, *A Leaf from the Yellow Book*, 32; and Egerton to her father, 14 Dec. 1893, Princeton University Library, Manuscript Division, Special Collections, Selected Papers of Mary Chavelita Bright (C0105), box 2, folder 17. Hereafter Bright Papers, Princeton.

[10] Egerton, 'A Keynote to *Keynotes*', 60.

problematic. It describes the existential anxiety of the cosmopolitan writer as citizen of nowhere: it expresses a very palpable sense of precariousness that is the other side of the coin of those confident statements about Irish provincialism and about her aesthetic superiority to the English.

In 1901, writing to her second husband from Norway, she set down her divided identity, repeating her conviction that the 'soul' cannot be bounded by nationality:

> I am home there. I am always alien here. I loathe England [. . .], the loveliest scene
> in England has an irritating effect. I feel the very language not my own. It is as if
> I were of another race—who had never learned my own tongue and always felt
> the one I learned to speak alien to the race in this soul in me.[11]

The arresting image of linguistic dispossession—particularly striking in a writer—alerts us to how Egerton's literary cosmopolitanism expressed itself as a psychological inner conflict: while she imagined literature as an appealing extraterritorial zone that gave her access to other languages and modes of feeling and alternative identities, she paradoxically associated the familiar setting of England with unfamiliarity and alienation. As an antidote to this aversion towards 'home' and rootedness, she sometimes fantasized about the literary profession as a kind of vagabondage: in 'A Keynote to *Keynotes*', she tells of how she 'would have liked to go in a caravan from hamlet to village, stopping to tell a story with a can for pennies'.[12] Like Arthur Symons—another cosmopolitan voice of the English *fin de siècle*—she idealized gypsies, whose wanderlust symbolized a type of intellectual freedom that stood in sharp contrast to the social and commercial realities of modern England.[13]

Most importantly, for Egerton, fantasies of unhindered mobility always clashed against the supremely hard reality of gender. In a letter written shortly after the one about her loathing of England, she bitterly mused: 'I was only kept from following the bent of my adventurous spirit by my sex—Had I been a youth I should have gone gaily round the whole world without a coin in my pocket.'[14] As we shall see, Egerton's writings show women simultaneously being socially liberated and made vulnerable by cosmopolitan uprooting. At the height of her fame in the 1890s, Egerton became a key translator and mediator of Scandinavian literature into English. Her Scandinavian interests provided Egerton, culturally and also very materially, in terms of personal contacts and networks, with the wider

---

[11]  Egerton to Reginald Golding Bright, 29 Mar. 1901, Bright Papers, Princeton, box 2, folder 19.

[12]  Egerton, 'A Keynote to *Keynotes*', 57. For Egerton's idealization of gypsies in her fiction, see the story 'A Cross Line' in *Keynotes*.

[13]  Cf. Katharina Herold, '"Against Civilisation": Symons, the Gypsy Lore, and Politicised Aestheticism', in Elisa Bizzotto and Stefano Evangelista, eds, *Arthur Symons: Poet, Critic, Vagabond* (Cambridge: Legenda, 2018), 145–159.

[14]  Egerton to Reginald Golding Bright, 2 Apr. 1901; quoted in Stetz, 'George Egerton', 7.

perspective for which she yearned in the middle of her English 'exile'. To read Egerton from this transnational perspective is therefore to restore an important part of her complex profile and, at the same time, to understand her key contribution to the cosmopolitan opening of the literary culture of the English *fin de siècle*.

## The Myth of the North: Egerton's Women of the World

What was controversial about Egerton was the way she wrote as much as what she wrote about: her highly self-conscious style, influenced by aestheticism and decadence, marked a decisive break from nineteenth-century realism. In particular, her handling of the short-story form relied heavily on the use of ellipsis and fragmentation in order to experiment with the portrayal of psychology, moods, and the emotions. Many of the stories in the early collections, *Keynotes* and *Discords*, examined difficult and potentially scandalous themes favoured by the naturalists such as extra-marital sex, addiction, and domestic abuse—all viewed from a distinctly, sometimes polemically, female perspective. However, Egerton's lyrical and ruptured style, which drew attention to the inconstancy of reality and moral relativism, departed from the scientific model privileged by naturalist authors, pointing instead to a philosophical engagement, especially, as we shall see, with Nietzsche.

In a famous passage from 'A Keynote to *Keynotes*', she explained her choice of the female point of view as a moment of breakthrough in literary history: 'I realised that in literature, everything had been better done by man than woman could hope to emulate. There was only one small plot left for her to tell; the *terra incognita* of herself, as she knew herself to be, not as man liked to imagine her—in a word to give herself away, as man had given himself in his writings.'[15] The cartographical metaphor reflects Egerton's practice of mapping questions of identity onto landscape. In her psychological narratives, women's spiritual journeys into what Egerton called the *terra incognita* of their inner selves often coincide with physical journeys through international space: in crossing national boundaries, Egerton's women experience displacement in both body and mind, straying beyond the horizons of expectation of their contemporary society, sometimes to their own detriment, often rejecting respectability and bourgeois social conventions. Egerton often concentrates on uprooted character: wonderers, strangers, or women who are caught between nations, often because of mixed parentage or international marriages. In terms of genre, the conventions of the short story form do not allow for the long build-up of social relationships, such as we find in realist and naturalist novels: the short narratives are instead a perfect

---

[15] Egerton, 'A Keynote to *Keynotes*', 58.

medium to focus on causal encounters, separations, rendezvous, and mobility broadly conceived.[16]

In the map of *fin-de-siècle* literary cosmopolitanism Egerton brings to light different geographical connections that make her work distinctive in the English-speaking world. While Wilde looked mainly to France and Hearn to Japan and the East, Egerton's gaze was pointed northwards. Her interest in Northern Europe reached from Scandinavia to Ireland and Holland, but Norway was the country to which she was most intensely drawn and the foreign setting she used most frequently in her fictions. In *Keynotes* alone, five of the eight stories are set in Norway, making the collection one of the most extensive treatments of modern Norway in the English *fin de siècle*. Other popular treatments such as Marie Corelli's extremely successful *Thelma: A Norwegian Princess* (1887), which had gone into forty-seven editions by 1916,[17] displayed none of Egerton's literary sophistication and extensive local knowledge.

In a perceptive review of *Keynotes* the critic William Sharp placed Egerton alongside French author Rachilde, Spanish Emilia Pardo Bazán, and Italian Matilde Serao as representing a transnational, militant 'New Spirit' in literature bent on laying bare 'the inner life of woman'. Sharp noted the influence of the Norwegian author Bjørnstjerne Bjørnson and the prevalence of a 'northern' sentiment in *Keynotes*, claiming that Egerton had been 'won by the witchery of the North—a witchery that is like none other, whose appeal, when felt at all, is irresistible, and which to those who love it seems the most beautiful, the most alluring thing in literature'.[18] Egerton herself spoke of the 'witchery' of Norway in *Keynotes*, comparing it to a 'love-philter' that infiltrates the blood stream.[19] Several stories in that collection contained vivid descriptions of the Norwegian landscape that interwove realism and myth:

> It was getting dusk, the luminous dusk of the north, as if a soft transparent purple veil is being dropped gently over the world. The fjord was full of lights from the different crafts at anchor, and the heaven full of stars, and the longer one looked up there, the more one saw myriads of glimmering eyes of light, until one's brain

---

[16] On the connection between mobility and modernity in Egerton, see Gerd Bjørhovde, *Rebellious Structures: Women Writers and the Crisis of the Novel 1880–1900* (Oslo: Norwegian University Press, 1987), 135; and Sally Ledger, 'Introduction', in George Egerton, *Keynotes and Discords* (London: Continuum, 2003), pp. ix–xxvi (p. xviii).

[17] C. B. Burchardt, *Norwegian Life and Literature: English Accounts and Views Especially in the Nineteenth Century* (London and Edinburgh: Oxford University Press, 1920), 65. It is revealing of Egerton's neglect as cultural mediator that in this major early twentieth-century study Egerton is only mentioned in a footnote to the conclusion (193).

[18] William Sharp, '*Keynotes*. By George Egerton', *The Academy*, 1137 (17 Feb. 1894), 143–144. It is worth noting that Symons had mentioned Pardo Bazán and Serao in 'The Decadent Movement in Literature' the previous year.

[19] George Egerton, *Keynotes and Discords* (London: Virago, 1983), 73. Subsequent references will be made in the text.

seemed full of their brightness, and one forgot one's body in gazing. Long silvery streaks glistened through the heaving water, like the flash of feeding trout, and lads and lasses in boats rowed to and fro, and human vibration seemed to thrill from them, filling the atmosphere with man and woman. And the silken air caressed my face as the touch of cool soft fingers. I had a feeling of perfect well-being; one does not get many such moments in one's life, does one?    (p. 49)

Like Hearn's Japan, Egerton's Scandinavia was simultaneously a real place—which the British had, in fact, already discovered as a popular tourist destination—and an idealized landscape that provided an attractive alternative to metropolitan industrial modernity. This is why her investment in this space reached deeper than the leisure-seeking mentality of a tourist looking for unspoilt nature and clean air. Over one hundred years before Egerton, Mary Wollstonecraft had used the Nordic landscape as a foil for female emotion in her Scandinavian travelogue, *Letters written during a short Residence in Sweden, Norway and Denmark* (1796). Egerton built on this important feminist precursor. Her short reveries on landscape concealed moments of intense introspection, in which the geography of the North provided a mirror for the *terra incognita* of female psychology. In *Keynotes* the Norwegian landscape is frequently used as a space of transformation, where the boundaries of the self are made pliable as the body enters into perfect harmony with the natural elements. In these moments the North becomes, as Martha Vicinus puts it, 'a place of possibilities',[20] that is, it promises personal freedom, spiritual regeneration, and an altogether preferable alternative to life back home, with its domesticated sociability and narrow civilization based on repression and restraint. The strong desire that pervades this vision has, as often in Egerton, a distinctly sexual stamp, here described as the 'human vibration' that radiates outwards from the courting couples in the rowing boats to fill the entire word-picture. The proto-Freudian diagnosis of a clash between civilization and the instinctual (sexual) drives of the individual, to which Egerton herself would draw attention later on, hardly needs glossing for twenty-first-century readers.

The return to nature, as fantasized by Egerton, has a strong dose of essentialism. However, it also discloses an idealist dimension in her work, by means of which she critically interrogates ideas of home and national identity. It is important to notice that the fantasy of the North is created and sustained from a distant or foreign point of view: the transformative potential of Egerton's Nordic landscapes is available only to those who are not rooted in them—foreignness and mobility are the keys to regeneration (one of Egerton's favourite words). It is therefore significant that in lyrical passages such as the previous quotation from 'Now

---

[20] Martha Vicinus, 'Rediscovering the "New Woman" of the 1890s: The Stories of "George Egerton"', in Vivian Patraka and Louise A. Tilly, eds, *Feminist Re-Visions: What has been and might be* (Ann Arbor: University of Michigan Press, 1983), 12–25 (16).

Spring has Come', the prime elements of the Norwegian landscape appear to be water and air rather than earth, as though to signify the evanescent and transitory nature of the vision, but also to push desire away from the land and its symbolism of rootedness. In naturalist fiction the soil provided a powerful symbol for the inescapable forces of heredity and the environment, notably in Zola's *Earth* (*La Terre*, 1887), which had recently been at the heart of a literary scandal in Britain after the prosecutions for obscenity of its translator and publisher Henry Vizetelly. Egerton's fascination with the sea as a means of connection with far-away places, just like her metaphor of the *terra incognita*, is a constant reminder of new worlds and alternative lives that are within the reach of her fictional characters: it is a way of questioning the very strategies for understanding human nature that the naturalists identified with the soil and of rejecting their claims to objectivity in fiction. When early reviewers (and sometimes later critics) compared Egerton to Zola because of her sexual frankness they therefore obscured a fundamental aspect of her work. It is true that she sometimes used a similar essentializing imagery, for instance in the story 'Virgin Soil' in *Discords*, where a girl who was given away to marry without sexual knowledge eventually decides to leave her adulterous husband; but even this tale ends with an idealistic turn that is deeply at odds with naturalist plot structures—the girl's decision to embark on a 'long journey' of liberation and self-discovery (p. 150).

Back to 'Now Spring has Come', the narrator is a classic Egerton character, who prides herself on having 'trotted the globe without male assistance' (pp. 42–43). She recounts how she picked up a copy of an advanced work of modern fiction from a Norwegian bookshop against the advice of the shop owner; and how she then became so haunted by what she calls the 'abstract ego of the novel' (p. 40) that she contrived to arrange a meeting with the author in a hotel in a Norwegian coastal town. The epiphanic apprehension of the Northern landscape occurs at this charged moment in the narrative, after the narrator's first meeting with the Norwegian writer, when she is exhilarated by the intellectual and sexual energy generated by the encounter. A second meeting takes place the following spring but that, unfortunately, goes less than well. They meet once again in a hotel and they talk about Tolstoy, Ibsen, Strindberg, and Nietzsche; this time they kiss, even. But the chemistry between them has gone and eventually they part coldly, the writer promising to burn the love letters the narrator had written to him in the intervening months, for the sake of propriety.

As several critics have pointed out, 'Now Spring has Come' is a thinly veiled fictionalization of Egerton's relationship with the Norwegian author Knut Hamsun, whom she had met in the summer of 1890, at the end of her two years in Norway.[21]

---

[21] The fullest account is Peter Fjågesund, 'Knut Hamsun and George Egerton: Factual and Fictional Encounters', in Bjørn Tysdahl et al., eds, *English and Nordic Modernisms* (Norwich: Norvik Press, 2002), 41–59.

The dangerous book that triggers the events in the story is thus Hamsun's *Hunger* (*Sult*, 1890), which, as we shall see later in this chapter, Egerton translated on her return from Norway, most probably before starting work on *Keynotes*, and eventually published in 1899. At the time of his first meeting with Egerton, Hamsun was making his reputation as the *enfant terrible* of Norwegian literature, having come back from a failed attempt to emigrate to America. In a provocative article titled 'From the Unconscious Life of the Soul' ('Fra det ubevisste sjelliv') published in the newly founded journal *Samtiden* in September 1890, he attacked realism and naturalism, calling instead for a psychological turn in literature that should seize on the unknown and the unexplainable as its primary objects of enquiry. Hamsun's polemic was first and foremost an attack on the internationally famous Norwegian writers of the previous generation, Bjørnson, Alexander Kielland, and Henrik Ibsen. He continued the confrontation in a series of public lectures the following year, dismissing their works as 'social poetry' ('samfundsdigtning').[22] In *Hunger*, the semi-autobiographical tale of the inner life a young author experiencing starvation on the streets of Christiania, he put his theories into practice. With its dissolution of plot, self-indulgent lyricism, and blunt irrationality, the novel marked a turning-point in Scandinavian literary modernity. It is easy to see how Hamsun's radical ideas should have appealed to the budding author of *Keynotes*, who was to pick up Hamsun's challenge to invent a new literary form capable of capturing the unconscious, albeit, in her case, from an explicitly gendered point of view. The story of the epistolary exchange and romance in 'Now Spring has Come' was based on the all-too-real attraction that Egerton developed for the charismatic and hypermasculine Hamsun, who liked to encourage female admirers but who, in the rather dismissive words of a recent biographer, 'realised that [Egerton] was very different from the paragon he imagined he had been writing to and about'.[23]

For these reasons, 'Now Spring has Come' held a special significance for Egerton. She intended it to be the opening story in *Keynotes*, following her dedication of the volume to Hamsun, '*In memory of a day when the west wind and the rainbow met. 1892–1893*'. This was her way of paying tribute to the writer who had influenced her most, even after their tense parting that, as she wrote to her father, had a 'miserable effect' on her.[24] In fact, 'Now Spring has Come' is the foundational narrative of Egerton's self-creation as an emancipated cosmopolitan author, anchored to a plot of sexual awakening. In the story, reading, writing, and international travel are what brings together these two 'unconventional' characters

---

[22] Knut Hamsun, 'Norsk Literatur', a lecture held on 7 Oct. 1891 in Christiania, reprinted in *Paa Turné: Tre foredrag om litteratur*, ed. Tore Hamsun (Oslo: Gyldendal, 1960), 17–44.
[23] Ingar Sletten Kolloen, *Knut Hamsun: Dreamer and Dissenter*, tr. Deborah Dawkin and Erik Skuggevik (New Haven and London: Yale University Press, 2009), 69.
[24] Egerton to her father, 26 Feb. 1891, Egerton Correspondence, Clark Library, box 2, folder 17. Eventually John Lane persuaded her to start instead with the more iconic 'A Cross Line'.

from different countries (p. 48) in the spiritualized Northern landscape, sus-
pended between myth and reality.

Over the next few years Egerton rewrote the very personal plot of 'Now Spring
has Come' several times. In 'The Regeneration of Two', in *Discords*, a foreign
'woman of the world' (p. 165) living in Norway comes across a Hamsun-like figure
of a poet-'vagabond' (pp. 200–201) and spiritually redeems him by making him
fall in love with her. The story concludes with the man kneeling at the woman's
feet, domesticated in her house, sobbing with joy, as the snow falls thick outside.
More remarkably, in the uncollected 'A Christmas Idyl', published in 1900 in the
*Universal Magazine*, Egerton reversed the gender roles: this time it is the man—a
wealthy Norwegian émigré named Einar Holt who returns to Christiania after a
long absence—who picks up a book written by a former sweetheart, Aagot, whom
he left behind when he emigrated. There are several clues in the narrative that
point to Hamsun as the original for Einer: the early emigration to America and the
references to circumstances that caused his 'semi-starvation of body, entire starvation of soul' conjure the protagonist of *Hunger*.[25] His nervousness and effeminacy are, however, psychological characteristics that are quite alien from the
young, swaggering Hamsun Egerton knew in the early 1890s. Equally, there is
more than a vague autobiographical feel in Aagot, the woman writer and translator (she translates from English to Norwegian) who struggles to make ends meet.
Despite its less experimental style, 'A Christmas Idyl' is striking for being a very
rare example of Egerton's exploration of masculine consciousness, as Einer is a
psychologized, male counterpart to her female characters in *Keynotes* and
*Discords*. With Einer, the man who had 'knocked about from one corner of the
globe to another',[26] Egerton creates a male analogue to her cosmopolitan female
protagonists, who are emancipated but also made socially and emotionally vulnerable by geographical dislocation: Einer has become a foreigner in his own
country, checking in at the international Grand Hotel in Christiania, the sound of
his mother tongue now striking 'unfamiliarity into his ears', and his own
Norwegian broken by an American accent that draws attention to him in
shops.[27] However, unlike most of the stories in *Keynotes* and *Discords*, 'A
Christmas Idyl' is a tale of homecoming: the reunification of the two estranged
lovers in the sentimental happy ending suggests a too easy reconciliation of
cosmopolitanism and rootedness, maybe in order to comply with the generic
conventions of commercial magazine publishing (Egerton was writing a
Christmas story for a Christmas number).

---

[25] Egerton, 'A Christmas Idyl', *Universal Magazine*, 2 (1900), 213–221 (214). Margaret D. Stetz has
drawn attention to this 'unjustly forgotten story' as a reworking of 'Now Spring has Come'; Stetz, 'New
Women Writing beyond the Novel: Short Stories', in H. A. Laird, ed., *The History of British Women's
Writing, 1880–1920* (Basingstoke and New York: Palgrave Macmillan, 2016), 215–231 (226–227).
[26] Egerton, 'A Christmas Idyl', 214.     [27] Ibid. 216.

As these fictional reworkings of her relationship with Hamsun demonstrate, Egerton combined a mythic portrayal of the North as an idealized, denationalized space of spiritual regeneration with a realistic and knowledgeable depiction of Norway as a location of literary modernity. In 'The Regeneration of Two', Christiania is a modern metropolitan capital, complete with fashionable shops and Cockney 'Cookies' (that is, a British group on a Thomas Cook package tour) who make 'unflattering remarks, at the top of their voices, on some of the idiosyncrasies of national costume, with a characteristic disregard of the fact that every second Norwegian understands them' (pp. 171–172). In 'The Little White Elf', one of the best-known stories in *Keynotes*, Christiania is again an international city where the streets and cafés teem with students and foreigners. Here the city is also, explicitly, a world literary capital where authors of international fame, Ibsen and Bjørnson, inhabit the public realm. The narrator is a classic Egerton woman split between two nations and two identities: half English half 'Norsk' (p. 75), she acts as a bi-cultural guide for English readers, priding herself on being able to 'see under the surface' of the city (p. 70); at the same time, though, she is reproached by her Norwegian cousin for being 'anglicised' and for only seeing the 'ridiculous side' of Norwegian customs (p. 74). This double perspective (depth/surface, proximity/distance) is the narrative standpoint from which 'The Little White Elf' is told. Dislocation is what both creates the narrator's distinctive authority and makes her social position precarious; crucially, it is what gives her the potential for self-fashioning that is a recurrent feature of Egerton's cosmopolitan female characters. In this story, most of the narrative takes place on board a steamer en route from Norway to England, where the narrator befriends an emancipated British woman—a strikingly masculine professional writer who has just been to Christiania to look up references in the National Library; she also reads Russian books, is an expert on Finnish sagas and 'Esquimaux marriage songs' (p. 84), and writes for the aptly named '*World's Review*' (p. 87), as well as reading Nietzsche in 'pragtbind', as she says, that is, in art binding (p. 85). The sea-journey becomes a transitional space where the two women can engage in a same-sex flirtation, and where the British woman frankly discusses her unconventional marriage and inability to have children. The Little White Elf of the title is the English woman's nickname for a child she has adopted, who is nurtured by her husband—an equally unconventional man who 'stays at home and grows good things to eat' while she 'go[es] out and win[s] bread and butter' (p. 80). The conclusion is characteristic of Egerton for being open-ended and ambiguous: the erotically tinged encounter with the emancipated masculine woman convinces the narrator, who at the beginning of the story described herself as not having the 'vocation' for marriage (p. 69), to slot into traditional gender expectations, accepting the marriage proposal of a Norwegian cousin she had previously rejected and embracing the hope to have children. At the same time, though, the narrator's decision is not exactly a straightforward act of domestication: in a brief coda we see the Anglo-Norwegian narrator about to emigrate to Cincinnati, where her fiancé now lives, thus opening a further story of uprooting and dislocation the outcome of which is left purposefully untold.

One last story, although not set in Norway, illustrates Egerton's interest in exploring the link between gender and cosmopolitan identities. 'A Psychological Moment at Three Periods' is the longest tale in *Discords*. It is a mini-*Bildungsroman* comprising three snapshots taken respectively from a woman's childhood in Ireland, her girlhood in the Netherlands, and finally her adulthood split between London, the South of France, and Paris. By the third part of the story, the little Irish girl has become what Henry James refers to as a *'femme du monde'*, with the term's mixed connotations of independence and sexual impropriety that place her on the margins of polite society:[28] she is the itinerant mistress of a married Irishman who has a wife back in Dublin. In the denouement Egerton stages a confrontation between the protagonist and her lover's wife that has clear parallels with the steamboat scene in 'The Little White Elf'. In 'A Psychological Moment at Three Periods' a Parisian hotel room provides the extraterritorial setting that enables the two women (who turn out to be former schoolmates) to embark on an intimate exchange in which their positions of authority are shockingly reversed. The legitimate wife complains of her unhappy marriage and portrays herself as the victim of the bigotry and narrow-mindedness of Catholic Ireland, confessing to envying the other's 'courage' and 'truth' (p. 54). The *femme du monde*, for her part, refuses to be cast into a position of guilt, rejecting the standard arguments for the moral condemnation of adultery and launching into a rousing speech about women's freedom. There is something of Ibsen's Nora in Egerton's protagonist, who becomes liberated when she is at her most vulnerable, having taken the decision to break up with her lover and venture into the unknown. Her parting speech exhorts women in particular to develop their individuality despite the social constraints imposed on them: 'I don't think people realise how much of the world belongs to them' (pp. 62–63). And: 'All that is best, and strongest, and most beautiful, because most love-worthy [. . .] in the world is a common inheritance, and I mean to take my share of it' (p. 63). This new idea of the world as desirable, full of opportunities, and, crucially, available to the women who want it, carries with it an imperative to let go of local identities, birth ties, and oppressive moral microclimates—which are all in this case identified with Ireland.

The hedonistic individualism expounded by Egerton in this story is reminiscent of Lord Henry Wootton's doctrine of a 'new Hedonism' in Wilde's *Picture of Dorian Gray*.[29] It also chimes closely with a controversial article by Grant Allen that appeared in the *Fortnightly Review* exactly at the same time as *Discords*, where

---

[28] Cf. Introduction, 'At Home in the World'.
[29] Oscar Wilde, *The Picture of Dorian Gray*, in *Complete Works*, iii: *The Picture of Dorian Gray: The 1890 and 1891 Texts*, ed. Joseph Bristow (2005), 187.

this influential critic, who had an association with Egerton through their publisher John Lane, hailed the hedonists as 'the pioneer[s] of a loftier faith' that, although particularly needed in Britain due to its puritan heritage, was destined 'hereafter to transform humanity'.[30] For Egerton as for Allen, hedonism was a progressive social philosophy that combined atheism and sexual reform, and found a particularly effective outlet in literature. Most tellingly, Egerton's strategic appeal to hedonism in 'A Psychological Moment at Three Periods' looks forward to Gide's journey of spiritual rebirth in *Les Nourritures terrestres* (1897), where the character of Ménalque—often recognized as a veiled portrait of Wilde—schools the narrator on how to sever domestic and familial ties, overcome Christian ethics, and enjoy and possess the world, in its infinite variety, by trusting his instincts and the senses: 'You must act without *judging* whether the action be good or bad. Love without worrying whether it be good or evil.'[31]

The links with Gide point to the influence of Nietzsche's philosophy, which, as Daniel Brown has shown, Egerton adapted as a progressive discourse for the emancipation of her female characters.[32] As in Wilde and Gide, in Egerton the new hedonism of the 1890s went hand in hand with sexual liberation: in the two male writers the focus was on homosexual emancipation, while in Egerton it was on liberating female sexuality from narrow codes of social propriety. Like Nietzsche and Gide, Egerton developed her philosophical arguments in a series of strong statements of individualism—'*always you must come back to yourself*' (p. 64, italics in the original)—and aphoristic swipes at organized religion—'We are all so busy building up wretched little altars to hold the shabby gods of our devotion, that our years pass away and we are laid to rest without ever having tasted life for the span of a day' (p. 63). In 'A Psychological Moment at Three Periods' the protagonist's cosmopolitan identity is thus initially depicted as a position of weakness—a frustrating vagabondage from one foreign town to another, from hotel to hotel. But in the course of the story the very ideal of a female cosmopolitanism is positively reconfigured, bolstered by the philosophies of hedonism and individualism. Spiritually regenerated, at the end of the story Egerton's worldly woman is described as 'an undaunted spirit waiting quietly for the dawn to break, to take the first step of her new life's journey' (p. 66). Needless to say, this is not an act of Christian redemption such as we find in conventional fallen-woman narratives. Egerton's philosophical engagement is important

---

[30] Grant Allen, 'The New Hedonism', *Fortnightly Review*, 327 ns (Mar. 1894), 377–392 (379). Allen's novel *The Woman Who Did* (1895) was published in the Bodley Head's Keynotes Series.

[31] André Gide, *Les Nourritures terrestres* (Paris: Gallimard, 1921), 16 ('Il faut agir sans *juger* si l'action est bonne ou mauvaise. Aimer sans s'inquiéter si c'est le bien ou le mal').

[32] Daniel Brown, 'George Egerton's *Keynotes*: Nietzschean Feminism and *Fin-de-Siècle* Fetishism', *Victorian Literature and Culture*, 39.1 (2011), 143–166. Much of Brown's interesting essay is focused on unearthing a connection between Nietzsche's and Egerton's proto-psychoanalytic techniques. In fact, the important shared precedent for both Egerton and Gide is the Swedish author Ola Hansson, who is examined in the next section of this chapter.

because it gestures towards an alternative to the ethical/political framing of cosmopolitanism in the Kantian tradition. At the same time, it puts the spotlight on the gendered bias of the male writers and thinkers who, theorizing world citizenship as an abstract ideal, underplay the embodied reality of women's position in society.

What emerges from Egerton's extensive portrayal of women's mobility in her fiction is that the cosmopolitan ideal is both the means to an attractive empowering individualism that frees women from traditional social and moral ties, and something that exposes them to the practical and emotional dangers of dislocation. Her stories do not offer an easy solution. What seems undeniable, though, is that cosmopolitan mobility is the necessary condition of literary modernity in Egerton's writing: it is what gives her access both to the mythology of the North as a supranational space of spiritual regeneration and to the modern ideas and techniques pioneered by Scandinavian writers that she imported into Britain by way of her fictions. In order to gain a more nuanced picture of Egerton's activity of cosmopolitan mediation, it is therefore important to investigate further her immersion in Scandinavian literature and commitment to making it known to English readers, starting from her translations.

## A Labour of Love: Ola Hansson and the Cultural Politics of Translation

Egerton's work as a translator of modern Scandinavian literature has been unjustly overlooked by critics. In one of the most influential theories of translation to have emerged in recent years, Lawrence Venuti has argued that in Britain and the United States translators have been forced into a position of invisibility, that is, they have, historically, been made to erase their presence from the text in order to guarantee its legibility by their English-speaking target audience.[33] By a similar mechanism, translations have by and large been excluded from processes of national canon-formation or, for that matter, of revision to existing canons. This explains why Egerton's translations have become all but invisible even in the midst of the rediscovery of her work that has taken place over the last decades, no doubt following the widespread perception of translation as second-order work, derivative and inferior in terms of quality and originality. Yet Egerton certainly did not mean to make herself invisible through the act of translation, as was likely the case for less ambitious nineteenth-century women translators who used their knowledge of modern languages as a way into a low-key, and therefore safe, literary profession that did not expose them to public scrutiny. She

---

[33] Lawrence Venuti, *The Translator's Invisibility: A History of Translation* (London and New York: Routledge, 2002), esp. 1–17.

did not approach it as a utilitarian form of literary work, aimed at economic profit. If anything, translation became for her an act of dissent against the rules of the British literary market, which then as now favoured original work in the national language. Neither did Egerton conceive of translation as a passive or mechanical activity, driven by choices imposed on her by editors and publishers, as she always herself chose the authors she wanted to translate. On the contrary, Egerton's Scandinavian translations are an integral part of her most creative period in the 1890s, when she produced the works of fiction for which she is best known today. Translation provided her with ways to forge literary connections with Scandinavia: it enabled her to enter into actual, epistolary, and textual dialogues with writers with whom she felt an affinity, which in turn deeply affected her own creative practices as a writer of fiction. In this way literary translation became for Egerton, both in the private and public spheres, a means of collaboration and productive contamination with foreign cultures and, as such, a fundamental part of what it meant for her to be a cosmopolitan author. Her example shows that in the study of literary cosmopolitanism translation should be considered as an equal alongside other modes of authorship that have traditionally commanded more academic prestige, such as 'creative' literature and criticism.

It is noteworthy that, at the height of her success after the publication of *Keynotes* and *Discords*, Egerton decided to switch to translation. In the early 1890s, as we have seen, she had translated at least a part of Hamsun's *Hunger*, but she had laid that aside to concentrate on her short stories. Now that she had become famous, she put fiction to the side in order to translate the 1892 cycle of prose poems *Ung Ofegs Visor* (*Young Ofeg's Ditties*) by the Swedish author Ola Hansson, who was practically unknown in the English-speaking world. The translation appeared in 1895, one year after *Discords*, with John Lane. In the opening of her short 'Introductory Note', Egerton went straight to the heart of the question of literary value:

> It has been urged upon me by many that translation is an unworthy form of literature; and with this view I entirely agree, if the translator be not in such sympathy with the writer he endeavours to give in his own tongue, as to make translation a labour of love, and not merely a branch of literary trade.[34]

Describing translation as a form of 'sympathy' and a 'labour of love', Egerton encouraged readers to view the task of the translator in ethical terms, as related to the love of strangers that plays such an important part in the cosmopolitan imagination. Disentangling herself from commercial motives, which, extending

---

[34] Egerton, 'Introductory Note', in Ola Hansson, *Young Ofeg's Ditties*, tr. George Egerton (London: John Lane; Boston: Roberts Bros, 1895), 5–13 (5). Subsequent references to this work in the main body of the text.

Egerton's metaphor, would render this love mercenary or even meretricious, she grounded her work in a double bond that brought together the private and public missions of the writer: her 'individual admiration' (p. 6) of Hansson's writings and the desire to make them known to English-speaking readers.

The 'Introductory Note' is an important document in Egerton's evolving identity as an author: the successful fiction writer now staged her public debut as a cosmopolitan critic and expert on Scandinavian literature. Even in subordinating her authority to Hansson's, as is customary in the relationship between translator and author, Egerton clearly gave the impression that she was the one in charge: she—not Hansson—determined the international value of the text as it migrated from one culture to another. This sense of agency was reinforced by the typographical design of the title-page, where Egerton's name was clearly visible, in the middle of the page, in a font that was only a little smaller than that used to print Hansson's own name (illustration 3.1). Moreover, unusually for a translation, the inside cover advertised Egerton's own previous works, *Keynotes* and *Discords*, now running in their sixth and third editions respectively, as though to reinforce the sense of Egerton's ownership of this foreign text by stressing the connections with her previous books. Beardsley's decorations in the lower half of the page furthered this sense of domestication by associating Hansson with the English symbolist and decadent authors—including, obviously, Egerton—published by John Lane; in fact they bore a strategic resemblance to the design Lane had used for the title-page of *Discords* only the previous year, underscoring further the sense of continuity and parity between translator and author. *Young Ofeg's Ditties* came out in early 1895, only months before Wilde's arrest would steer Lane away from pursuing risky projects associated with literary decadence. For now, though, Wilde's works featured prominently in the advertisements at the back of the book, including the English translation of *Salomé*, with drawings by Beardsley, which Lane had issued the previous year. Indeed, the two translations worked together to strengthen the Bodley Head's cosmopolitan credentials and its commitment to international decadence.

*Young Ofeg's Ditties* is a cycle of allegorical prose poems that describe the spiritual quest of the protagonist, Ofeg, as he moves through a series of heavily symbolical natural landscapes. Written in a highly lyrical style and mixing intense psychological focus and philosophical discussion, the book makes a sustained attack on the prominent materialist, positivist, and naturalist schools. A couple of examples will be enough to illustrate how Hansson promotes, in their stead, a form of extreme individualism. Poem XIX, for instance, describes Ofeg's encounter with a sea monster who prophesies that, in the future, '[a]ll things shall be reduced to the same level, the level of mediocrity'; Ofeg rebuts this view with his individualist doctrine: 'I believe in the one. I believe in myself. The God to whom I could bring myself to kneel dwells in my own soul' (p. 116). Later in the book, in

**Illustration 3.1** Title page of George Egerton's translation of *Young Ofeg's Ditties*, private collection

poem XXIII, Ofeg finds himself in a community which lives in a valley encircled by high hills; as he climbs up those hills, the men and women below, absorbed in their daily tasks, appear to him smaller and smaller just as he gradually learns to distance himself emotionally from them, ceasing to be concerned about whether the figures he can now barely make out in the distance are addressing greetings or hurling insults and threats at him. Finally, he emerges above a thick layer of clouds that isolates him from what goes on below, and his gaze rests triumphantly on the highly symbolic 'sun-tipped snow peak of the mountain, thither where the path led' (p. 135). In these examples and throughout *Young Ofeg's Ditties*, Hansson employs images and tropes that anticipate (or, given the time lag of the English translation, reinforce) Egerton's themes in *Discords*: the rejection of roots and enclosure, the symbolism of the journey and the 'new world', the adoption of a detached position as a privileged aesthetic and ethical perspective. But Hansson's route to spiritual regeneration goes through a much more aggressive form of individualism, which brings the protagonist to see fellow humans repeatedly as 'slaves' (e.g. pp. 30, 31, and 82) and even 'rats' (p. 66). His ideal of renewal cannot be achieved without such rhetorical iconoclasm.

It is easy to see that *Young Ofeg's Ditties* was heavily influenced by the writings of Nietzsche, especially *Thus Spoke Zarathustra* (*Also sprach Zarathustra*, 1883–5), which it resembled both in content and form.[35] In the early 1890s Hansson had been an active promoter of Nietzsche's philosophy: his pioneering short monograph *Friedrich Nietzsche: Seine Persönlichkeit und sein System* (1890) was followed by a series of articles in the Berlin magazine *Die Gegenwart*, later collected as *Friedrich Nietzsche und der Naturalismus* (1891). Hansson praised Nietzsche as an anti-naturalist thinker, arguing that his doctrine of individualism should replace Zola and Ibsen as an inspiration for writers. Hansson wrote both these important works in German as his intention was that the Germans should be the first to embrace Nietzsche's philosophy, before triggering an international reception. His enthusiastic championing occurred at a time before Nietzsche's works became widely noted within literary circles and, for this reason, he has earned the label of Nietzsche's first discoverer.[36]

In her introductory note, Egerton singled out Hansson's demonstration of Nietzsche's 'triumphant doctrine of the ego' (p. 5) as the main interest of *Young Ofeg's Ditties*. Her own work of translation now added another segment to the international chain of transmission of Nietzsche's ideas from Germany to Scandinavia and now to Britain, where Egerton's discussion of Nietzsche in the introduction to *Young Ofeg's Ditties* anticipated by over one year Havelock Ellis's important 1896 series of essays in *The Savoy*, which is otherwise widely held as the onset of Nietzsche's English reception.[37] In this way, the publication of her translation of Hansson helped to bring into focus Egerton's *own* interest in Nietzsche that had been quite prominent in *Discords* but in fact dated as far back as *Keynotes*, translator and author becoming partners in a transnational

---

[35] David R. Hume, *The German Literary Achievements of Ola Hansson* (Bern and Frankfurt a.M.: Peter Lang, 1979), 85.

[36] Wieńczysław A. Niemirowski, *Der Schriftsteller Ola Hansson in Berlin 1890–1893* (Lublin: Wydawnictwo Uniwersytetu Marii Curie-Skłodowskiej, 2000), 64.

[37] These ran from *The Savoy*, 2 (Apr. 1896) to 4 (Aug. 1896).

network that spread Nietzsche's ideas within literary culture. Egerton, however, tried to soften the hard philosophical edge of *Young Ofeg's Ditties* by drawing attention to Hansson's psychological interests: she stressed his skill in capturing 'the elusive emotions that flit like shadows across the hearts and minds of men', and called him 'a pathological hunter in the terra incognita of the human soul' (p. 10). This first public use of the image that she will later adopt to describe her own work provides another striking instance of the way in which she blurred her identities as translator and author.

Hansson had regarded Nietzsche as primarily a poet.[38] Likewise, Egerton wanted English readers to appreciate Hansson as a 'poet' (p. 13) and 'an aristocrat in letters' (p. 11), claiming that the 'peculiar rhythm of his prose adapts itself to his moods, fixes the fleeting expressions, the changeful colours, and the scarcely audible undertones of life' (p. 11). Egerton's double emphasis on form and psychology underscored Hansson's proximity to symbolist and decadent literature, especially to the genre of the prose poem associated with Baudelaire. In setting up Hansson in such terms, Egerton was first of all marking the arrival into English of a new wave of Scandinavian literature, pioneered by herself, which had rejected the social realism of Ibsen and Bjørnson in favour of what she called 'psychological mysticism' (p. 7) and 'the nervous life of to-day', of which she saw Hansson as the 'incarnation' (p. 10). As we have seen with reference to her use of Hamsun in 'Now Spring has Come', Egerton had already introduced this new school indirectly in her short fiction by means of intertextuality and allusion, but she now did so explicitly, adopting the different voice of translator and critic. However, Egerton also wanted to ensure that this new Scandinavian school should not be perceived as a marginal phenomenon confined to one of Europe's geographical peripheries. Her claim that Hansson's 'numerous lyrical and critical works have been translated into most European languages, and every new issue of his pen is hailed with eagerness' (pp. 8–9) was overstated. Yet it was certainly true that in Germany, where *Young Ofeg's Ditties* was serialized before its appearance in book form, the work met with great critical acclaim.[39] In France, a partial translation had appeared in the prestigious *Mercure de France* as early as 1892, tantalizingly introduced by the French translator as 'a lyrical expression of anarchist philosophical doctrines and Nietzsche's authoritarian personalism'.[40]

[38] See Harold H. Borland, *Nietzsche's Influence on Swedish Literature, with Special Reference to Strindberg, Ola Hansson, Heidestam, and Fröding* (Gotheborg: Wettergren & Kerbers, 1956), esp. 58.

[39] The prose poems that would make up *Young Ofeg's Ditties* started appearing in 1889 in the *Deutschland*. For their German reception see Hume, *German Literary Achievements*, 35.

[40] Ola Hansson, 'Les Chants d'Ofeg', tr. Jean de Néthy, *Mercure de France*, 30 (June 1892), 103–113 (103) ('une expression lyrique des doctrines philosophiques anarchistes et du personnalisme autoritaire de Nietzsche'). De Néthy—in many ways a counterpart to Egerton—played a key role in introducing Scandinavian literature to *fin-de-siècle* France. She would also translate some of Knut Hamsun's works. Her short essay on Hansson was clearly a very important source for Egerton's introduction to her own translation, which shows how closely Egerton, like Wilde and Hearn, followed the French press. I compare translations by Egerton and de Néthy in 'The Time of Ola Hansson: Translating

Equally importantly, Hansson himself was an extremely active cultural mediator. Following a hostile domestic reception of his early work, in 1892 he had moved to Germany, where he wrote an influential series of essays on Scandinavian literature for the *Magazin für die Literatur des In-und Auslandes* and enthusiastically promoted Nordic literature, especially his friend August Strindberg, among German readers, using his connections with literary and theatrical circles in Berlin. Some of these essays were republished in the French press, where Hansson even had a public exchange with Max Nordau on the topic of decadence, following the appearance of the French translation (1894) of *Degeneration*.[41] At the same time, he played a key role in introducing German (Nietzsche) and French authors (Bourget and Huysmans) to Scandinavian readers.[42] Through all these activities, Hansson became the nodal point in an important anti-naturalist network that brought together German, French, and Scandinavian literatures. With her translation, Egerton extended that international network to England, reducing the distance between cosmopolitan readers in London and their counterparts in Paris, Berlin, and the Scandinavian capitals.

However, the act of translation also entailed an important personal dimension. For, as she had done with Hamsun, Egerton clearly developed a sense of emotional proximity to Hansson that bordered on flirtation.[43] Their letters record an exchange of ideas, books, and photographs that started when Egerton approached Hansson in early 1894, asking for permission to translate his book. Hansson then sent her a very complimentary reaction to *Keynotes*, singling out for special praise the first part of the Norwegian trilogy 'Under Northern Sky', which he thought managed to be both English and Scandinavian at the same time. He told Egerton that he admired her lyrical temperament, which he ascribed to her Irish background, and observed that 'the newest English culture' was witnessing a breakthrough of 'the Celtic temperament'.[44] It was also Hansson who suggested to her for the first time the cartographic metaphor she would use as a memorable expression of self-definition, when he referred to his early work *Sensitiva Amorosa* (1887)

Scandinavian Decadence in *Fin de Siècle* France and England', in Pirjo Lyytikäinen et al., eds, *Nordic Literature of Decadence* (New York and Oxford: Routledge, 2020), 205–222.

[41] See Ola Hansson, 'Mouvement littéraire en Suède', tr. Jean de Néthy, *Revue des revues*, 4 (July 1893), 481–489; and Ola Hansson, 'La Maladie dans la littérature actuelle', *Revue des revues*, 5 (June 1894), 353–358.

[42] On the French connections see Hume, *German Literary Achievements*, 47; and George C. Schoolfield, *A Baedeker of Decadence: Charting a Literary Fashion, 1884–1927* (New Haven and London: Yale University Press, 2003), 44.

[43] In her dealings with these Scandinavian authors Egerton replicated the model of 'ambiguously amorous friendships' she established with her main British literary contacts, Lane and Richard LeGallienne, which Margaret D. Stetz sees as a survival strategy in the male-dominated book market of the 1890s. Stetz, '*Keynotes*: A New Woman, her Publisher, and her Material', *Studies in the Literary Imagination*, 30.1 (1997), 90–106 (98).

[44] Hansson to Egerton, 1 May 1894, Dublin, National Library of Ireland, Letters to George Egerton from Ola Hansson, MS 10946 (17) ('det keltiska lynnet bryter igenom i den nyaste engliska kulturen').

as mapping a 'terra incognita' in the study of human psychology.[45] Hansson was no feminist but *Sensitiva Amorosa*, a decadent collection of lyrical vignettes that explored male sexuality and libido, can indeed be seen as a Swedish precursor to *Keynotes*, written from the point of view of the male psyche. It appears from their correspondence that Egerton had not come across *Sensitiva Amorosa* at the time of writing *Keynotes*, but she must have been deep in her reading of Hansson at the time of finalising *Discords*, which, as the analysis of 'A Psychological Moment at Three Periods' has shown, bears the intellectual imprint of the Swedish author, especially in its references to Nietzsche's philosophy, mysticism, and individualism. One topic that Egerton and Hansson clearly had in common was the feeling of being culturally dislocated. With a mixture of melancholy and pride, Hansson confided in Egerton that more of his work had appeared in German and Norwegian translations than in his native Swedish; he told her that Swedish critics' attacks on *Sensitiva Amorosa* caused him to feel 'superfluous in [his] own country', forcing him to seek exile in Germany.[46] Egerton would retell this story in her introductory note to *Young Ofeg's Ditties*, speaking of the 'storm of opprobrium and scurrilous personal attacks' (p. 8) that met the publication of *Sensitiva Amorosa* and calling that book the 'key' (p. 11) to all of Hansson's subsequent work.

Hansson was thrilled with the translation. Egerton sent him a copy to check through before going to press but he did not want anything changed. He thought the English version fully preserved the mood of his prose poetry; that it had 'the soul' ('själen') of his work in it.[47] He told Egerton that reading her English version was like hearing an 'old melody' ('en gammal melodi') that brought him back to an intimate side of himself with which he had now lost touch, and that experiencing his work through the medium of a different personality and another language was like finding oneself again. He thought, in other words, that translation restored the original freshness of his work, making it new and exciting again three years after its original publication. He added: 'I think that it is unbelievable how my individuality rings straight out of the English, which, however, must also be your personal, your own most intimate property.'[48] There could not have been more welcome praise for Egerton's debut as translator. Hansson's words corroborated what she wrote in the introductory note about her work being a 'labour of love'. The passage from one language to another did not cause his work to lose content; on the contrary, it created new meanings and 'nuance' according to Hansson. The translated text retained the essence of the author's self and yet

---

[45] Hansson to Egerton, 30 June 1894, National Library of Ireland, MS 10946 (17).
[46] Hansson to Egerton, 3 Apr. 1894, National Library of Ireland, MS 10946 (17) ('Jag var öfverflödig i mitt hemland'). Hansson never returned to Sweden, living in Germany first and then moving from one European country to the other until his death at Buyukdere, in Turkey, in 1925.
[47] Hansson to Egerton, 14 Nov. 1894, National Library of Ireland, MS 10946 (17).
[48] Ibid. ('Jag tycker, det är otroligt, hvad min egenart klingar rent ut i detta engelska, som dock tillika måste vara ert personliga, er egen intimaste egendom').

was, at the same time, the 'most intimate property' of the translator. It belonged fully to both author and translator, creating a special bond of intimacy between them; to both Sweden and Britain, opening a new channel of communication between the two countries. It is no wonder that Egerton would proudly (mis)remember Hansson's endorsement over thirty years later: 'He said: "It's like hearing some melody one whistled as a boy hummed by a new voice with a note added"—at least to that effect.'[49]

British critics were predictably less lyrical. Following its earlier caricatures of Egerton as Borgia Smudginton, author of 'She-Notes', *Punch* published a spoof titled 'Blind Alley-gories. By Dunno Währiar', claiming to be a translation from the Lappish by the paper's own 'Hyperborean Enthusiast'.[50] It included a parody of Egerton's introductory note that mocked her admiration for modern Scandinavian literature and her efforts to import this material into Britain. The 'impressionable' Währiar, said to be 'the most remarkable personality that his native Lapland has yet produced', was described 'casting off the shackles of conventionality and escaping to Sweden in his sledge-perambulator' at the age of 4. *Punch* satirized the obscurity of Hansson's work, which, it claimed, was incomprehensible to ordinary readers, and the translator's perverse effort to preserve in English 'the mystical unintelligibility of the original'. The bogus 'Introductory Note' was followed by the parody of one of the allegorical ditties ('The Lost Backbone'), in which Young Garnaway, 'the Pessimistic Prose Poet', encounters the 'God of the Period' in his back-garden and laments humanity's loss of its 'perception of the ridiculous, which is the backbone of real enjoyment'. The *Punch* spoof illustrates the dynamics of the public confrontation between cosmopolitan author (here both Egerton and Hansson) and a conservative national press that styled itself as defending British common sense. *Punch* equated foreignness with incomprehensibility and drew a clear boundary between the domestic and the foreign in matters of literary taste. In this scenario where the differences between nations were essentialized and exaggerated for comical effect, the implication was that translation was always ultimately bound to failure.

*Punch* set the tone for the book's British reception. Its satire was echoed in serious reviews in high-brow journals, where Egerton was accused of 'overshoot[ing] the mark of English taste',[51] and Hansson's work of being 'incoherent', 'unintelligible', and 'obscurely aphoristic'.[52] For all this, what emerges as a clear pattern from the English reviews of *Young Ofeg's Ditties* is that the translator was anything but invisible to critics, most of whom devoted an equal amount of space to her as to the author, analysing her motives for bringing Hansson to the

[49] Egerton to Terence de Vere, 23 Feb. 1930, Bright Papers, Princeton, box 2, folder 25.
[50] [Anon.], 'Blind Alley-gories. By Dunno Währiar', *Punch*, 108 (20 Apr. 1895), 184. All quotations in this paragraph are from the same page.
[51] George Cotterell, 'New Novels', *The Academy*, 1196 (6 Apr. 1895), 293–294.
[52] [Anon.], 'Translations', *The Athenæum*, 3596 (26 Sept. 1896), 415–416 (415).

English public and the relationship between the two literary figures. The critic of the *Saturday Review* was explicit: 'to us the greatest interest [in *Young Ofeg's Ditties*] is in the fact that George Egerton has translated them'. The same critic was also perceptive on the continuity between Egerton's work as translator and author, connecting *Young Ofeg's Ditties* to Egerton's own turn to 'erotic mysticism' in *Discords*.[53]

Hansson had hoped that *Young Ofeg's Ditties* would 'vex' English readers.[54] Apart from *Punch*'s ironic dismissal and the odd praise for the book's 'beauty of form',[55] he—and Egerton—seem to have succeeded. The *Daily Chronicle*, after berating Egerton for exhibiting poor critical judgement in selecting this book for translation, compared Hansson unfavourably to Turgenev, provided its own parody of one of the ditties (following *Punch*'s example), and concluded by declaring that there is 'throughout this book a great deal more pretentiousness than profundity, a knack of decking semi-cynical commonplaces in nightmare-like imagery, and here and there a revelling in nightmare for nightmare's sake'.[56] The *Athenæum* called it an 'unspeakably nauseous and offensive little book', pointing to a 'total lack of equilibrium, an hysterically sensitive and corruptly morbid imagination, and a vanity so excessive as to be scarcely sane'.[57] The imagery of degeneration that creeps into the last review is telling, for, as already anticipated, the first reception of *Young Ofeg's Ditties* coincided with the time and immediate aftermath of the Wilde trials and the appearance of the English translation of Nordau's *Degeneration*, which worked together to create an atmosphere of suspicion and intolerance for experimental foreign literature. The toxic combination of nationalism and degeneration theory is most evident in a sadly notorious article by Hugh E. M. Stutfield entitled 'Tommyrotics', published in *Blackwood's Magazine* shortly after Wilde's imprisonment. Following Nordau both in his main line of argument and hysterical tone, the author denounced the dangers of a new literature variously identified with decadence, aestheticism, new hedonism, and anarchistic socialism, calling for a public 'boycott [of] morbid and nasty books and plays' and appealing to the police to put an end to their circulation.[58] Egerton's translation of *Young Ofeg's Ditties* (which he described as a series of 'confused and idiotic bubblings' fuelled by Nietzsche's egomania) was one of the books Stutfiled singled out for special vituperation as having outdone Ibsen

[53] [Anon.], [Double review of *Discords* and *Young Ofeg's Ditties*], *Saturday Review*, 30 Mar. 1895, 416–417 (417).

[54] Hansson to Egerton, 25 Feb. 1895, National Library of Ireland, MS 10946 (17) ('Måtte boken förarga').

[55] [Anon.], 'Young Ofeg's Ditties', *Bookman*, 48 (Sept. 1895), 172.

[56] [Anon.], 'Sounding Brass and Tinkling Symbols', *Daily Chronicle*, 6 May 1895, 3.

[57] [Anon.], 'Translations', *The Athenæum*, 415.

[58] Hugh E. M. Stutfield, 'Tommyrotics', *Blackwood's Edinburgh Magazine*, 157 (June 1895), 833–845 (844).

in stoking up social revolt.[59] Swedish author, German philosopher, and English translator were bundled together as conspiring against the moral health of English readers: 'the "triumphant doctrine of the ego," which Miss George Egerton finds so comforting, appears to be the theory of a German imbecile who, after several temporary detentions, was permanently confined in a lunatic asylum'.[60]

What is particularly revealing about Stutfield's attack is the way in which he presented degenerate modern literature and what he called 'decadentism' as foreign phenomena, rooted on the Continent—mainly in France but, as we have seen, also in Germany and Scandinavia—and consistently described their British exponents as 'debased admirers' and 'imitators'.[61] In the eyes of this critic, Egerton's practice of blurring the line between creative literature and translation (he also saw a straightforward continuum between *Young Ofeg's Ditties* and *Discords*) was not only sloppy but politically calculated to weaken the moral fibre of English readers. Stutfield's politics are clear enough: in his paranoid vision, the responsibility for importing these dangerous foreign tastes and ideas rested with a small number of individuals, such as Egerton and Wilde, who sought to undermine a healthy, native English literary tradition. Stutfield's real target, in other words, was literary cosmopolitanism. Worried by the free circulation of literature across borders, he wanted to launch a nationalist reaction that erected strong and secure boundaries around English, policed by critics who upheld the moral values of the nation and, when necessary, by the intervention of state censorship. His attack was a direct rebuff to the opening toward world literature that, as we have seen in the Wilde chapter, had been gathering momentum in Britain since the late 1880s. In his view, the penetration of foreign literature was a form of invasion that tested the limits of Victorian liberalism, and called for a policy of cultural self-defence: 'Ours is a free country, no doubt, but the claim for liberty to disseminate morbid abomination among the public ought not to be entertained for a moment.'[62] By a similar logic, the cosmopolitan writer is equated with the anarchist—the other invisible enemy of the nation in the popular imagination of the *fin de siècle*: 'The one works with the quill, the other with the bomb; and the quill is the more dangerous weapon of the two.'[63] What is more, women writers and readers seemed to Stutfield especially liable to spread noxious foreign literature: the gendered cosmopolitanism represented by Egerton therefore became a particularly strong social and political threat.

Hysterical though it undoubtedly was, 'Tommyrotics' is representative of a soaring nationalism that took hold of public discourse at this point.[64] Hansson had hoped that his book would have a wide resonance in England and that his

[59]   Ibid. 838 n. 2.      [60]   Ibid. 838.      [61]   Ibid. 841, 838.      [62]   Ibid. 844.
[63]   Ibid. 841.
[64]   Cf. the anonymous attack on Wilde in the *Daily Telegraph* discussed in Chapter 1, at n. 97.

poetry would work as something 'not altogether foreign' to English readers.[65] In the event, it was precisely its foreignness that attracted hostile attention. As a result, Hansson started to worry that the negative English reviews—notably the attack and parody in the *Daily Chronicle*—were reaching back to Sweden, where they could do further damage to his already precarious reputation.[66] Egerton too, despite being almost universally praised as a translator, clearly felt that, given the change of atmosphere that followed the Wilde trials, this was not the right time to try and feed more Hansson to a hostile British public. She therefore scrapped a plan to bring out a translation of his collection of essays *Tolkare och siare* (Interpreter and Seer), which she had announced in her introduction to *Young Ofeg's Ditties* and seems to have nearly completed in the months following the publication of that book.[67] Egerton was exasperated by the xenophobic reactions to *Young Ofeg's Ditties*, which embittered her sense of marginalization and made her wish for an impossible alternative identity outside of her mother tongue. As she wrote to John Lane, 'I would never write another word in English if I could write in any other language.'[68] Yet she must also have realized that translation was more needed than ever in post-Wilde Britain, where the rise of literary nationalism risked stifling writers' freedom. In September of that same year she therefore announced to Lane that she had revised her translation of Knut Hamsun's 'celebrated novel' *Hunger* and was having it type-written, with a view to publication.[69] Together with *Young Ofeg's Ditties*, *Hunger* was to be her second major intervention into the cultural politics of translation of the English *fin de siècle*.

### Translation as Cosmopolitan Intertextuality

The events relating to the 'Englishing' of *Hunger* have been lucidly analysed by Tore Rem.[70] After keeping the manuscript for over a year, despite Egerton's continuous pressure, Lane finally turned it down, no doubt because he was worried that the enterprise would be detrimental both in financial and reputational terms. After another rejection by Grant Richards, Egerton eventually turned to Leonard Smithers, who brought out *Hunger* in 1899. Smithers, whom Wilde described as 'the most learned erotomaniac in Europe',[71] ran a double line in

---

[65] Hansson to Egerton, 25 Feb. 1895, National Library of Ireland, MS 10946 (17) ('icke alldeles främmande').
[66] See his letter to Egerton, 29 May 1895, National Library of Ireland, MS 10946 (17).
[67] See Egerton's postcard to John Lane, 1 Aug. 1895, Egerton Correspondence, Clark Library, box 7, folder 71.
[68] Egerton to Lane, 13 Mar. 1895, Egerton Correspondence, Clark Library, box 7, folder 58.
[69] Egerton to Lane, 5 Sept. 1895, Egerton Correspondence, Clark Library, box 7, folder 72.
[70] Tore Rem, 'The Englishing of *Hunger*: Knut Hamsun, George Egerton and Leonard Smithers', in Tysdahl et al., eds, *English and Nordic Modernisms*, 61–76.
[71] Wilde to Reginald Turner, 10 Aug. [1897], in *Complete Letters*, 924.

advanced literature and pornography, which he published under the imprint of the Erotika Biblion Society. After the debacle of the Wilde trials, which caused Lane to become much more cautious in his choice of authors, Smithers was the most risk-prone publisher in London, and the one that more than any other continued to represent the 'foreign' literary sensibility denounced by Stutfield and critics of the nationalist ilk. He published the short-lived cosmopolitan literary magazine *Savoy* (1896), and his authors included Arthur Symons, Beardsley, and the disgraced Wilde, whose *Ballad of Reading Gaol* (1898) was advertised at the back of *Hunger*. His foreign authors in translation were almost exclusively French and included Balzac, Choderlos de Laclos, and Stendhal. Egerton's translation of *Hunger* was the only Scandinavian title published by Smithers but it is worth noting that, like Ola Hansson's *Young Ofeg's Ditties*, the novel had recently drawn attention to itself in France: the French translation of *Hunger* that came out in 1895 was, in all likelihood, what motivated Egerton to return to her unfinished draft and make her unsuccessful approach to Lane.[72]

Like all Smithers's books, *Hunger* circulated within a small but influential subculture linked to decadent, symbolist, and cosmopolitan milieus. Wilde, who read it in France after his release from prison, fancied that William T. Horton's cover illustration, which featured a haggard-looking young man meant to evoke the book's starving protagonist, bore a resemblance to the English decadent poet Ernest Dowson, one of Smithers's authors who was then living in Paris under financial hardship.[73] As it happened, Egerton had her own reservations about the book's cover, thinking that it did not reflect the 'modernity' of the novel, and had vainly tried to persuade Smithers to change it.[74] Whether we take it, like Wilde, as a meta-commentary on English decadence or as pioneering modernism, Egerton's translation of *Hunger* became connected with a decadent-leaning English literary avant-garde just as *Young Ofeg's Ditties* had been four years earlier, partly by association with Smithers, partly due to Egerton's own reputation. This, as Rem notes, constitutes a pecularity of Hamsun's English reception, as in Scandinavian literary histories Hamsun, unlike Hansson, is not associated with decadence, but rather tends to be read as an individualist who worked outside literary currents.[75]

Once again Egerton reclaimed her critical ownership of the foreign text in a short 'prefatory note'. Ironically, given the fact that *Hunger* would come to be recognized as a classic of world literature, Egerton appeared more nervous in her advocacy of Hamsun than in her introduction to *Young Ofeg's Ditties*, almost asking the reader to make allowances for the fact that *Hunger* was Hamsun's first attempt at a novel. No doubt this was in response to the changed cultural climate

---

[72] Knut Hamsun, *La Faim*, tr. Edmond Bayle (Paris: Langen, 1895).
[73] Wilde to Leonard Smithers [6 June 1899], in *Complete Letters*, 1151.
[74] Egerton to Smithers, 20 Apr. 1899, Bright Papers, Princeton, box 2, folder 18.
[75] Rem, 'Englishing of *Hunger*', 72.

that had compelled her to seek a somewhat shady publisher (Smithers went bankrupt only a few months after the publication of *Hunger*). Introducing his work in English for the first time, she wanted to give an impression of Hamsun as a difficult author who had 'something alike magnetic and repellent' and whose rewards were therefore at first hard to see.[76] It is possible that Egerton's brief portrait entailed a projection of her own difficult personal relationship with Hamsun, fictionalized in 'Now Spring has Come'. In any case, she drew particular attention to two features which she believed to be the main characteristics of Hamsun's work: his interest in psychology, which made him 'a master at probing into the unexplored crannies in the human soul, the mysterious territory of uncontrollable, half-conscious impulses' (p. viii); and his aestheticism. She described him as a 'stylist' who had 'a superb contempt for everything that was not of aesthetic value in his own eyes' (p. vi) and an almost Parnassian ability to treat language as a 'plastic material' (p. vii). By focusing on these features, Egerton brought Hamsun close to her own early work in *Keynotes*, which, it is worth remembering, was dedicated to him, and to that of Ola Hansson, which she had brought to the English public years earlier. It is as if Egerton wanted to show that the three authors had all this time been working together across space and languages in pursuit of a common literary ideal that translation now made apparent. The more so since Egerton emphasized Hamsun's own commitment to cosmopolitanism, citing a Norwegian critic's view that his work had introduced an American note new to Norwegian literature. This time, though, Egerton was more guarded about translation, repeating twice within a short space that, in the case of Hamsun, the style of the original must necessarily be 'sacrificed' (pp. vii, ix), thus drawing attention to the loss of artistic content in her English version.

Reviewers readily seized on Egerton's sense of insecurity. One critic accused the translation of being 'unidiomatic', regretting the fact that Egerton 'should write English which never fails to remind us that it is only a translation'.[77] Another critic went the opposite way, arguing that 'her individuality is so strong that she has made it felt even in a translation'.[78] It is easy to see how *Hunger* should have confused turn-of-the-century English critics: reading Egerton's translation today, it is still striking how starkly modernist it is in its staccato effect full of sudden shifts of perspective. Egerton's translation also abounded in the abrupt shifts in tense that were such a recognizable characteristic of her own style ever since *Keynotes*, together with the use of parataxis and plunges into individual consciousness that produced the 'smudge' parodied by *Punch*. Once again, as in the

[76] Egerton, 'Prefatory Note', in Knut Hamsun, *Hunger*, tr. George Egerton (London: Smithers, 1899), pp. v–x (p. v). Subsequent references will be given in the text.
[77] [Anon.], [Review of Knut Hamsun, *Hunger*], *Literature*, 5 (15 July 1899), 54.
[78] [Anon.], [Review of Knut Hamsun, *Hunger*], *Black and White*, 19 Aug. 1899, 242.

case of *Young Ofeg's Ditties*, translation could be seen retrospectively to provide an 'original' for Egerton's fiction.

In her translation, Egerton did not excise content that could be found offensive on sexual or religious grounds, in contrast to standard practices of bowdlerization adopted by other late Victorian women translators (e.g. Georgina Harding's contemporaneous translations of D'Annunzio).[79] The English press was quick to note that, of course, and to link it with Egerton's own transgressive reputation. In a review that overplayed Hamsun's naturalism, the critic of the *Academy* called the book 'a fragment of life itself, hacked apart and flung at the reader all raw, bleeding, crude, and amorphous'.[80] The most interesting part of the review concerns the literary relations between England and Norway:

> The translator says that *Hunger* made a sensation in Christiania. We can believe it. [*the critic then cites as proof the narrator's near-seduction scene of the mysterious Ylajali*] Not many London publishers would have passed such a scene. Yet London will probably not experience the slightest sensation over *Hunger*. At once less keen for novelty, and more secure in its critical poise, London will accept *Hunger* with a cold, inimical calm. For the unlettered will ignore it, and the lettered will perceive that, though it may be surgery, it is not fiction.[81]

In order to dismiss the book, the reviewer set up a dichotomy between metropolitan London and the peripheral Scandinavian capital, where the reading public was allegedly less literate and altogether less modern, and therefore eager to mop up what London viewed as ineffectual or passé. If diagnosing the modernism of *Hunger* as old-fashioned was an evident blunder, it did however prove true that the novel was not widely noted in the English press, where it attracted fewer reviews than *Young Ofeg's Ditties*. It is probably due to this lack of response that the translation of *Hunger* was Egerton's last major effort to bring modern Scandinavian authors to English readers.[82]

---

[79] Egerton's translation has withstood the passage of time very well and is more accurate than its first follower, Robert Bly's American translation of 1967. The most recent translator of *Hunger*, Sverre Lyngstad, has accused Egerton of expurgating the text in order to comply with 'the Victorian censor that must have been operating at the back of her mind'; 'Translator's Trap: Knut Hamsun's *Hunger* in English', in Knut Hamsun, *Hunger*, tr. Sverre Lyngstad (Edinburgh and London: Canongate, 2001), 223–241 (223). However, this claim has been rebutted by Rem, 'Englishing of *Hunger*', 69.

[80] [Anon.], [Review of Knut Hamsun, *Hunger*], *The Academy*, 56 (24 June 1899), 682–683 (682).

[81] Ibid. 682–683.

[82] Egerton would return to translation later in her career, when she became a translator and adapter of French boulevard theatre using contacts procured by her second husband, Golding Bright, who was often in France on business: these included Henry Bernstein's *The Whirlwind* (*La Rafale*, 1905, tr. 1910); and *The Attack* (*L'Asssaut*, 1912, tr. 1912), both of which attracted some success in the 1910s, and Pierre Loti and Judith Gautier's Chinese play *The Daughter of Heaven* (*La fille du ciel*, 1911, tr. 1912).

Yet, the translations of Hansson and Hamsun were important turning points in Egerton's career that cannot be divorced from her fiction if we are to gain a full understanding of her work and public reputation. Soon after finishing her translation of *Young Ofeg's Ditties*, Egerton told John Lane that Ola Hansson got 'at fibres in [her] as no one else'.[83] This striking expression conveys the sense of intimacy that translation enabled Egerton to achieve with Scandinavian writers—a bodily and almost erotic experience that had a stimulating effect on her as an author. For Egerton, translation was not confined to the act of rendering the foreign text into English: it became a continuous process of close engagement that spilled into her own creative works and fed and shaped the very fibres—to redeploy her organic metaphor—of her writing. If *Keynotes* and *Discords* were profoundly influenced by Hamsun, whose novel she had started to translate before embarking on her own fiction, *Fantasias* (1898) bore the unmistakable mark of *Young Ofeg's Ditties*: within this collection of allegorical tales, 'The Futile Quest' in particular details a spiritual journey similar to that of Hansson's protagonist, describing the impulse that drives the dreamer to 'the world outside' and 'the unknown.'[84] Two years later, as we have seen, the uncollected 'A Christmas Idyl' went back to her relationship with Hamsun, staging a romance between a returning Norwegian emigrant and a translator. A similar erotic transposition of the author–translator relationship took place again the following year in *Rosa Amorosa* (1901), Egerton's autobiographical book of love letters to a Norwegian man, whose title evidently pays homage to Hansson's *Sensitiva Amorosa*. Earlier she had also borrowed the title of one of Hamsun's novels in her short story 'Pan' in *Symphonies* (1897), as if to underline their shared views on the social hypocrisy of civilization.[85] In the course of this long public dialogue with Hansson and Hamsun, Egerton's role of translator morphed into that of imitator, advocate, critic, ally, and rewriter. When we reinsert the translations alongside the 'English' writings on which critics habitually focus in their discussions of Egerton, we can see that her work in the 1890s is in fact a layered oeuvre, in which she switched between translation and fiction. In so doing, she also erased the distance between the two, blurring foreign original and domestic copy into a form of cosmopolitan intertextuality.

Hansson and Hamsun got at the 'fibres' of Egerton's subjectivity as reader and author in many ways. But perhaps what drew her most to these two Scandinavian writers was that both, in their different manners, kept going back to the themes of homelessness and exile, wondering and travel, that were also, as we have seen, such an important part of her own work and identity. Hamsun's exploration of the

[83] Egerton to Lane, 24 Dec. 1894, Egerton Correspondence, Clark Library, box 7, folder 40.
[84] Egerton, *Fantasias* (London and New York: John Lane, 1898), 81.
[85] Fjågesund sees a parallel use of the Pan myth in Hamsun's *Pan* and Egerton's 'The Regeneration of Two' in *Discords*; Fjågesund, 'Knut Hamsun and George Egerton', 49. He also argues that the character of Kamma in Hamsun's *Mysteries* is based on Egerton (44).

psychology of the foreigner and outsider in his novels *Mysterier* (1892) and *Pan* (1894) anticipated Egerton's fictions of cosmopolitan mobility analysed earlier in this chapter. While Hansson's insistence in his letters on his alienation from the Swedish literary establishment enabled Egerton to view her own perceived marginality to English literary taste as a sign of distinction. The same sense of dislocation was also shared by Hamsun who, following the publication of *Hunger*, spent several years in self-imposed exile in Paris, where, as a French reviewer put it, he found 'a haven of work and solitude' that protected him from the 'calumnies' of Norwegian critics.[86] Indeed, *Hunger*'s portrayal of the writer as a social outcast caught in an almost existential struggle with the bourgeois press provided a fictional mirror for Egerton's own situation in literary London. The parallel would hardly have escaped Egerton, especially at the time that Lane kept her manuscript for over a year, dithering over whether he wanted to commit to publication. Egerton's correspondence with John Lane, preserved in the William Andrews Clark Memorial Library, is full of poignant and sometimes ironic echoes of the humiliating relationship between Hamsun's fictional protagonist and his newspaper editor in Christiania—Egerton constantly complaining about her financial hardships and staining her letters with tears.

Writing under the influence of Nietzsche, both Hansson and Hamsun compounded their views on cosmopolitanism with a staunch idealistic belief in individualism and an attack on the materialism of modern society. In his early account of his experiences in America (1889), which Egerton knew and judged 'wrong-headed',[87] Hamsun linked the difficult integration of non-Anglo-Saxon immigrants with America's hostility towards foreign literature, notably Zola. He noted the paradox that the country with the 'greatest crossing of cosmopolitan elements' should also be the one that was culturally most closed to what went on outside its borders.[88] His position was conflicted. While he attacked American patriotism and xenophobia, he also exposed his own racial prejudices: Hamsun shared degeneration theorists' fear that miscegenation would pose a threat to the cultural vitality of the nation. It is a well-known fact that in the twentieth century he would get closer and closer to nationalist thought, eventually embracing Nazi ideology. Indeed, the author of *Hunger*, who first kindled Egerton's enthusiasm for Scandinavian literature, would one day be courted and celebrated by the Führer himself as a model of pure Germanic values.[89] Hansson's literary

---

[86] Henri Albert, 'Les Letters Scandinaves: Knut Hamsun', *Revue blanche*, 8 (1895), 188–190 (189) ('Paris lui est devenu contre les calomnies un refuge de travail et de solitude').

[87] Egerton, 'Prefatory Note', in *Hunger*, p. v.

[88] Knut Hamsun, *Fra det moderne Amerikas Aandsliv* (Copenhagen: Philipsen, 1899), 22 ('Det er forbeholdt Amerika, hvor der er større Krydsning af kosmopolitiske Elementer end i noget andet Land i Verden, at planmæssig holde sig borte fra Udenverdenens modern Kulturstrømninger').

[89] See Tore Rem, *Knut Hamsun: Rejsen til Hitler* (Oslo: Cappelen Damm, 2014); and Peter Sjølyst-Jackson, *Troubling Legacies: Migration, Modernism, and Fascism in the Case of Knut Hamsun* (London and New York: Continuum, 2010). Sjølyst-Jackson stresses the importance of the early experience of

cosmopolitanism, too, eventually shaded into right-wing politics: writing outside his native Sweden, his works fed into the growing movement of pan-Germanism, a transnational ideology that in fact reinforced nationalism and exclusion, and showed marked anti-Semitic tendencies.[90] In this sense his evolution was similar to that of Jean Moréas, discussed earlier in relation to Wilde, who went from the heart of cosmopolitan Parisian symbolism to founding the nationalist *école romane*. The Italian Gabriele D'Annunzio followed the same trajectory from decadent cosmopolitanism to extreme nationalism, his celebration of Latin culture and Italian identity becoming for the Italian Fascists what Hamsun's work was for the Nazis. It is clear that Egerton was heavily drawn towards the culture of the Germanic North of Europe and waxed lyrical about spiritual rebirth against the backdrop of an unspoilt Northern landscape. Yet, perverted though she judged the urban and materialist orientation of American and British societies, she did not seek a spiritual alternative in idealized visions of ethnic purity. Her close alliance with Scandinavian authors did not translate into ethnocentric nationalism, just as her sceptical stance towards Ireland prevented her from embracing unproblematically the Celtic element that Ola Hansson judged so pronounced in her work.

## The Scandinavian Field

Egerton's championing of Hamsun was vindicated when he was awarded the Nobel Prize for Literature in 1920. The prize, which followed the publication of *Growth of the Soil* (*Markens Grøde*, 1917), sealed Hamsun's reputation as a world author and caused an immediate demand for more English translations—nothing had appeared since Egerton's *Hunger* apart from a belated 1914 version of his relatively minor novel *Shallow Soil* (*Ny Jord*, 1893) by C. C. Hyllested. Now *Hunger* was reissued on both sides of the Atlantic with an additional translator's note in which Egerton congratulated herself on having been 'somewhat of a seer' when she introduced Hamsun to English readers in the 1890s.[91] Hamsun's international success in the 1920s triggered a delayed English reception of *Hunger* at the time when the home-grown experimental modernism of Joyce and Woolf created a more hospitable context for its challenging style. Egerton's feeling of anachronism in relation to her fateful anticipation of psychoanalysis—'I came too soon'—would certainly also apply to her translations.

migration in Hamsun's works and provides an analysis of Hamsun's use of chilling racist arguments in *From the Cultural Life of Modern America*.
  [90]  See Niemirowski, *Ola Hansson in Berlin*, 84–129.
  [91]  Egerton, 'Translator's Note', in Hamsun, *Hunger*, tr. George Egerton (London: Duckworth, 1921), pp. v–x (p. v).

If we view Egerton's mediation of Scandinavian literature from the larger transnational perspective of the 'united literary field' or world literary space described by Casanova,[92] we can read the friction between Egerton and her English critics as a struggle over the symbolic capital associated with literary modernity. When the *Academy* reviewer dismissed *Hunger* as provincial and passé in 1899, s/he chastised the translator for importing out-of-date goods, as it were, and implicitly reasserted the superiority of a larger metropolitan literary culture (England or, even, the English-speaking world) over an allegedly provincial one (Norway). The award of the Nobel Prize to Hamsun—the ultimate symbolic consecration in world-literary terms—validated Egerton's hunch that the clock of modernity needed to be reset: Scandinavia was, in fact, 'ahead' of London in the *fin de siècle*. Throughout the 1890s, Egerton worked hard to promote the smaller Scandinavian literatures into the English-speaking world, contributing to a global process of resettlement of Scandinavia within world literary geography that took place at this time.

In order to gain a proper understanding of Egerton's unique intervention, it is necessary to consider the state of Scandinavian literature—and in particular Norwegian literature—in England in the 1890s. In her classic epistolary Scandinavian travelogue cited earlier, Mary Wollstonecraft described the Norwegians as a people with little 'taste for literature', who were just then 'arriving at an epoch which precedes the introduction of the arts and the sciences'.[93] This was 1796, a time in which Norway, in a political union with Denmark, still did not possess a university of its own and its de facto cultural capital was Copenhagen. Half a century later, in 1840, the English outlook on the country did not seem to have changed much: in a sociological study, Cambridge scholar and Norwegian enthusiast R. G. Latham complained that Norwegian civilization was 'exceedingly underrated' and protested that the Norwegians wished 'to be known as something better than hardy peasants and hospitable mountaineers', stressing the similarities between Christiania and London or Paris for an audience that he clearly deemed predisposed to think otherwise.[94] By the end of the century, however, the international literary reputation of Scandinavia, and Norway in particular, had undergone a radical change. If, in Britain, Bernard Shaw sounded tentative when, in 1889, he described the Norwegians as 'commencing to be thought of as a people with a vast modern literature', in France Maurice Barrès unhesitatingly singled out Ibsen and Scandinavian drama among the most powerful foreign influences in the cosmopolitan reorientation of French literary taste.[95]

---

[92] Casanova, *World Republic of Letters*, 103.
[93] Mary Wollstonecraft, *Letters Written in Sweden, Norway, and Denmark*, ed. Tone Brekke and Jon Mee (Oxford and New York: Oxford University Press, 2009), 42.
[94] R. G. Latham, *Norway and the Norwegians*, 2 vols (London: Bentley, 1840), i. 1, 2.
[95] George Bernard Shaw, 'The Performance of Grieg's *Peer Gynt* in London', *Dagbladet* (18 Mar. 1899), repr. in *Shaw's Music: The Complete Musical Criticism*, ed. Dan H. Laurence, 3 vols

What caused this change in perception was the so-called modern breakthrough ('det moderne gennembrud'), an expression used by the Danish critic Georg Brandes to refer to the double process of internationalization and modernization that he wanted Scandinavian literature to undergo. In a series of influential works and notably in his lectures collected as *Main Currents in Nineteenth-Century Literature* (*Hovedstrømninger i det nittende Aarhundredes Litteratur*, 1872–90), later translated into several European languages, Brandes denounced the provincialism of Danish and Scandinavian literature and exhorted his contemporaries to open up to influences from abroad. Brandes set the example by producing translations, networking with foreign authors, and writing for the international press. Through all these activities he emerged as one of the most cosmopolitan writers of the century since Goethe. His work had two connected aims: to make foreign literatures and ideas current in Scandinavia (for instance by promoting Nietzsche's philosophy) and, at the same time, to make modern Scandinavian authors known abroad.[96] In other words, Brandes pushed Scandinavian literature to enter the global networks of confrontation and exchange to which the larger nations had traditionally had easier access, and to participate fully in international literary modernity. Following Goethe, Brandes saw the arrival of world literature as an inevitability. However, he also conceded that the end of the nineteenth century was witnessing a sharp increase in national feeling that posed a setback to Goethe's cosmopolitan ideal.[97]

The mobility and visibility of Scandinavian authors that Brandes yearned for became a reality in the last years of the nineteenth century. In the cases of Ola Hansson and Hamsun, this was, in the first instance, the result of domestic conflict: both fled the pressures of hostile criticism in their native countries and relocated to more metropolitan settings in Berlin and Paris. Brandes himself went into a self-imposed exile in Berlin (1877–83), alienated by nationalist and anti-Semitic reactions to his work. The problem for these polyglot and internationally

---

(London: Max Reinhardt, Bodley Head, 1981), i. 582; and Barrès, 'La Querelle des nationalistes et des cosmo-polites', 1.

[96] See Svend Eric Larsen, 'Georg Brandes: The Telescope of Comparative Literature', in Theo D'haen, David Damrosch, and Djelal Kadir, eds, *The Routledge Companion to World Literature* (London and New York: Routledge, 2012), 21–31; and Peter Madsen, 'World Literature and World Thoughts: Brandes/Auerbach', in Christopher Prendergast, ed., *Debating World Literature* (London and New York: Verso, 2004), 54–75. Brandes started writing about Nietzsche as early as 1889. His advocacy of the German philosopher brought him into conflict with Ola Hansson, who as we have seen was another prominent Scandinavian Nietzsche enthusiast. Brandes would later accuse Hansson of plagiarism. See Borland, *Nietzsche's Influence on Swedish Literature*, 58; and Niemirowski, *Ola Hansson in Berlin*, 54.

[97] Georg Brandes, 'World Literature', in Theo D'haen, César Domínguez, and Mads Rosendhal Thomsen, eds, *World Literature: A Reader* (London and New York: Routledge, 2013), 24–27. The essay was originally published in both Danish and German as 'Verdensliteratur'/'Weltliteratur' (1899). Original quotations are from Georg Brandes, 'Verdensliteratur', in *Samlede Skrifter*, 18 vols (Copenhagen: Gyldendal, 1899–1910), xii: *Tænker om Liv og Kunst. Politik og Nationalitet. Nogle Taler. Ungdomsvers. Slutningsord. Register* (1902), 23–28.

successful Scandinavian authors (and their critics) became how to negotiate their double identities as, at the same time, cosmopolitan and national voices: in order to be successful internationally, they had to retain the expression of a local, Nordic character that was prized by cosmopolitan foreign readers. Brandes captured this double perspective in an essay on world literature (1899), where he argued that '[t]he world literature of the future will become all the more captivating the more the mark of the national appears in it'.[98] No one exemplified this dynamic better than Ibsen: starting from the 1880s, his dramas were welcomed into cosmopolitan literary circles all over Europe precisely because they were perceived to bear the strong national mark that Brandes talked about, projecting Norway onto the international stage. As Narve Fulsås and Tore Rem have argued, Ibsen's phenomenal success showed that the supposedly provincial identity of Scandinavian writers could be turned into a vantage position.[99] Indeed, following Ibsen, 'peripheral' Scandinavia more generally became central to debates over world literature and literary cosmopolitanism in the *fin de siècle*. We have already seen the important role played by Scandinavian drama in the *querelle* between cosmopolitans and nationalists started by Barrès. In an 1894 review of a French translation of modern Scandinavian short stories (including works by Hamsun and Ola Hansson), the critic Léon Bazalgette went even further by claiming that modern Scandinavian translations were hastening the arrival of the *'universal world literature* predicted by Goethe'.[100]

In Britain too the modern breakthrough produced a sense of excitement around Scandinavian literatures as relative newcomers on the international scene, coupled with the problem of how exactly to understand their modernity. It is worth remembering that, in Britain at least, the Scandinavian languages were not taught in institutions of learning and knowledge of them among the general public was exceedingly rare. Brandes himself recognized minority language as a serious hindrance to the international reputation of Scandinavian writers.[101] Neither were there systematic library holdings of literature produced in the Nordic countries after the Viking age; and an attempt to set up an English Scandinavian Society in 1875 was short-lived.[102] In these circumstances, the

---

[98] Brandes, 'World Literature', 27 ('Fremtidens Verdensliteratur vil blive des mere fængslende, jo stærkere det nationale Præg fremtræder i den', 28).

[99] Narve Fulsås and Tore Rem, *Ibsen, Scandinavia, and the Making of a World Drama* (Cambridge and New York: Cambridge University Press, 2018), esp. 7–8 and 237–238. Cf. also Toril Moi, *Henrik Ibsen and the Birth of Modernism: Art, Theatre, Philosophy* (Oxford: Oxford University Press, 2006), esp. 37–66.

[100] '[L]a *littérature universelle* prédite par Goethe commence à s'ordonner et à prendre corps, embrassant les *littératures nationales* fraternellement unies sur son vaste sein.' Léon Bazalgette, 'Nouvelles Scandinaves, traduites par Jean de Néthy', *L'Ermitage*, 8 (Aug. 1894), 136–137 (136). As we have seen, de Néthy was Egerton's French counterpart in promoting Scandinavian authors.

[101] Brandes, 'World Literature', 25.

[102] See Brian W. Downs, 'Anglo-Norwegian Literary Relations 1867–1900', *Modern Language Review*, 47.4 (1952), 449–494 (471–472).

British public had to rely on a small number of key mediators or experts who effectively secured a monopoly on the field.

The most important figure was Edmund Gosse, who in the 1870s, in parallel with Brandes's writings on the modern breakthrough, brought out a series of pioneering periodical articles collected in *Studies in the Literature of Northern Europe* (1879), dedicated to Brandes, in which he set out to introduce 'a new literature' to English readers.[103] Gosse was clearly inspired by Brandes's comparative method. His ultimate aim in making Nordic literature known at home was that English literature should also be viewed and studied as inextricably embedded in a web of world literature—which for him meant European literature—within which the literatures of the European North were in close communion. Gosse's greatest achievement in the book, however, was his 'discovery' of Ibsen, who was essentially unknown in Britain in the 1870s and whom he introduced alongside Bjørnson, in a detailed essay, as the foremost Norwegian living writer and a 'modern European'.[104] In the following decade Ibsen would eclipse Bjørnson (whose works were extensively translated into English in the 1870s and 1880s), becoming the most important phenomenon in nineteenth-century Anglo-Scandinavian literary relations. Ibsen's growing reputation was aided by William Archer's competent translations, a series of controversial productions (the single first performance of *Ghosts* at the Royalty Theatre, London, on 13 March 1891 caused particular outrage), and the support of leading critics including, beside the ubiquitous Gosse, Havelock Ellis, Arthur Symons, and George Bernard Shaw. While Bjørnson, whom a contemporary critic described as the 'Muscular Christian' of Norway,[105] tended to appeal to a more conservative taste, Ibsen, as Shaw showed, split the English critical establishment, half of which hailed him as a moral force, the other half as unwholesome and even obscene.[106]

In the introduction to a landmark edition of three of Ibsen's social dramas in translations by Archer and Eleanor Marx, Havelock Ellis traced the emergence of Scandinavia into world literature. According to Ellis, the current reputation of the Scandinavian countries should be compared to that of early nineteenth-century Germany, home to languages that foreigners regarded as 'little more than barbarous' and to peoples that appeared 'innocent

---

[103] Edmund Gosse, *Studies in the Literature of Northern Europe* (London: Kegan Paul, 1879), p. vii. Gosse's definition of 'Northern Europe' comprised Holland as well as Scandinavia. For Gosse as 'imperial mediator' of Ibsen, see Fulsås and Rem, *Ibsen, Scandinavia, World Drama*, 142–144.

[104] Gosse, *Studies in the Literature of Northern Europe*, 36.

[105] C. F. Keary, *Norway and the Norwegians* (London: Percival, 1892), 363.

[106] George Bernard Shaw, *The Quintessence of Ibsenism* (London: Walter Scott, 1891), 5. For analyses of the British reception of Ibsen's dramas within a comparative framework see Philip Ross Bullock, 'Ibsen on the London Stage: Independent Theatre as Transnational Space', *Forum for Modern Language Studies*, 53.3 (2017), 360–370; Casanova, 'The Ibsen Battle'; Fulsås and Rem, *Ibsen, Scandinavia, World Drama*, 159–174 and *passim*; and Kirsten Shepherd-Barr, *Ibsen and Early Modernist Theatre, 1890–1900* (Westport, CT: Greenwood Press, 1997).

and primitive'.[107] Yet, as was the case with Germany in the age of romanticism, this seeming primitivism hid an 'intense literary activity' (p. vii) that
promised to bring a wave of renewal to the metropolitan centres of European
letters, notably, in this case, London. The peripheral Scandinavian nations and
especially Norway—the country that more than the others marked 'the
extreme Northern limit of European civilisation' (p. viii)—were the place
where literature had best come to terms with 'the burning questions of the
modern world' (p. vii). According to Ellis, Ibsen was the figurehead of literary
Scandinavia because he was the most representative of its extreme contrasts:
he revealed the clash between the primitivism of the Norwegian landscape and
its pockets of extreme literary modernity; he was the embodied paradox of the
'European significance' (p. xiv) of the individual writer operating within the
still 'provincial' (p. xii) culture of his native country. Emerging from this
dynamic world, Ibsen should therefore be seen, in Ellis's view, as a late-
century Goethe—a figure that succeed in making a quintessentially local
literature part of the international exchange of ideas, promoting the flow of
a new world literature in the sense that Brandes would discuss the following
year. 'Ibsenism', as later defined by Shaw, thus became one of the transnational
literary 'isms' of the *fin de siècle* alongside naturalism, symbolism, individualism, cosmopolitanism, etc. In the eyes of hostile critics, all of these movements
blurred into a dangerous literary internationalism that blended avant-garde
artistic practices and progressive social ideas. This is why Nordau in
*Degeneration* could bracket together Ibsen and Nietzsche as 'egomaniacs',
despite the glaring differences between the two writers.[108]

When Egerton made her debut with *Keynotes*, the English literary perception of
Scandinavia was dominated by the controversial presence of Ibsen.[109] As a writer
with an obvious double interest in modern Norway and in women, she was
naturally associated with Ibsenism: Ibsen's name was frequently invoked in
early reviews of her work and of course featured prominently in the famous
*Punch* caricature of Egerton as 'Donna Quixote', where an open book in the
foreground simply marked 'Ibsen' sent out an unmistakable signal. Yet, Ibsen's
visibility in the public sphere also eclipsed Egerton's true alliances which, as we
have seen, were in fact chiefly with Hamsun, the writer who was busy, as she put it,
'behead[ing] the literary idols of the day'—that is, attacking those very writers,
including Ibsen, who had brought Scandinavian literature to international

---

[107] Havelock Ellis, 'Preface', in Henrik Ibsen, *The Pillars of Society and Other Plays*, tr. William
Archer, Henrietta Frances Lord, and Eleanor Marx-Aveling (London: Walter Scott; New York:
Whittaker, 1888), pp. vi–xxx (p. vi). Subsequent references will be made in the text.

[108] 'As in Ibsen ego-mania has found its poet, so in Nietzsche it has found its philosopher.' Max
Nordau, *Degeneration* [tr. anon.] (London: Heinemann, 1895), 415.

[109] Fulsås and Rem date the period of the British 'Ibsen battles' between 1889 and 1893; Fulsås and
Rem, *Ibsen, Scandinavia, World Drama*, 145.

prominence.[110] With her first-hand experience of modern Norway and her rare ability to read Norwegian—and, through Norwegian, Danish and Swedish— Egerton introduced to Britain new influences and ideas which none of her reviewers were knowledgeable enough to spot.

By promoting Hamsun and Ola Hansson, Egerton headed a new phase of the English assimilation of Scandinavian literary modernity, no longer associated with social realism, but rather with individualism, decadence, Nietzsche's philosophy, interests in the unconscious and abnormal psychology, as well as, crucially, a new form of literary cosmopolitanism. Faced with change, those same English pioneers of the Scandinavian modern breakthrough who had endorsed its challenges to middle-class taste could now act as severe gatekeepers. In the late 1890s Gosse, for instance, complained that the 'tendency among the youngest [Norwegian] writers is, so far as I can judge, rather too cosmopolitan for home consumption', blaming Hamsun and naturalist feminist writer Amalie Skram for what he called a 'literature of disease and horror' that perverted the mission of realism to be true to life.[111] Implicitly contrasting their work with Ibsen's and the first generation of modern-breakthrough literature, he regretted that the palette of these new writers was 'wilfully loaded with unnatural colours' and called the new school 'another ill-result of that condensation of European streams of style into one artificial channel which is so much to be deplored'.[112] Gosse wanted Norway to remain provincial in the eyes of English readers. His attempt to disentangle a pure, as it were, national Norwegian literature from the cosmopolitan tendencies of world literature was aimed at protecting the version of Scandinavian modernity that he had helped to promote, which by the end of the century was in increasing danger of looking outdated. We have already seen how Egerton's translation of Ola Hansson came under attack in the British press by critics who repressed cosmopolitan literary tendencies by means of degeneration theory. But even a champion of modern Nordic literature like the critic and translator Robert Nisbet Bain—who was the author of a biography of Hans Christian Andersen and, as we will see in Chapter 4, wrote a series of well-informed articles on 'Contemporary Scandinavian Belles Lettres' for the international journal *Cosmopolis*—denounced Ola Hansson's work as morbid, hysterical, and stylistically overdone, and showing the 'nastiness' of French naturalism and the 'erotomania characteristic of all Decadents'. Almost in the same breath, he also castigated Hamsun's 'very pronounced taste for nastiness'.[113] Gosse's article appeared just a few months before Egerton's translation of *Hunger*; Nisbet Bain's the year after her translation of *Young Ofeg's Ditties*. It

---

[110] Egerton, 'Prefatory Note', in Knut Hamsun, *Hunger*, p. v.
[111] Edmund Gosse, 'Norway Revisited', *North American Review*, 167 (Nov. 1898), 534–542 (539).
[112] Ibid. 540.
[113] Robert Nisbet Bain, 'Contemporary Scandinavian Belles Lettres', *Cosmopolis*, 4.11 (Nov. 1896), 355–369 (359, 360).

seems that the writers Egerton chose went against the grain of what English critics expected from Scandinavia at this point.

In order to promote her favourite Scandinavian writers, Egerton used the same formula of national character/international reputation that had aided the internationalization of Scandinavian literature in the modern breakthrough. Ola Hansson was thus the embodiment of his native Swedish province of Skåne—a periphery within a periphery—and, at the same time, he was the darling of metropolitan Europeans who read his works in translation and awaited with eagerness 'every new issue of his pen'.[114] Hamsun was the Norwegian 'son of the people' whose work was discussed by the most advanced critics in Germany and France.[115] The same was true of the Norwegian writer Arne Garborg, about whom Egerton wrote a short but pioneering English article in 1898—one of her extremely rare forays into criticism. Garborg was well-known in Norway as a champion of *landsmål*, the emerging literary language based on a fusion of Norwegian dialects, which would later be called *nynorsk* or 'new Norwegian'. Egerton wanted English readers to appreciate Garborg, whose works were not yet translated into English (like Hamsun, he would become more widely known in the 1920s), as 'the most national' of contemporary Norwegian writers and 'the least influenced by foreign thoughts and tendencies'.[116] She described him as a 'peasant's son [...] in whom the hold of the soil has never slackened' and his writings as 'ore, dug out of the very brown heart of Norwegian soil'.[117] And yet, this very same symbolism of the soil that Egerton used to characterize Garborg's uniquely Norwegian identity also, at the same time, put Garborg within a very international canon of naturalist fiction that comprised the foundational Zola and counted exponents pretty much in every corner of Europe. Indeed, on the strength of the *fin-de-siècle* international vogue for naturalist fiction, Garborg's writings had by this point already been extensively translated into German and met with a positive reception in German-speaking countries, largely thanks to the support of Ola Hansson.[118] What interested Egerton in the case of Garborg's international success was that what appeared to be most quintessentially Norwegian was also eminently translatable—or, to put it in socio-economic terms, that the national was an international currency in the European literary market of the 1890s. Moreover, Egerton suggested that writers came to be, as she put it, 'most national' not by spontaneously absorbing the cultural inheritance of their people or by shutting themselves off from foreign influences; rather, only by a careful study of 'every phase of European culture' did authors learn how to distil and project their native culture onto the international stage.[119] Garborg's work reflected this natural

---

[114] Egerton, 'Introductory Note', in Hansson, *Young Ofeg's Ditties*, 9.
[115] Egerton, 'Prefatory Note', in Hamsun, *Hunger*, p. vi.
[116] Egerton, 'Arne Garborg', *Outlook*, 2.34 (24 Sept. 1898), 240–241 (240).    [117] Ibid. 241.
[118] See Schoolfield, *Baedeker of Decadence*, 88–89; and Niemirowski, *Ola Hansson in Berlin*, 184.
[119] Egerton, 'Arne Garborg', 240.

alignment of the national and the cosmopolitan: he was equally committed to capturing the authenticity and uniqueness of Norwegian life, for instance in his poem cycle *Haugtussa* (1895) that Egerton singled out for special praise, and to translating foreign works into 'new Norwegian', including classics such as Homer and Shakespeare as well as Ola Hansson's book on Nietzsche. By the same token, Egerton refused to see a stark opposition between a vital national literature close to the soil and a cosmopolitan literary culture that thrived on international exchanges and collaborations.

As all these examples show, Egerton was deeply aware that what constituted modern Scandinavian literature in the eyes of the wider world was not determined domestically (that is, inside Scandinavia) but abroad, especially in Paris and Berlin. She therefore kept an eye on what went on in those capitals by reading foreign literary periodicals such as the *Revue blanche*,[120] and using her Scandinavian contacts in Germany, like Ola Hansson, to gain knowledge about new trends and opinions. In the *fin de siècle*, France and Germany both experienced a notable influx of Scandinavian literature, but they received it in very different ways. As we have seen, in France, the reception of Scandinavian drama (notably Ibsen) got caught up in the debate on literary cosmopolitanism, where, alongside Russian fiction, it was routinely mentioned as one the most prominent foreign imports: using a telling territorial metaphor, Barrès spoke of the growing 'empire of Ibsen and Dostoevsky' in order to convey how the popularity of these authors encroached on and almost threatened domestic literary culture.[121] While French readers were attracted by the North's radical difference from the Latin heart of French culture and by its invigorating 'barbarism', German readers were drawn to Scandinavia by its deep-set similarity to their native culture, its shared Germanic core. In the wake of the Franco-Prussian war, Scandinavian realist and naturalist writers in particular represented a Germanic substitute for decadent French naturalism, capable of bringing the Germans back to their racial roots, paradoxically better preserved in Scandinavia than in Germany itself. This alliance of Scandinavian modernity and German nationalism could take on sinister undertones, as in Leo Berg's *Henrik Ibsen und das Germanenthum* (1887), which portrayed Ibsen's (allegedly) fundamentally Germanic spirit as a healthy alternative to French and Jewish influences. In any case, thanks to the great popularity and impact of Scandinavian literature, most Scandinavian authors, including Hamsun and Ola Hansson, used Germany as their first stepping-stone to the international arena.

Britain was caught between the French and German models. Through the second half of the nineteenth century, a steady growth in English translations of

---

[120] Egerton to Lane, 29 Jan. 1894, Egerton Correspondence, Clark Library, box 7, folder 16.

[121] Barrès, 'La Querelle des nationalistes et des cosmopolites', 1 ('l'empire d'Ibsen et de Dostoïevski').

medieval Nordic literature, such as the sagas, had promoted a rediscovery of Germanic roots, which some commentators regarded as a more vigorous model than the Mediterranean, decadent, and potentially queer, classical civilization.[122] And yet, when it came to translating modern Scandinavian literature, Britain was far less receptive than Germany. William Archer denounced this situation in the mid 1880s, with particular reference to Norwegian authors: he compared unfavourably the few and unsatisfactory translations that were available in Britain to Germany's 'excellent translations' of the great modern Norwegians (the so-called *fire store*, or 'four greats'—Ibsen, Bjørnson, Alexander Kielland, and Jonas Lie—but also Garborg). He blamed this situation on the intrinsic hybridity of the English language: 'Our Latinised idiom has not, on the whole, the receptivity and pliancy which render German translations at once so faithful and so readable, and I confess that such English renderings as I have seen of modern Norwegian books seem to me to give but a mediocre reflex of the original.'[123] Whether or not we accept this linguistic argument, which flirts with ideas of essentialism and racial purity, Archer was right in exposing the inadequacies of some English translations, notably of Ibsen. He was also right in pointing to a broader resistance, within English literary culture, to domesticating Scandinavian literature on the German model. For all the fact that the social realism of Ibsen and the modern breakthrough could be grafted onto the existing English realist tradition, most English responses tended to follow the French, emphasizing the exoticism of the North and its sense of foreignness to a more metropolitan English culture, as we have seen in Ellis's introduction to Ibsen's social dramas. It is telling that, with both of her major Scandinavian translations, Egerton used France as a barometer of English taste, presenting writers who had recently been introduced to French audiences. She also stressed the cosmopolitan credentials of her authors, alongside their national significance, in order to make it clear that what Scandinavia could offer English readers was not a way backwards into mythicized notions of a shared pre-Norman past, but forwards into an interconnected, internationalist literary modernity.

---

[122] For data on Old Norse translation see Andrew Wawn, 'Early Literature of the North', in *The Oxford History of Literary Translation in English*, 5 vols (Oxford and New York: Oxford University Press, 2005–), iv: *1790–1900*, ed. Peter France and Kenneth Haynes (2006), 274–285. For modern Scandinavian translation in this period, see Robert E. Bjork, 'A Bibliography of Modern Scandinavian Literature (Excluding H. C. Andersen) in English Translation, 1533–1900, and listed by Translator', *Scandinavian Studies*, 77.1 (2005), 105–42. For decadent or queer British classicism see, among others, Linda Dowling, *Hellenism and Homosexuality in Victorian Oxford* (Ithaca, NY: Cornell University Press, 1994); Stefano Evangelista, *British Aestheticism and Ancient Greece: Hellenism, Reception, Gods in Exile* (Basingstoke and New York: Palgrave Macmillan, 2009); Jennifer Ingleheart, *Ancient Rome and the Construction of Modern Homosexual Identities* (Oxford and New York: Oxford University Press, 2015); and Daniel Orrells, *Classical Culture and Modern Masculinity* (Oxford and New York: Oxford University Press, 2011).

[123] William Archer, 'Norway Today', *Fortnightly Review*, 38 (Sept. 1885), 413–425 (425).

## The Northern Light Series

What English readers now needed, given the growing interest in Scandinavian writing, was a specialized forum—a journal or publisher that would systematically promote the literature of modern Scandinavia. Around the mid-1890s, after the appearance of her translation of Ola Hansson, Egerton and John Lane worked together to create such a forum within the Bodley Head. After the commercial success of *Keynotes*, Lane had launched the Keynote Series, which was intended to showcase daring new fiction that, like Egerton's, took radical views on contemporary social issues, particularly to do with gender.[124] Building on that successful model, he now wanted to start a new series dedicated to translations of modern Scandinavian literature, which was to be called the Northern Light series. The title 'Northern Light' cleverly captured the double attraction of Scandinavia for English readers: it simultaneously conjured the exoticism of the North and its promise to provide enlightenment on modern questions, for instance, about the relations between the sexes. Unfortunately, the plan never materialized, but the Bodley Head archives in the Harry Ransom Center reveal a spate of activity in which the principal actors, besides Lane and Egerton, were Richard Le Gallienne's Danish wife Julie Nørregaard and Hermione Ramsden, an otherwise rather obscure figure associated with the Bodley Head (she also published an article in the *Yellow Book*) who was able to translate from German as well as the Scandinavian languages. Egerton, Nørregaard, and Ramsden were all well plugged into the Scandinavian scene: they scouted potential new titles for Lane and reviewed manuscripts submitted for the series. In their different ways—for they clearly had different tastes and priorities—they all belonged to an international network of culturally mobile women whose important, but materially ephemeral, work of mediation gets all too easily erased from literary history: anonymous reports and translations leave a very faint trace. It was characteristic of Lane to rely on an entirely female network of collaborators, whose professional opinions he trusted, whom he probably did not pay very well, and whom he put in competition with each other. So, for instance, Egerton wrote the reader's report for an anthology of Norwegian short stories translated by Ramsden (comprising tales by Magdalene Thoresen, Jonas Lie, Hans Aanrud, and Kristian Elster), which she recommended for publication, approving both of the 'judicious' introduction and the fluent translation;[125] while Ramsden acted as the press's reader for Egerton's translation of *Hunger*, which she thought a 'coarse' book, clearly influencing Lane's decision

---

[124] For the importance of the Keynote Series alongside the *Yellow Book*, also published by Lane, in promoting decadence in Britain, see Kirsten MacLeod, *Fictions of British Decadence: High Art, Popular Writing, and the Fin de Siècle* (Basingstoke and New York: Palgrave Macmillan, 2006), 116–134.

[125] Egerton, reader's report in a letter to Lane, 20 Sept. 1895, Egerton Correspondence, Clark Library, box 7, folder 75.

to turn it down.[126] She later also spoke publicly against the Scandinavian mysticism favoured by Egerton, comparing the impression of reading Ola Hansson's *Young Ofeg's Ditties* to 'a severe attack of delirium'.[127] Both Egerton and Ramsden wrote lukewarm reports for an English translation of Selma Lagerlöf's *Gösta Berlings Saga* (1891), now considered a modern classic of Swedish literature, that Lane also discarded—the book was eventually published by Chapman and Hall in a partial translation by Lillie Tudeer in 1898.[128] In fact, the Northern Light series appears to have failed to take off partly because Lane's aides were all too keen to guard their separate territories.

Lane was wary of translation, which was financially riskier to publish than original English fiction. Even the commercially strong Keynote Series had included only one foreign title, Dostoevsky's *Poor Folk*, translated by Lena Milman (1894). Yet he was clearly prepared to make an exception for Scandinavia at this point, thinking that he would find interested readers and, crucially, a valuable market. Always hyper-aware of her publisher's eye for profit, Egerton tried to persuade Lane to branch out more into translation by pointing out that his London competitor William Heinemann was making a feature of 'books from foreign sources, and not I fancy from love of letters solely or philanthropical motives'.[129] The venture to which Egerton refers here is Heinemann's International Library, which was launched in 1890 under the general editorship of Edmund Gosse. In the editor's note to the first volume, which was in fact a Scandinavian novel—Elizabeth Carmichael's translation of Bjørnson's *In God's Way* (*Paa Guds Veje*, 1889)—Gosse explained that the purpose of the series was to correct what he regarded as the English public's complete ignorance of contemporary European fiction (he thought that the one exception was the Russian novel, of which the English had lately learnt to become 'partly aware'). Writing for a domestic public that was increasingly well-versed in foreign travel while remaining distinctly insular in literary taste, he described the series as a 'guide to the inner geography of Europe'. The guiding principle of selection was, however, disappointingly conservative: Gosse was to include works that were 'amusing' and 'wholesome', while promising 'to discard all which may justly give offence'.[130] Heinemann's International Library thus endeavoured to present a domesticated foreignness that would not challenge readers at home (Gosse seems to have been particularly keen to steer clear of naturalism).

---

[126] Hermione Ramsden to Lane, 29 Oct. [1895], Harry Ransom Center, The University of Texas at Austin, John Lane Company Records, 14.5. Hereafter Lane Company Records, Harry Ransom Center.

[127] Hermione Ramsden, 'The New Mysticism in Scandinavia', *Nineteenth Century*, 47 (Feb. 1900), 279–296 (289).

[128] For the reports see, respectively, Egerton Correspondence, Clark Library, box 7, folder 75; and Ramsden to Lane, 9 Oct. [1895], Lane Company Records, Harry Ransom Center.

[129] Egerton to Lane, 5 Nov. 1894, Egerton Correspondence, Clark Library, box 7, folder 36.

[130] Gosse, 'Editor's Note', in Bjørnsterne Bjørnson, *In God's Way*, tr. Elizabeth Carmichael (London: Heinemann, 1890), n. p.

Competitively priced at 3s. 6d. and reassuringly bland in intent, the series was a commercial success, reaching its twentieth volume by 1897. Unsurprisingly given Gosse's interests, Scandinavian titles featured prominently: beside the opening volume, the series also included Bjørnson's *The Heritage of the Kurts* (*Det flager i Byen og paa Havnen*, 1884, tr. 1892), and Lie's *The Commodore's Daughters* (*Kommandørens Døtre*, 1886, tr. 1892) and *Niobe* (1893, tr. 1897). Gosse's personal commitment to making Bjørnson known in Britain is also reflected in his thirteen-volume edition of *The Novels of Bjørnstjerne Bjørnson*, which started appearing in 1895, also with Heinemann.

Issued by the most avant-garde publisher of literary London and overseen by Egerton, who was always likely to spark controversy, the Northern Light series was to capitalize on the appetite for modern Scandinavian literature without pandering to the little-Englandism exemplified by Gosse. It was moreover to package Scandinavian modernity in the beautiful editions for which Lane was famous, which emphasized the preciousness of the contents (Ola Hansson, for one, was greatly impressed by the physical appearance of the Bodley Head books[131]). The Bodley Head's and Egerton's associations with progressive gender politics and international decadence, recently amplified by the reception of her translation of *Young Ofeg's Ditties*, were both the selling points and the bane of the projected series, which crumbled into dust when Lane became much more guarded as a result of the Wilde trials and the reactionary nationalistic backlash that followed them. Yet, the aborted Northern Light series not only remains an important episode in Egerton's often invisible career as mediator of Scandinavian literature into the English-speaking world, but it also enables us to piece back together an international network of women writers in which Egerton played a central role.

It was no coincidence, and a testimony to Lane's commitment to Egerton, that the series was to be launched by Ramsden's translation of Laura Marholm Hansson's *Das Buch der Frauen: Zeitpsychologische Porträts* (1895), rendered into English as *Modern Women* (1896), a book that in the event came out as part of Lane's general list.[132] Laura Marholm was married to Ola Hansson and, like her husband, was an important link between Scandinavia and Germany. She translated both Hansson and Brandes into German, but her main commitment was to creating an international perspective on the woman question that was then bubbling up in different countries, and which she saw as the most urgent problem in modern literature. In 1890 Marholm wrote an important series of articles on women in Scandinavian poetry for the German magazine *Freie Bühne für modernes Leben*, in which she analysed different types of female psychology introduced by Ibsen, Bjørnson, and Strindberg. This early work already displayed the

---

[131] Hansson to Egerton, 28 Dec. 1894, National Library of Ireland, MS 10946 (17).
[132] See Ramsden to Lane, 18 Dec. [1895], John Lane Company Records 14.5, Harry Ransom Center.

characteristic brand of Marholm's problematic feminism—or anti-feminism according to some of her early critics[133]—in that she reproached Scandinavian women writers for dilettantism and accused them of wanting to assume the male role. In *Das Buch der Frauen/Modern Women* she developed this hard-core essentialist line, rejecting the arguments for the social emancipation of women put forward by the male writers of the modern breakthrough. As Ramsden put it in her introduction: 'According to Ibsen, a woman is first of all a human being, and then a woman; [Marholm] places the woman first, the human being last. Bjørnson believes that an intellectually developed woman with a life-work can get on very well by herself; Laura Marholm maintains that, apart from man, a woman is nothing.'[134]

Marholm drew six critical portraits of modern women from different nations who had gained international distinction in different artistic and scientific fields. One of her portraits, 'Neurotic Keynotes', focused on Egerton, whom Marholm used to illustrate her own essentialist beliefs. *Keynotes* was, according to Marholm, 'the book of a devoted wife, who would be inseparable from her husband if only he were not so tiresome, and dull, and stupid' (p. 63); even Egerton's prose exhibited the indelible mark of gender, 'spring[ing] backwards and forwards as restlessly as a nervous little woman at her toilet' (p. 62). Marholm read *Keynotes* as a vindication of woman's deep-seated natural desires and as a cry against the weakness of modern men. Its great achievement was that it did not seek to imitate men's literature and its point of view and, for that reason, was 'quite independent of any previous work; it is simply full of a woman's individuality' (p. 68). Marholm moreover emphasized Egerton's cosmopolitan identity, asserting that her real strength came from the way she straddled the Celtic and English 'races' (p. 90), writing *across* the two cultures but never from within.

Marholm's take on feminism was certainly eccentric and her praise of Egerton as a 'neurotic writer' (p. 84) was not without a double edge. The views of this opponent of female suffrage and universal education were likewise not always easy to reconcile with Egerton's equally complex attitude towards women's emancipation. Yet Marholm clearly thought that the significance of Egerton's work was such that it deserved to reach beyond the boundaries of English, and she even went to the trouble of adding fresh material on Egerton in a revised edition of *Das Buch der Frauen* that came out after the publication of *Discords* (this was the version that provided the source text for the English translation). In any case, the outcome of *Das Buch der Frauen*, which attracted considerable attention not only in Germany but throughout Europe, was that Egerton now found herself projected onto the international stage as the 'English' representative of a transnational

---

[133] Cf. Hedwig Dohm, *Die Antifeministen: Ein Buch der Verteidigung* (Berlin: Dümmlers, 1902).

[134] Laura Marholm, *Modern Women*, tr. Hermione Ramsden (London: Bodley Head; Boston: Roberts Brothers, 1896), p. vii. Subsequent references in the text.

network of talented women who worked across the arts, science, and politics. In *Modern Women*, Egerton figures as the peer of notable female personalities from across the Continent: the pioneering Russian-born scientist, author, and activist Sonia Kovalevsky, the first woman ever to have held a university professorship in mathematics; the Italian diva Eleonora Duse, then at the height of her international success; the Norwegian writer Amalie Skram, whose hard-edged naturalism troubled Gosse but whom Marholm singled out as the best among contemporary Scandinavian women writers; Marie Bashkirtseff, the French-based Russian artist whose diary—'a perfect gold mine for all that has to do with the psychology of young girls' (p. 149)—had caused an international sensation in the late 1880s; and Anne Charlotte Leffler, the chief Swedish exponent of women's rights. Marholm argued that all these women succeeded in their different fields of activity thanks to the way in which they embodied 'womanly feelings' (p. xiv), sometimes despite their efforts to repress them. On a meta level, Marholm showed that the category of 'woman' was a more powerful and meaningful marker of identity than nationality: what all these women also had in common with each other and with the polyglot Marholm was their cosmopolitan orientation, reflected in their shared ability to exist across languages and cultures. The book thus set up a tension between gender essentialism and cosmopolitanism: women, so essentialized and biologically determined in Marholm's view, were also capable of profiting most from uprooting themselves from home and the nation. In other words, Marholm suggested that their essential gender characteristics empowered women to embrace a cosmopolitan identity—a position that echoed the stance that Egerton put forward in her own stories.

Egerton, who got to know Marholm and her work during her epistolary exchange with Ola Hansson, facilitated the translation of *Modern Women*. She persuaded Lane to accept it on the grounds that it would boost her own reputation in Britain and hence, obviously, his sales: 'it may be worth your while to show what a foreign opinion of my book or myself as "Poetess of the neurotic" (the Lord save us!) is, and justify your publishing my things to those in England who rather resent it'.[135] Even if Egerton clearly thought that Marholm's portrait of her was sensationalist and possibly ill-judged, she saw that it was helping her work to gain the international reach she yearned for. Through Marholm, English readers would now be able to see that there was more to Egerton than fashionable smudge: her proper place was among a transnational intellectual elite of women 'of European note, and a modern note', as she again wrote to Lane.[136] After the publication of *Modern Women*, Marholm's work continued to attract attention in Britain, two more of her books appearing simultaneously in 1899 (one of them, *We Women and our Authors*, again with John Lane and in Ramsden's translation). These later

---

[135] Egerton to Lane, 5 Nov. 1894, Egerton Correspondence, Clark Library, box 7, folder 36.
[136] Ibid.

works radicalized the gender essentialism of *Modern Women*, leaning heavily on degeneration theory and denouncing the dangers of miscegenation with a single-minded conviction that borders on hysteria. As we have seen in the cases of Ola Hansson and Hamsun, for Marholm too cosmopolitanism, while attractive and even inevitable, also became a potential threat that unleashed racist and anti-Semitic language—she repeatedly claimed that the mixing of German and Jewish blood resulted in a weakening of healthy masculinity.[137]

The ties between Egerton, Ola Hansson, and Laura Marholm were lost in translation in the course of time, but to trace them again now is to recognize an active and powerful international network that spanned Scandinavia, Germany, and Britain. Thanks to their access to influential publishing outlets such as the German *Freie Bühne* and the Bodley Head, their joint efforts were crucial in creating the conditions for the international circulation of public and private writings about the woman question, decadence, anti-naturalism, Nietzsche's philosophy, and of course literary cosmopolitanism. The collaboration between Egerton and her Scandinavian contacts resulted in complex patterns of influence: just as Egerton imitated Ola Hansson, Marholm identified with Egerton, especially on the controversial question of the need to write frankly about female sexual libido, and took her as a literary model.[138] They also helped to promote each other's works internationally by means of criticism and translations. Egerton was able to offer Scandinavian authors the increasingly high cachet that Britain enjoyed on the world literary stage: Hansson, Marholm, and Hamsun were all keen to get translated into English in order to access a new global market for their works, which was different from Germany and rivalled France in terms of its size and prestige. At the same time her Scandinavian contacts facilitated the reception of Egerton's work outside English-speaking countries, benefiting from the growing visibility that Scandinavian literature enjoyed internationally: the popularity of the German translation of *Keynotes* by Adalbert von Hagen (*Grundtöne*, 1895) rode on the back of the country's interest in Scandinavian, as much as English, literature, going into three editions in its first year; while in Sweden, Marholm's *Modern Women* was brought out at the same time as the Swedish translation of Egerton's *Keynotes*, both published by Adolf Bonniers in 1895.

Unsurprisingly for someone who felt so alienated from the English public, Egerton set an enormous importance on her foreign translations and she followed the internationalization of her readership with great pride. As she wrote to Lane, 'My friends grow apace. This is perhaps the best of writing.'[139] She must have been especially pleased to receive a fan letter from New Zealand, in which a man named

---

[137] Laura Marholm, *The Psychology of Woman*, tr. Georgia A. Etchison (London: Grant Richards, 1899). There are many instances of this deeply troubling strain, e.g. 239, 243, and 245.
[138] See Ebba Witt-Brattström, *Dekadensens kön: Ola Hansson och Laura Marholm* (Stockholm: Norstedts, 2007), 282.
[139] Egerton to Lane, 19 Nov. 1894, Egerton Correspondence, Clark Library, box 7, folder 38.

W. F. Howlett told her of how he had read out *Keynotes*, translated into pidgin English, to Scandinavian immigrants in the settlement of Makaretu. Even with their sketchy command of English, the migrants were apparently 'much impressed. They thought that in some fashion Satan was made flesh & came to dwell among us.'[140] This glimpse of an unexpected colonial reading scene where *Keynotes* is used to bridge the cultural gap between Anglo-Saxon settlers and Scandinavian migrants is reminiscent of the well-known image of Wilde speaking of aestheticism to the miners in Leadville, Colorado, or Hearn's unrecorded conversations with farmers and fishermen in the impoverished districts of rural Japan. It shows how vernacular global encounters endowed metropolitan modern literature with new meanings and possibilities of expression. It also shows that, important though it is to understand how individual authors embodied, discussed, and put into practice the cosmopolitan ideal, we also need to go beyond the category of the author as it is traditionally viewed and constructed within the narrow prism of the nation. The remaining two chapters of the book therefore shift the focus onto how different kinds of networks reflected literary cosmopolitanism around the turn of the century, starting from an analysis of how cosmopolitanism became a specialized field within the periodical press.

---

[140] W. F. Howlett to Egerton, 22 Sept. 1895, Bright Papers, Princeton, box 1, folder 29.

# 4

# Controversies in the Periodical Press

## *Cosmopolitan* and *Cosmopolis*

> These journals, as they win an ever wider public, will contribute in the most effective way towards that universal world literature for which we are hoping.
>
> (Johann Wolfgang Goethe, 'Edinburgh Reviews')
>
> He had the real cosmopolitan spirit, the easy imagination of strangeness surmounted.
>
> (Henry James, 'Wolcott Balestier')

This book so far has focused on individual authors, examining how their identities, literary practices, and careers were shaped by the desire to reach beyond national cultures. In order to express their cosmopolitan orientation, Wilde, Hearn, and Egerton had to contend with the embodied reality of the periodical press, where many of their works appeared for the first—and sometimes the only—time, and from which, like many of their contemporaries, they derived a good deal of their income.[1] We have seen how Wilde positioned himself at the margins of English society in a series of interventions staged in the form of newspaper interviews and open letters, and how the reception of *Salomé* developed against the background of heated literary controversies over nationalism and cosmopolitanism in the French press. In a different context, the *Harper's Magazine*'s commission to travel to Japan completely changed Hearn's career; and his life-long collaborations with American periodicals enabled him to cultivate an English-speaking readership from across the world by showcasing some of the essays that would later make up his Japanese books. Egerton also used the periodical press to recalibrate public perceptions of her work and to construct herself as an expert on Scandinavian literature. As these examples show, the story of these authors' literary cosmopolitanism could be told again, differently and in illuminating ways, from the perspective of the magazines and newspapers with which they collaborated: the *Pall Mall Gazette*, *Woman's World*, *The Outlook*, the *Yellow Book*, *Universal Magazine*, the New Orleans *Times-Democrat*, and the

---

[1] Laurel Brake, *Subjugated Knowledges*; Josephine M. Guy and Ian Small, *Oscar Wilde's Profession*; Margaret D. Stetz, 'Publishing Industries and Practices', in Gail Marshall, ed., *The Cambridge Companion to the Fin de Siècle* (Cambridge and New York: Cambridge University Press, 2007), 113–130.

*Literary Cosmopolitanism in the English* Fin de Siècle: *Citizens of Nowhere*. Stefano Evangelista,
Oxford University Press. © Stefano Evangelista 2021. DOI: 10.1093/oso/9780198864240.003.0005

*Atlantic Monthly*, to name but the most important. Periodicals such as these provided a platform from which authors projected their cosmopolitan credentials and curated their public personae. Indeed, as a discursive phenomenon that bridges the aesthetic and social spheres, the literary cosmopolitanism analysed in this book could hardly have come into being without the material support of the periodical medium.

For the study of literary cosmopolitanism, the periodical press provides important material in two related ways. It makes available a rich archive of interventions in the public debate around literature and national identity—an archive that is the more useful precisely because of its potentially frustrating open-endedness. And, at the same time, it brings to light network-like structures that stretched across borders, enabling authors to operate internationally, for instance by reviewing foreign literatures or being reviewed or discussed by foreign critics, by circulating their work in translation, or simply by being published side by side with writers from different countries. Periodicals, in other words, created a dynamic international space within which literary culture appeared less coextensive than ever with national culture.[2]

In a classic historical study, Benedict Anderson observed that the press played a determining role in shaping the nation as 'an imagined political community'.[3] In particular, Anderson identified the defining periodicity of newspapers and reviews as creating an experience of simultaneity that was fundamental for developing a feeling of shared national identity among the reading public. While Anderson's argument remains powerful and persuasive, it is also the case that periodicals empowered readers to forge imaginary ties that went beyond the limits of the nation. Many quality nineteenth-century periodicals, in Britain and elsewhere, promoted an international outlook by publishing translations and setting up specific features dedicated to foreign news items and, crucially, foreign literatures.[4] Goethe's remark on periodicals' important contribution to world literature, quoted as an epigraph to this chapter, referred to two British journals—the *Edinburgh Review* (1802–1929) and the *Foreign Quarterly Review* (1827–46, then merged with the *Westminster Review*)—which, he believed, were making enormous progress in acquainting British readers with the literatures of other

---

[2] See Caroline Levine, 'From Nation to Network', *Victorian Studies*, 55.4 (2013), 647–666 (esp. 649). Levine expands her formalist theory of networks in *Forms: Whole, Rhythm, Hierarchy, Network* (Princeton: Princeton University Press, 2015), 112–131. Cf. also Birgit Van Puymbroeck, who, with reference to the interwar period, outlines the advantages of adopting the methodology of *histoire croisée* in studying international networking in the periodical press. Van Puymbroeck, '"The Age of Mistaken Nationalism": *Histoire Croisée*, Cross-National Exchange, and an Anglo-French Network of Periodicals', *Modern Language Review*, 107.3 (2012), 681–698.

[3] Benedict Anderson, *Imagined Communities*, 6.

[4] For a comparative assessment of British and French examples from the earlier part of the century, see Juliette Atkinson, 'Continental Currents: Paris and London', in Joanne Shattock, ed., *Journalism and the Periodical Press in Nineteenth-Century Britain* (Cambridge: Cambridge University Press, 2017), 224–244.

countries.[5] Circulating internationally, Goethe went on, such journals also made Germans aware of how the British viewed German literature, prompting further connections and stimulating new opinions. As the century drew towards its end, the global connectivity noted by Goethe increased further thanks to improved transport and communication technologies, which generated yet more opportunities to reorganize the periodical press and make it an even more effective medium of internationalization.

In the English-speaking world, this new international orientation of the *fin-de-siècle* 'industry' is best reflected in the monthly *Review of Reviews*, founded in 1890 by W. T. Stead, the former editor of the *Pall Mall Gazette*. Stead, who was a leading figure of turn-of-the-century journalism and a committed political activist, was deeply interested in international traffic and travel (he famously died in the sinking of the *Titanic*). The idea behind the journal, which Stead claimed to have had during a conversation with Tolstoy,[6] was that modern readers needed a guide to navigate the vast ocean of print that was now being produced each month, not only nationally but all over the world. The *Review of Reviews* aimed to provide English-speaking readers with an affordable and intelligent digest of the international press in the form of summarized articles, annotated lists and checklists, and even condensations of new international literature that would keep 'its salient features and best scenes intact'.[7] If each periodical can be understood as a network-like structure, the *Review of Reviews* was a meta-network that cemented the interdependence of the national presses. Its eclectic contents were selected by the interventionist editor, whose published 'Programme' for the review was to 'enable the busiest and poorest in the community to know the best thoughts of the wisest; to follow with intelligent interest the movement of contemporary history; and to understand something of the real character of the men and women who rank among the living forces of our time'.[8]

At the same time, however, the *Review of Reviews* also shows that the internationalism of periodical markets and technologies must not be too readily conflated with the liberal ideology of cosmopolitanism represented by Goethe. In the first issue, the editor's address 'To All English-Speaking Folk' stressed the democratizing ethos of the *Review of Reviews*, reflected in its affordable retail price of six pence (to put this into perspective: a copy of *The Times* sold for three pence

[5] Fritz Strich, *Goethe and World Literature*, 350 ('Diese Zeitschriften, wie sie sich nach und nach ein größeres Publikum gewinnen, werden zu einer gehofften allgemeinen Weltliteratur auf das wirksamste beitragen', 398–399).

[6] See J. O. Baylen, 'W. T. Stead as Publisher and Editor of the *Review of Reviews*', *Victorian Periodicals Review*, 12.2 (1979), 70–84 (71); also James Mussel, '*Review of Reviews* (1890–1936)', in Laurel Brake and Marysa Demoor, eds, *Dictionary of Nineteenth-Century Journalism* (Ghent: Academic Press; London: British Library, 2009), 537–538.

[7] [Anon.], 'Programme', *Review of Reviews*, 1.1 (Jan. 1890), 14. Condensed literature published by the journal included Tolstoy's *Kreutzer Sonata*, Mark Twain's *Connecticut Yankee*, and *The Journal of Marie Bashkirtseff*.

[8] Ibid.

in 1890). However, the journal was also perfectly clear about its belief in the right to global dominance of 'the English-speaking race', which the *Review of Reviews* would now help to fulfil its destiny. The journal aimed 'to promote by every means a fraternal union with the American Republic, to work for the Empire, to seek to strengthen it, to develop it, and when necessary to extend it'.[9] The *Review of Reviews* thus compounded internationalism with imperialism, in dialogue with contemporary ideas of an Imperial Federation, discussed in the Introduction, and Greater Britain. It is significant that the spiritual agent that held the journal's ideology together was Stead's evangelical Christianity, which was invoked repeatedly in the address 'To All English-Speaking Folk', rather than the Enlightenment ideal of world citizenship, which was not mentioned at all. This missionary championing of Anglo-Saxon civilization was fundamentally at odds with Kant's philosophical tradition, as much as with a liberal cosmopolitanism committed to diversity and what Appiah calls 'cultural hybridization'.[10]

We will come back to Stead in the course of this chapter and the next, which examines his important contribution to the Esperanto movement. For the moment, it is enough to note that in the *fin de siècle* the power of the periodical medium to question or affirm national identities was very much in the public eye. On 13 April 1895, a spoof advert in *Punch* publicized 'Le "Yellow Book"' as specializing in 'romans pour les anglophobes', ridiculing the cultural pretensions of the contributors and readers of this iconic periodical, which crystallized a distinctly English but also cosmopolitan brand of decadence (illustration 4.1). The mock cover illustration, featuring a Beardsley-esque androgynous caricature of the French Marianne and a John Bull Figure in a desert setting, refers to colonial disputes in Africa between the two European superpowers (the joke is that this is a special 'Africain' edition published under the 'imprint' of the French politicians Alexandre Ribot and Gabriel Hanotaux). What is most striking is the seamless way that the perceived cosmopolitanism of the *Yellow Book*—a journal, it is worth remembering, which did publish rare items in French but otherwise contained very few foreign authors, hardly any translations, and no political commentary— is projected into the political field of international relations, and associated with a betrayal of patriotism. The cosmopolitan love of strangers (here, the *Yellow Book*'s Francophilia) is turned into a sentiment of hatred, as the caricaturist perniciously ascribes to the *Yellow Book* the xenophobic rhetoric that was, in fact, a prerogative of *Punch*. As with the illustration of 'Britannia à la Beardsley' discussed in the Introduction, the aim of this caricature—published during the Wilde trials—was to discredit the progressive literary milieu that gravitated around John Lane (including, of course, Egerton) by depicting them outside of the national

---

[9] [Anon.], 'To All English-Speaking Folk', *Review of Reviews*, 1.1 (Jan. 1890), 15–20 (16).
[10] Appiah, 'Cosmopolitan Patriots', 619.

**Illustration 4.1** 'Le "Yellow Book" (Africain) Officiel', *Punch*, 13 April 1895. Punch Cartoon Library/TopFoto

consensus. Both caricatures provide a snapshot of a polarized literary culture, divided between groups with strong cosmopolitan and national allegiances, who are mistrustful of each other. In particular, the satire on 'Le "Yellow Book"' implies that the periodical medium should fulfil the specific responsibility of upholding national identity and national feeling.

This chapter focuses on two monthly journals launched at the *fin de siècle*. The American *Cosmopolitan* and the European *Cosmopolis* stood out for the way in which they staked an explicit claim to cosmopolitanism in their titles, packaging it as the subject interest of specialized reader groups.[11] Both journals presented cosmopolitanism as an inescapable condition of modernity and both defined themselves in relation to the shifting ideas and aspirations that cosmopolitanism embodied in this transitional period. They were, however, profoundly different

---

[11] For a list of other journals that referenced cosmopolitanism in their titles, see Agathocleous, *Urban Realism*, 55. These included *Philogene's Cosmopolitan Political and Statistical Review* (1839–60, London, weekly), *The Cosmopolitan Review* (1861, London, monthly), *The Cosmopolitan* (1865–76, London, New York, and Paris, weekly), and *The Cosmopolitan Critic and Controversialist* (1876–7, London, monthly and then quarterly).

journals in terms of look, editorial style, target readership, and marketing policies. *Cosmopolitan* was a richly illustrated, commercial, general-interest magazine addressed to a middle-class audience; it became increasingly sensationalist and fashion-oriented, and of course specifically targeted at a female market, in the course of its long and successful history that stretches uninterrupted into the twenty-first century. By contrast, *Cosmopolis* was a high-brow international venture that published literature, as well as cultural and political commentary, in three languages, and had a total lifespan of little less than three years. More than the work of any single author, *Cosmopolitan* and *Cosmopolis* expose the differences and dissonances in the discursive construction of literary cosmopolitanism—in particular, the tension between the politico-philosophical ideals of world citizenship inherited from the eighteenth century and filtered via Goethe's notion of world literature, and the fast-developing new understanding of cosmopolitanism inflected by consumer culture. In examining *Cosmopolitan* and *Cosmopolis*, the focus will therefore be on how cosmopolitan idealism interacted with the material reality of the *fin-de-siècle* periodical market: what was the relationship between literary cosmopolitanism and journalistic practices? How did periodicals shape the construction of literary cosmopolitanism in the public sphere? *Cosmopolitan* and *Cosmopolis* enable us to formulate answers to these questions while considering the complex positioning of a cosmopolitan English literary culture in relation to transatlantic and European space.

### *Cosmopolitan*: The University of Democracy

'The World is my Country and all Mankind are my Countrymen': in March 1886, the motto inscribed on the cover of the first number of *Cosmopolitan* was modelled on the slogan of the American abolitionist newspaper, *The Liberator*. The new magazine—a quality monthly published by Schlicht & Field in Rochester, New York—thus harked back to a distinctly American vision of world citizenship based on the civil rights movement.[12] Over the next few years, the changes to the cover design of *Cosmopolitan* reflected its search for a distinctive identity. The all-American iconography of the initial issues, which prominently featured the Statue of Liberty, gave way first to a stylized globe (the motto had disappeared and the contents list was moved inside), which, in its abstract simplicity, signalled a move away from the American focus and a turn towards a high-brow aesthetics. Then, after less than a year, came the blue and red cover which was to become the public face of *Cosmopolitan* into the twentieth century. Here, the abstracted globe was subsumed into a title design that was more redolent of the arts and crafts

---

[12] *The Liberator*, edited by William Lloyd Garrison, was first published on 1 Jan. 1831; its motto read 'Our country is the world—our countrymen are mankind'.

movement, revealing the stylish aspirations of the magazine. In practical terms, the most significant change in these early years occurred when John Brisben Walker took over as editor at the end of 1888. Historians of *Cosmopolitan* credit Walker with an ability to implement effective innovations, some of them borrowed from the more sensational world of newspaper publishing, and to take clever marketing decisions.[13] There is no doubt that his talent was behind the remarkable commercial success that *Cosmopolitan* experienced in the *fin de siècle*. By January 1893, Walker could claim to have increased the circulation from the estimated 25,000 at the time of his takeover to 150,000 copies, of which around 50,000 seem to have been destined for Britain.[14] Later that year the magazine, which by now had moved offices to New York and owned its own printing-house, decided to cut its already affordable price by half (to 12½ cents per month), which led to a further increase in its circulation to an estimated 200,000 by 1894.

These sales figures show that there was nothing experimental or niche about *Cosmopolitan*. The magazine explicitly aimed to appeal to a large family audience: a short editorial in the first number announced that it would contain 'the best, the liveliest, the most interesting, and the most valuable reading matter for all classes, that money can procure', with the aim of becoming 'indispensable to every household in the land'.[15] It proudly added that the articles would be 'short and bright, never long and tedious as is usually the case' and would comprise art and literature, as well as science, politics, and society. *Cosmopolitan* thus presented itself as exciting but safe, wide-ranging, concise, and affordable. Indeed, at $2.50 per year, *Cosmopolitan* certainly offered value for money, especially given its lavish use of high-quality illustrations that accompanied every article. The emphasis on the brevity of the articles, which would characterize the magazine all through its early decades, implied a target audience of busy practical people rather than literary intellectuals—or simply a new audience drawn from the increasingly large class of educated readers who were pressed for time. The formula of brevity and breadth was more than an editorial ploy aimed at stealing readers from established, traditional American periodicals such as *Harper's* and the *Atlantic Monthly*. It was at the heart of what being cosmopolitan, as understood by the magazine, was about: it embodied a vision of modernity shaped by the new speed of global transport and communications and informed by the

---

[13] James Landers, *The Improbable First Century of Cosmopolitan Magazine* (Columbia, MO, and London: University of Missouri Press, 2010), 38 and *passim*; and Sister Mary Damascene Brocky, 'A Study of Cosmopolitan Magazine, 1890–1900: Its Relation to the Literature of the Decade' (unpublished doctoral thesis, Notre Dame University, 1958).

[14] John Brisben Walker, 'The Making of an Illustrated Magazine', *Cosmopolitan*, 14.3 (Jan. 1893), 259–272 (259). The British circulation figure comes from a letter from William Dean Howells to Henry James, 23 Feb. 1892, cited in D. M. Rein, 'Howells and the *Cosmopolitan*', *American Literature*, 21.1 (1949), 49–55 (52).

[15] From an announcement on the inside of the front cover of the first issue, *Cosmopolitan*, 1.1 (Mar. 1886).

liberal ambition of extending world culture—the desire 'to be at the centre of the world', to quote Baudelaire's 'Painter of Modern Life'—beyond the elite.[16]

A survey of the contents of *Cosmopolitan* during the years of Walker's editorship (1888 to 1905) reveals an eclectic offering that ranged from literature to current affairs, foreign travel, exploration, and transport and communication technologies, especially developments in aerial navigation, which *Cosmopolitan* watched closely throughout the 1890s. In its coverage of foreign topics the magazine relied on a broad spectrum of experts that went from professional writers and journalists to former diplomats, politicians, and war correspondents. The latter partly explains why articles on military life became more and more frequent, and why these are only in apparent contrast with the ethos of peaceful relations ostensibly evoked by the magazine's title. With this varied coverage that stretched to almost every corner of the globe, *Cosmopolitan* addressed itself to a growing market of cultured readers with a *specialized* interest in the wider world— the contradiction in terms intuited by Baudelaire. Side by side with these cultural interests, the magazine gradually developed a focus on fashion and sophisticated modes of consumption. The reason for its success was that it presented this new 'cosmopolitan' lifestyle as within reach of its readers' aspirations, thanks to the ever-increasing power of American wealth. Celebrity was thus a frequent focus, with regular features, typically lead articles, on topics such as royals, actresses, and millionaires, accompanied by photographic illustrations and glamorous portraits on nearly every page. In the course of the 1890s, side-lining the radical and philosophical associations suggested by its first motto, *Cosmopolitan* did not simply reflect, but rather led the way in shaping the media construction of cosmopolitanism as a social identity—one that was increasingly feminized and linked to glamorous consumerism and *savoir faire*. This would become the linchpin of *Cosmopolitan*'s highly successful commercial brand in the twentieth century.

All through the period covered by this book, *Cosmopolitan* worked to redefine world citizenship as a social identity driven by materialistic desires that fed on global commerce. It is not surprising, therefore, that in 1893 the magazine offered detailed and lavishly illustrated coverage of the Chicago World's Columbian Exposition. This important symbolic event marked the 400th anniversary of Christopher Columbus's arrival on American soil and, at the same time, celebrated America's leading role in the modern global economy. *Cosmopolitan* capitalized on the symbolism of the World Fair: it dedicated to it an almost entire issue, breaking its policy of thematic eclecticism. Walker's enthusiastic opening editorial—another breach of customary practice—set the tone by hailing 'the vast change which this object lesson will make in the minds of the millions who visit it, broadening, opening, lighting up dark corners, bringing them in sympathy with

---

[16] Baudelaire, 'The Painter of Modern Life', 9 ('être au centre du monde', 352).

their fellow-men'.[17] Significantly, this lesson in cosmopolitan enlightenment now radiated from the heart of America, and not from old Europe. In the global village of the Chicago World Fair, as in all world exhibitions, visitors could become world citizens for one day for the cheap price of an admission ticket, admiring foreign goods and architectures in the various national pavilions, peering at strange people in purpose-built ethnological villages, tasting exotic foods. Looking back to the end of the nineteenth century from a Marxist perspective, Walter Benjamin famously criticized international exhibitions as 'places of pilgrimage to the commodity fetish': in his memorable formulation, by transforming commodities into an entertainment industry, international exhibitions eclipsed the real value of commercial objects, giving rise to a 'phantasmagoria of capitalist culture'.[18] Paraphrasing Benjamin, one could add that, at the same time, such exhibitions reduced the cosmopolitan diversity of world culture to a fetishism of cultural difference based on marketable goods. Emptied of the philosophical and cultural premises that constitute its spiritual soul, cosmopolitanism also becomes a phantasm when it is turned into a marketable experience.

There was none of this suspicion of the perverting power of capitalism in *Cosmopolitan*'s coverage of the Fair. Nor were there criticisms of the way in which international exhibitions empowered hosting countries in the developed West by projecting their political power around the world—an objection that was at the heart of an article by W. T. Stead, also printed in *Cosmopolitan*, on the Paris Exposition Universelle of 1900.[19] In *Cosmopolitan*, coverage of the Chicago World Fair was dominated by patriotic pride or even chauvinism—one contributor going as far as to claim that the Fair reflected 'the supremacy of the Anglo-Saxon race'.[20] Walker himself dubbed the Chicago Fair a 'University of Democracy': for him, the impressive neo-classical pavilions erected by the American government for the instruction of the people surpassed in magnificence the palaces that despots of past ages built for entirely egotistical ends.[21] The World Fair, therefore, provided Walker with a handy, transparent metaphor for what *Cosmopolitan* set out to do through the print medium: the magazine also aspired to be a university of democracy, where readers would imbibe a liberal humanism compounded with a sophisticated materialism that fed on global free trade. *Cosmopolitan* thus projected the phantasmagoric quality of global capitalism described by

---

[17] John Brisben Walker, 'Introduction: The World's College of Democracy', *Cosmopolitan*, 15.5 (Sept. 1893), 517–527 (517).

[18] Walter Benjamin, *The Arcades Project*, tr. Howard Eiland and Kevin McLaughlin (Cambridge, MA, and London: Harvard University Press, 2002), 21, 22. The original German is from Walter Benjamin, *Das Passagen-Werk*, in *Gesammelte Schriften*, ed. Rolf Tiedemann et al., 7 vols (Frankfurt a.M.: Suhrkamp, 1991), v: *Das Passagen-Werk*, ed. Rolf Tiedemann ('Weltausstellungen sind die Wallfahrtsstätten zum Fetisch Ware [ ... ] Phantasmagorie der kapitalistischen Kultur', 50, 51).

[19] W. T. Stead, 'The Paris Exposition', *Cosmopolitan*, 29.4 (Aug. 1900), 339–360 (357).

[20] John J. Ingalls, 'Lessons of the Fair', *Cosmopolitan*, 16.2 (Dec. 1893), 141–149 (147).

[21] Walker, 'World's College of Democracy', 524, 519.

Benjamin, packaging it in its illustrated articles. It entertained readers by creating for them a highly desirable virtual global space in which they experienced the world's different cultures in material terms, as 'object lessons', to use the editor's expression.

It would be unfair, however, to assume that its worldly materialism and the effort to appeal to a middle-class readership of would-be socialites and armchair travellers made *Cosmopolitan* incapable of taking socially progressive stances. Granted: *Cosmopolitan* hardly lived up to the socialist expectations raised by the new motto it adopted in 1892—'From every man according to his ability, to every man according to his needs'—which was taken from Marx's *Critique of the Gotha Programme* (*Kritik des Gothaer Programms*, 1875).[22] Nonetheless, throughout the 1890s, *Cosmopolitan* took its educational ambition extremely seriously. With its affordable price, the magazine aimed to bring a liberal education to those who did not have the resources to attend institutions of learning: the idea was that supplying such readers with high-quality but approachable discussions of a range of topics would help them build both their cultural knowledge and civic identities. Education and educational reform in America were also very much a focus of discussion, with more than 100 articles on these subjects during Walker's editorship.[23] Walker even hatched an ambitious plan to found his own university, the 'Cosmopolitan University', where teaching would be provided by correspondence free of charge.[24]

Another aspect of the magazine's social engagement was reflected in a number of articles that interrogated the history of abolition, examined current racial relations in the United States and elsewhere, or made efforts to represent the views of non-Anglo-Saxon immigrant communities. Particularly noteworthy in this respect was the early involvement of political activist Wong Chin Foo, a prominent member of the American Chinese community. Wong, who has been called 'an unsung hero in Chinese American history',[25] was expelled from China for political agitation. In the United States he started the weekly New York newspaper *Chinese America* (*Hua Mei Xin Bao*, 1883) and founded the first Chinese American voters association (1884); he was also a leading activist in the Chinese Equal Rights League set up to campaign for the repeal of the Chinese

[22] Karl Marx and Friedrich Engels, *Critique of the Gotha Programme* (London: Electric Book Co., 2001), 20.
[23] Landers, *Improbable First Century*, 80; Daniel A. Clark and Paul S. Boyer, *Creating the College Man: American Mass Magazines and Middle-Class Manhood, 1890–1915* (Madison, WI: University of Wisconsin Press, 2010), 52–53.
[24] [Anon.], 'A New University', *Cosmopolitan*, 23.5 (Sept. 1897), 463–464. Walker was the victim of his own success: the university became a practical impossibility because it attracted too many enrolments.
[25] Qingsong Zhang, 'The Origins of the Chinese Americanization Movement: Wong Chin Foo and the Chinese Equal Rights League', in K. Scott Wong and Sucheng Chan, eds, *Claiming America: Constructing Chinese American Identities during the Exclusion Era* (Philadelphia: Temple University Press, 1998), 41–63 (41).

Exclusion Act of 1882.[26] Shortly before starting his collaboration with *Cosmopolitan*, Wong had caused scandal with an article in the *North American Review* titled 'Why am I a Heathen', which denounced the hypocrisy of American Christians in their attacks on Chinese immigrant populations. The article provocatively ended by inviting Americans to 'come to Confucius' in order to improve their morals.[27] In *Cosmopolitan*, Wong contributed an article on the Chinese district in New York City and a serialized 'translation' of the Chinese historical novel *Wu Chih Tien, The Celestian Empress*, which was in fact a free adaptation or downright creation of Wong's.[28] Coming, as it did, just after his attack on the anti-Chinese bias of American Christians, Wong's involvement with *Cosmopolitan* demonstrates that the magazine was willing, especially in its early days, to provide a platform for progressive voices in the debate on ethnic diversity within American society. Most notably perhaps, in the pages of *Cosmopolitan*, Wong's double profile as (pseudo)translator and political activist connected two cosmopolitan identities that were otherwise seldom presented as contiguous: those of the migrant and of the literary mediator. The liberal ethos of the magazine was nowhere deployed more effectively than in creating a bridge between the socially abject experience of migration—in this case, the publicly vilified Chinese migration—and the position of cultural authority.

## A Flying Trip around the World

In its early years, under Walker's rule, *Cosmopolitan* was not strictly speaking a women's magazine. In fact, many items on sporting and military topics, among others, explicitly targeted a male readership. However, part of the early success of *Cosmopolitan* was due to the fact that it closely involved women in shaping the vision of cosmopolitanism that it projected: worthy items of domestic economy published in the first numbers soon gave way to more ambitious articles that glamorized women's position in society and showed them as empowered by knowledge, money, and fame. Crucially, *Cosmopolitan* also opened its doors to women as authors, that is, as active producers and not just consumers of culture

[26] Information on Wong Chin Foo comes from Judy Yung, Gordon H. Chang, and Him Mark Lai, eds, *Chinese American Voices: From the Gold Rush to the Present* (Berkeley and Los Angeles: University of California Press, 2006), 70. The Chinese Exclusion Act prohibited the immigration of Chinese workers for ten years and barred the Chinese from naturalization.

[27] Wong Chin Foo, 'Why I am a Heathen', *North American Review*, 145 (Aug. 1887), 169–179 (179).

[28] Wong Chin Foo, 'The Chinese in New York', *Cosmopolitan*, 5.4 (Aug. 1888), 297–311; *Wu Chih Tien, The Celestian Empress* was serialized in *Cosmopolitan* in 1889. For Wong's role as translator/author and the novel's subversion of 'Golden Age assumptions about history, race, and masculinity', see Hsuan L. Hsu, 'A Connecticut Yankee in the Court of Wu Chih Tien: Mark Twain and Wong Chin Foo', *Common-Place*, 2.1 (2010) <www.common-place-archives.org/vol-11/no-01/hsu> [accessed 17 May 2019].

and news. Emblematic in this respect was the contribution of Elizabeth Bisland, whom we have already encountered as Hearn's early editor and biographer. The connection between Hearn and Bisland went back to 1880s New Orleans, where both worked for the local press. Bisland was an admirer of Hearn's work and the two formed a close, flirtatious literary friendship—one of his first tokens was to lend her the copy of Gautier's poems that had travelled with him around the world.[29] She was later to celebrate the bohemian side of Hearn as a sworn enemy of American 'provincial propriety' in her posthumous edition of his Flaubert translation.[30] In the late 1880s, some time before Hearn left for Japan, Bisland moved to New York, where she quickly made a name for herself as a journalist and society hostess. This double profile was reflected in the work that she undertook for *Cosmopolitan* as literary author and editor. Bisland used her influence to secure two articles by Hearn on the West Indies.[31] In general, in terms of both content and style, she lifted the level of the magazine's journalism by introducing a vein of aestheticism—something that she also shared with Hearn—which is particularly in evidence in her early articles on American artists' circles.[32]

Bisland's defining contribution, however, occurred late in 1889 when, going as usual into the editor's office one day, she was unexpectedly asked to set off that very evening on a trip around the world, in a race against another journalist, the *New York Star*'s Nellie Bly. Bly had sailed to Europe earlier that morning aiming to break the fictional record set in Jules Verne's extremely popular adventure romance, *Around the World in Eighty Days* (*Le Tour du monde en quatre-vingts jours*, 1872). Both of them were to write about their experiences for their respective outlets. Over the next few weeks, the two women travelled in opposite directions: Bly making her way eastward while Bisland went west—from New York to San Francisco by train, then by steamer to Japan, on to Hong Kong, Singapore, Ceylon, Aden, and then through the Suez Canal into Brindisi, by rail to Britain, and finally back by steamer to New York. In the event, Bisland lost: while she had managed to beat Verne's Phileas Fogg by going round the world in just 76 days, Bly had made it back to New York in 72. Nonetheless, as an editorial issued on the tenth anniversary of the magazine was later to acknowledge, the serialization of her travels, 'A Flying Trip around the World', was a

---

[29] Nina H. Kennard, *Lafcadio Hearn*, 129. Hearn and Bisland drifted apart after he emigrated to Japan. They reconnected towards the end of his life, when they resumed their correspondence and he dedicated *A Japanese Miscellany* (1901) to her.

[30] Elizabeth Bisland, 'Introduction', in Flaubert, *The Temptation of Saint Anthony*, n. p.; cf. Chapter 2.

[31] Lafcadio Hearn, respectively 'A Study of Half-Breed Races in the West Indies', *Cosmopolitan*, 9.2 (June 1890), 167–172; and 'A Society of Many Colorings', *Cosmopolitan*, 9.3 (July 1890), 337–341.

[32] Elizabeth Bisland, 'The Studios of New York', *Cosmopolitan*, 7.1 (May 1889), 3–22; and 'A Nineteenth-Century Arcady', *Cosmopolitan*, 7.5 (Sept. 1889), 512–519.

milestone in the early history of *Cosmopolitan*, leaving a deep mark on its identity.[33]

In the monthly instalments of 'A Flying Trip around the World', Bisland borrowed the narrative tropes used by Verne in *Around the World in Eighty Days*, interweaving exotic vignettes, adventure romance, and the sense of suspense created by the feeling of constantly running against the clock. Verne's fictional narrative was now tested, in journalistic fashion, against the reality of a more efficiently connected world. In contrast to Verne, however, Bisland's serial was very much the story of a *woman's* world travel: she often paused over the special difficulties and opportunities she encountered on the ground of her gender, from the challenges of assembling an adequate travel wardrobe in a very short time to how to navigate the heavily gendered social spaces of boats and trains. An article published in *Cosmopolitan* to publicize her trip played up the feminist expectations by comparing her to 'the first woman who circumnavigated the globe'—a French cross-dresser who, in the eighteenth century, travelled under the assumed male name of Baré as a servant to the botanist Philibert Commerson, on board the ship *L'Étoile*.[34] Bisland, whose glamorous portraits featured widely in the illustrations that accompanied the serial, showed that women—that is, wealthy middle-class women—no longer needed a male disguise to be emancipated world travellers. Her contribution put a female face onto the *Cosmopolitan* brand.

The serialization of 'A Flying Trip around the World' transformed not only *Cosmopolitan* but Bisland's own career: from being a reporter of the glamorous ideal of female worldliness that the magazine marketed so successfully, she graduated to being its very embodiment. The publicity generated by the trip, which was widely reported in the American press, enabled her to launch an independent literary career. The instalments of her trip around the world came out in book form on both sides of the Atlantic and Bisland went on to become the author of a substantial body of essays and memoirs (sometimes under her married name, Wetmore) in which she projected the authorial persona she had fashioned in the pages of *Cosmopolitan*. In these later works she redeployed the very brand of the magazine that she had helped to create, portraying herself as a cosmopolitan American who rebelled, like Hearn, against the 'wearing provincialism' of American literature.[35] By so doing, Bisland re-elaborated the worldly aestheticism

---

[33] See Karen Roggenkamp, 'Dignified Sensationalism: *Cosmopolitan*, Elizabeth Bisland, and Trips around the World', *American Periodicals*, 17.1 (2007), 26–40. Roggenkamp sees Bisland as embodying the magazine's difficult negotiation of a traditional, genteel style of periodical publishing and modern sensationalism. See also Matthew Goodman, *Eighty Days: Nellie Bly and Elizabeth Bisland's History-Making Race around the World* (New York: Ballantine, 2013); and Jason Marks, *Around the World in 72 Days: The Race between Pulitzer's Nellie Bly and Cosmopolitan's Elizabeth Bisland* (New York: Gemittarius, 1993).

[34] Wm S. Walsh, 'In the Library', *Cosmopolitan*, 8.3 (Jan. 1890), 380–383 (383).

[35] Elizabeth Bisland, *At the Sign of the Hobby Horse* (Boston and New York: Houghton Mifflin, 1910), 2. See also Bisland, *The Secret Life: Being the Book of a Heretic* (New York: John Lane; London: John Lane, Bodley Head, 1906); and Bisland, *A Flying Trip around the World* (London: Osgood,

she had contributed to *Cosmopolitan*, circulating it within a transatlantic space independent of the magazine's label and marketing herself as a sophisticated amateur whose cosmopolitan identity straddled high and popular culture.

Besides being a testimony to the larger imprint that the magazine's ideal of cosmopolitanism left on literary culture, Bisland's contribution shows that *Cosmopolitan*'s commitment to liberal humanism entailed a progressive attitude to gender, later emphasized in articles by prominent feminist writers such as Sarah Grand and Olive Schreiner. However, Bisland's work also exposes unresolved tensions within the liberal model of the 'university of democracy' embraced by the magazine. In the last instalment of 'A Flying Trip around the World', which described the passage through Britain, Bisland realized that her world travels had taken place almost entirely within colonized territories, which were subject to British law and in which the English language was spoken. This realization prompted her to wax lyrical about 'the splendour of [the British] empire', gushing about Anglo-Saxon blood as the binding agent of the powerful Anglo-American alliance: 'In my veins, too, runs that virile tide that pulses through the heart of this Lord of the Earth—the blood of this clean, fair, noble English race!'[36] It is disappointing that Bisland's journey around the world should culminate in an endorsement of colonial exploitation, which she had undoubtedly witnessed first-hand during her travels. And it is puzzling that, for all her readiness to find fault with American chauvinism, Bisland should be seduced by the same sentiment when it came to Britain. Perhaps Bisland's prejudice simply reflected the fact that her world trip was not set up to enable her to engage with different cultures and immerse herself in foreign space, but as a test of the power and efficiency of the global transport and communication systems. The magazine's editorial policies of brevity and clarity are also to blame for the lack of sophisticated self-reflection, in Bisland, about the impact of international mobility on women's national and social identities, such as we have seen in Egerton's narratives in the previous chapter. Like the world fairs in which *Cosmopolitan* also recognized a model for itself, Bisland's world trip was a phantasmatic projection of capitalist modernity, in which the means of the interconnectedness of the globe became its end. This is why Bisland, like Verne in his avuncular way before her, ended up celebrating the empire as bringing economic and moral order to the world, overlooking the inequalities and suffering it caused. Her endorsement of the myth of the civilizing mission of the Anglo-Saxon 'race' is only the most glaring instance of the fact that 'A Flying Trip around the World' contained little in the way of cosmopolitan curiosity or sympathy with strangers. As we shall see, however, the

McIlvaine, & Co., 1891). However, Bly's story, also published in book form, was, and remains, the more famous of the two; Nellie Bly, *Around the World in 72 Days* (New York: Pictorial Weeklies, 1890).

[36] Elizabeth Bisland, 'A Flying Trip around the World', *Cosmopolitan*, 9.6 (Oct. 1890), 666–677 (670).

note of Anglophilia that she sounded at the end of her journey was itself highly controversial, as it became a charged topic in the journal's positioning of modern American literature on the world stage.

## Literary Controversies in *Cosmopolitan*

Bisland's contribution exemplifies the overlap between literature and journalism in *Cosmopolitan*. Through the 1890s, the magazine's literary content grew steadily both in quality and quantity. Issues typically carried several items of original short or serialized fiction, mostly by American and British authors. The considerable presence of British authors gave the magazine a decidedly transatlantic profile. *Cosmopolitan* included contributions by Arthur Conan Doyle, Sarah Grand, Thomas Hardy, Rudyard Kipling, Richard Le Gallienne, Ouida, Robert Louis Stevenson, and H. G. Wells, whose *War of the Worlds* was serialized there in 1897. This partial list reveals that the editorial policy was driven by fame and reputation. *Cosmopolitan* used the literary *cachet* of London to impress cultured American readers. It is telling of the 'prestige' use of British authors that, in an 1897 retrospective article on the history of the magazine, they singled out Le Gallienne's free rendering of the Rubáiyát of Omar Khayyám as a particular highlight.[37] British writers, for their part, saw *Cosmopolitan* as a medium to publicize their work across the Atlantic, encouraged in no small part by the magazine's high print-run.

Of even greater symbolic value for the magazine's literary profile was the occasional inclusion of foreign, almost exclusively French, fiction, in translation.[38] *Cosmopolitan*'s short but high-quality list during Walker's editorship included Guy de Maupassant, publicized as 'the most famous of short story writers',[39] and the Belgian Georges Rodenbach, whose 'The Story of a Portrait in Bruges' (1895), first printed in English in *Cosmopolitan*, predated the appearance of the French 'original' by several years.[40] French non-fiction included works by Maurice Barrès, Anatole France, Sarah Bernhardt, and Paul Bourget, who provided a foreign writer's take on the 1893 Chicago World Fair. The greatest coup in matters of foreign fiction was the serialization of Tolstoy's *The Awakening* (*Voskreseniye*), which *Cosmopolitan* was to

---

[37] [Anon.], 'Making a Magazine', *Cosmopolitan*, 23.5 (Sept. 1897), 465–482 (477).

[38] Apart from the articles by Francisque Sarcey discussed later in the chapter, *Cosmopolitan* was a strictly monolingual magazine. A rare exception is an article by the Franco-American actress Jane Hading, 'The Story of my Career', *Cosmopolitan*, 6.3 (Jan. 1889), 220–224, which is in both French and English. This was an experiment carried out by Walker early in his tenure as editor and immediately abandoned.

[39] [Anon], 'Making a Magazine', 478.

[40] Georges Rodenbach, 'The Story of a Portrait in Bruges', *Cosmopolitan*, 18.5 (Mar. 1895), 620–628. The story appeared in French as 'La Vie d'un portrait' in *La Nouvelle revue* in June 1900, and was collected in the 1914 edition of *Le Rouet des Brumes* (1901).

undertake simultaneously with Russian, English (*The Chronicle*), French, and German magazines in 1899. Persuaded by Tolstoy's reputation not only as a world author but as a spiritual leader with many followers around the globe, Walker committed to the serialization of the novel before reviewing the entire manuscript. The publication, however, came to an abrupt halt after only four months, when Tolstoy's agent objected to *Cosmopolitan*'s purging explicit sexual content from the translation. The controversy was aggravated by a certain degree of chaos in the international coordination between authors, agents, translators, and the magazine.[41] This embarrassing episode—which echoed an earlier one in which the magazine had been nearly swindled into publishing a forged novel by George Sand[42]—shows that *Cosmopolitan* stood on less secure footing when it dealt in high-brow international literature due to a lack of real expertise in the editorial team. It is instructive, in this sense, to compare the situation of *Cosmopolitan* to the remarkable difference that Hearn's contribution made to the New Orleans *Times-Democrat*, which, during his tenure as literary editor, published a more extensive and ambitious list of quality French literature in translation despite its local status and limited financial means. The Tolstoy debacle also shows that *Cosmopolitan*'s family orientation put quite a severe constraint on what content the magazine was prepared to include.

Criticism was initially less prominent in the pages of *Cosmopolitan*. As one would expect, there was discussion of the ubiquitous Ibsen and Zola. But, when the magazine ventured into less chartered territory, such as the Spanish naturalist Emilia Pardo Bazán, whom Arthur Symons named as the most important Spanish decadent, serious commentary was undermined by a sensationalist focus.[43] From 1893, however, an increase in quantity as well as quality of critical items testifies to a growing literary ambition. Starting from that year, the regular feature 'In the World of Art and Letters' promised to help readers 'to keep in touch with the intellectual movement of the world' (the related 'The Progress of Science' was to do the same for scientific topics).[44] In keeping with the ethos of the journal, the

---

[41] [Anon.], 'Discontinuance of Count Tolstoy's Novel', *Cosmopolitan*, 27.4 (1899), 447–449. The episode is also analysed by Landers, *Improbable First Century*, 65–66.

[42] The George Sand novel in question, titled *Princess Nourmahal*, was advertised as forthcoming in Sept. 1887, but two months later the magazine was forced to admit that it had been swindled. In an embarrassing note of apology, the editor (this was before the days of Walker's editorship) explained that Lew Vanderpoole, the presumed translator of this work, had approached the magazine claiming to be Sand's nephew and to be in possession of the unpublished novel, but was eventually found out to have been an impostor. Vanderpoole had already dabbled in literary fakes in the form of a forged interview with Kaiser Ludwig II of Bavaria, which had appeared in *Lippincott's* in Nov. 1886. See [Anon.], 'A Literary Adventurer: Lew Vanderpoole and the George Sand Manuscripts', *The Sun*, 21 Sept. 1887, 1.

[43] Sylvester Baxter, 'The First Woman of Spain', *Cosmopolitan*, 15.2 (June 1893), 228–234; cf. Arthur Symons, 'The Decadent Movement in Literature', in Symons, *Symbolist Movement in Literature*, 169–183 (181).

[44] [Anon.], 'In the World of Art and Letters', *Cosmopolitan*, 15.3 (July 1893), 378–381 (378). Further references in this paragraph are to the same page.

articles in this section had to be brief, and they were followed by lists of the selected twenty most important books and reprints of the month, which together provided a guide to world literature for busy practical people. The editor explained that the spiralling amount of publications and the intensified international circulation of literature presented a 'problem' for 'the man or woman occupied with the many cares of our nineteenth century civilization'. In order to help navigate this vast sea of information, *Cosmopolitan* would commission 'leading reviewers and critics of England, France, Germany, and the United States' to comment on what 'seems to [them] the most salient feature of the month'. The resulting articles, which became a feature in the mid 1890s, broadened the American focus of the magazine by providing a sense of actual connection with the living literatures of other nations—mostly, it has to be said, with France and Britain—embedding the literary content of *Cosmopolitan* more deeply into foreign space.

The British items of 'In the World of Art and Letters' were mostly covered by Andrew Lang and Israel Zangwill. Lang was a respected critic with extremely good links both to America—notably to regular *Cosmopolitan* contributor Brander Matthews, to whom we shall come back shortly—and to periodicals at home.[45] Zangwill was, in many ways, a more interesting choice: the young writer who had recently come to prominence with his novel *Children of the Ghetto* (1892) became the most prolific British contributor to *Cosmopolitan* in the mid-1890s, publishing not only literary news but also short fictions and poems. In his perceptive snapshots, Zangwill provided some of the most progressive literary coverage in *Cosmopolitan*, including topics relating to the leading aesthetic and decadent periodicals (*Yellow Book*, *The Savoy*, *The Evergreen*) and going beyond Britain when he wanted to highlight important international phenomena such as the writings of Maeterlinck and Max Nordau.[46] Sometimes Zangwill's criticism, like his short stories, explicitly focused on Jewish subjects.

For France, Walker chose the drama critic Francisque Sarcey who, while certainly extremely eminent, was also an outspoken sceptic of the influence of foreign authors on modern French theatre. In his reviews for *Cosmopolitan*, Sarcey was true to his reputation for cultural conservatism—something that the journal packaged as adding an authentic French note.[47] It is for this reason that Sarcey's brief articles were the only items that *Cosmopolitan* printed in two languages—French and English. In this way, they doubled up as French practice exercises, feeding into the pedagogic mission of the magazine (foreign language learning featured prominently in the advert pages). 'In The World of Art and Letters' also included frequent contributions from Hjalmar Hjort Boyesen, a

---

[45] See Marysa Demoor, ed., *Friends over the Ocean: Andrew Lang's American Correspondents* (Ghent: Universa, 1989).

[46] See Israel Zangwill, 'Minorities in Literature and Art', *Cosmopolitan*, 21.2 (June 1896), 213.

[47] See, for instance, Francisque Sarcey, 'In the World of Art and Letters', *Cosmopolitan*, 17.4 (Aug. 1894), 500–502. Here Sarcey is cynical about the Parisian fashion for Ibsen.

Norwegian American who was an expert on Scandinavian literature and also covered Germany.

When it came to literature, therefore, *Cosmopolitan* used foreign, especially British, authors, to increase its cultural capital and, simultaneously, to encourage its American public to become more international in its tastes. However, the magazine also stayed firmly committed to American literature—the vast majority of its authors were American—and used its pages to network domestic writers with prestigious foreign names. Indeed, the magazine liked to put the spotlight on questions of national identity, problematizing the cosmopolitan tendencies of modern American literature, notably as displayed in its relation with Britain. These dynamics can best be seen in the treatment of one of *Cosmopolitan*'s star authors: Henry James. James contributed both non-fiction and fiction to *Cosmopolitan* in the early 1890s, when he was already an established name. He was introduced by the writer William Dean Howells, who briefly acted as associate editor.[48] James's debut piece was an obituary of the American publisher Wolcott Balestier, who had died prematurely in Dresden in his late twenties. Balestier had formed a partnership with the London publisher William Heinemann, with whom, in 1891, he had launched the 'English Library' series as a competitor to the German firm Tauchnitz's extremely successful 'Collection of British Authors'. Books in the 'English Library' series were also aimed at British and American travellers on the Continent (or, indeed, European readers of English), they were cheap paperbacks like Tauchnitz, and, just like Tauchnitz, they had their head-quarters in Leipzig—a major publishing hub in Continental Europe.

James, who was a friend of Balestier, had been deeply affected by his death. His obituary was written from the perspective of a cosmopolitan American author commenting on another cosmopolitan literary American. It aimed to provide an appreciation of Balestier not simply as a clever businessman but as exemplary of a desire to straddle different worlds that James also shared. For this reason, James centred his portrait on Balestier's transformational encounter with London, which he described as the necessary transitional space for 'the "cultured American"' on a journey towards foreign places and ideas.[49] According to James, while most Americans saw London 'in the interest of leisure and shopping, or at the most of patriotism and consolation', Balestier understood that London could provide 'an extension without being a substitution' of America: 'It "took in," as it were, the great agglomerations he had left behind the sea, and added others to them.'[50] Like

[48] Rein, 'Howells and the *Cosmopolitan*', 52–53.

[49] Henry James, 'Wolcott Balestier', *Cosmopolitan*, 13.1 (May 1892), 43–47 (44). James reused the obituary in his introduction to Ballestier's posthumously published fiction *The Average Woman* (1892). According to Adeline R. Tintner, James's friendship with Balestier inspired his positive portrayal of cosmopolitanism in his short story 'Collaboration' (1892); Tintner, 'Rudyard Kipling and Wolcott Balestier's Literary Collaboration: A Possible Source for James's "Collaboration"', *Henry James Review*, 4.2 (1983), 140–143.

[50] James, 'Wolcott Balestier', 44.

his own fictional Americans, the deceased publisher in James's view experienced Europe as a space of freedom and self-development—a space whose greatest lesson, as James would show in *The Ambassadors*, was to teach them how to become men of the world.

The final summing up of Balestier's character provided James with an opportunity to present the 'cosmopolitan spirit' that he shared with Balestier as inevitably bound with modern trends in literature and society:

> There was something in him so actively modern, so open to new reciprocities and assimilations, that it is not fanciful to say that he would have worked originally, in his degree, for civilization. He had the real cosmopolitan spirit, the easy imagination of strangeness surmounted. He struck me as a bright young forerunner of some higher common conveniences, some greater international transfusions. He had just had time to begin, and that is exactly what makes the exceeding pity of his early end.[51]

James's striking definition of cosmopolitanism as 'the easy imagination of strangeness surmounted' emphasized the liberal ideal of opening up to foreign cultures and assimilating different ideas and ways of life. His metaphor of transfusion likewise portrayed the 'cosmopolitan spirit' positively, in no ambiguous terms, as a revitalizing force for the collective organism of humanity.

Such a distinctively American type of cosmopolitanism that combined cultural distinction and commercial success seemed perfectly attuned to the ethos of *Cosmopolitan*. However, in the same number, readers also encountered an article by one of the journal's house critics, Brander Matthews, which completely contradicted James's views on the need for 'greater international transfusions'. In a review of contemporary American essayists, Matthews quoted with approval 'Colonel' Thomas Wentworth Higginson's saying that 'to be really cosmopolitan a man must be at home even in his own country';[52] and he recommended Higginson's collection, *Concerning All of Us* (1893), as a tonic to those Americans who wavered in their cultural patriotism or had doubts about the healthy state of literature and the arts in their country. By contrast, Matthews slighted the work of the aesthetic Anglophile writer Agnes Repplier for being too embedded in English models and perversely ignoring the writer's 'own' American literature: 'Colonialism is scarcely an adequate explanation for this devotion to the first-rate, second-rate and third-rate writers of a foreign country to the neglect of the first-rate writers of her own.'[53] In open contrast with James, who, as we have

---

[51]   Ibid. 47.
[52]   Brander Matthews, 'Concerning Certain Some American Essayists', *Cosmopolitan*, 13.1 (May 1892), 86–90 (87).
[53]   Ibid. 89.

seen, also presented Britain as America's stepping-stone into the wider world, Matthews argued that, in order to become truly cosmopolitan, American literature should undergo a full process of decolonialization that, counterintuitively perhaps, must start from asserting its own national culture domestically and abroad.

In a later issue Matthews further clarified his views on national and cosmopolitan literary identities, this time by explicitly attacking James. Reviewing recent American short stories, he contrasted what he saw as the false cosmopolitanism of Paris, which was really based on diffidence towards and ignorance of foreign cultures, with the cultural openness of New York, which embodied a true cosmopolitanism that was to him an inherent component of American identity: 'We come of stocks so varied, and as yet so ill fused, that although the new American begins to emerge, he is surrounded and encompassed about by men of every heredity; and he is receptive perforce; and he is not hostile to the foreigner; and he cannot but be cosmopolitan.'[54] American writers should therefore look for material inside the nation, with all its breadth of life experiences and local varieties, rather than abroad. James, whose *The Lesson of the Master and Other Stories* (1892) was one of the volumes under review, was held as the exemplar of a misguided American xenophilia:

> By accident of birth Mr. James is an American, and as we read these very clever tales we wonder whether he would not have greater strength to wrestle with the problems of art if he touched his native land more often. [. . .] Of course the charge that Mr. James has become an Englishman is silly enough; his opinion of the British is sufficiently obvious to all who care to look for it; but perhaps there is ampler warrant for the charge that he has ceased to be an American. He seems to have lost his interest in American character, his relish for it. [. . .] He has expatriated himself, and like all exiles he cannot but lose touch with his own country.[55]

This stigmatization of James as a citizen of nowhere is couched in the same rhetoric that we have seen in English attacks on Wilde and Hearn. The difference is that, from Matthews's American perspective, England is now the source and not the victim of subversive foreign influences that undermine a healthy national culture. The anti-English sentiment displayed here is part of a postcolonial moment in the American *fin de siècle* that harks back to a romantic, Herderian nationalism in order to encourage the growth of an independent and strong national culture. But the language of dispossession and ostracism that Matthews unleashes against James reveals that, no matter how much he tried to portray his

---

[54] Brander Matthews, 'More American Stories', *Cosmopolitan*, 13.5 (Sept. 1892), 626–630 (626).
[55] Ibid. 630.

point of view as socially progressive, his cultural patriotism was tainted by a chauvinistic nationalism that also comes across in his critical writings.[56]

Jessica Berman has rightly argued that *Cosmopolitan* is the embodiment of a turn-of-the-century America caught between expansiveness and 'expansionism'.[57] Her assessment is borne out by the dispute between James and Matthews, which also reveals the symbolically charged role played by Britain and English literature in this transitional moment. Anglophile writers such as James, Bisland, and Agnes Repplier all believed, in their very different ways, that the English heritage of American literature constituted a precious tie with Europe that writers could use as a bridge to the wider world. By contrast, Matthews—whose interests were by no means provincial, having published on French drama and Ibsen among other things—believed that American literature should emphasize its difference from Britain, and he condemned American Anglophilia as a form of provincialism. *Cosmopolitan* tried to manage the competing energies that traversed this highly complex landscape against the backdrop of tense national debates on immigration and various geo-political crises in which America got involved in this period. However, the journal also made most of their differences in order deliberately to stoke up controversy. Matthews's review of American essayists, for instance, greatly exaggerated the abrasiveness of Higginson's patriotism, which in fact took a much softer stance towards the cosmopolitan 'adaptiveness' of American national identity than his critic made out.[58] By a similar token, shortly after Matthews's slighting of Agnes Repplier, *Cosmopolitan* took on the latter as a regular reviewer of English literature, giving her a platform to broadcast the very Anglophilia that the magazine had criticized—all of this while continuing to encourage the collaborations of British authors.

James would again be sacrificed on the altar of literary controversy later that year (1892). This time, his story 'The Wheel of Time'—one of the most formally accomplished texts ever published in *Cosmopolitan*—was directly juxtaposed with an article titled 'A Colonial Survival', written by none other than the future American president Theodore Roosevelt. Roosevelt's essay praised patriotic literature in fairly blunt and predictable terms, but his verbal aggression towards American cosmopolitanism is worth pausing on, especially in the light of his future political career. Roosevelt, who was a close friend of Brander Matthews, voiced his deep concern at 'the queer, strained humility towards foreigners, and especially towards Englishmen, shown by certain small groups of Americans'.[59]

---

[56] See, for instance, Brander Matthews, *The American of the Future and Other Essays* (New York: Charles Scribner's Sons, 1910).

[57] Jessica Berman, *Modernist Fiction*, 31 ff.

[58] Cf. Thomas Wentworth Higginson, 'A New National Temperament', in *Concerning All of Us* (New York: Harper & Bros, 1893), 131–138 (137).

[59] Theodore Roosevelt, 'A Colonial Survival', *Cosmopolitan*, 14.2 (Dec. 1892), 229–236 (230). Further references in this paragraph are to the same page.

And he singled out two cosmopolitan types that he found particularly disruptive: the 'vulgar rich', who used their American wealth to make their way into the high society of other countries; and 'their antitypes, the refined, fastidious people of weak fibre, the artists and literary men of more cultivation than intellect, and more intellect than character'. The 'brainless woman of fashion' and 'the émigré novelist' were two sides of the same coin for Roosevelt, who regarded both, in eugenic terms, as 'feeble [. . .] folk', whose self-chosen exile was in fact a good thing for the moral fibre of the nation: 'they simplify the solution of our difficult national problem by eliminating therefrom certain unimportant but objectionable factors'. Coming, as it did, right after James's text (with only a one-page poem as a buffer zone), this phobic attack read as an indirect commentary on 'The Wheel of Time' and its anglicized author, who belonged to the class of exiled Americans that Roosevelt abhorred and who had made a successful literary career of writing about them. Roosevelt rewrote James's definition of cosmopolitanism as the 'easy imagination of strangeness surmounted' into 'the queer, strained humility towards foreigners', emphasizing hierarchy and exclusion where James had striven to promote a liberal vision of the self as pliable and receptive to foreign influences. Roosevelt attempted to quash James's 'queer' cosmopolitanism by means of a programme of social hygiene based on manliness, understood simultaneously as a gender category (straight masculinity) and civic identity. The images of weakness and degeneracy that he attached to the literary cosmopolite fed into discourses of degeneration that were already in the air (Nordau's book was published in German that same year), to which Roosevelt contrasted his own vision of the healthy body of a sealed national culture. The homophobic message was clear enough for those who wanted to pick up on it.[60]

The result of the journal's editorial choices was that James's cosmopolitanism acquired a power of resistance that his overtly apolitical aestheticism otherwise makes difficult to see. Not only his endorsement of the cosmopolitan practices of the publisher Balestier but his very *style* came to embody the liberal cosmopolitan imagination that Roosevelt vilified as noxious and queer, and tried to crush through his blunt, virile, anti-intellectual rhetoric. As we have seen with Wilde, hostile commentators blurred cosmopolitan and queer identities in order to relegate authors to the margins of society. In this charged space, 'The Wheel of Time'—a story in which the cosmopolitan theme plays no significant part— became *about* the values of cosmopolitanism in the pages of the magazine: James's voice embodied, in its very essence, the qualities of 'cleverness' and 'cultivation' satirized by Matthews and Roosevelt as inherently inimical to the manly and straight-talking style upon which a patriotic, truly national literature

---

[60] Philip Horne has analysed the later biographical overlap between James and Roosevelt in '"Reinstated": James in Roosevelt's Washington', *Cambridge Quarterly*, 37.1 (2008), 47–63. As Horne shows, in 1901 James would call Roosevelt 'a dangerous and ominous Jingo' (51).

ought to be built. These clashes over literature and national identity lent a controversial topicality to the notion of cosmopolitanism, showing that it was not a minority concern, but rather went right to the heart of what it meant to be a modern American. In staging these debates, *Cosmopolitan* participated in America's emergence as an autonomous power inside what Casanova calls the 'world literary space', where its closest and, at the same time, most antagonistic relation was with Britain.[61] The journal was tasked with having to manage this difficult process of recalibrating hierarchies of symbolic power, arbitrating between different, clashing visions of how to build a strong and distinctive identity for American literature at home and internationally.

## *Cosmopolis*: A Sense of Closer Fellowship

Unlike *Cosmopolitan*, the short-lived, ambitious *Cosmopolis* never printed a motto on its austere title-page, and its elusive editor, the Belgian Fernand Ortmans, never wrote editorials that explicitly laid out the journal's policy. Nonetheless, in an interview for *The Sketch* publicizing the launch of the new journal, Ortmans explained that the aim of his 'international review' was to 'enable different peoples and different nations "to see ourselves as others see us."'[62] An English advertising prospectus further clarified this mission: 'by its independence and impartiality; by its moderation and urbanity of tone', *Cosmopolis* hoped to 'help to bring about a sense of closer fellowship between the nations—a larger sympathy making, slowly, no doubt, but effectually, for the far-off goal of perfect culture: peace and concord'.[63] *Cosmopolis* thus looked back to Kant's philosophy and the Enlightenment idea of the Republic of Letters, believing that serious, sceptical, and impartial dialogue between the best minds of different countries would foster a common culture and shared ethics, and eventually lead to what Kant called 'perpetual peace'.[64] However, Ortmans and his contributors were also very aware of living in a profoundly different world than that of the previous century. Now, the mass international circulation of people and print meant that cosmopolitanism was not a utopian notion confined to a small intellectual elite, but rather a very present and material condition of the modern world that the journal should reflect. In this respect the journal, as Frederik Van Dam has argued, set out to perform a diplomatic mission.[65] In particular, *Cosmopolis* was to be the pioneering

---

[61]  Cf. Casanova, *World Republic of Letters*, esp. 82–87.
[62]  [Anon.], 'An International Review and its Editor', *The Sketch*, 1 Jan. 1896, 6.
[63]  Advertising prospectus enclosed with *Cosmopolis*, n. p. Bodleian Library, Oxford, Per. 3974 d.41.
[64]  Kant, 'Perpetual Peace: A Philosophical Sketch', in *Kant's Political Writings*, 93–130.
[65]  Frederik Van Dam, 'Resonant with a Whole World of Meaning: The Diplomatic Aesthetic of *Cosmopolis*', *Victoriographies*, 8.2 (2018), 170–186.

voice of the new era of international arbitration, when conflict could be resolved and replaced by effective and constructive communication.

A programmatic article titled 'The true Cosmopolis', printed during the journal's first year, encapsulated its idealism. Here, the eminent British positivist historian Frederic Harrison exposed a frustrating paradox that complicated the task of *Cosmopolis*: 'We *hear* about our neighbours far more than ever. We have less *sympathy* with foreign thought, we have far less of the Cosmopolitan genius that was common in the most fertile epochs of the human mind.'[66] In particular, Harrison bemoaned the disappearance of the 'cosmopolitan citizenship of the Middle Ages' and formulated a modern system of 'inter-citizenship' that would help the present age to get rid of some of the rampant chauvinism fanned by imperialism and ambitions of world dominance.[67] Harrison was careful to stress that his ideal of world citizenship by no means called for the obliteration of patriotic sentiment, noting that the young *Cosmopolis* had already been enthusiastically welcomed by 'patriotic men in all parts of Europe and America'.[68] Nonetheless, he warned that national habits, feelings, and interests should not stand in the way of a higher liberal ideal of intellectual progress and international solidarity that he rousingly summed up in his conclusion: 'The philosopher, the historian, the poet, the romancer, the artist, need always to have before them an ideal of *the best*—the best that ever has been—the best that they can give. And this *best* never is, never can be, in a narrow sense, *national*. This is the true cosmopolis!'[69] Taking inspiration from the increasingly international culture of modern science, *Cosmopolis* brought together enlightened contributors who were able to think and write beyond the nation. This different perspective was intended to generate new ideas and create new encounters, transnational alliances, and patterns of networking that promoted excellence in journalism and literature.

This strong commitment to high culture aimed to appeal to a radically different public than the busy 'family' audience of *Cosmopolitan*: *Cosmopolis* addressed itself to people who were willing to invest time in reading its long, high-brow articles unrelieved by illustrations. For such readers, being cosmopolitan meant to immerse oneself deeply into high-quality items written by authors of international standing, rather than consuming foreign cultures through the exotic images that populated the pages of *Cosmopolitan*, or reading digests and condensed literature such as were provided by the *Review of Reviews*. Unlike *Cosmopolitan*, moreover, *Cosmopolis* ignored fashion and commercial interests. If anything, its networking of intellectuals from different countries had an uneasy relation with the networks of international capitalism. Launched on the fiftieth anniversary of the repeal of the Corn Laws, which became known in Britain as the Jubilee of Free Trade,

---

[66] Frederic Harrison, 'The True Cosmopolis', *Cosmopolis*, 8 (Aug. 1896), 325–340 (325). Emphasis in the original.
[67] Ibid. 329.      [68] Ibid. 352.      [69] Ibid. 340.

*Cosmopolis* adopted an ambivalent attitude to Richard Cobden's legacy, with several contributors questioning the belief that free trade would pave the way for world peace. Harrison, for instance, dismissed free trade as 'a dream from the ivory gate', which gave way all too quickly under pressure from nationalist ideology, with which the majority of the people were readier to empathize.[70] Other contributors, even when writing from liberal perspectives, separated cosmopolitan idealism from free trade and identified commerce with negative forms of international competition or even with war.[71]

*Cosmopolis* used its high-brow profile and prestigious list of contributors— which included top journalists, writers, editors, and academic experts—to fight a tough, if brief, battle against the mounting nationalism in the European press. In one of the early numbers, the former editor of the *Fortnightly Review*, T. H. S. Escott, noted with approval that in Britain as in France and Germany quality newspapers and magazines shared 'an honest desire to improve, socially or politically, the relations between their own and other European countries'.[72] However, he accused the popular press of sensationalizing and exaggerating international tensions, stoking up chauvinistic feelings and turning the print medium into an agent of division. This volatile situation called for careful managing:

> the intellectual public of Europe, notwithstanding the geographical divisions of mountain ranges and seas, acquires more of unity and solidarity as the end of the century approaches. The press consequently tends more and more to become, if an arithmetical simile may be adopted, a common denominator in European thought. As such, notwithstanding periodical tendencies to patriotic chauvinism, a newspaper public co-extensive with the civilised world must, if wisely controlled, generally be favourable to the prevention of national misunderstanding, and therefore to the promotion of international amity.[73]

In this moment of increased traffic and communication between European nations, an international review was more needed than ever to correct the 'patriotic chauvinism' of the national presses. *Cosmopolis* aimed to provide such a platform, where liberal readers from all nations could find common ground in the form of intelligent and impartial commentary.

---

[70] Ibid. 337.
[71] For instance, among the English contributions, Frederick Greenwood, 'The Safeguards of Peace Considered', *Cosmopolis*, 5 (May 1896), 346–360; and Henry Dunckley, 'The Jubilee of Free Trade', *Cosmopolis*, 6 (June 1896), 643–659.
[72] T. H. S. Escott, 'The Press as an International Agency', *Cosmopolis*, 3 (Mar. 1896), 664–677 (668).
[73] Ibid. 667.

Attacks on the perverting agency of the popular press were by no means uncommon in the late nineteenth century. In the English context, the most notable instance of this phenomenon was Matthew Arnold's campaign against W. T. Stead's 'new journalism'—while, ironically, Stead's ambition for the *Review of Reviews*, 'to make the best thoughts of the best writers in our periodicals universally accessible', emulated Arnold's well-known definition of culture.[74] What was new was that *Cosmopolis* now brought together the voices that were speaking against populism on a domestic level to form a joined-up international network of resistance. Escott's call against jingoism found many echoes in the pages of *Cosmopolis*. Writing about socialism and international relations, for instance, the pseudonymous German contributor 'Ignotus' despaired about a nationalistic press that gathered under the slogan 'Right or wrong, my country' (in English in the original).[75] Liberals and socialists occasionally joined hands within the covers of the journal. The idea was that, by recruiting the best high-quality journalism from every nation, the journal would nurture an intellectual elite whose knowledge would be democratized by the periodical medium, with its high circulation and relatively affordable price of half a crown (3.25 francs or 2.50 German marks). Resolutely keeping away from the commercialism of *Cosmopolitan*, *Cosmopolis* stood firm by an ethical and intellectual ideal of world citizenship that would be capable, now more than ever, to fight the way in which populists and nationalists manipulated the sentimental appeal of patriotism. Its ultimate aim was to denationalize knowledge and the very idea of culture.

## Trilingualism and Translation

Each issue of *Cosmopolis* was simultaneously published in London, Paris, Berlin, Vienna, St Petersburg, Amsterdam, and New York. In this way, the journal projected internationally the material condition of simultaneity that Anderson deemed so crucial to the nation-building power of the periodical press: accessing the same debates and ideas at the same time, readers across this vast area of the Western hemisphere could imagine themselves as part of a now no longer national, but cosmopolitan community, that shared specific interests and outlooks. The major innovation of the journal, however, and the most distinctive feature of its cosmopolitan idealism, was that it was printed in three languages:

---

[74] [Anon.], 'Programme', 14. On 'new journalism', see Matthew Arnold, 'Up to Easter', *Nineteenth Century*, 21 (May 1887), 629–643.

[75] Ignotus, 'Politisches in deutscher Beleuchtung', *Cosmopolis*, 9 (Sept. 1896), 909–924 (913). See also Frederick Greenwood, 'Sentiment in Politics', *Cosmopolis*, 10 (Oct. 1896), 340–354, which blames newspapers for introducing into British politics a type of emotionalism that is the enemy of Europeanist idealism (347).

every number carried groups of articles in English, French, and German. The language clusters were roughly equal in length and were typically each split into original fiction, criticism, and politics/international relations. The three languages of *Cosmopolis* represented the most culturally and politically dominant nationalities in Europe and gave them equal weight. However, the positioning of English before French, besides reflecting the larger extent of the British Empire in terms of size and population, sent a clear signal about the mounting international prestige of Britain as a European and global centre of literary innovation and publishing. The British pre-eminence in the journal was material as well as symbolic, though, for *Cosmopolis* was printed in London (and then distributed in the other capitals) and had its de facto headquarters there, in spite of the fact that most authors writing in a foreign language did so in French (Georg Brandes, the Italian writer Angelo De Gubernatis, Tolstoy, etc.). It is worth remembering that the editor, Ortmans, was a Belgian and that therefore this linguistic policy might be a reflection of a special Belgian Anglophilia and wish to counterbalance French cultural dominance. Viewed from an English perspective, the addition of Germany to the Anglo-French axis that was covered by the *Yellow Book* and *The Savoy*, allowed *Cosmopolis* to provide readers with a fuller and more internationally integrated treatment of German culture than any of the existing English-language periodicals. Stimulating though it undoubtedly was, the simultaneous presence of the three languages came at a high expense: readers who were not competent in all three 'wasted' a substantial number of pages per issue. Nonetheless, trilingualism was essential to the identity of the journal and to the cosmopolitan experience it aimed to offer: readers of *Cosmopolis* were meant to step on foreign soil even as they scrolled down the contents list of each issue.

The political significance of the multilingualism of *Cosmopolis* emerges most clearly if we compare it with the unselfconscious monolingualism of *Cosmopolitan* or, especially, with the imperialistic monolingualism of the *Review of Reviews*. The latter was created with the explicit aim of bolstering the global power of the 'English-speaking man', whom Stead's journal believed to have been destined to lead 'the van of civilisation'.[76] In other words, the *Review of Reviews* used the English language as a binding agent for an imperial identity, which it did by simultaneously publishing editions in Britain, America, and 'Australasia'. By contrast, *Cosmopolis* used foreign languages to celebrate cultural diversity and to show that it was possible to foster an imagined community, to go back to

---

[76] [Anon.], 'To All English-Speaking Folk', 15. Cf. Laurel Brake, 'Stead Alone: Journalist, Proprietor, and Publisher, 1890–1903', in Laurel Brake et al., eds, *W. T. Stead: Newspaper Revolutionary* (London: British Library, 2012), 77–97 (84); Simon J. Potter, 'Journalism and Empire in an English-Reading World: The *Review of Reviews*', in Shattock, *Journalism and the Periodical Press*, 281–298. Stead's preference would have been for an 'English-speaking re-union' of the British Empire and America into a single mighty world power; see Estelle W. Stead, *My Father* (London: Heinemann, 1913), 239.

Anderson's terms, that transcended the boundaries of the nation and the mother tongue. The comparison with *Cosmopolitan* also shows that multilingualism was not a viable strategy to enlarge the potential audience of *Cosmopolis* by multiplying it by three: rather, counterintuitively perhaps, it could shrink its public by making it more specialized.

In the first issue, several of the French contributors specifically addressed the challenges and advantages of writing as a foreigner or for foreign readers, suggesting that they were doing so in response to a precise request from the editor. The theatre critic Francisque Sarcey, whom we have already encountered in the pages of *Cosmopolitan*, argued for the importance of foreign critics in making the French see their national literature through 'different eyes', revealing to them details and aspects of texts that natives may pass by without paying attention.[77] While the critic Emile Faguet reflected that writing beyond the national border demanded a different type of sincerity, an act of careful and honest introspection which was absolutely necessary for the success of a journal like the present one.[78] He therefore expressed the hope that English and German critics would be equally honest when discussing French literature, citing the saying of an unspecified French critic: 'posterity begins abroad'.[79] The journal made much of this foreign point of view, especially when it came to culture: French art and literature were discussed by English and German critics; Italian, Scandinavian, and Russian authors were introduced from English, French, and German perspectives. Throughout, foreignness was not equated with a condition of ignorance but with clarity of judgement: it was the repository of a desirable knowledge that *Cosmopolis* now made available to its readers by broadcasting voices from across the border. At the same time, the international recognition attested by inclusion in *Cosmopolis* increased the domestic prestige of the authors who wrote or were written about in the journal.

*Cosmopolis* did not publish translations. Indeed, several contributions explicitly or implicitly portrayed translation as a ground of misunderstanding. For instance, the journal proudly printed Tolstoy's French version of an article that he had originally written in Russian and that had then appeared in such a sloppy French translation that the ageing writer decided to rewrite it in French.[80] And, again writing in French, Georg Brandes—to whom we shall return in the next section—argued that Ibsen's poems were 'intraduisibles' and that Goncourt's mistaken criticism of Ibsen's language as 'livresque' should, in fact, best be

---

[77] Francisque Sarcey, 'Alexandre Dumas', *Cosmopolis*, 1 (Jan. 1896), 171–183 (171) ('autres yeux que les nôtres').
[78] Emile Faguet, 'Cronique littéraire', *Cosmopolis*, 1 (Jan. 1896), 184–195 (184) ('par-dessus la frontièr de mon pays').
[79] Ibid. ('l'étranger, c'est le commencement de la postérité').
[80] The article in question was titled 'Le Non-Agir', and was (re)published as Léon Tolstoï, 'Zola et Dumas', *Cosmopolis*, 3 (Mar. 1896), 761–774.

interpreted as revealing the bookish quality of the art of literary translation as such.[81] Anticipating today's theories of 'untranslatability' in literary studies, such interventions gestured towards a model of intercultural relations that rejected easy notions of equivalence.[82] Rather than engendering familiarity through translation, *Cosmopolis* asked its readers to immerse themselves into the strangeness of the foreign idiom, capturing its unique nuances and mentality, if they were fluent in it, or struggling with its difficulty if they only had an imperfect knowledge. The evident challenge presented by this reading experience was intrinsic to the journal's high-brow, intellectual profile. In other words, multilingualism was the material condition of the ethics of international coexistence advocated by the journal. A secondary effect of this politics of non-translation, however, was that it emphasized the differences between cultures, flirting with essentialism and creating an international landscape in which borders became highly visible and, in fact, multiplied. This is reflected in the contributors' occasional tendency to write, self-consciously, as representatives of their country.

More pressingly, the journal's trilingualism was simultaneously the sign of its cosmopolitan opening and of its limitations. The international dialogue conducted in *Cosmopolis* was largely confined to Britain, France, and Germany, whose monopoly over the journal was not only linguistic but also extended to the sphere of interest of the majority of the articles. The result was that *Cosmopolis* drew a map of Europe divided into major and minor, centre and periphery—an English contributor tellingly describing Spain as 'the most foreign country of Europe'.[83] By the same token, the world outside the European continent was imagined, if at all, as coextensive with the colonized territories of the three major empires. A planned gradual expansion of the journal was to correct this tendency by enabling it to reach different language areas within Europe: from the second year, there was a Russian supplement published in St Petersburg, which was given together with the journal to Russian subscribers and could also be obtained for an extra fee by subscribers in other countries. In its third year, *Cosmopolis* was to have extended this new feature to Scandinavia, Holland, Italy, Spain, and Greece. In the event, despite its impressive initial circulation of 24,000,[84] the journal collapsed before achieving the further linguistic expansion, revealing the underlying tension between its utopian ambition and the reality of the market.

[81] Georg Brandes, 'Henrik Ibsen en France', *Cosmopolis*, 13 (Jan. 1897), 112–124 (118).
[82] Cf. Apter, *Against World Literature*, 3–4 and *passim*; Barbara Cassin, ed., *Dictionary of Untranslatables: A Philosophical Lexicon*, tr. Steven Rendall et al. (Princeton: Princeton University Press, 2013).
[83] Charles Whibley, 'Spain at the New Gallery', *Cosmopolis*, 3 (Mar. 1896), 678–683 (679). Whibley was the Paris correspondent of the *Pall Mall Gazette*.
[84] Figure quoted in Mark W. Turner, '*Cosmopolis: An International Review* (1896–98)', in Laurel Brake and Marysa Demoor, eds, *Dictionary of Nineteenth-Century Journalism in Great Britain and Ireland* (Ghent: Academia Press; London: British Library, 2009), 145–146 (146).

## A Cosmopolis of World Literature

We have seen that Goethe believed that periodicals would hasten the opening of national literary cultures, enabling the free circulation of ideas and texts that he called world literature. However, he was also careful to point out that this increased international circulation would not lead to a flattening of world cultures. In the same entry in which he praised the work undertaken in Britain by the *Edinburgh Review* and the *Foreign Quarterly Review*, he added that 'there can be no question of the nations thinking alike, the aim is simply that they shall grow aware of one another, understand each other, and, even where they may not be able to love, may at least tolerate one another'.[85] He believed that an enlightened understanding of cultural differences through world literature would bring an enormous social benefit to humanity, in that it would ultimately lead to peaceful relations between the nations. Not only were several of Goethe's reflections on world literature prompted by his reading of foreign journals, including—aside from the British examples—the French *Globe* (1824–32) and the Italian *Eco* (1828–35). But he also used his own periodical, *Über Kunst und Altertum* (1816–32), from which the previous quotations are taken, as a medium to broadcast his ideas of literary cosmopolitanism and world literature.

Although it never claimed so explicitly, the mission of *Cosmopolis* was deeply shaped by Goethe's ideal of world literature. Particularly important was Goethe's belief that the periodical press could strengthen the power of literature to promote tolerance or, as the journal's advertising pamphlet put it in terms that closely followed Goethe, create a 'larger sympathy' between the nations, which would in turn lead to 'peace and concord'.[86] Like the English Goethe Society discussed in Chapter 1, *Cosmopolis* belongs to a *fin-de-siècle* momentum to find new relevance for world literature as Goethe conceived it: both the society and the periodical sought to gather together and nurture a self-consciously cosmopolitan class of readers, for whom an interest in foreign literatures constituted a specialized taste and distinctive cultural identity. The English prospectus identified the journal's target readership as 'those whose knowledge of modern languages enables them to follow closely and directly the various literary, political, artistic and scientific movements actually shaping the life of foreign countries'.[87] The alliance with the English Goethe Society was symbolically sealed when the newly founded *Cosmopolis* published the society's presidential address for 1896, which marked the tenth anniversary of Max Müller's lecture on Goethe and Carlyle.[88]

---

[85] Strich, *Goethe and World Literature*, 350 ('nur wiederholen wir, daß nicht die Rede sein könne, die Nationen sollen überein denken, sondern sie sollen nur einander gewhar werden, sich begreifen, und wenn sie sich wechselseitig nicht lieben mögen, sich einander wenigstens dulden lernen', 399).
[86] Advertising prospectus for *Cosmopolis*. See n. 63 of this chapter.      [87] Ibid.
[88] Edward Dowden, 'The Case against Goethe', *Cosmopolis*, 6 (June 1896), 624–642. The *Review of Reviews* published extracts of Dowden's address, declaring that 'the editor of *Cosmopolis* [was]

*Cosmopolis* expressed its commitment to world literature in two fundamental, related ways: by publishing authors of international acclaim—modern classics, as it were—and by privileging comparative approaches in criticism. Its ambition to feature world authors was amply borne out by the fact that, during its brief life span, the journal carried items by at least six future Nobel laureates: Anatole France, Paul Heyse, Kipling, Theodor Mommsen, G. B. Shaw, and W. B. Yeats. Even outside this Olympian circle, its literary offerings, while geographically limited to Western (mostly male) authors, were impressive. They included English works by, among others, Henry James, Joseph Conrad, George Gissing, Rudyard Kipling, and R. L. Stevenson; French works by Paul Bourget, Pierre Loti, and Mallarmé; and German works by Theodor Fontane and Arthur Schnitzler.[89] Some of these authors, it should be noted, contributed essays rather than original literature. As regards criticism, the comparative slant was particularly evident in the many essays that focused on reception and international circulation, highlighting the agency of mediators and the special significance of moments of encounter between different national literatures. As we have already seen, the journal made a feature of representing the distant and comparative look of the foreign observer. In the very first issue the Danish critic Georg Brandes set the tone by writing in French about an English drama, Shakespeare's *Othello*, as a work of world literature.[90] Later issues would occasionally carry mini clusters of essays, in different languages, marking literary events deemed of international significance, such as the death of the French dramatist Alexandre Dumas *fils* (February 1896) or the hundredth anniversary of the birth of Heinrich Heine (December 1897). In addition to its varied offering of literary essays, *Cosmopolis* also provided readers with regular literary chronicles that kept them up to date with major literary trends and debates in the three main language areas covered by the journal: Andrew Lang took care of the English ones, flanked by the French critic Emile Faguet and the Austrian Anton Bettelheim—all established figures with solid connections to quality periodicals in their respective countries. All this activity contributed to bring into relief a busy, shared literary culture that existed on a supranational level.

True to the journal's policy of neutrality, Ortmans never set an explicit critical agenda. However, several key contributors explicitly or implicitly revisited some of the classic arguments about world literature. For instance, in a programmatic

fortunate in securing the full text'. [Anon.], '"The Case Against Goethe": A Severe Indictment', *Review of Reviews*, 13 (June 1896), 523.

[89] On the international relations of German literature in *Cosmopolis*, see Julia Schroda, '*Cosmopolis*—drei Jahre *Internationale Revue* im Dienst der europäischen Verständigung (1896–98)', in Michel Grunewald and Uwe Puschner, eds, *Krisenwahrnehmungen in Deutschland um 1900: Zeitschriften als Foren der Umbruchszeit im wilhelminischen Reich/Receptions de la Crise en Allemagne au début du XXᵉ siècle: Les Périodiques et la mutation de la societé allemande à l'époque wilhelmienne* (Bern and Berlin: Peter Lang, 2010), 419–437 (428–429).

[90] Georg Brandes, 'Othello', *Cosmopolis*, 1 (Jan. 1896), 154–170 (esp. 165–166).

article on contemporary French culture that ran across the first two issues, the Swiss critic Edouard Rod—another prolific international mediator—described Europe as a space of free circulation and productive exchange in terms that looked back to Goethe's legacy:

> There is already in place a *European literature*, a continuous free exchange that is not stopped either by customs erected by officials or by borders erected by strongholds. Tomorrow there will be a *world literature*: ideas will arrive from the most far-flung corners of the globe, they will crowd, they will fight one another, they will chase one another with ever-increasing rapidity, cluttering our memories, developing around our imaginations a mobile panorama in which we will hardly have time to fix their fugitive aspects [. . .].[91]

Goethe's ideal, locally realized on a European level, now awaited its full realization as the literatures of Europe opened themselves to influences and voices from other parts of the globe, multiplied and propelled towards the old continent by the acceleration of global connections. For Rod, who saw literary cosmopolitanism ('cosmopolitisme littéraire') as a defining characteristic of modern culture,[92] the notion that literatures were kept separate by the political boundaries of the nations was outdated and preposterous. Following Goethe, he also stressed that literature's inevitable post-national trajectory would not entail erasing its distinctive national characteristics. That is, for instance, French literature would not in the future become less and less French. Rather, literary modernity consisted everywhere in the ability to manage multiplicity and complexity, conjugating local traditions with the centrifugal forces that came from abroad. At this crucial moment of cosmopolitan opening, the challenge for periodical culture was simultaneously to encourage and regulate the potentially overwhelming flow of ideas.

In the same issue, the French historian Gabriel Monod, founder of the *Revue historique*, offered a complementary take on questions of national and global identities. In an article that celebrated the twentieth anniversary of the Bayreuth Festival, Monod noted the apparent paradox that this most international event was established by Richard Wagner with the explicit aim of promoting a German *national* art. On the basis of this, he proceeded to deconstruct the false opposition between the national and universal in literature: 'What is more Greek than Homer, more Latin than Virgil, more Italian than Dante, more Spanish

---

[91] Edouard Rod, 'Le Mouvement des idées en France: L'Esprit littéraire', *Cosmopolis*, 2 (Feb. 1896), 447–456 (451–452) ('Il y a déjà une *littérature européenne*, un libre-échange continu que n'arrêtent ni les douanes hérissées de fonctionnaires ni les frontières hérissées de forteresses. Il y aura demain une *littérature mondiale*: des idées viendront des coins les plus reculés du globe, se presseront, se combattront, se chasseront avec une rapidité toujours croissante, encombrant nos mémoires, développant autour de nos imaginations un panorama mobile dont nous aurons à peine le temps de fixer les aspects fugitifs').

[92] Ibid. 447.

than Cervantes, more English than Shakespeare, more French than Molière, more Russian than Tolstoy? At the same time, what is more universal?'[93] The argument that great authors are representative of a specific culture and, at the same time, the shared property of readers everywhere—that is, that they are denationalized by the very virtue of embodying something that is profoundly national and local—is another *locus classicus* of theories of world literature that acquired increased topicality in this age of rising nationalism (Gide would use the same argument, and almost the same examples, in his anti-fascist speech at the 1935 International Writers' Congress for the Defence of Culture).[94] Just as the Bayreuth Festival, which started as a celebration of German music, now gathered an international public that Monod described as 'a new race, unknown by ethnographers and explorers, the polyglot race of the Wagnerians', *Cosmopolis* would shape a new race of polyglot readers who looked to literature and the arts as the proof that 'national differences can be an element of harmony and union'.[95]

Earlier in the chapter we saw that the *Cosmopolitan* magazine liked to present cosmopolitanism as a topic of debate and controversy. In a similar fashion, in order to showcase new and sometimes discordant perspectives, *Cosmopolis* occasionally opened its doors to controversial ideas, such as the so-called 'renaissance latine' and pan-Germanism. For instance, the journal published an article by Ola Hansson in which the Swedish writer spoke of a Germanic earth spirit as the binding agent of the peoples of Northern Europe (we have seen in Chapter 3 how Hansson's pan-Germanism fed into anti-Semitic discourses).[96] The most long-lasting controversy in *Cosmopolis*, however, related to the international circulation of Scandinavian literature, reflecting nationalist concerns that were bubbling up in various parts of Europe at this point. In June 1896, a moderately anti-Ibsen piece by Francisque Sarcey, which invited readers to treasure the 'qualités natives' of French literature,[97] was juxtaposed with an article by Edmund Gosse, in which the English critic accused the French Jules Lemaître of literary chauvinism. In a recent essay on the influence of Scandinavia, Lemaître—a proponent of the Latin renaissance—had provocatively suggested that Ibsen had added nothing to

---

[93] Gabriel Monod, 'Le Jubilé des Nibelungen', *Cosmopolis*, 2 (Feb. 1896), 471–493 (493) ('Qu'y a-t-il de plus grec qu'Homère, de plus latin que Virgile, de plus italien que Dante, de plus espagnol que Cervantès, de plus anglais que Shakespeare, de plus français que Molière, de plus russe que Tolstoï? Qu'y a-t-il aussi de plus humain?').

[94] An English version of Gide's speech was published in the *Left Review* in 1935. See Ben Tran, 'Queer Internationalism and Modern Vietnamese Aesthetics', in Mark Wollaeger and Matt Eatough, eds, *The Oxford Handbook of Global Modernisms* (Oxford and New York: Oxford University Press, 2012), 367–387 (370–371).

[95] Monod, 'Le Jubilé des Nibelungen', 477, 493 ('race nouvelle, inconnue des ethnographes et des explorateurs, la race polyglotte des Wagnériens'; 'les diversités nationales peuvent être un élément d'harmonie et d'union').

[96] Ola Hansson, 'Hans Thoma', *Cosmopolis*, 7 (July 1896), 249–270 (252). The anti-Semitic tendencies of pan-Germanism were already pronounced in Julius Langbehn's foundational *Rembrandt als Erzieher* (1890).

[97] Francisque Sarcey, 'Henrick Ibsen', *Cosmopolis*, 6 (June 1896), 738–752 (751).

French literature that was not already there in George Sand and Dumas *fils*.[98] Gosse, who was an important mediator of Ibsen and Scandinavian literature in the English context, now denounced Lemaître as a 'McKinley of literature, depreciating foreign goods in the hope of raising the price of native produce'.[99] Gosse reactivated the metaphors of world literature as free trade picked up by Marx and Engels and Max Müller, and connected them to the very contemporary phenomenon of American economic protectionism, of which he also clearly disapproved. He concluded in no uncertain terms that Lemaître's incitement to '"une réaction du génie latin," [. . .] is fit to make us weep'.[100] Over the following months, the English translator Robert Nisbet Bain and the German author Lou Andreas Salomé amplified the controversy by adding contrasting views from the English and German angles—Bain deploying familiar phobias and clichés about naturalism and decadence, while Salomé emphasized progressive elements such as the cosmopolitan orientation of Scandinavian writers and their interest in gender.[101]

The defining contribution on Scandinavia and world literature, however, came from the pen of Georg Brandes. The Danish critic used his authority as one of Europe's most respected—and sometimes controversial—critics to respond, in the name of Scandinavians, to French critics who lamented the excessive influence of Scandinavian writers on French literature. Brandes subverted the terms of the debate by declaring at the outset that, in fact, what had been exported so far from Scandinavia—but also, by extension, from any country—was 'nothing or next to nothing'.[102] He thus implied that the real cosmopolitan turn in literature was still to come; that translators, mediators, and comparatists had a long way ahead of them. Brandes attacked ideologies of nativism and literary sovereignty, which, he stressed, were present in Scandinavia as much as in France and other European countries. Against the rhetoric of invasion, competition, self-sufficiency, and protection of native cultures used by nationalists, Brandes defended the value of

---

[98] Jules Lemaître, 'L'Influence récente des littératures du nord', in *Les Contemporains: Études et portraits littéraires*, 6th ser. (Paris: Lecène, Oudin, et Cie, 1896), 225–270 (235–239).

[99] Edmund Gosse, 'Current French Literature', *Cosmopolis*, 6 (June 1896), 660–677 (677).

[100] Ibid. The soon-to-be American president William McKinley, who was elected into office later that year, had come to prominence as a strong advocate of raising tariffs on foreign imports in order to protect the American economy.

[101] Robert Nisbet Bain, 'Contemporary Scandinavian Belles-Lettres', *Cosmopolis*, 11 (Nov. 1896), 355–369 (359 and *passim*); and Lou Andreas Salomé, 'Skandinavische Dichter', *Cosmopolis*, 11 (Nov. 1896), 552–569. It is worth noting that Bain was particularly scathing about Ola Hansson's *Young Ofeg's Ditties* but made no mention of Egerton's recent translation. See also his later 'Scandinavian Current Belles-Lettres', *Cosmopolis*, 33 (Sept. 1898), 673–683. The controversy over Ibsen's alleged borrowings from George Sand would be taken up one more time in Victor Basch, 'Ibsen et George Sand', *Cosmopolis*, 26 (Feb. 1898), 466–492. Basch pointed out the symbolic importance of the controversy as 'une question de littérature comparée qui peut présenter un certain intérêt aux lecteurs de cette Revue cosmopolite' (467) and called for an approach that would understand and value cultural difference.

[102] Brandes, 'Henrik Ibsen en France', 112 ('A vrai dire ce q'on est approprié de nous est rien ou presque rien').

literary 'hospitality' that harked back to classical Kantian cosmopolitanism.[103] There was a deeply personal dimension to this argument for, as we have seen, Brandes had been marginalized in his native Denmark and forced to pursue his literary career abroad. Writing in French in *Cosmopolis* was a gesture of social and political activism by means of which Brandes reclaimed the cosmopolitan right to hospitality, which he believed fundamental to the ethics of world literature.[104]

This is also where Brandes proceeded to reveal a series of misunderstandings and errors generated in the process of translating Ibsen into French, as we have seen in the previous section. His purpose was not pedantically to correct mistakes but to show that the criticism of foreign literatures called for special skills and, at the same time, for special sensitivity and humbleness. He demanded that foreign authors be treated with respect—the respect that is due to guests according to the rules of hospitality. Brandes laid down an ethics of critical practice for the conduct of international literary relations: he satirized readers, like Sarcey, who 'find everywhere equivalences and similarities, rather like certain amateur etymologists take pleasure in deriving French words from Turkish words that sound vaguely similar'.[105] While the amateur critic attempted to domesticate foreign literatures by spotting presumed points of contact with the domestic, a truly cosmopolitan perspective should start from acknowledging the state of interdependence of national literatures, respecting difference within interconnectedness. Source-finding and the search for origins should therefore be seen as fraught methods beloved by nationalist critics who wanted to reinforce ideologically loaded ideas of originality and purity. The ulterior aim of such approaches was to keep literatures apart, erecting false boundaries between them. Instead, the eyes of the cosmopolitan critic should be on the dynamics of flux and networking. Brandes's conclusion brought him surprisingly close to one of the main principles of Wilde's cosmopolitan criticism in 'The Critic as Artist': 'the absolutely new does not exist in literature as such'.[106]

Brandes expanded this argument in his better-known essay 'World Literature' ('Verdensliteratur', 1899). There, he explicitly compared the present to the age of Goethe, concluding that the turn of the twentieth century, despite the increasing internationalization of the press and a more widespread circulation of translations, was a time of 'ever stronger and more bellicose nationalism'.[107] The result of

---

[103] Ibid. 113.

[104] According to Svend Erik Larsen, Brandes's activism is precisely what makes his work particularly relevant to comparative and world literature today. Larsen, 'Georg Brandes', in Theo D'haen et al., eds, *The Routledge Companion to World Literature*, 22.

[105] Brandes, 'Henrik Ibsen en France', 122 ('trouvant partout des équivalents et des ressemblances, à peu près comme certains étymologistes dilettanti et spirituels s'amusent a dériver des mots français de mots turcs, dont le son présente quelque analogie').

[106] Ibid. 124 ('l'absolument nouveau n'existe pas dans la littérature proprement dite').

[107] Brandes, 'World Literature', 27 ('I de sidste Aartier af det 19de Aarhundrede har en stedse stærkere og hidsigere Nationalfølelse trængt disse Tanker tilbage', 28).

this political situation was that literatures everywhere had become 'ever more national'.[108] National and cosmopolitan loyalties should not, however, be seen as excluding one another: the 'world literature of the future' would create its universal spirit out of respect for the variety and diversity of local literatures.[109] This was by no means an endorsement of cultural nationalism, which Brandes observed with discomfort. Rather, Brandes developed Goethe's Herderian, cultural relativist position that world literature did not mean 'the nations thinking alike', using it as a warning for modern authors: any deliberate attempt to write for a large international public would result, according to him, in bland ephemeral works—he cited the example of Zola, whose recent trilogy Lourdes-Rome-Paris had failed precisely because he had aimed to write not for France but for 'the entire world'.[110] In order to achieve universal and lasting value, literature should be rooted in local knowledge and preserve a local flavour. In this later work, published both in Danish and German, the ethical question of respect for the foreign element in literature discussed in *Cosmopolis* led Brandes to write scathingly against the distorting power of translation, and to criticize the imbalance between small and large nations—or, to be precise, between small and large languages—when it came to gaining world literature status. He noted that France still had a disproportionate influence in determining a work's international standing, followed by England and Germany: as he conceded somewhat despondently, 'It is only the writers in these three lands who can hope of being read in the original by the most educated in all nations.'[111] This complaint about the unfair advantage of French, English, and German can be read as a materialist critique of the vision of world literature embraced by *Cosmopolis*, which had already gone under at that point, for perpetuating a hierarchical mentality that was in fact untrue to Goethe's ideal.

Nonetheless, Brandes's own example shows that *Cosmopolis*, despite its biases and limitations, did, during its short life span, take on the role that Goethe hoped periodicals would play in facilitating and intensifying international literary relations. In a sense, the debate over Scandinavian literature staged by the journal in 1896 was old news, rehearsing as it did arguments that had already been aired in the national presses in France, Britain, and other countries. What was different was that, in the pages of the international periodical, disputes that had taken place on a local level were contextualized and relativized within a larger cultural space, where foreign voices could participate directly, as agents, and not merely as objects of debate. A related case in point was Yeats's only contribution to *Cosmopolis* in the last year of the journal's run: 'The Celtic Element in Literature' was a delayed reply to Matthew Arnold's 'On the Study of Celtic Literature' (1866), originally

---

[108] Ibid. 27 ('Literaturerne bliver i vore Dage bestandigt mere nationale', 28).
[109] Ibid. 27 ('Fremtidens Verdensliteratur', 28).   [110] Ibid. 26 ('for den hele Jord', 28).
[111] Ibid. 25 ('Det er kun Skribenterne i disse tre Folkeslag, der kan haabe paa at blive læste i Originalen af de mest Dannede i alle Nationer', 25).

published in the *Cornhill Magazine*. Arnold's essay was attracting renewed attention in Britain in the context of the Irish literary revival of the 1890s. Publishing in an international review, Yeats was able to shift the debate on the so-called Celtic renaissance from the narrow and highly politicized prism of Anglo-Irish relations, projecting it instead onto a broader, European set of alliances and exchanges. It is telling that, while Arnold's essay focused on English cultural identity, Yeats connected Celtic literature to international symbolism, associating it with the writings of Villiers de l'Isle-Adam, Mallarmé, Ibsen, and D'Annunzio among others.[112] In this sense, the most powerful contribution that *Cosmopolis* made to world literature was to enable authors to write from 'home' but, simultaneously, from a different perspective, creating a space that mediated between the national and international spheres.

## *Cosmopolis* and the English *Fin de Siècle*

In his interview for *The Sketch* quoted earlier, Ortmans declared that *Cosmopolis* would be 'above all else [. . .] a literary review' and that it would aim to publish the best living authors writing in English, French, and German.[113] In keeping with the journal's commitment to world literature, the English list suggests that Ortmans targeted a mixture of famous authors and writers who specialized in foreign and international themes. The latter included the important Ibsen critic and translator William Archer, Edmund Gosse (who wrote as an English expert on French literature), Vernon Lee, George Moore, A. Mary F. Robinson (who published under her married name of M.me J. Darmesteter), G. B. Shaw, and Helen Zimmern. Arthur Symons contributed some travel essays that would later form part of his collection *Cities* (1903), and Max Müller a series of biographical pieces. The high calibre of the English fiction selected for inclusion was already very much in evidence in the opening number, which featured the first instalment of a posthumous work by the world-famous R. L. Stevenson ('Weir of Hermiston') and the first half of one of James's very best short stories, 'The Figure in the Carpet'. In Britain, Ortmans gained a reputation for treating his authors well—Henry James remembered that he was paid a handsome sum and that, on top of that, Ortmans entertained him 'gorgeously at the Savoy'.[114]

---

[112] W. B. Yeats, 'The Celtic Element in Literature', *Cosmopolis*, 30 (June 1898), 675–686 (685–686). On national identity in Arnold, see Joep Leerssen, 'Englishness, Ethnicity, and Matthew Arnold', *European Journal of English Studies*, 10.1 (2006), 63–79.
[113] [Anon.], 'An International Review and its Editor', 6.
[114] James, letter to Violet Hunt, 8 Jan. 1902, quoted in Robert Secor, 'Henry James and Violet Hunt, the "Improper Person of Babylon"', *Journal of Modern Literature*, 13.1 (1986), 3–36 (10). Hunt published her own story '"The Truth, the Whole Truth—"' in *Cosmopolis*, in Sept. 1896.

Even more importantly, Ortmans was prepared to entrust his star authors with a high degree of freedom. Mallarmé published in *Cosmopolis* one of his most experimental works, the poem 'Un coup de dés', which played with typographical layout in a daring, unprecedented way.[115] Nothing as outrageous came from the journal's English contributors. However, one way that Ortmans distinguished himself from his English competitors was by willingly accepting novellas—too long to fit into one single issue but too short for book publication—that many English journals were reluctant to print. Looking back on the 1890s periodical market, James characterized this longer short-story form as fundamentally alien to English culture:

> It was under the star of the *nouvelle* that, in other languages, a hundred interesting and charming results, such studies on the minor scale as the best of Turgenieff's, of Balzac's, of Maupassant's, of Bourget's, and just lately, in our own tongue, of Kipling's, had been, all economically, arrived at—thanks to their authors', as 'contributors', having been able to count, right and left, on a wise and liberal support. It had taken the blank misery of our Anglo-Saxon sense of such matters to organise, as might be said, the general indifference to this fine type of composition. In that dull view, a 'short story' was a 'short story', and that was the end of it.[116]

The fact that both stories James published in *Cosmopolis*—'The Figure in the Carpet' and 'John Delavoy'—fell into this awkward category shows that the international review was able practically to provide that 'liberal support' that James struggled to find within the domestic market.

It is significant that, in his recollections of the challenges of the *nouvelle* form, James put his contributions to *Cosmopolis* together with the stories he published in the *Yellow Book* ('The Death of the Lion', 'The Coxon Fund', 'The Next Time'), building a connection between these outwardly dissimilar journals. In January 1896, *Cosmopolis* came into the market at a charged moment in the history of English literary periodicals. The quarterly *Yellow Book* was still prominent but it had been badly hit by the Wilde trials, as a result of which it had got rid of its iconic arts editor, Aubrey Beardsley. That same month saw the launch of *The Savoy*—also initially a quarterly—where Beardsley had now migrated, which promised to provide a home for the progressive and controversial content from which the *Yellow Book* had started to shy away, and to be even more Francophile

---

[115] Stéphane Mallarmé, 'Un coup de dés jamais n'abolira le hasard', *Cosmopolis*, 17 (May 1897), 417–427.

[116] Henry James, 'The Lesson of the Master, The Death of the Lion, The Next Time, The Figure in the Carpet, The Coxon Fund', in *Literary Criticism: French Writers, Other European Writers, The Prefaces to the New York Edition* (New York: Literary Classics of the United States; Cambridge: Press Syndicate of the University of Cambridge, 1984), 1225–1237 (1227).

in outlook. *Cosmopolis* entered the English scene as a potential competitor to these two important literary journals, which also addressed themselves to a cosmopolitan readership.

James's prominent presence in the inaugural number of *Cosmopolis* directly invited a comparison with the *Yellow Book*, which, in its first issue, had also featured a James story—'The Death of the Lion', a self-reflexive tale on modern publishing and the status of literature in the marketplace. As Philip Horne has pointed out, James's stories for the *Yellow Book* and *Cosmopolis* shared formal and thematic features that set them apart from the works that he was placing in other journals at this time: not only did they stretch the short-story form notably in terms of length, as James was later to remember, but they were also the tales where he 'most forcefully [put] forward his dismay at the stupidity and vulgarity of the new literary world of inflationary advertising and "personalities"'.[117] The connection between the two journals was reinforced by Andrew Lang, who, also in the opening issue of *Cosmopolis*, praised the *Yellow Book* for fighting against the low standards of modern literary journalism:[118] the international review and the domestic decadent magazine shared ground in seeking to stem the flow of the excessive commercialization of the periodical market.

The extent of *Cosmopolis*'s overlap with the English little magazines is best shown by the fact that, over the next three years, Ortmans recruited some of the most prominent authors who orbited around the *Yellow Book* and *The Savoy*: besides James, these included Gissing, Gosse, Lee, George Moore, Shaw, Symons, and Yeats. The same interaction with the progressive scene of the *petites revues* was also true of the German and French lists—Mallarmé, for instance, set aside his close collaboration with the *Revue blanche* in order to publish 'Un coup de dés' in *Cosmopolis*.[119] Despite these productive exchanges, however, *Cosmopolis* failed to embed itself in the English literary culture of the 1890s to the same extent as the *Yellow Book* and *The Savoy*, which soon came to be regarded as iconic of the special zeitgeist of the decade.[120] Operating as it did on an extraterritorial level, the international review never established the strong actual links with cultural institutions and social spaces (cafés, salons, galleries, theatres, music venues) that were crucial in helping the authors of little magazines build a sense of collective identity and shared mission.

---

[117] Philip Horne, 'Henry James and the Economy of the Short Story', in Warren Chernaik, Warwick Gould, and Ian Willison, eds, *Modernist Writers and the Marketplace* (Basingstoke: Palgrave Macmillan, 1996), 1–35 (13).

[118] Andrew Lang, 'Literary Chronicle', *Cosmopolis*, 1 (Jan. 1896), 70–87 (70).

[119] Gordon Millan, 'La Publication d'*Un coup de dés* dans *Cosmopolis*', *Études Stéphane Mallarmé*, 1 (2003), 21–28.

[120] Koenraad Claes, *The Late-Victorian Little Magazine* (Edinburgh: Edinburgh University Press, 2018), 107–142; Ian Fletcher, 'Decadence and the Little Magazines', in Ian Fletcher, ed., *Decadence and the 1890s* (London: Edward Arnold, 1979), 173–202; Margaret D. Stetz and Mark Samuels Lasner, *The Yellow Book: A Centenary Exhibition* (Cambridge, MA: Houghton Library, 1994).

Nothing encapsulates the limitations of the journal's neutral, denationalized space more clearly than its strict policy of non-illustration. By refusing to print images and resolutely sticking to a conservative design, *Cosmopolis* distanced itself from the image-saturated commercial end of the market but also, crucially, from the sleek visual idiom of the little magazines. Around the turn of the century artists positively drove the orientation of many small but influential literary journals. As we have seen with the *Punch* caricatures analysed in the Introduction and earlier in this chapter, Beardsley's distinctive style became a visual prompt for the cosmopolitan sympathies of the English aesthetic and decadent circles that gathered around the *Yellow Book* and *The Savoy*. Similarly, the *Revue blanche* (1889–1903) enlisted the help of the Nabi school, the German *Pan* (1895–1900) employed Berlin-based arts-and-craft artists, and the Austrian *Ver Sacrum* (1898–1903) developed close connections with the Vienna Sezession. The minimalism of *Cosmopolis*, which made it look old-fashioned, serious, and demanding, was a deliberate rejection of this trend: it signalled that the journal was determined to operate above fashions and artistic coteries, indeed almost above time and space. This is why *Cosmopolis* struggled to fit into the lively scene of the little magazines that proliferated in these years and why, despite its outstanding cast of contributors, it was later side-lined in literary histories, which are typically written from national perspectives.[121]

This peculiar position between national marginality and international visibility made *Cosmopolis* a congenial environment for authors who, like James, operated from within Britain but had broader intellectual allegiances. Key in this respect was the role played by Thomas Fisher Unwin, the journal's English publisher.[122] Fisher Unwin was extremely well connected to liberal and progressive circles through his wife, the prominent anti-imperialist and suffragist Jane Cobden, daughter of the Victorian advocate of international free trade, Richard Cobden. Together with his collaborator Edward Garnett, Fisher Unwin was instrumental in attracting to *Cosmopolis* two of his most promising, internationally oriented house authors: Joseph Conrad and Israel Zangwill. Conrad published one of his very first stories in *Cosmopolis*, 'An Outpost of Progress' (June and July 1897), which introduced some of the ideas that he would later develop in *Heart of Darkness* (1899). Also a long short story of the kind that James thought awkwardly suited to the English market, 'An Outpost of Progress' portrayed the moral degeneration of two European commercial agents posted to a remote trading station in central

---

[121] *Cosmopolis* is not examined in the otherwise impressive Peter Brooker et al., eds, *Oxford Critical and Cultural History of Modernist Magazines*, 3 vols (Oxford and New York: Oxford University Press, 2009–13), where contributions are organized by nation. See however Carol de Saint Victor, '*Cosmopolis*', in Alvin Ed Sullivan, ed., *British Literary Magazines: The Victorian and Edwardian Age, 1837–1913* (Westport, CT: Greenwood Press, 1984), 85–92. Most of the existing scholarly articles on *Cosmopolis* examine the specific involvement of individual authors.

[122] The French and German publishers of *Cosmopolis* were, respectively, Armand Colin (Paris) and Rosenbaum & Hart (Berlin).

Africa, where they agree to selling locals into slavery in return for ivory. The setting of the novella echoed the journal's interest in European colonial policies in Africa, explored in several political essays.[123] But Conrad's critique of the moral corruption of European colonialism was more scathing than anything else in the journal. With bitter irony, 'An Outpost of Progress' exposed the hollowness of a Western ideal of 'progress' based on colonial exploitation. In particular, it eviscerated the notion that 'civilisation follows trade' by showing the degrading effects of an exploitative and dehumanizing form of global capitalism on both African and European populations.[124]

Equally significant was the inclusion of five stories by Israel Zangwill, which made him one of the most prolific contributors to *Cosmopolis*. As we have seen, Zangwill had risen to fame with his novel *Children of the Ghetto*, which gave a sympathetic portrayal of Jewish immigrants by domesticating them through the quintessentially English literary form of the working-class novel *à la* Gissing. In 1896, Fisher Unwin brought out Zangwill's collected essays *Without Prejudice*, which addressed questions of, among others, Jewish identity, cosmopolitanism and patriotism, and contemporary literature, building up Zangwill's profile as cultural critic as well as author.[125] In his short fictions for *Cosmopolis*, Zangwill furthered his ambition to bring Jewish subjects into mainstream and world literature. The accomplished story 'Chad Gadya' in particular focused on the generational conflict between a pious elderly Venetian Jew and his emancipated son. The son, through whose eyes we see the unfolding of the events, is a pleasure-seeking aesthete, who has escaped 'the joyous slavery of the Ghetto' by going to live in Vienna and becoming 'an adept in the forbidden'.[126] On a visit to his family during Passover, hearing his father sing the 'Chad Gadya' (a song that is sung at the end of the ritual *Seder*) brings him to reflect on his own identity, which is torn between the idealism of his father's traditional Judaism and the materialism of the cosmopolitan lifestyle that he has chosen for himself. Overcome by his internal conflict, the son commits suicide by throwing himself into the lagoon. Surprisingly perhaps, 'Chad Gadya' projects a fundamentally pessimistic outlook on cosmopolitanism as a doctrine that divests the world of moral purpose and precludes the individual from developing a sense of community. In so doing, Zangwill subverts stereotypes about Jewish identity against the backdrop of a fictional narrative that is extremely aware of the long history of anti-Semitism endured by Venetian Jews: he shows that it is not the Jew who is a citizen of nowhere because of the millennial exile of the Jewish people, but the extreme individualist, adrift in the ethical chaos of modernity. Profoundly different though

---

[123] Laurence Davies, '"Don't you Think I am a Lost Soul?" Conrad's Early Stories and the Magazines', *Conradiana*, 41.1 (2009), 7–28 (21).
[124] Joseph Conrad, 'An Outpost of Progress', *Cosmopolis*, 19 (July 1897), 1–15 (14).
[125] Israel Zangwill, *Without Prejudice* (London: Fisher Unwin, 1896).
[126] Zangwill, 'Chad Gadya', *Cosmopolis*, 7 (July 1896), 1–17 (4, 2).

their stories were in terms of setting and tone, Conrad and Zangwill performed a similar task: they both put pressure on the ideas of civility, progress, and diplomacy that informed the liberal ideal of cosmopolitanism as 'closer fellowship' embraced by *Cosmopolis*. Their stories, in other words, stretched and questioned the limits of the metropolitan European perspective of the journal from within.

The conflict between idealism and materialism captured in Zangwill's story provides a good way of framing the radical differences between *Cosmopolis* and *Cosmopolitan*. The European periodical embodied a fundamentally idealistic vision of cosmopolitanism that resisted the reality of the turn-of-the-century periodical industry: it deliberately looked back to the Enlightenment and Goethe's notion of world literature in order to protect a liberal ideal that it believed threatened by political conflicts and by the spread of consumer culture. By contrast, *Cosmopolitan* embraced the opportunities offered by the market, making skilful use of technical innovations in order to reach as wide an audience as possible. In this process, it seized on and broadcast an image of cosmopolitanism that fused social privilege, glamour, and materialism. Such an image was to have a strong impact on the media construction of cosmopolitanism in twentieth-century popular culture internationally. While *Cosmopolis* stood firm in its commitment to anti-nationalist critique, *Cosmopolitan* occasionally provided a platform for nationalist and chauvinistic views in its carefully staged debates on American identity and on the relationship between English and American literature.

However, the fact that the two periodicals shared a number of key contributors—Bourget, James, Lang, Sarcey, Stevenson, Zangwill—also shows that it would be wrong to think that the different visions and practices of cosmopolitanism they 'sold' their readers were totally discreet or indeed antithetical. Zangwill's experience, in particular, shows that literature created a shared space between the two different types of readership the journals cultivated: his collection *Dreamers of the Ghetto* (1898) was made up of stories that he had published in *Cosmopolis* and *Cosmopolitan* almost simultaneously. Similarly, the long lists of adverts for hotels, casinos, and glamorous spa resorts in *Cosmopolis* show that the international review also explicitly targeted a public of well-to-do travellers and worldly socialites: despite its efforts to uncouple cultural and financial capital, its metropolitan identity and outlook entangled the journal in the networks of free-trade capitalism. When he predicted that the future of literary cosmopolitanism would be driven by periodicals, Goethe could not have foreseen the different material circumstances of the much larger and more powerful public sphere of the end of the century. Connecting English literature to transatlantic and European networks, *Cosmopolitan* and *Cosmopolis* created a dynamic space for the diffusion of literary cosmopolitanism driven by the different social aspirations and attitudes to cultural capital of the heterogeneous, fractured, and fast-growing global reading public of English-language periodicals at the *fin de siècle*.

# 5

# Those Who Hoped

## Literary Cosmopolitanism and Artificial Languages

> I am a citizen of the world. [ ... ] I speak Esperanto, which is the language of my country.
>
> (Gaston Moch, quoted in the *Review of Reviews*)
>
> Oh, patriotism, patriotism, when will people finally understand your true meaning! When will your holy name cease to be a weapon in the hands of various liars!
>
> (Ludvik L. Zamenhof, address in the London Guildhall, 21 August 1907)

*Cosmopolitan* and *Cosmopolis* were not the only periodicals that staked an explicit claim to cosmopolitanism in their titles. In 1891, a different *Cosmopolitan* magazine was launched in Sydney with the mission of promoting 'the brotherhood of mankind by assisting all men to understand one another'.[1] Undaunted by a fire that had destroyed the manuscript of the projected first number the previous year, the journal proclaimed that, as world nations moved away from 'established customs' and old religious feuds, '[s]ome will look forward to the future with anxiety and dread; but others will keep a trustful heart and gild the future with prophetic rays of hope'.[2] In the course of its brief life in the 1890s, the Australian *Cosmopolitan* fostered this optimistic vision of global unity and enlightenment by promoting an internationalist outlook in matters of politics as well as literary taste: it published new translations of major foreign authors such as Pushkin and Mérimée, as well as works from 'minor' languages such as Swedish, Basque, Hungarian, and Malay. A distinctive feature of the Australian *Cosmopolitan* was that it was fully bilingual—a choice that drew attention to the importance of language and translation in matters of international communication. Its real peculiarity, though, was that, aside from English, it was not written in any of the established world languages, like *Cosmopolis*, or in one of the languages associated with the Australian immigration, but in a brand-new, artificial language

---

[1] [Anon.], 'Editorial Notice', *The Cosmopolitan/Kosmopolan*, 1 (Feb. 1891), 1–3 (1).
[2] George Walters, 'All's well that Ends Well/Whither?', *The Cosmopolitan/Kosmopolan*, 1 (Feb. 1891), 4.

*Literary Cosmopolitanism in the English* Fin de Siècle: *Citizens of Nowhere*. Stefano Evangelista,
Oxford University Press. © Stefano Evangelista 2021. DOI: 10.1093/oso/9780198864240.003.0006

that was meant to be the very embodiment of the journal's cosmopolitan optimism: Volapük.

Although it is now mostly forgotten or regarded as an historical eccentricity, Volapük was a visible presence in the cultural landscape of the *fin de siècle*. The Australian *Cosmopolitan*—or *Cosmopolitan/Kosmopolan*, as its full bilingual title actually ran—was part of a Volapük network that stretched across continents and is estimated to have numbered fourteen journals, 253 local clubs, and almost 900 certified teachers.[3] Nor was Volapük an isolated experiment. Other artificial languages invented around this time include Pasilingua (1885), Spelin (1888), Spokil (1889), Mundolingue (1889), and, of course, Lingvo Internacia (1887), later known as Esperanto, whose uninterrupted history stretches right to the present day. These linguistic inventions were accompanied by attempts to revive Latin in updated or simplified forms: Universal Latein (1902), Reform Latein (1902), and Latino sine Flexione (1903) are only three of a number of experiments that used the one-time lingua franca of European intellectuals and scientists as the basis for a common language of the future. In 1903, French scholars Louis Couturat and Léopold Leau mapped the large and growing field of artificial languages in their *Histoire de la langue universelle*, which provided an extensive classification of old and new attempts. For Couturat and Leau the necessity of a universal language was no longer a matter for dispute, but something that 'was becoming increasingly urgent and self-evident because of the development in all sorts of relations between civilized nations'.[4] Estimates vary, but scholars now believe that the new, artificial (or, as some scholars prefer to call them, planned or created) languages that saw the light of day in this period number between 150 and 250.[5] Movements of spelling reform, phonetic languages, typewriting, and stenography—which generated their own dedicated schools and magazines—were part of the same effort to make language a more efficient technology and to break down barriers between speakers of different national idioms.

This search for a universal language was not a new phenomenon of the turn of the century. In pre-Enlightenment times, the aim of language creators had been to

[3] Roberto Garvía, *Esperanto and its Rivals: The Struggle for an International Language* (Philadelphia: University of Pennsylvania Press, 2015), 47. These figures refer to what Garvía identifies as the historical 'peak' of Volapük in 1889, shortly preceding the launch of *Cosmopolitan/Kosmopolan*.

[4] Louis Couturat and Léopold Leau, *Histoire de la langue universelle* (Paris: Hachette, 1903), p. vii ('[E]lle s'impose avec une evidence et une urgence croissantes, à mesure que se développent les relations de toute sorte entre les nations civilisées').

[5] Grace Brockington has calculated that around 150 new languages were invented between 1860 and 1920, with peaks in the 1880s and between 1905 and 1915. Brockington, 'Introduction: The Expanded Universal Language Movement', in Charlotte Ashby et al., eds, *Imagined Cosmopolis: Internationalism and Cultural Exchange, 1870s–1920s* (Oxford and Bern: Peter Lang, 2019), 351–378 (369). Markus Krajewski quotes an even higher figure, claiming that the number of artificial languages in existence around 1900 was approximately 250. Krajewski, 'Organizing a Global Idiom: *Esperanto, Ido* and the World Auxiliary Language Movement Before the First World War', in W. Boyd Rayward, ed., *Information beyond Borders: International Cultural and Intellectual Exchange in the Belle Époque* (Farnham and Burlington, VT: Ashgate, 2014), 97–108 (98).

find a perfect language that would enable speakers to formulate thoughts in a more precise way than what was available to them through the demotic and allegedly corrupted natural languages, in order to get closer to philosophical truth or to the essence of things.[6] Now, however, the prime goal was universal communication: the artificial languages of the *fin de siècle*, like Volapük and Esperanto, were meant to enable people of different nationalities to speak to each other effectively and on equal terms. As both the Australian *Cosmopolitan* and Couturat and Leau testify, the need for a universal language was seen as a direct consequence of processes of globalization and modernization: in a world that advanced at an ever faster pace, where times, weights, and measures were largely standardized, and where people were more mobile than ever, it seemed imperative that knowledge and information should circulate internationally unhindered by linguistic barriers. Importantly, this practical objective very often went together with a type of utopianism: the belief that the adoption of a universal language would aid international relations and, ultimately, pave the way to world peace. Idealistic though they were, modern promoters of universal languages believed that they had an advantage over their earlier counterparts, whose efforts, driven by philosophical or religious ambitions, were often clouded in mysticism. Now science was revolutionizing linguistic knowledge, while modern communication and transport technologies—print, mail, the telegraph, railways, steamships—could boost the spread of a new language in unprecedented ways.

Universal languages were therefore intended to lay down a practical route to world citizenship. Directly or indirectly, they built on the philosophical tradition that went back to Kant's ideal of a 'great federation' of world nations, which their speakers and promoters believed was now closer to realization than ever before.[7] In common with other forms of cosmopolitan activism, universal language movements shared an ethical commitment to securing equality among different nations and races, dialogue, fraternity, and justice. For their exponents, language was where differences between peoples and nations were most indelibly encrypted: it was the framework that needed to be questioned and dismantled most urgently if divisive nationalisms were to be effectively opposed. Although, as we shall see, the radical aims of these movements by no means included the abolition of national languages or their literary heritage, universal languages did overthrow normative ways of relating language and national identity rooted in Herder. According to the view that Herder put forward in the 'Treatise on the Origin of Language', the organic evolution of a language was inextricably bound with the identity and destiny of a people. It followed that language expressed a people's unique spiritual essence: it

---

[6] Umberto Eco, *The Search for the Perfect Language* [1993], tr. James Fentress (London: Fontana, 1997). Eco provides an accessible overview of attempts to create a priori and a posteriori universal languages, from a perspective that merges philosophy and linguistics.
[7] Kant, 'Idea for a Universal History', 47.

was the ultimate embodiment of what differentiated it from other peoples, providing a natural justification for the division of humanity into national groups. Herder saw languages as natural, living organisms and was highly sceptical of attempts to regulate them from above. He rhetorically asked: 'what can the philosopher and philologist in his dead museum improve in a language which *lives* in all its efficacy?'[8] At the turn of the twentieth century, the inventors and proponents of universal languages worked within that 'dead museum', contravening the process of natural development as Herder saw it by working backwards from the late stages of language evolution: artificial languages like Volapük and Esperanto were written before they became oral; they had recorded rules before they were even used; they moved, to use Herder's organic metaphor, from death to life. They did so deliberately, of course, in order to break apart some of the nationalist mythology that had accrued around romantic theories of language over the course of the nineteenth century.

Criticizing the ideological manipulation of language by nationalist groups, E. J. Hobsbawm has pointed out that national languages are in fact 'almost always semi-artificial constructs' and 'the opposite of what nationalist mythology supposes them to be, namely the primordial foundations of national culture and the matrices of the national mind'.[9] As we have seen in the Introduction, the ideologically charged notion of a 'national' language aided the emancipation of oppressed minorities (such as the Irish, for instance, or the Italians who lived under Austro-Hungarian rule), who could use it to boost a communal identity and resist pressures to conform with dominant cultures; but it could also be used to draw and enforce boundaries, to exaggerate differences between nations, and to propagate myths of mutual incomprehensibility that entrenched feelings of division and hostility. Conscious of this fact, promoters of universal languages believed that, if people around the world could be persuaded to adopt a single shared language, they would see that those differences could easily be overcome.

Why, then, could not one of the *existing* world languages be adopted for universal use? At the end of the nineteenth century, in Europe and beyond, French remained the international language of diplomacy and, to a large extent, culture; English had established itself as the lingua franca of commerce; and German was increasingly laying claim to science. Arguments in favour of the universal adoption of English repeatedly came up against objections that its spelling was too eccentric and its pronunciation too complicated for non-natives to master. It was with this in mind that, in 1888, Alexander Melville Bell (the father of Alexander Graham Bell—credited as the inventor of the telephone) devised a system that he called 'World-English', which kept the sound and

---

[8] Herder, 'Treatise on the Origin of Language', 136 ('was kann denn der Philosoph und Philolog in seinem toten Museum an einer Sprache verbessern, die in aller ihrer Würksamkeit *lebt*?', 779).
[9] E. J. Hobsbawm, *Nations and Nationalism*, 54.

grammar of the language intact but regularized spelling by introducing a host of new symbols:

> evėri wun haz hėʌd ov ḓi bùç̧èʌ, hū, åftėr a loŋ sèʌç̧ foʌ hiz nɪf, at last fåùnd it in hiz måùţ. sō, spēkèʌz ov iŋgliṣ hav bin sēkiŋ for a yùnivė'ʌsal laŋgwij, ꭓen lō! it iz in ḓèʌ måùḓz! ḓi intelijibi'liti ov wuʌdz haz bin obskyù'ʌd bɪ a dens mist ov letèʌz. ḓis iz nåù dispè'ʌst in wuʌld-iŋgliṣ; and ḓi laŋgwij standz rēvē'ld— bēyo'nd kompa'risun klēʌ, simpl, kōpius, and kozmòpo'litan—ḓi fitiŋ tuŋ ov ꭓùma'niti. [10]

Bell believed that it was impossible to invent an artificial language that would surpass English 'in grammatical simplicity, and in general fitness to become the tongue of the World'.[11] But what that 'general fitness' exactly consisted in was clearly a subjective question. More worryingly, his claim that English was somehow in essence the 'fitting tongue of Humanity' had clear imperialistic overtones. To make matters worse, Bell envisaged a two-caste system, where 'non-scholastic learners' and foreigners would use World-English, while educated, metropolitan English speakers in Britain and America would still operate in what he calls 'Literary English'.[12] Such a hierarchy of power further undercut the language's claim to true universality by entrenching class and national divides. Indeed Bell's experiment shows that trying to elevate any existing language to a universal status risked inflating, rather than putting an end to, the competition between nations for political and cultural supremacy.

The great advantage of artificial languages, beside their grammatical regularity that supposedly made them easier to learn, was that they existed outside national frameworks. They were, so to speak, neutral territories on which the foundations for 'the brotherhood of mankind'—to go back to the opening number of the Australian *Cosmopolitan*—could be laid afresh, unconditioned by pre-existing histories and present asymmetries. What they conspicuously lacked was the immediacy of affect possessed by natural languages—the spontaneous and intimate links with emotion, heritage, and, ultimately, reality that Herder had attributed to the mother tongue. Bell, for one, was aware of this and argued that a great

---

[10] Alexander Melville Bell, *World-English: The Universal Language* (London: Trübner & Co., 1888), 29 ('Every one has heard of the butcher, who, after a long search for his knife, at last found it in his mouth. So, speakers of English have been seeking for a Universal Language, when lo! it is in their mouths! The intelligibility of words has been obscured by a dense mist of letters. This is now dispersed in World-English: and the language stands revealed,—beyond comparison clear, simple, copious, and cosmopolitan,—the fitting tongue of Humanity.').

[11] Ibid. 7.     [12] Ibid. 8.

advantage of World-English was that it did not do away with 'the glorious associations with the forms of our words'.[13] Again, he seemed blind to the fact that this nationalist sentiment ('glorious associations'!) contradicted the spirit of universalism that he overtly professed. In this respect, however, it is also import-ant to take into account that the proliferation of universal languages in the *fin de siècle* occurred simultaneously with attempts to revive virtually dead languages, such as Irish and Hebrew, for nation-building purposes. If those long-forgotten languages could be successfully made to embody shared feelings and identities, why not Volapük or Esperanto? Did the fact that these languages were artificially created inevitably preclude them from becoming a living, natural organism in Herder's sense? Could they not provide a practical alternative to a theory of *Volkesgeist* that was increasingly co-opted in the service of divisive and belligerent nationalisms? Most artificial languages were, after all, built on roots borrowed from various existing languages. Did they not, in their eclecticism, simply reflect the reality of an increasingly interconnected world where exchanges between speakers of different languages were becoming more and more common? Did they not, in other words, mark a natural new step in the ongoing evolution of humanity from a local to a global organization?[14] Such fundamental questions about the relationship between language and identity were deeply relevant to debates around literary cosmopolitanism.

Far from aiming to provide an exhaustive analysis of this complex phenom-enon, this chapter examines how artificial universal languages intersected with the turn-of-the-century literary cosmopolitanism mapped out in this book. We have already seen that the Australian *Cosmopolitan* circulated Volapük translations of literary works from 'minor' languages that were not otherwise accessible in English. As that example shows, the Volapük and, especially, Esperanto move-ments made strategic use of literature and print media in their efforts to unite their sympathizers scattered around the globe and endow them with a shared identity. Their ambitious aim was to create a new type of cosmopolitan literacy that would aid the cause of universal communication. However, despite their flurry of activity, universal language movements remained minority phenomena that oper-ated very much in the margins of mainstream literary culture. In fact, the large majority of writers—internationally oriented ones no less so—saw the new arti-ficial languages as inherently anti-literary. Of the authors discussed in previous chapters, only Hearn admitted to being lured by the 'dream of an universal language'.[15] And, even as he wrote this, Hearn did not have Volapük or

---

[13] Ibid. 7.

[14] Approaching artificial languages through this evolutionary framework, Will Abberley investigates how they shaped utopian fiction of the turn of the century. Abberley, *English Fiction and the Evolution of Language, 1850–1914* (Cambridge and New York: Cambridge University Press, 2015), 22 ff.

[15] Lafcadio Hearn, 'English the Universal Tongue of the Future', in *Editorials*, 166–168 (168). The article was originally published in the New Orleans *Item* on 23 Oct. 1881. Hearn was responding to an

Esperanto in mind. If anything, his 'dream' of a universal language was inspired by his love of the Creole of Louisiana as a language of contamination and border-crossing, which was the demotic, democratic property of the people rather than the bureaucratic instrument of states and governments. Joseph Conrad's flat dismissal of Esperanto as 'a monstrous jargon' was more characteristic of the prevalent negative attitude to artificial languages that, as Kaori Nogai has shown, survives until today even among contemporary theorists of cosmopolitanism.[16] At the turn of the twentieth century, as in the twenty-first, many believed that artificial languages embodied a misguided universalism that flattened human diversity. Given this history of controversy, this chapter starts by investigating an instance of hostile reception in the work of one of the otherwise most cosmopolitan writers of the period, Henry James. James's references to Volapük in one of his stories provide a clear indication of how visible this phenomenon was within mainstream culture, and of the assumptions and prejudices that had become attached to it. In the late 1880s, Volpük was overtaken by Esperanto, the most successful artificial language ever created and the one that made most vigorous use of literature and print media. After examining the key features of the literary cosmopolitanism of Esperanto, the chapter closes with an analysis of the Esperanto movement in turn-of-the-century Britain, focusing on its overlap with artistic and literary cultures.

## Henry James contra Volapük

Henry James's short story 'The Pupil' (1891) is about good and bad forms of cosmopolitanism.[17] The plot is typical of James's so-called international theme. The Moreens, an American family who have settled in Europe, employ another transplanted American, Pemberton, to tutor their adolescent son. The latter, Morgan, is a precocious child who suffers from a serious heart condition. It soon becomes clear that the Moreens live beyond their means: they move from

---

article by the evolutionary philosopher John Fiske published in the *Atlantic Monthly*, in which Fiske predicted that, one hundred years into the future, English would be spoken all over the world.

[16] Conrad to J. R. Pinker, 10 Mar. 1913, in *The Collected Letters of Joseph Conrad*, ed. Frederick R. Karl, 9 vols (Cambridge and London: Cambridge University Press, 1983–2008), v: *1912–1916*, ed. Frederick R. Karl and Laurence Davies (1996), 188. Kaori Nogai, '"The New Bilingualism: Cosmopolitanism in the Era of Esperanto', in Janet Wilson, Cristina Şandru, and Sarah Lawson Welsh, eds, *Rerouting the Postcolonial: New Directions for the Millennium* (London and New York: Routledge, 2010), 48–59 (48). Nogai cites hostile remarks by Robert Pinsky, and goes on to reclaim Esperanto as a 'culture of cosmopolitanism' with specific relevance to postcolonial studies (49).

[17] 'The Pupil' was originally published in two parts in *Longman's Magazine*, 17 (Mar. 1891), 512–531; and (Apr. 1891), 611–632. References in this chapter are to this first periodical edition, and appear in parentheses in the main body of the text. 'The Pupil' was first collected in *The Lesson of the Master and Other Stories* (1892). This is the volume that attracted a negative review by Brander Matthews in *Cosmopolitan*; cf. Chapter 4.

one European city to the next in increasingly shabby accommodations and cannot afford to remunerate Pemberton for his services. The equally impoverished Pemberton, through whose perspective we see the unfolding of the events, is frustrated by this situation, yet he lets himself get trapped in an abusive relationship with the family because he develops a very strong attachment to the boy, whom he cannot bear to leave. He has, in fact, made it his moral mission to save the young Morgan from the corrupt and neglectful ways of his parents. Morgan, for his part, is only too glad to have found a potential saviour. Master and pupil wander together around Nice, Venice, and Paris, walking arm in arm, doing Greek lessons, and buying books and presents for each other. All the time, they plot their escape, fantasizing about a not-too-distant future in which they will live together, away from the Moreens, Pemberton supporting the boy on his private tutoring. Finally, in a moment of particularly acute financial difficulties, it is the Moreens themselves who suggest that they want to entrust the boy to Pemberton. As Mrs Moreen puts it with a characteristic veneer of genteel hypocrisy, '"We've struggled, we've suffered [ . . . ] but you've made him so your own that we've already been through the worst of the sacrifice"' (p. 631). However, just as master and pupil are about to realize their dream, the boy's life is cut short by a heart attack.

In the preface to the American edition, James explained that he conceived of the Moreens as ambiguous relics of the 'golden age' of international travel in the mid-nineteenth century.[18] Ignoring how much the world had moved on since then, they clung to the adulterated last remnants of the romance and glamour of that bygone age. As such, they provided very interesting material 'for the social chronicler, any student in especial of the copious "cosmopolite" legend'.[19] Even without James's guidance, the cosmopolitan theme would be hard to miss. Mr Moreen is described as 'a man of the world' no less than ten times—the epithet becoming an ironic refrain that systematically unveils the character's pretensions, hypocrisy, and moral shortcomings. In the tragic conclusion to the story in particular, Mr Moreen's acceptance of his bereavement 'as a man of the world' (p. 632) is hardly a sign of distinction, revealing instead his lack of real empathy for the death of his child. Caught between a romanticized past and the present age of mass travel and materialism, the Moreens embody a debased cosmopolitan ideal that is entirely based on consumption, social ambition, and display. Indeed, their worldliness is connected to their fraudulent treatment of Pemberton and their constant running away from creditors, from country to country. Having given up America—not only physically, but also in terms of the moral grounding that some of James's other characters derive from their American roots—and, at the same time, unable to belong properly to Europe, the Moreens have ended up in

---

[18] Henry James, 'What Maisie Knew, The Pupil, In the Cage', in *Literary Criticism*, 1156–1172 (1167).
[19] Ibid. 1166.

an emotional and ethical vacuum, plainly revealed by their inability to care for their son. As the pupil bursts out to Pemberton in a moment of frustration, his parents are 'so beastly worldly' that even he is totally ignorant of who or what they really are (p. 614). This negative portrayal of the Moreens as citizens of nowhere enables James to scrutinize cosmopolitanism as a concept marked by ambiguities and historical tensions. Pemberton himself doubts whether 'the term "cosmopolite"' adequately captures the family's shifty social identity (p. 517). To the Yale- and Oxford-educated Pemberton, who has come to Europe in order to escape America's narrow horizons, the word 'cosmopolite' denotes an altogether more high-minded ideal, which is certainly not reflected in the Moreen family's snobbishness and amateurish pursuit of foreign fashions. His relationship with Morgan embodies a contrasting model of world citizenship, enacted through intellectual dialogue and education, which looks back to the classical origins of the cosmopolitan ideal, channelled through the references to their Greek lessons.

The two conflicting models of cosmopolitanism—the Moreens' materialism and Pemberton's ethical idealism—come to a clash over the body of the pupil. Both the brilliant product and victim of a rootless upbringing that has precociously acquainted him with different countries, languages, and social conventions, Morgan Moreen is a vulnerable being, whose talents need to be properly fostered, his health looked after. Pemberton's real love for Morgan and his willingness to sacrifice himself for his pupil easily make the tutor's behaviour ethically superior to the fake and opportunistic affect of the parents. His desire to settle with the child is portrayed as a welcome alternative to the Moreen family's precariousness and neglect. Ultimately, however, the play between bad and good cosmopolitanism in 'The Pupil' is not a clean-cut affair. For it is evident that, despite his sense of ethical superiority, Pemberton is at heart seduced by the unconventional lifestyle of the Moreens, who, as he begrudgingly admits to himself, 'were so out of the workaday world and kept him so out of it' (p. 618). Even more poignantly, his attachment to the boy and desire to mould the upbringing of this 'pale, lean, acute, undeveloped little cosmopolite' (p. 520) are troubled by a mounting queer longing, awkwardly repressed by the narrative, which is amplified in a series of scenes of emotional and physical intimacy.[20] Master and pupil constitute an alternative, cosmopolitan queer family (the classical Greek intertext is again crucial here) whose existence the story envisages but does not bring itself to realize, leaving open questions as to its ethical propriety.

Language plays a crucial role in the tangle of cosmopolitan identities and modes of affect represented in 'The Pupil'. The narrative is hyper-aware of what people

---

[20] The homosexual content of James's story, which was included as the opening item in Edmund White's *Faber Book of Gay Short Fiction* (1991), has been the object of much critical scrutiny. For different views, see Helen Hoy, 'Homotextual Duplicity in Henry James's "The Pupil"', *Henry James Review*, 14.1 (1993), 34–42; and Philip Horne, 'Henry James: The Master and the "Queer Affair" of "The Pupil"', *Critical Quarterly*, 37.3 (1995), 75–92.

speak and how, and of the importance of fluency and accent in a world where
everyone is expected to be a polyglot. In the absence of more concrete assets, the
Moreens' mastery of foreign languages provides them with their main form of
capital: it enables them to move between countries and grants them access to
upper-class society. In fact, the only mention in the story of a possible source of
family income is a reference to Mrs Moreen's former career as a literary
translator—an activity that would, however, hardly have been very lucrative.
The Moreens not only speak excellent French and Italian but can even imitate
dialects for jocular effect. However, the most remarkable feature of the Moreens'
linguistic habits is the fact that they have developed a private family language they
call 'Ultramoreen'. Readers are never offered transcriptions of this eclectic language, but we must presume that it saturated the oral world of the everyday life of
the characters: it is the medium in which members of the family communicate
with each other, and which the master needs to learn in order to get close to the
boy. This explains the striking comparison of Pemberton's process of getting to
know the young Morgan Moreen to a work of translation:

> During the first weeks of their acquaintance Morgan had been as puzzling as a
> page in an unknown language—altogether different from the obvious little
> Anglo-Saxons who had misrepresented childhood to Pemberton. Indeed, the
> whole mystic volume in which the boy had been bound demanded some practice
> in translation. To-day, after a considerable interval, there is something phantas-
> magoric, like a prismatic reflexion or a serial novel, in Pemberton's memory of
> the queerness of the Moreens.   (p. 516)

The young Morgan is a philological exercise that, if properly executed, can unlock
the way into an attractive new world of feeling and perception. At the same
time, translation and standardization are metaphors for Pemberton's moral cru-
sade to save the boy from his biological family's dilettantism and bad affect.
Pemberton's wish to translate the boy mirrors his desire to domesticate him,
that is, to create a stable home for him; while the Moreens' habit of corrupting
language is part and parcel of their corrupted cosmopolitanism—the pun on
the name of the exotic pigment 'ultramarine' captures the family's pretentious
habit of self-mythologizing. Indeed, the entire retrospective, written narrative of
'The Pupil'—recorded, as we learn here, 'after a considerable interval' from the
events—translates and standardizes the rich cosmopolitan idiom of the Moreens'
world into literary English. Only the odd foreign word is allowed to survive here
and there in order to add a studied colour effect.

It is striking that, when Pemberton first hears the eccentric cosmopolitan idiom
of the Moreens, he mistakes it for Volapük. This throwaway reference, which
would have struck a more familiar chord in 1891 than it does today, helps James to
add fuel to his satire of cosmopolitan pretence. As we know, the family language

turns out to be something else, but the associations conjured by Volapük, which is mentioned three times in the original version of the story, remain enveloped in the mists of the Moreens' dubious identity, compounded with all that makes the family phoney and strange. Conversely, like the fictional Ultramoreen, the all-too-real Volapük is lampooned as a 'spoken cypher' (p. 517), a way of turning language into a code that impedes, rather than facilitates, natural communication. The artificial language, in other words, partakes of the negative moral connotations attached to the artificiality of the Moreens in their social dealings. Like Ultramoreen, Volapük belongs to the linguistically hybrid spoken world of international society that the story conjures only in order to reduce it to standard literary English.

James's slights against Volapük are intended for comic effect. But they are part of a rhetoric of language purity that ushers more troubling ideas into the narrative. In the same paragraph in which he describes Morgan as 'a page in an unknown language', James compares the Moreens to 'a band of gipsies' and, later, to 'Jews at the doors of clothing-shops' (pp. 517, 617). These analogies are meant to deflate the family's worldly pretensions by associating them with socially marginal groups. But they do so by leveraging widespread ethnic prejudices against peoples who were marked out not only for their perceived lack of rootedness but also, significantly, for their use of hybrid idioms. Years later, as Jonathan Freedman has shown, James would worry explicitly about the potential threats that Jewish migrants posed to the English language.[21] In 'The Pupil', these glimpses of social discrimination and anti-Semitism reveal a darker side of James's project of sorting out good and bad cosmopolitan identities, as the linguistic cleansing enacted by the narrative flirts with racist imagery.

We can try to unpack the set of associations evoked by James by taking a closer look at the meteoric history of Volapük that was still unfolding at the time of publication of 'The Pupil'. Invented in 1879 by a Bavarian Catholic priest called Johann Martin Schleyer, Volapük was intended to facilitate universal communication between people of different nationalities and, in that way, to aid commercial and scientific transactions. Volapük literally meant 'world language', but Schleyer, who claimed to have created the language by an act of divine inspiration, drew heavily on Germanic—especially English—word roots. These were modified by means of a rational and extremely regular system of prefixes and affixes in order to create the different parts of speech (nouns, verbs, adjectives) and to show number, gender, tense, and so on. Schleyer's preference for simplifying roots and his elimination of the letter *r*—he thought Chinese speakers would find it too hard to pronounce—meant, however, that words were often difficult to recognize, even

[21] Jonathan Freedman, *The Temple of Culture: Assimilation and Anti-Semitism in Literary Anglo-America* (Oxford and New York: Oxford University Press, 2000), 121 and *passim*. Freedman refers to James's comments on Jewish migrants in *The American Scene* (1907).

for people who were familiar with the language from which they were derived (for instance, *vol* for world, from the English; *bel* for mountain, from the German 'Berg'). Moreover its grammar—the use of affixes in particular—presented substantial complications, which brought Alexander Bell, predictably perhaps, to compare it unfavourably with English.[22] These difficulties notwithstanding, Volapük was the first universal language to achieve any degree of success: in the course of the 1880s, its speakers managed to create a truly global network which met in dedicated schools, clubs, and societies, and which communicated across continents by means of journals that promoted the new language and printed commercial and cultural items of potential interest to their cosmopolitan readers. The bilingual adverts in an issue of the Australian *Cosmopolitan* published the same year as 'The Pupil' provide an effective snapshot of the mixture of business interests and international social networking that formed the core of the Volapük movement (illustration 5.1).

James's lampooning of Volapük in 'The Pupil' is a tribute to just how visible this relatively new phenomenon had already become. In Britain, Volapük had just received a prestigious public endorsement from the Philological Society, which recommended it as a fit practical medium for both commercial and scholarly international communication. The Society's vice-president, the esteemed phonetician Alexander J. Ellis, declared that Volapük displayed 'great ingenuity in its construction' and commended its 'vast organisation' that he estimated to be by the hundred thousand.[23] Ellis reviewed several of the artificial languages that were then in existence, including Bell's World-English, but he concluded that the fact that Volapük was already so established gave it an enormous advantage over all the others, whatever its linguistic weak points. Ellis's intervention was important because it highlighted one of the prime historical grounds for the perceived need for a universal language, namely the lack of an effective global network of connections between the scientific societies scattered around the world—a state that, he believed, posed a real hindrance to the advancement of scholarship.[24] From our point of view, however, this important endorsement is especially significant for the way it brought out into the open the spectre of race that haunts 'The Pupil'. Ellis questioned the belief that a universal language should be based on the principles of the 'Aryan stock', arguing that artificial languages 'should be

---

[22] Alexander Melville Bell, 'Volapük', *Science*, 11 (27 Jan. 1888), 39–40.

[23] Alexander J. Ellis, 'On the Conditions of a Universal Language, in Reference to the Invitation of the American Philosophical Society of Philadelphia, U.S., to Send Delegates to a Congress for Perfecting a Universal Language in an Aryan Basis, and its Report on Volapük', *Transactions of the Philological Society*, 21.1 (Nov. 1890), 59–98 (96, 97). The article was based on a lecture that had been delivered in London on 15 June 1888, and was subsequently also reported in the mainstream press and reprinted in pamphlet form; see, for instance, [Anon.], 'Volapük as a Universal Language', *The Academy*, 850 (18 Aug. 1888), 107.

[24] Ellis, 'Conditions of a Universal Language', 61. This was a matter raised by the American Philosophical Society, which had solicited the help of the philologists in perfecting 'a language for learned and commercial purposes, based on the Aryan vocabulary and grammar in their simplest form' (60).

**Illustration 5.1** *Cosmopolitan/Kosmopolan*, 3 (1 October 1891), 64. Österreichische Nationalbibliothek, Sammlung für Plansprachen, 703.731-C

constructed quite independently of any racial considerations'.[25] Indeed he warned that universal could not and should not mean 'West European'.[26] However, he went on to undermine this argument by dismissing certain artificial languages as reminiscent of 'breaks down, nigger language, talkee-talkee'.[27] Ellis was referring to those universal languages based on simplified versions of existing ones, such as

---

[25] Ibid. 64.     [26] Ibid. 76.     [27] Ibid. 80.

varieties of reformed Latin. His scientific reasoning was that a universal system of communication ought not to undo the work of linguistic evolution: that it ought not to sacrifice sophistication for the sake of comprehensibility. However, the racist sentiment that crops up in this remark transcends scientific and linguistic questions, and goes right to the heart of cosmopolitan universalism. Like the condescending asides on Gypsies and Jews in 'The Pupil', the negative reference to African American and Caribbean cultures in Ellis draws a clear line of separation between a desirable form of cosmopolitanism that is the domain of educated elite groups, and the socially abject cosmopolitan identities of oppressed minorities. Such demarcations aimed to assuage the powerful fears of miscegenation that were alive even in progressive liberal circles connected with science and literature. They were meant indirectly to reassure critics and proponents alike that the adoption of a universal auxiliary language would not mean disbanding the privileges that dominant social groups enjoyed on the grounds of their birth and ethnicity.

The fact that philologists treated Volapük as a matter of serious scientific interest did not stop others from making fun of it. With its endless rows of ä's, ö's, and ü's, long compounds, and regular stress on the last syllable of every word that lent it a characteristic sing-song quality, Volapük was an easy target. In France, *Le Figaro* satirized Volapük as 'a fruit salad of languages, a stew of various dialects, a Russian salad of different patois [ ... ] the revenge of the Tower of Babel';[28] and it caricatured deluded Volapükists talking amusing gibberish: 'Dansk patatos cara rini va te fair fich nia da potam ebeni zong zong rataplan. Tir tir!'[29] It was of course funny to see all the skill and effort required to build a highly complex artificial language system collapse into childish nonsense. In Britain, the satirical magazine *Fun* also lampooned Volapük as a confusing hotchpotch of tongues aimed at gullible cosmopolites:

> Farewell, farewell, O, Mother Tongue,
> In which this bard so oft hath sung!
> No more in English will he sing,
> Because it will not be the thing.
> The universal language craze
> Demands that he should sing his lays
> (By which so many have been struck)
> In *Bal Ninô* and *Volapuk*!
>
> These tongues or dialects would seem
> To form a grand new language scheme,

[28] Labruyère, 'Le Volapuk', *Le Figaro*, 17 Sept. 1886, 1 ('une macédoine de langues, une olla-podrida de plusieurs dialectes, une salade russe de patois différents [ ... ] la revanche de la Tour de Babel').
[29] Albert Millaud, 'Carnet d'un interviewer: Sur le volapuk', *Le Figaro*, 15 Feb. 1888, 2.

By which all folks may understand
The jargon of each other's land.
You take all languages, no doubt,
And stir them up and round about,
And then you'll grasp (if you've the luck),
The *Bal Ninô* and *Volapuk!*

Now, Mr. WORLD, likewise his wife,
Methinks (ere you can utter 'knife')
May straight, without the least complaint,
Adopt this language—and they mayn't.
You beat all languages to pulp,
Then swallow all with one swift gulp,
And Fortune may reward your pluck,
With *Bal Ninô* and *Volapuk!*[30]

[...]

However ephemeral, such satires show artificial languages moving out of what Herder called the 'dead museum' of philology, and into metropolitan settings and fashionable salons, where the 'universal language craze' reached the likes of James's Moreens. Satirists responded to this process of social transformation by denying artificial languages any claim to cultural capital: while Volapük may be useful for commercial purposes, it could never aspire to the realm of poetry—literature was and ought to remain the exclusive province of the 'mother tongue'. The outwardly benign humour was moreover designed to activate patriotic sentiments aimed at defending the primacy of English, at home and internationally, protecting it from foreign challenges (in Britain as in France, Volapük remained heavily associated with its 'native' Germany).[31]

Volapükists rebutted some of these tendentious opinions from the pages of their own specialized periodicals, which started to appear around the mid-1880s. In the French journal *Le Volapük*, for instance, the critic Robert de la Sizeranne argued that the hostility to Volapük was part of a conservative aversion towards progress and novelties of all kinds: the enemies of Volapük were also set against decadents, anarchists, wagnerites, and impressionists.[32] The strategic link with the avant-garde artistic movements of the time was meant to show that Volapük was more than just a language: it was a progressive culture that overlapped with progressive movements in the arts. In his regular contributions to *Le Volapük*,

---

[30] [Anon.], 'More Universal Language', *Fun*, 7 Apr. 1886, 151.

[31] Cf. Garvía, who concludes that many French public satires of Volapük had an openly anti-German agenda. Garvía, *Esperanto and its Rivals*, 34–38.

[32] Robert de la Sizeranne, 'Volapükistes et anti-Volapükistes', *Le Volapük*, 12, supplement (Nov.–Dec. 1887), 1 ('les décadents, les anarchistes, les incohérents, les wagnériens, les impressionistes').

the same writer also refuted the idea that the spread of universal languages posed a threat to literature: he reassured readers that Volapük did not aim to become a substitute for established literary languages, but rather to work alongside them in order to increase the global circulation of literature and promote a cosmopolitan literacy among its speakers. Other Volapükists went even further. An article in the German Volapük journal *Rund um die Welt* argued that Volapük was helping to realize Goethe's idea of world literature thanks to its increasing use as an intermediary language for translation.[33] It referred to the popular 'Volapük als Dolmetsch' (Volapük as interpreter) exercises, in which someone would translate a short piece of literature, from any language, into Volapük and then someone else would translate the Volapük into a third language, without any knowledge of the original. These games were meant to demonstrate the flexibility and efficacy of Volapük as a 'bridge language' that was capable of forging an actual, living connection between two natural languages that would otherwise not be able to communicate directly with each other. In their most striking form, such 'Volapük als Dolmetsch' exercises could be conducted across continents. Thus, for instance, the poem 'The Thought Ever Troubles me' by the Hungarian national poet Petőfi Sándor was translated into Volapük by the Hungarian Volapükist Madrassy Pál and published in a Volapük magazine in Naples; the Volapük version, 'Tik at obi egelo vexadom', was then translated into several national languages by Volapükists with no knowledge of Hungarian, and published in various Volapük magazines around the world, including the first issue of the Australian *Cosmopolitan*, where it appeared in a bilingual version.[34] English-speaking Australians thus had access to Petőfi, in *English* translation, thanks to Volapük; or, to put it differently, the first English translation of this work by the pre-eminent Hungarian nineteenth-century poet was made not only via Volapük, but because of the very existence of Volapük.

Looking at the literary translations published in the Australian *Cosmopolitan* during the journal's brief lifetime, we can also see another important emerging trend: works of literature selected for translation into Volapük show recurring themes, in particular the celebration of political liberty (such as in Petőfi's poem, which is a hymn to the 'Sacred Freedom of the World') and cosmopolitan humanism. A later issue, for instance, featured the Volapük translation of Leigh Hunt's poem 'Abou Ben Adhem' (1838), which celebrates the love of 'one's fellow men' as the highest moral sentiment—equivalent, if not superior,

---

[33] Siegfried Lederer, 'Volapük im Dienste der Weltliteratur', *Rund um die Welt: Zeitschrift für Volapükisten und solche, die es werden wollen*, 4.9–10 (Aug. 1891), 146.

[34] Alexander Petőfy [sic], 'This Thought Ever Troubles me/Tik at obi egelo vexadom', tr. Madrassy Pál/[George Walters], *Cosmopolitan/Kosmopolan*, 1 (Feb. 1891), 6. A note by the English translator explains that the Volapük version comes from the journal *Valabled*, printed in Naples. Siegfried Lederer tells the story of the global circulation of this poem in 'Volapük im Dienste der Weltlitteratur'.

to the love of God.[35] This phenomenon of thematic selection is important because it shows that Volapükists were constituting themselves as a specialized readership who wanted to read about issues close to their hearts, especially issues connected to the ethical and political aspects of cosmopolitanism. They were, in their marginal and haphazard way, using the new language in order to assemble a world literary canon—an international body of literature that they could use to build and foster a shared identity. Nor should it surprise us to see romantic nationalism (Petőfi) and cosmopolitanism (Leigh Hunt) share the pages of the Volapük press: the promoters of universal languages argued precisely that their purpose was to harmonize the two sentiments.

News of Volapük reverberated in public places, creating an unprecedented amount of interest in the phenomenon of universal artificial languages more generally. In 1903, Couturat and Leau, summarizing the historical significance of Volapük, found that its greatest merit was to have given the first, incontrovertible proof that a written and spoken artificial language was a practical possibility. They also noted, however, that its greatest fault was to have created a prejudice against international languages: while the word Volapük had become almost synonymous with universal language, it also implied a negative judgement, if not a downright condemnation.[36] This is how Volapük made its way into 'The Pupil', where James channelled some of the widespread prejudice against the language and its users to add colour to his narrative of the decline of the 'cosmopolite "legend"', as he put in the preface to the New York edition. It is telling that, when he revised 'The Pupil' for that edition in the early twentieth century, he took out two of the three original references to Volapük, clearly believing that its cultural associations were no longer as powerful as in 1891. The only reference that was allowed to stand was to Ultramoreen as 'the family Volapük', in which the artificial language is used as a metaphor and no longer as something that the Moreens could actually have spoken. Nonetheless, even a quick survey of the activities of the Volapük community in the 1880s shows that its members worked in great earnest, not only to learn this admittedly complicated language and build social and print networks, but also to put their language into the service of literature. In a way, the Volapükists' very devotion to their cause was precisely what brought the whole movement down. By the time 'The Pupil' was published in 1891, Volapük was already riven by an internal conflict between reformists and conservatives that led to a veritable schism. The powerful Association française pour la propagation du Volapük took the view that the language ought to be simplified; while its inventor, Schleyer, sustained by a newly

[35] Leigh Hunt, 'Abou Ben Adhem', tr. John F. Davis, *Cosmopolitan/Kosmopolan*, 6 (July 1892), 84. Leigh Hunt's poem was itself based on a creative translation of a story from Barthélemy D'Herbelot's *Bibliothèque Orientale* (1781). See *The Poetical Works of Leigh Hunt*, ed. H. S. Milford (London and New York: Oxford University Press, 1923), 707.
[36] Couturat and Leau, *Histoire de la langue universelle*, 162–163.

constituted language academy, insisted that Volapük should stick by its original form.[37] The ongoing tensions led to splits, resignations of prominent members, and general loss of steam. Even more determining for the demise of Volapük, however, was the arrival of a powerful competitor: Esperanto, the new universal language of hope.

## Dr Esperanto's Literary Cosmopolitanism

The controversy around universal languages was not simply played out between supporters and satirizers. While supporters all wanted the same thing—a created auxiliary language that would be mastered around the world by as many people as possible in order to facilitate communication, commerce, and cultural transactions—they disagreed bitterly over what such a language should look like. In this dynamic field, which comprised linguists, learned societies, intellectuals, and business people, universal languages fought each other for supremacy, trying to win the support of influential figures and initiate grass-roots movements. As Roberto Garvía has argued, 'the battle of artificial languages was entwined with the intellectual dilemmas of the time, reflecting the anxieties that traversed the European mindset amid the drastic economic, social, and political transformations taking place in every corner of the continent'.[38] The three main competitors to address the social and cultural anxieties that Garvía talks about were Volapük, Esperanto, and Ido (a reformed Esperanto created in the early twentieth century). Of these, Esperanto easily emerged as the winner, even though it never achieved its ultimate goal of becoming a global, working lingua franca.[39]

Esperanto was invented by the Polish ophthalmologist Ludwik Lazarus Zamenhof, who in 1887 published a pamphlet in Russian, immediately translated into Polish, French, and German, titled *Lingvo internacia* (international language), in which he concisely outlined the purpose and grammar of the new language. A first, heavily unidiomatic, English translation by Julius Steinhaus was issued in Warsaw the following year.[40] This was soon followed in 1889 by two much improved versions by the Oxford linguist Richard Henry Geoghegan (also printed in Warsaw) and Henry Phillips Jr, secretary of the American Philosophical Society (published in New York). Zamenhof signed himself 'Doktoro Esperanto', or Dr Hopeful, and his invention soon took the memorable *nom de plume* of its creator. Zamenhof identified three conditions that an artificial language must fulfil

---

[37] For an excellent concise account of the competition between Volapük and Esperanto, see Garvía, *Esperanto and its Rivals*, 47.
[38] Ibid. 3.     [39] Ibid.
[40] Dr Esperanto [L. Ludwik Zamenhof], *Dr Esperanto's International Tongue*, tr. J. St. [Julius Steinhaus] (Warsaw: Kelter, 1888).

in order to be truly universal: it must be easy to learn; people who learn it must be capable of being understood by people of other nations; and it must be promoted as a living, spoken language, not just a written one to be deciphered with the aid of a dictionary. Esperanto grammar, as laid out by Zamenhof in the foundational document that would come to be called *Unua Libro* (First Book), was totally regular and extremely simplified. Zamenhof claimed that it could be learnt in one hour. The pronunciation was also regular and the spelling phonetic, while the vocabulary drew on a number of existing languages, with a proportional bias in favour of the Latin tongues. Zamenhof attempted to make Esperanto as universal as possible by selecting for inclusion words—or, to be precise, roots—that recurred in as many European languages as possible. This Eurocentric bias is to this day a matter of dispute.[41] The First Book also included a basic vocabulary list and a number of small 'pledge' coupons that readers were meant to fill, cut out, and send to Zamenhof himself, promising that they would learn the new language. In this way, Zamenhof could keep a tab on the growth of his followers, registering their names in an address book known as the *adresaro*.

From the beginning, and increasingly so when Esperanto started gaining ground across the world, Zamenhof stressed the political neutrality of his project, which was not meant to interfere with established forms of government. Neither was Esperanto intended to replace national languages. It was to be a universal second language designed, like Volapük, to bring advantages to science and trade. In Zamenhof's utopian vision, one day all humans would be bilingual speakers of a national language, which they would employ, as it were, domestically, and Esperanto, which would be used for the purposes of international communication. Much as Zamenhof stressed the neutrality of his invention, however, the utopianism of Esperanto—the 'hope' that was at the heart of its *raison d'être*—had far-reaching political implications. The very fabric of the language went against the principles espoused by Herder and romantic philology, according to which the organic growth of languages was a natural mirror of the uniqueness and particularity of a people. Contrary to this view, Zamenhof saw all languages as hybrid and intertwined with one another: his view of languages knew no natural borders. He therefore worked to collect elements that were shared across languages, using those as the building-blocks for his project. In the First Book, he pointed out that foreign words and expressions formed part of everyone's native language, no matter how successfully these may have been domesticated in the course of time. Moreover, far from being fully detached from others or complete or perfect

---

[41] Those who challenge charges of Eurocentrism tend to base their arguments on the practical consideration that Esperanto has had a notable uptake in some non-European countries, notably Japan and Vietnam. See Brockington, 'Introduction: The Expanded Universal Language Movement', 368. Brockington cites the support for Esperanto by Iranian and Japanese diplomats, and Gerald Chan, 'China and the Esperanto Movement', *Australian Journal of Chinese Affairs*, 15 (Jan. 1986), 1–18.

in itself, every language existed in a state of 'relative poverty'.[42] As he put it, 'we are so often obliged to appropriate, from foreign sources, words and phrases; if we do not, we run the risk of expressing ourselves inexactly, and even of thinking incorrectly'.[43] In other words, the boundaries we erect between languages are arbitrary. The hybrid and neutral nature of Esperanto in this sense simply restituted a natural cosmopolitanism of language that was, in fact, also true of so-called national languages. Esperanto thus brought to the surface a substratum of shared foreignness that was inside all apparently discrete and mutually exclusive national identities.

In order to see the full political import of Zamenhof's idea, it will be sufficient to compare it briefly with what Max Nordau had to say about linguistic identity and international relations shortly before the publication of Esperanto. Within literary studies Nordau is mostly remembered today for his attacks on decadence in *Degeneration*, which we have analysed in relation to Egerton.[44] But his previous collections of essays, *Conventional Lies of our Civilisation* (*Die conventionellen Lügen der Kulturmenschheit*, 1883) and *Paradoxes* (*Paradoxe*, 1885), had already made his name known across the world, including in English-speaking countries. In 'Nationality'—one of the essays in *Paradoxes*—Nordau staunchly defended the role of language in creating and protecting national identities. He noted that, while it was possible to become a 'naturalized' citizen of a nation other than that of one's birth, the mother tongue clung to the individual as the ultimate proof of his or her essential spiritual loyalty: 'It is through his language that the individual becomes the adopted child and heir of all the thinkers and poets, the teachers and leaders of the people; it is language that brings him beneath the spell of that universal suggestion which is exerted upon all the individuals who compose a people by its literature and history, and is the cause of their similarity in sentiment and action.'[45] It followed that the act of adopting a foreign language was like 'crawl [ing] into a strange skin' ('in eine fremde Haut kriechen')—an unnatural act that betrayed the basic principles of communal identity.[46] Nordau was thinking primarily of situations in which linguistic minorities were pressed to accept the language forced on them by an oppressive state. Yet, his argument illustrates how the Herderian, romantic idea of a national language as means of self-determination could become radicalized into a form of chauvinism. Nordau rejected outright the vision of a future in which 'mankind will resolve itself into

---

[42] Dr Esperanto [Ludwik L. Zamenhof], *An Attempt towards an International Language*, tr. Henry Phillips Jr (New York: Holt & Co., 1889), 6.
[43] Ibid.    [44] Cf. Chapter 3.
[45] Max Nordau, 'Nationality', in *Paradoxes* [tr. anon.] (Chicago: Schick, 1886), 344–365 (350) ('Durch die Sprache wird es Adoptivkind und Erbe aller Denker und Dichter, Lehrer und Führer des Volks; durch die Sprache gelangt es unter die Wirkung der allgemeinen Suggestion, die von dem Schrifttum und der Geschichte eines Volks auf dessen sämtliche Glieder ausgeübt wird und sie einander im Empfinden und Handeln ähnlich macht').
[46] Ibid. 355.

large groups, like vast families or moderate sized communities', or in which the nations will be persuaded to 'accept a universal language'.[47] In place of these utopias, he envisaged a violent global, Darwinian struggle for linguistic supremacy, in which the strongest nations would in due course come to dominate the world politically and culturally, exerting their power through their language:

> The struggle for language is another form of the struggle for existence, and must be fought as that is: one kills the enemy or is killed by him, or else seeks safety in flight. The struggle between nationalities is the finishing up of a process that began centuries ago [ ... ], and all this time has been, as it were, frozen up, but is now at last thawing out and hastening to its conclusion.[48]

In this brutal scenario, the world's linguistic diversity provided not only an explanation but a rightful justification for violence. Like a prophet of gloom, Nordau watched the approach of the, to him, inevitable 'catastrophe' of a linguistic Armageddon with satisfied smugness: 'It will be cruel and hard, but hard and cruel is the fate of all that lives, and existence is a conflict where no mercy is shown.'[49]

The Esperanto movement set out to undo these gloomy predictions by offering a practical solution to the world's linguistic divisions. Just as importantly, it substituted the rhetoric of hatred and pessimism embodied by Nordau with optimism and, literally, a language of hope. It is significant that both Nordau and Zamenhof came from multilingual Jewish backgrounds in European land empires—Austro-Hungary in the case of Nordau, Russia in Zamenhof's. Their experiences of multi-ethnic societies, however, led them to radically different positions: Nordau became a leading Zionist close to Theodor Herzl, while Zamenhof, after a youthful spell of activism, became disillusioned with Zionism, and with both Yiddish and Hebrew as unifying languages for Jews around the world. Zamenhof expressed his disagreement with Zionist principles in an alternative philosophy he called 'Hillelism' or 'Homaranism', divulged pseudonymously as 'Homo Sum' in 1901.[50] Otherwise he stood firm in his commitment to the

---

[47] Ibid. 358, 359 ('die Menschen formen größere Gruppen, gleichsam erweiterte Familien oder mäßig umfangreiche Gemeinden [ ... ] Annahme einer Weltsprache').

[48] Ibid. 360 ('Der Kampf um die Sprache ist eine andere Form des Kampfes ums Leben und muß wie dieser geführt werden; man tötet den Feind oder man wird von ihm getötet oder man flieht. Der Kampf der Nationalitäten ist die Abwicklung eines Prozesses, der vor Jahrhunderten [ ... ] begonnen hat und nur all die Zeit her gleichsam eingefroren war, jetzt aber endlich auftaut und seinem Abschlüsse entgegeneilt').

[49] Ibid. 362 ('Sie wird grausam und hart sein, aber hart und grausam sind die Geschicke alles Lebenden und das Dasein ist ein Kampf ohne Erbarmen').

[50] On Hillelism see Andreas Künzli, *L.L. Zamenhof (1859–1817): Esperanto, Hillelismus (Homaranismus), und die 'jüdische Frage' in Ost- und Westeuropa* (Wiesbaden: Harrassowitz, 2010), 165–177. On Zamenhof's Jewish identity, see also Hesther Schor, *Bridge of Words: Esperanto and the Dream of a Universal Language* (New York: Holt & Co., 2016), 59–94. Biographical information in this

broader liberal universalism reflected in Esperanto. In his correspondence, the desire to break free from the yoke of nationalism, inherent in the Esperanto project, is presented as a product of his Jewish experience:

No one can feel the misery of human division as strongly as a Jew from the ghetto. No one can feel the need for a neutral language free of a sense of nationality as strongly as the Jew who is obliged to pray to God in a language long dead, who receives his upbringing and education in the language of a people that rejects him, and who has fellow-sufferers all over the world but cannot communicate with them.[51]

And in propagandist literature Zamenhof spoke frequently of his upbringing in the multi-ethnic city of Białystok in the Russian Empire, where he quickly realized that '*humanity* does not exist, that there are only Russians, Poles, Germans, Jews, etc. This thought ever deeply troubled my boyish mind—although many may smile at the thought of a lad sorrowing for humanity.'[52] This lived, painful experience of linguistic diversity and ethnic division encouraged him to begin comparing the words he saw and heard everywhere around him and, 'inspired by love and hope', to devise a key for simplifying and rationalizing them into a workable system.[53]

What stands out most in Zamenhof's accounts is the intensely personal, romanticized experience of language. In this era of professionalized language science and comparative linguistics, the creation of the most successful international language was not the work of a linguist but of an amateur—a medical doctor from provincial Poland who was meant to have set out the basics of his system when he was little more than a child. This narrative of 'a lad sorrowing for humanity', with its powerful, immediate emotional appeal, shows that Esperanto did not simply provide its followers with a language but a veritable structure of feeling—a cosmopolitan affect that was the foundation stone for a wider ethics. Inbuilt in the very fabric of the artificial language was a different way of looking at

chapter comes from Marjorie Boulton, *Zamenhof, Creator of Esperanto* (London: Routledge & Kegan Paul, 1960).

[51] Letter from Zamenhof to the influential French Esperantist Alfred Michaux, 21 Feb. 1905; in Ludwik L. Zamenhof, *Leteroj de L. L. Zamenhof*, ed. Gaston Waringhien, 2 vols (Paris: Sennacieca Associo Tutmonda, 1948), i. 107 ('La malfeliĉon de la homara disiĝo neniu povas senti tiel forte, kiel hebreo el la ghetto. La necesecon de lingvo sennacia, neŭtrale homa neniu povas senti tiel forte, kiel hebreo, kiu estas devigata preĝi al Dio en jam longe mortinta lingvo, ricevas sian edukadon kaj instruadon en lingvo de popolo, kiu lin forpuŝas, havas samsuferanojn en la tuta mondo kaj ne povas kun ili kompreniĝadi').

[52] Ludwik L. Zamenhof, 'The Birth of Esperanto (Freely translated, from an Esperanto version of a Private Letter of Dr. Zamenhof written in Russian, by John Ellis)/Eltiro el privata letero de D-ro Zamenhof al S-ro B., Presita kun permeso de ambaŭ korespondantoj, en jaro 1896. Tradukis el lingvo rusa V. G.', *The Esperantist*, 1.5 (Mar. 1904), 76–78; and 1.6 (Apr. 1904), 87–90 (76).

[53] Ibid. 78.

the world that rejected Nordau's nationalist model of conflict and struggle for domination just as much as the shallow and affected cosmopolitanism that James satirized in 'The Pupil'.

In effecting this emotional reorientation, literature played a very important role. In the First Book, Zamenhof complemented his discussion of linguistic matters with excerpts of literary translation (from Genesis, Heinrich Heine, the Lord's Prayer) as well as some original poetry that he had himself composed in the new language. As we have seen with Volapük, literary translation was extremely important for artificial languages because it proved that they were capable of handling complex subjects and feelings, strengthening their claim to cultural value and helping to foster a sense of community among their speakers. But while the Volapük movement came to literature in a second phase of its development, Esperanto used literature as a starting point.

Zamenhof's poem 'Mia penso' ('My thought'), included in the First Book, gave a highly emotional picture of the creator of Esperanto as having been cast out of society by his cosmopolitan idealism. Speaking in the first person, Zamenhof described how his dedication to his ideal became his constant 'thought and torment' ('penso kaj turmento'), provoking a mixture of 'sorrows and hopes' ('doloroj kaj esperoj') to which he sacrificed the pleasures of companionship and youth.[54] The image of the lover of humanity being marginalized by his very desire to connect with strangers captures the paradoxical condition of the citizen of the world as citizen of nowhere. In propagandist literature Zamenhof frequently went back to his experience of social isolation. He described the psychological strain of his secret project and the relief offered by writing poetry:

> Compelled to carefully conceal my thoughts and plans, I went scarcely anywhere, took no part in anything, and the most enjoyable part of my life— the student-years—was, for me, the saddest. Sometimes I endeavoured to find distraction in society, but I felt myself a stranger, sighed and went away, and from time to time eased my heart by writing poems in the language I was elaborating.[55]

The universal language designed to bring the whole world together was simultaneously a language of extreme individualism, introspection, and withdrawal into the self.

Zamenhof recast his idealistic mission in a major key in his later poem 'Espero' ('Hope'), which celebrates the arrival of the cosmopolitan 'new sentiment' ('nova sento') of Esperanto and its journey from land to land; here, he compared Esperanto to a 'mighty voice' ('forta voko') that brings the hope of peace and

[54] [Zamenhof], *An Attempt towards an International Language*, 28–29.
[55] Zamenhof, 'The Birth of Esperanto', 89.

harmony.[56] Esperantists are called to fight the spectre of a divisive nationalism by peaceful means, gathering together under the 'sacred banner of hope' ('la sankta signo de l'espero') and using linguistic neutrality as their weapon. 'Espero' gave poetic expression to Zamenhof's belief that the world's common humanity was not only fragmented but impeded in its course by linguistic and national differences. The poem, which became the official hymn of the Esperanto movement, played with conventional images and tropes of the literatures of romantic nationalism—what it resembles most is a national anthem—but it turned them on their head by celebrating cosmopolitanism as a higher ethics than national loyalty. Like a national anthem, its cultural value is not so much within the text as in the emotional force that accrued around it as it travelled in time and space, in endless reprints in periodicals and promotional materials and performances in Esperanto gatherings and congresses, where it helped to cement the shared identity of Esperantists. 'Espero' performatively asserts the fact that the Esperanto language and anti-nationalist sentiment are one and the same thing.

The cosmopolitan affect of Zamenhof's original writings was echoed in the many sentimental narratives that circulated in propagandist literature. There was, for instance, the story of the two Swedish friends Valdemar Langlet and E. Etzel, students at the university of Uppsala, who in the spring of 1895 journeyed through Russia, meeting Esperantists wherever they went. The two young men reported feeling 'all the time in the happiest frame of mind and the best of humors, just as two brothers might be, who, separated since birth by unscalable walls, schould [sic] see them vanish in a twinkling. Never before as during those five weeks had we felt so much "men" [sic], members of a common family, mighty and composed of brothers.'[57] Translated into multiple languages and printed in promotional material that circulated internationally, such tales were meant to show that Esperanto was not a pastime for language geeks but something for people who sought authentic human contact. The motifs of hospitality and sociability highlighted in the tale of the Swedish friends were typical features: the act of communicating in the artificial language, in which there was no separation or hierarchy between natives and foreigners, put strangers on equal

[56] Ludwik L. Zamenhof, *The International Language 'Esperanto': Complete Instruction-Book with Two Vocabularies*, tr. R. H. Geoghegan (Uppsala: Nya Tidnings, 1898), 11. The first two stanzas read: 'En la mondon venis nova sento, / Tra la mondo iras forta voko; / Per flugiloj de facila vento / Nun de loko flugu ĝi al loko. // Ne al glavo sangon soifanta / Ĉi la homan tiras familion: / Al la mond' eterne militanta / Ĝi promesas sanktan harmonion.' (Geoghegan's literal translation: 'A new sentiment has come into the world, / A mighty voice goes through the earth: / On wings of light wind / Let it now fly from place to place. // Not to the blood-thirsty sword / Does it drew [sic] the human family: / To the ever-warring world / It promises peace and harmony').
[57] Ludwik L. Zamenhof, *A Few Words on the International Language 'Esperanto'*, tr. Richard Henry Geoghegan (Uppsala: Nya Tidning, 1898), 17. Langlet was a leading Swedish Esperantist and internationalist, who would play a key role in helping Jews escape to Sweden from Hungary during the Holocaust. See 'Valdemar Langlet', in Geoffrey Sutton, *Concise Encyclopedia of the Original Literature of Esperanto 1888–2007* (New York: Mondial, 2008), 43.

footing, and this neutral zone fostered the growth of a characteristic affect—the brotherliness experienced by Laglet and Etzel—that marked out the spiritual ideal of world citizenship.

In effect, the early Esperantists behaved in ways that closely resembled a nation-building movement: they devised not only a language but, as we have seen, a hymn, as well as a recognizable symbol (the green star, which they used in public places to make themselves known to other speakers), a flag, and even, later on, a currency. Theirs, however, was a nation that was to end all nations or, at least, that was to put an end to the chauvinistic attitudes that separated one nation from the other.

Most importantly, Esperantists made very good strategic use of the medium of periodicals to constitute themselves into an efficiently networked community. From the launch of the first Esperanto journal, *La Esperantisto*, in Nuremberg, in 1889, the turn of the century saw the birth of dozens of Esperanto reviews and magazines, across Europe and beyond, issued both from large metropolitan centres and provincial locations. Typically, Esperanto magazines contained an eclectic mixture of international news and news about the progress of the Esperanto movement, linguistic questions (these were especially prominent, given the young age of the language and the fact that most magazines were aimed at learners), translations, and cultural items. Most of them included lists of other Esperanto associations, publications, clubs, and societies, which served the important purpose of building a virtual network, fostering a sense of connection and collaboration among members of a community that was spread thinly over a very large geographical area. Zamenhof himself frequently contributed articles and letters that bounced internationally, from one review to the other. By the early twentieth century, the Esperanto press was so well established that it could afford to specialize further, producing journals aimed at dedicated sub-groups, such as *Espero pacifista* (from 1905) and *Espero katolika* (from 1906). The majority of early Esperanto periodicals were bilingual or even, as in the case of the pioneering *La Esperantisto*, trilingual. The multilingualism of the Esperanto press served a practical purpose: readers could use different versions of the same article to practise the new language. But the simultaneous presence of universal and national languages on the same page also implicitly made the point that, like Volapük, Esperanto did not aspire to replace any of the existing languages but rather to exist alongside them in order to facilitate international dialogue and connections. Unlike the multilingualism of *Cosmopolis* explored in the previous chapter, which was based on respecting the uniqueness and separate identity of different languages by keeping them strictly apart, the multilingualism of the Esperanto press adopted a principle of universal translatability as the ethical foundation of its cosmopolitanism.

In the First Book, Zamenhof outlined the practical and political benefits of Esperanto as a universal language of translation:

How much time, trouble and money are wasted in the translation of the literary work of a nation, and yet how small a portion of its literature has ever been so reproduced or will be, even more or less unfaithfully. But, if there were in existence an international language, all translation could be made into it, and even works written therein, which could possess, *ipso facto*, an international character. The impassable wall that separates literatures and peoples would at once crumble into dust, and all that was written by another nation would be as acceptable as if in our own mother tongue; reading would prove common to all, and with it would advance education, ideals, convictions, tendencies—the whole world would be as one family.[58]

It is worth paying attention to Zamenhof's repeated emphasis on literature in this foundational statement. Literature is both the desire for connection that imaginatively projects different peoples towards one another and what keeps them apart, bringing them to face the hard reality (the 'impassable wall') of mutual incomprehension. Zamenhof's idea was that, in a world in which Esperanto has become the universal auxiliary language of international communication, the global circulation of literature would increase in both volume and efficiency, as there would be no need for further translations into other languages once a work has been translated into Esperanto. This would bring particular benefit to literatures written in minor languages. It is worth noting in this respect that translation into Esperanto was also qualitatively different from existing practices: because of the extraterritoriality of the universal language, translations were all made *out of* the mother tongue rather than into it as was (and is) otherwise almost inevitably the case. In this way, while certain practices of translation can reinforce the formation of national identity and even bolster nationalist thinking, Esperanto translation embodies, in its very essence, the desire to break free from the logic of nations and states, sidestepping regressive urges of the cultural politics of domestication highlighted by Venuti.[59] In Zamenhof's utopia where everyone in the world uses Esperanto as a second language—to which Esperantists gave the name of 'fina venko' (final victory)—linguistic differences cease to embody essential differences between the people. This focus on literary translation had important consequences for the literary identity of the Esperanto movement, whose impressive activity of translation was much more systematic and extensive than that undertaken in Volapük during the relatively brief spell of that language's popularity. Zamenhof set the example by publishing translations of the Old Testament and *Hamlet*, which are now considered foundational documents of Esperanto

---

[58] [Zamenhof], *An Attempt towards an International Language*, 5.
[59] Cf. Lawrence Venuti, 'Local Contingencies: Translation and National Identities', in Sandra Bermann and Michael Wood, eds, *Nation, Language, and the Ethics of Translation* (Princeton and Oxford: Princeton University Press, 2005), 177–202 (180 and *passim*); and, on domestication, Venuti, *Translator's Invisibility*, 14–15.

literature, as well as works by Dickens, Gogol, Molière, Goethe, Schiller, Hans-Christian Andersen, and the Polish novelist Eliza Orzeszkowa, who was also the author of an important essay on patriotism and cosmopolitanism (*Patriotyzm i kosmopolityzm*, 1879).

There is also another significant element that emerges from Zamenhof's remarks on translation in the First Book: he clearly, from the very start, placed a great deal of importance on literature in the development of Esperanto as a working, living language, which he conceived as destined to produce its own original literature. Once again, there would be an inherent qualitative difference in works written in the universal language: the fact that authors would not be writing for a national group but for the whole of humanity would bring them—force them, almost—to adopt broader sympathies and perspectives. In 1903 Zamenhof raised the bar in the *Fundamenta krestomatio de la lingvo Esperanto* (Fundamental Chrestomathy of the Esperanto Language), an anthology of Esperanto writings, including literary translations, which was designed to provide stylistic guidance and prevent the language from fragmenting into different dialects.[60] In the late nineteenth century, this idea that an artificial language would be able to have its own style and literary canon was totally untested and easy to deride. Promotional Esperanto material the world over loved to cite an endorsement by Tolstoy, who had tried his hand at learning Esperanto and praised it as furthering the causes of 'mutual comprehension' and world peace.[61] Tolstoy, however, much as he commended the study of Esperanto as 'a Christian labour, which hastens the coming of the kingdom of God',[62] stopped short of using it for literary purposes. The question of the literariness of the universal language was one that divided even its supporters. On the one hand, the leading French Esperantist Louis de Beaufront called Esperanto the language of the 'expression juste', which not only had nothing to envy existing languages in terms of suppleness and richness, but surpassed them when it came to clarity of expression.[63] On the other, the British economist R. J. Lloyd, who advocated the teaching of Esperanto in schools, regarded it as the language of 'bare fact'—suitable for business transactions but not for the intricacies of literary expression.[64] Indeed, Tolstoy aside, explicit support among writers was rare.

---

[60] Ludwik L. Zamenhof, *Fundamenta krestomatio de la lingvo Esperanto* (Paris: Hachette, 1903), p. v.

[61] Tolstoy, letter dated 25 Apr. 1894; quoted in Zamenhof, *A Few Words*, 13. Tolstoy had been approached to give his opinion on Esperanto by the Russian journal *Posrednik*, and Zamenhof originally drew attention to his reply in *La Esperantisto*, 92 (1895). Tolstoy's involvement eventually led to the temporary censorship of *La Esperantisto* and Esperanto publications in the Russian Empire from 1895 to 1905. See Peter G. Forster, *The Esperanto Movement* (The Hague and Paris: Mouton, 1982), 64–65.

[62] Tolstoy, quoted in Zamenhof, *A Few Words*, 15.

[63] Louis de Beaufront, 'L'Esperanto peut-il être littéraire?', *L'Esperantiste*, 1.4 (Apr. 1898), 54–56 (55). Beaufront would later be one of the leaders of the Ido secession from the Esperanto movement.

[64] R. J. Lloyd, 'On the Economic Value of an International Business Language', *Westminster Review*, 160 (Dec. 1903), 673–683 (683).

Starting from the 1890s, the fear of cultural decline that had previously been attached to Volapük was projected onto Esperanto; and, like Volapük, Eseranto soon gained currency as a term of caricature and abuse. As we have seen, Esperanto was, in Conrad's terms, a 'monstrous jargon'.

In the early twentieth century, observing the growing interest in Esperanto among scholars, the American critic Brander Matthews flatly rejected the idea that an artificial language was 'ever likely to have a literature of its own'.[65] Matthews, whose nationalistic views were discussed in the previous chapter, went on to ground his objection in a radicalized Herderian argument on the organic inter-dependence of language, emotion, literature, and individual and national identity:

> Will anybody ever use any invented dialect by the fireside and when he goes courting? Will children baby-talk in any book-made vocabulary? Will any mother ever croon a lullaby over her cradled child in Esperanto? Will school-masters thruout [sic] the world combine to instruct youth in a language without a past and only a doubtful future? And can any language made to order in the study ever possess the vigor and the variety of a language which has been evolved slowly thru the ages in response to the needs of men, like a tool shaping itself slowly to the hand that wields it?[66]

Normative images of a healthy family life are mobilized to quash the cosmopolitan affect of Esperanto and protect the sanctity of the nation. Matthews's openly post-Herderian and evolutionary view of the relationship between language and national identity rested, like Nordau's, on competition and violence. He made no secret in this respect that he thought that English (no doubt in the simplified spelling of which he was an advocate) would one day emerge victorious on the world stage; and, as examples of how writers from 'the smaller races' were already turning to English, he cited the cases of the then popular Dutch author Maarten Maartens and of Joseph Conrad.[67]

In keeping with their utopian mentality, Esperantists tried to overturn the nationalistic discourse exemplified by Matthews by shifting the focus from inher-ently conservative arguments about heritage and the past, to looking into the future. The British Esperanto translator Joseph Rhodes, for instance, claimed that Esperanto speakers found themselves 'in possession of an instrument whose potentialities stretch out before them like a Newtonian ocean; and it will only be when a Shakespeare or a Dante comes into or grows up within the movement that the possibilities of this euphonious instrument can be adequately explored'.[68]

---

[65] Brander Matthews, 'English as a World Language', in *The American of the Future*, 194–215 (203–204).

[66] Ibid. 204.    [67] Ibid. 208.

[68] Joseph Rhodes, 'Progress and Prospects of Esperanto', *North American Review*, 184 (Feb. 1907), 282–291 (287).

Rhodes censured Esperantists who doubted whether 'a hotchpotch of a language is fit for literary expression', reminding them that such objections 'might lead to some awkward questions as to how our own hotchpotch tongue has come into being, or why a language which selects the excellencies of several should necessarily be inferior to any of them'.[69] The next one hundred years would prove that Rhodes's predictions about the future of Esperanto were not misguided. While Esperanto might not have had its Shakespeare or Dante, it did gradually acquire its own literature—an especially important milestone was the launch, in Budapest, of the cultural magazine *Literatura Mondo* in 1922—as well as critical literature and literary histories.[70]

## Esperanto in Britain: Max Müller, W. T. Stead, Felix Moscheles

Despite the early efforts of the Oxford linguist Richard Henry Geoghegan, who, as we have seen, translated the First Book in 1889, Britain came to Esperanto later than Zamenhof's native Russian Empire, France, or the Scandinavian countries. It nonetheless played an important role internationally in its early development. The first British Esperanto Society was founded in Keighley, Yorkshire, in 1902, shortly followed by the London Esperanto Club and a number of other regional associations, which eventually gathered under the umbrella of the British Esperanto Association in 1904. In 1903 the first British periodical, *The Esperantist*, was launched, later supplemented by, and eventually merged with, the *British Esperantist*. By 1907, the British Esperanto network was clearly developed and internationally prominent enough to volunteer to host the third World Esperanto Congress, which, as we shall see, took place that year in Cambridge. Zamenhof himself explained the strategic importance of Britain to the Esperanto cause in a recorded phonograph message that was played at a meeting of the London Esperanto Club in January 1904: 'The nations will listen with attention to the voice issuing from the centre of the English-speaking world. When such a powerful nation as the English begins speaking of the brotherhood of nations and the neutrality of international relations, the world will applaud with enthusiasm, and that sacred Cause for which we contend will march forwards with

---

[69] Ibid.
[70] The bibliography is very large. Good overview or introductory material includes William Auld, *The Development of Poetic Language in Esperanto* (Rotterdam: Universala Esperanto-Asocio, 1976); *Esperanta antologio: Poemoj 1887–1981*, ed. William Auld (Rotterdam: Universala Esperanto-Asocio, 1984); Margaret Hagler, 'The Esperanto Language as a Literary Medium: A Historical Discussion of Esperanto Literature, 1887–1970, and a Stylistic Analysis of Translated and Original Esperanto Poetry' (unpublished doctoral thesis, Indiana University, 1970); Pierre Janton, *Esperanto: Language, Literature, and Community*, tr. Humphrey Tonkin, Jane Edwards, and Karen Johnson-Weiner (Albany, NY: State University of New York Press, 1993); K. R. C. Sturmer, *Esperanto in Literature: Notes and Impressions* (London: Esperanto Publishing Co., 1930); and Sutton, *Concise Encyclopedia*.

great strides.'[71] Like the French, the English generally felt that they already *had* a world language that enabled them to communicate effectively with foreigners. Domestically, this posed an additional challenge to Esperanto: the artificial language could be seen to aspire to the role that, according to Brander Matthews and critics of his ilk, was otherwise destined for English; but this counter-cultural *cachet* also increased its appeal among social radicals including, as Kaori Nogai has shown, groups connected to the Celtic revival and other forms of anti-colonial struggle.[72]

As in other countries, the success of Esperanto in Britain in this crucial early phase was largely due to the work of a number of highly dedicated, idealistic individuals whose names are hardly remembered today outside Esperanto circles: these included Harold Bolinbroke Mudie, active in the London Esperanto Club and editor of *The Esperantist*; Joseph Rhodes, founder of the Keighley Club, journalist, and Esperanto translator; John Pollen, Colonel in the British Army and president of the British Esperanto Association; and Eliza Ann Lawrence, secretary of the London Club, private secretary to W. T. Stead, and crucial intermediary between Zamenhof and British Esperanto circles. These people hosted social gatherings, attended and gave language classes, held talks, printed leaflets and magazines, exchanged information, and corresponded with Esperantists in foreign countries—all in pursuit of the cosmopolitan cause of establishing a common auxiliary language for humanity that would promote international exchange and mutual understanding. Their activities, however, would have had a much more limited outreach without the support of three key public figures—two of whom we have already encountered in different contexts— who built bridges between the work of the Esperanto community and mainstream culture, broadcasting the former's message and ambitions on a larger scale: the linguist Max Müller, the journalist W. T. Stead, and the painter and writer Felix Moscheles. Studying the involvement of these three personalities throws light on the cultural and social networks of the early British Esperanto movement, and enables us to situate it within the broader cosmopolitan culture examined in the previous chapters.

Of the three, Max Müller was the one who had, at the same time, the least direct contact with Esperanto circles and the most international visibility. When Esperanto came into being, Müller was nearing the end of an extremely distinguished career as a professional linguist at Oxford. He was also, as explained in Chapter 1, a prominent cosmopolitan figure, reflected in his appointment as first

[71] Quoted in [Anon.], 'President's Speech at Annual Meeting, Dr. Zamenhof's Greetings by Phonograph', *The Esperantist*, 1.4 (Feb. 1904), 49–52 (52). The meeting was held at Essex Hall, London, on 14 Jan. 1904.
[72] Nogai, '"The New Bilingualism"', 51–52. On the social composition of the British Esperanto movement, and especially on the perceived support among members of subversive groups and 'cranks', see Forster, *Esperanto Movement*, 9–10, 266, and *passim*.

president of the English Goethe Society. Müller's influential work in comparative linguistics had also striven to find a universal language, although his gaze was turned to the past rather than the future—to the disappeared tongue of the 'Aryan' peoples, the original common language out of which the modern Indo-European languages developed into separate branches. Indeed, in his inaugural address to the Goethe Society, Müller built on his philological research in order to flip the question of world literature back to the past, arguing that 'the rudiments of a world-literature' are to be found in the very oldest surviving written records, Egyptian and Babylonian inscriptions. Those, he claimed, were addressed to the whole of humanity rather than a single nation.[73]

In his mid-century lectures on the science of language, Müller had already contemplated the possibility that humanity may, one day, return to using a single common language. There he declared that 'to people acquainted with a real language, the invention of an artificial language is by no means an impossibility, nay, that such an artificial language might be more perfect, more regular, more easy to learn, than any of the spoken tongues of man'.[74] Although it was formulated with reference to John Wilkins's seventeenth-century philosophical experiments, Müller's endorsement was extremely important to the artificial language movement, and was prominently cited in a number of key places that went from Couturat and Leau's *Histoire de la langue universelle* to Zamenhof himself.[75] Indeed, in Esperanto literature worldwide, Müller was only second to Tolstoy as the most frequently cited international authority to have bestowed their seal of approval, indirect though that be, on the new language. It is easy to see why. Just as Tolstoy conferred cultural capital on Esperanto by associating it with the prestigious field of literature, Müller lent it scientific legitimacy by putting a scholarly imprimatur on a language that was invented by an amateur linguist and was taken up largely outside academic institutions and centres of learning. Müller, who corresponded with Zamenhof in the early 1890s,[76] always remained somewhat aloof from Esperanto circles and, as we shall see, his attachment to Esperanto was rather romantic in nature, and never translated into activism. Nonetheless, his cautious support was of great symbolic importance for the new language, both in Britain and internationally.

A decidedly more practical and enthusiastic form of involvement came from W. T. Stead, who was among the earliest to espouse the Esperanto cause in Britain

---

[73] Müller, 'Goethe and Carlyle', 775; cf. Chapter 1.

[74] Max Müller, *Lectures on the Science of Language, Delivered at the Royal Institution of Great Britain, Second Series* (London: Longman, Green, Longman, & Roberts, 1864), 61.

[75] Cf. Couturat and Leau, *Histoire de la langue universelle*, p. x; and Zamenhof, *The International Language 'Esperanto'*, 15. Zamenhof quoted Müller's letter to the Russian literary association Posrednik, in which he stated that he 'should certainly place the Esperanto system' above the other existing artificial languages.

[76] Ludwik L. Zamenhof, *Zamenhof Leteroj*, ed. Adolf Holzhaus (Helsinki: privately printed, 1975), 25–26.

with the zealousness that marked out his social crusades since the time of 'The Maiden Tribute of Modern Babylon' (1885). Stead first came across Esperanto when travelling in Germany in 1902.[77] The following January he chose Esperanto as the topic for one of his Mowbray House Friday at Homes—themed salon-like afternoon gatherings to which he invited friends and contacts from the extended circle of the *Review of Reviews*. From then on, Stead not only provided a focal point for the networks of sociability that built around the new language, hosting the London Esperanto Society in his office and acting as treasurer; but he also, crucially, turned the *Review of Reviews* into the unofficial organ for the promotion of Esperanto in the English-speaking world, at a time before the existence of dedicated journals and indeed paving the way for the launch of *The Esperantist* in November 1903. Regularly from the start of 1903, the *Review of Reviews* advertised Esperanto classes, addressed language questions, occasionally printed short items in Esperanto, and charted the spread of the movement in Britain and internationally. In this way, knowledge about Esperanto first reached English-speaking readers not, as in most countries, through the channels of small dedicated magazines but in a big commercial title with an established large network of readers and powerful social contacts.

The *Review of Reviews* rehearsed the usual arguments designed to persuade and reassure: Esperanto was meant to facilitate the advancement of knowledge by bringing together 'the best minds of all nations',[78] and it was not intended to replace national languages or lessen the spiritual ascendancy of the mother tongue.[79] In Stead's mind, Esperanto was ideally suited to the readership of the *Review of Reviews*—busy practical people who had no time or inclination to gain in-depth knowledge of foreign languages but nonetheless wanted to be in touch with foreign and global trends. Such people more than anyone needed a 'universal key language', as the journal called it, 'which every year will fit the wards of more and more locks all over the world'.[80] The *Review of Reviews* primarily viewed Esperanto as a technology that, like the telegraph and the periodical press itself, helped to circulate information quickly and to form large and efficient international networks (it particularly commended Zamenhof's invention of the *adresaro*[81]). The journal also energetically championed the universal language as a support for literacy among the blind, on the grounds that it was easier to learn through Braille than any existing foreign language, and it therefore opened up a new world of communication and socialization to the visually impaired.

[77] Frederic Whyte, *The Life of W. T. Stead*, 2 vols (London: Jonathan Cape; New York: Houghton Mifflin, 1925), ii. 67.
[78] [Anon.], 'Esperanto: The Next Step', *Review of Reviews*, 30 (Sept. 1904), 310.
[79] [Anon.], 'Esperanto', *Review of Reviews*, 27 (May 1903), 504.
[80] [Anon.], 'Esperanto: The Next Step', 310.
[81] See [Anon.], 'Esperanto', *Review of Reviews*, 27 (Feb. 1903), 168.

Like the *Review of Reviews* itself, the journal's vision of Esperanto was internationalist without necessarily adhering to the principles of a liberal cosmopolitanism. While it supported the idea that Esperanto's neutrality made it preferable to any language, including English, as a means of international communication, the *Review of Reviews* also found a way of marrying Esperantism with its imperialist convictions, in a manner that was quite alien to Zamenhof's outlook. A review of Couturat and Leau's *Histoire de la langue universelle* argued that Esperanto was especially needed at a time when 'every part of the world is colonised by Europeans'—a state of affairs that the author of the review clearly deemed proper and natural.[82] Esperanto had, after all, come into being out of the multi-ethnic social fabric of the Russian Empire as an attempt to solve the problems of communication and social integration to which Zamenhof repeatedly referred in his letters and interviews. It was perhaps inevitable that in Britain, too, its potential would be transferred onto imperial ground.

The overlap with colonial networks emerges most clearly in the activities of the skilled linguist John Pollen, who served as the first president of the British Esperanto Association. Pollen came to Esperanto by way of his experience in the Indian Civil Service, where he had been exposed to several local languages and had witnessed the utility of Hindustani and Urdu as 'artificial' means of communication between different groups. Like Stead, he combined interests in Esperanto and in Russia, serving on the Committee of the Anglo-Russian Literary Society and producing translations of Russian literature.[83] After working to promote Esperanto in Britain, Pollen went back to India in 1907 in order to lecture on Esperanto around the country. On his outward journey, he even appears to have managed to persuade the captain of the HMS *Marmora* to allow him to fly the Esperanto flag on the way from Jedda into Bombay.[84] A postcard commemorated this epic event by depicting Pollen in the setting of colonial India—a traditional temple and elephants are visible in the background—wearing a fez and wrapped in the Esperanto flag (illustration 5.2). The iconography reveals the awkward positioning of Esperanto on colonized territory, where, as the British flag planted on the temple inescapably reminded viewers, its cosmopolitan message could hardly be separated from the British imperial politics of domination.

---

[82] [Anon.], 'A Universal Language', *Review of Reviews*, 28 (Dec. 1903), 633.

[83] John Pollen, *Rhymes from the Russian, Being Faithful Translations of Selections from the Best Russian Poets: Pushkin, Lermontof, Nadson, Nekrasof, Count A. Tolstoi, Tyoutchef, Maikof, Lebedef, Fet, K. R., etc.* (London: Kegan Paul, Trench, & Trübner, 1891). On Pollen's involvement in the Anglo-Russian Literary Society, see Rebecca Beasley, *Russomania: Russian Culture and the Creation of British Modernism 1881–1922* (Oxford and New York: Oxford University Press, 2020), 82–83.

[84] [Anon.], 'British Esperanto Association', *British Esperantist*, 1.7 (July 1905), 99; [anon.], 'Our President's Movements', *British Esperantist*, 3.5 (May 1907), 83; [anon.], 'Lecture by Colonel Pollen. "To India with the Flag"', *Cambridge Daily News*, 15 Aug. 1907, 3.

**Illustration 5.2** 1907 postcard featuring Colonel John Pollen, private collection. The postcard was printed for the Cambridge World Esperanto Congress of 1907

The question of empire came up in the stand-out piece of Stead's Esperanto journalism in the *Review of Reviews*—an interview with Zamenhof, made during the first World Esperanto Congress in Boulogne-sur-Mer in 1905. The long article also comprised a full English translation of the hymn 'Espero' and several illustrations. As Stead explained, the congress represented a milestone for the fledgling

Esperanto movement, as it marked the first time that adherents from different nations had come together in large numbers, testing the practicality of the spoken language and its efficacy as a social binding agent. Stead brought up imperialism straight away, suggesting to Zamenhof that Esperanto could be used to save the Austro-Hungarian Empire from the threat of dissolution caused by the resurgent nationalisms of its different constitutive language groups, notably the Hungarians. Zamenhof, however, resisted Stead's attempt to put Esperanto in the service of imperialism, speaking cautiously about romantic nationalisms and generally trying, as he always did, to disengage Esperanto from politics.[85] Despite this difference of opinion between interviewer and interviewee, Stead drew a warm character portrait of Zamenhof as a modest, even reticent man with an ardent nature consecrated to the dream of bringing humanity together: with a possible nod to Thomas Carlyle's Teufelsdrockh, he described Zamenhof as 'an absent-minded professor of the old German type. [ ... ] His idea is his real world. Great world capitals, magnificent palaces, stately monuments—all these are but shadows in the Land of the Idea.'[86] Stead wanted to explain that the idealistic cosmopolitanism of the Esperanto movement had little to do with schemes of private gain or the glamorous worldliness that filled the pages of *Cosmopolitan*, or the attitude of 'chanciness' that James had satirized in 'The Pupil'. For this reason, following the established narrative trope, he lingered on Zamenhof's struggle to realize his dream in the midst of personal and political adversity, depicting the creator of Esperanto as a sentimental hero and encouraging readers to view his life as 'a romance of our latter day'.[87] However, the most striking feature of Stead's carefully constructed portrait—the fullest in English at that date—was that the narrative of hope that encapsulated both the Esperanto movement and Zamenhof's private identity was unequivocally Christianized. Stead made no mention of Zamenhof's Jewishness and described the latter's boyish dream of eliminating differences between languages as a fight against the 'Anti-Christ' and the devil, inspired by 'the promise of the City of God'.[88] This metamorphosis of Zamenhof into a Christ-like figure clearly shows the extent to which the advocacy of Esperanto in the *Review of Reviews*, no less than other aspects of the journal's cosmopolitan interests, was eccentrically coloured by the editor's imperialist and Christian beliefs, which risked to damage the Esperanto cause even as his powerful journalistic network gave it a platform to reach English-speaking readers worldwide.

By this point, however, the *Review of Reviews* was no longer the only voice of the British Esperanto movement. Since November 1903, the dedicated journal *The Esperantist* had endeavoured to bring Britain up to speed with the progress that had already been made in other nations. Stead himself wrote the lead article of the

---

[85] [W. T. Stead], 'Character Sketches: Dr. Zamenhof, the Author of Esperanto', *Review of Reviews*, 32 (Sept. 1905), 255–263 (256).
[86] Ibid. 259.      [87] Ibid. 256.      [88] Ibid. 257.

opening issue, giving a number of good reasons for becoming an Esperantist. These included belief in progress, business advantages, and the opportunity to gain a truly global cultural outlook: 'We are Esperantists because the adoption of Esperanto will enable men and women of every nation to share with all others the best contributions which each has been able to make to the thoughts and know-ledge of the world.'[89] *The Esperantist* followed the by-now established format of specialized magazines in other countries, publishing a mixture of bilingual Esperanto news, language problems and exercises, readers' correspondence, and other information that would be useful for networking purposes. As Stead had announced in the first issue, culture, and especially literature, was a special focus. In its short life span of less than two years, *The Esperantists* published translations of, among others, poems by Felicia Hemans, W. H. Henley, Thomas Moore, and Tennyson; extracts from George Eliot's *Silas Marner*, Edwin Arnold's *The Light of Asia*, and the 'Rubaiyat of Omar Khayyam' (from Fitzgerald's translation); stories by Dickens and H. G. Wells; and serializations of Bunyan's *Pilgrim's Progress* and Shakespeare's *The Tempest* and *Richard III*, as well as several items of original Esperanto literature. Zamenhof had translated *Hamlet*, in spite of his limited knowledge of English, because he wanted English to be prominently represented in the new Esperanto literature. Now British Esperantists turned their own hands to English literature, producing a first canon based on a mixture of classics and popular texts. The amount of literary translation in *The Esperantist*, which was impressive even by the standards of other European Esperanto journals, shows that British Esperantists were among the most zealous followers of Zamenhof's admonishments on the importance of literary translation. These first Esperanto translations of English literature functioned as linguistic exercises, which tested the adaptability and expressive power of the new language and, simultaneously, they embodied the ethos of cosmopolitan hospitality of the Esperanto movement, where native speakers foreignized and, as it were, de-territorialized their domestic works, turning them into a gift for strangers who did not speak their language.

Literary activity was more limited in the second specialized journal, the *British Esperantist*, into which *The Esperantist* eventually merged in 1905. Here, however, the radical political connections of the early Esperanto movement emerged more clearly, even from the cover, which was the work of Walter Crane (illustration 5.3). In the Introduction, we saw Crane's subtle questioning of the capitalist foundations of British imperialism and of its claim to a cosmopolitan identity in the *Imperial Federation Map* of 1886. For the *British Esperantist*, Crane went back to the iconography he had used in that map, recasting the image of Britannia that he had drawn nearly twenty years earlier: blown up against a green background, the angel-like winged figure wore the same draped garment and still sat on the

---

[89] W. T. Stead, 'Esperanto', *The Esperantist*, 1.1 (Nov. 1903), 1–2 (2).

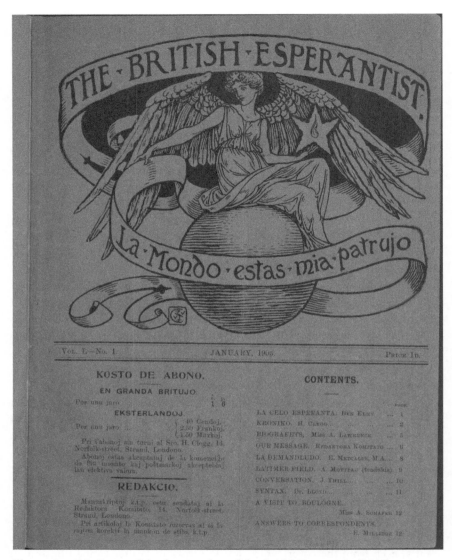

**Illustration 5.3** Cover of the first number of the *British Esperantist* (1905). Österreichische Nationalbibliothek, Sammlung für Plansprachen, 700-072-B-C.Esp

globe in the same posture but, stripped of the war-like attributes of British supremacy (helmet, trident, Union-Jack shield), she now bore the five-pointed star of the Esperanto movement. The motto printed on her banner—'La Mondo estas mia patrujo' (the world is my country)—evoked Diogenes's famous saying that he was 'a citizen of the world', presenting the Esperanto movement within a long tradition of philosophical cosmopolitanism that stemmed from classical antiquity, now filtered through international socialism. While Britannia stood for hierarchy and control in the *Imperial Federation Map*, the cover of the *British Esperantist* was visually dominated by this abstracted, universal figure whose features were gentler than her predecessor's, and who represented peace. The globe on which she sat was also pointedly void of all political and geographical markers to signify the ideal of a world without borders.

Crane was not a committed Esperantist and, as Grace Brockington has argued, he rather believed that mutual understanding and world peace could be fostered by means of the 'universal language of design'.[90] Nonetheless, his intervention shows us the productive triangulation between Esperanto, arts and crafts circles, and internationalist socialism that was a distinctive feature of early Esperanto culture in Britain. Crane's association with socialism was well-known: he had, for instance, designed the cover for Edward Carpenter's *Chants of Labour* (1888) and his drawing 'Solidarity of Labour', published in the *Commonweal*—the journal of the British Socialist League—in 1890, featured a winged allegorical female figure that is strikingly similar to his illustration for the *British Esperantist*.[91] Going back to the *Imperial Federation Map*, it is significant that, in remodelling his design for the *British Esperantist*, Crane also removed the figure of Atlas that bore the burden of the globe on 'human labour', as if to say that the cosmopolitan utopia of Esperanto would also bring the end of the exploitation of the working class. These associations with utopian socialism constructed through visual allusions were reinforced in the message from the editorial committee included in the first issue, which noted how 'all around us, girting the land belt-like, groups, clubs, and societies have arisen, emulous and indefatigable. Earnest workers have shared in the labour of propaganda. Earnest, whole-souled men and women have fostered and watched over the destinies of the great mission, a mission to which they have generously and devotedly given their time and their best energies.'[92] Such rhetoric echoed the language employed by the socialist press, notably in describing Esperantists as 'workers' and appealing to the adherents' spiritual commitment.

The key connecting figure between Esperantist, artistic, and activist milieus was the artist Felix Moscheles. Born into a German family with strong ties to international music circles (his father was the well-known virtuoso and composer Ignaz Moscheles), Moscheles was very conscious of being linguistically, culturally,

---

[90] Grace Brockington, 'Rhyming Pictures: Walter Crane and the Universal Language of Art', *Journal of Verbal/Visual Enquiry*, 28.4 (2012), 359–373 (359). See also Morna O'Neill, *Walter Crane: The Arts and Crafts, Painting, and Politics, 1875–1890* (New Haven and London: Yale University Press, 2010), 15. O'Neill compares Crane's interest in creating a 'new mode of communication' based on decorative design to G. B. Shaw's interest in phonetic English.

[91] Elizabeth Carolyn Miller provides a helpful exploration of Crane's involvement in the *Commonweal* in the context of that journal's commitment to utopian and revolutionary socialism. Miller, 'William Morris, Print Culture, and the Politics of Aestheticism', *Modernism/Modernity*, 15.3 (Sept. 2008), 477–502 (486–488).

[92] Editorial Committee, 'Nia Alparolo/Our Message', *British Esperantist*, 1.1 (Jan. 1905), 6–7 (6).

and socially in-between. In his autobiography, he recounts his experience of xenophobic bullying as a child—both in England, where he was teased and marginalized for being German, and in Germany, where his schoolmates targeted him for being English.[93] As a young man, Moscheles moved in Pre-Raphaelite circles (Rossetti's father gave Italian lessons to his sisters[94]) and, in time, he became a respected portrait painter and memoirist of the *fin de siècle*. Aside from his reminiscences of famous figures such as Rossini and Mazzini, he also published the autobiographical *In Bohemia with Du Maurier* (1896), a spin-off from the great popular success of *Trilby* (1894), where he collected anecdotes from his time as an art student in Paris.[95] As befits a memoirist, Moscheles was an excellent networker: his literary connections included George Du Maurier and Robert Browning, while in the art world he was close, among others, to Lawrence Alma-Tadema and Crane—the latter probably came to collaborate with the *British Esperantist* via Moscheles. Moscheles was among the first to take up Esperanto in Britain, clearly believing that the international language would provide ways to fulfil his own cosmopolitan identity and social ideals. As early as 1892, he was already exchanging letters (in German) with Zamenhof, to whom he spoke of his interest in Esperanto and willingness to promote its cause in Britain.[96] When British Esperantists finally started to organize themselves over ten years later, he was a pioneering activist, serving as first president of the London Esperanto Club and vice-president of the British Esperanto Association, as well as contributing to both British Esperanto journals. Moscheles, who painted Zamenhof's finest existing portrait (illustration 5.4), also acted as a direct point of contact with the founder of the Esperanto movement: the two corresponded all through these important early years, and it was via Moscheles that Zamenhof sent the phonograph recording that was played out in London in 1904.

Moscheles worked closely with Stead and also befriended Max Müller after virtually meeting him in the pages of *Cosmopolis*, where Moscheles published a memoir of Mazzini and Müller contributed several scientific and autobiographical pieces. Moscheles and Müller shared a similar German emigré background and connections to the musical world—Müller's father was the poet Wilhelm Müller, author of the lyrics for *Die schöne Müllerin* (1821) and *Winterreise* (1823), set to music by Franz Schubert. In an early article in *The Esperantist*, published three years after Müller's death in 1900, Moscheles recounted a visit to Müller in Oxford, during which the eminent linguist confirmed to him in private that a universal language was indeed 'possible' and that 'Esperanto [was] the best attempt at a universal language yet made'.[97] However, the most revealing memory

---

[93] Felix Moscheles, *Fragments of an Autobiography* (London: James Nisbet & Co., 1899), 23.
[94] Ibid. 40.      [95] Felix Moscheles, *In Bohemia with Du Maurier* (London: Fisher Unwin, 1896).
[96] Zamenhof to Felix Moscheles, 20 Oct. 1892, in *Zamenhof Leteroj*, 79–80.
[97] Felix Moscheles, 'Kion Max Müller diris/What Max Müller Said', *The Esperantist*, 1.2 (Dec. 1903), 19–20 (19).

**Illustration 5.4** Felix Moscheles, portrait of Ludwik L. Zamenhof. The painting now hangs in the headquarters of the Esperanto Association of Britain in Barlaston, Staffordshire

of the visit was a little German poem that Müller himself composed and inscribed in Moscheles's album as a parting gift:

> Felix Mendelssohn:
> Wenn Menschen aus einander gehn
> So sagen sie, Auf Wiedersehn,- auf Wiedersehn.
> Felix Moscheles:
> Die Sprachen sind auch aus einander gegangen,
> Drum theilen sie alle dasselbe Verlangen
> Auf Wiedersehn, auf Wiedersehn!
>
> F. Max Müller[98]

---

[98] Ibid. 20. The poem could be translated as: 'Felix Mendelssohn: / When people from each other part / They say, we shall meet again, we shall meet again. / Felix Moscheles: / The languages have also from each other parted, / That's why they all share the same desire / to meet again, to meet again!'

The famous composer Felix Mendelssohn, who set to music the lines that Müller quotes here, was Moscheles's godfather. Paying homage to his family history and to their families' shared experiences of migration, Müller portrayed Moscheles's belief in the emotional reunion of the world's languages through Esperanto as an echo of Mendelssohn's romantic music.

Müller was right to see a deep streak of romantic idealism in Moscheles. Aside from his Esperanto activism, Moscheles fought for the causes of social justice, international relations, and world peace, serving as an important link between these worlds. He moved in Fabian circles, through which he met Crane,[99] was involved in the Berne International Peace Bureau, and sat on the executive committee of the Peace Society, as well as serving as president of the International Arbitration and Peace Association. His radicalism was reflected in his close friendship with the Ukrainian revolutionary socialist Sergey Stepniak-Kravchinsky, who was, like Zamenhof, one of Moscheles's portrait subjects, and who acted as an important medium for the dissemination of Russian literature through his connection with Constance Garnett.[100] Indeed, Moscheles's London studio, where the artist held concerts and social gatherings, was a space where art and activism fused into a single whole: in the late 1880s the International Arbitration and Peace Association used to hold its meetings there; and later, in the 1890s, it provided the setting for annual Peace Day gatherings where activists mingled with prominent guests from the artistic and literary worlds such as the pianist Mark Hambourg and G. B. Shaw.[101]

Moscheles's commitment to international arbitration in particular reveals the strong ethical and political core of his cosmopolitanism. Under the umbrella of the International Arbitration and Peace Association, Moscheles worked closely with George Herbert Perris, whose attacks on the sentimental appeal of nationalist mythology were discussed in the Introduction. Moscheles also wrote pamphlets, published by the Association, in which he denounced the way in which patriotic sentiment was easily perverted into a negative feeling of hostility in school curricula, in the press, and in literature, citing Tennyson as an example.[102] He admitted that patriotism could be a virtuous sentiment, when it worked to bind together the citizens of one country; but he warned that, in an era of increased international relations, patriotism must be regarded as no more than 'collective

---

[99] Walter Crane, *An Artist's Reminiscences* (London: Methuen, 1907), 262.

[100] Arthur Warren, *London Days: A Book of Reminiscences* (Boston: Little, Brown, & Co., 1920), 48–49. On Stepnyak and Russian literary émigrés in London, see Carol Peaker, 'We are Not Barbarians: Literature and the Russian Émigré Press in England, 1890–1905', *19: Interdisciplinary Studies in the Long Nineteenth Century*, 3 (2006), 1–18 (4–9). <https://19.bbk.ac.uk/issue/115/info/> [accessed 31 July 2020].

[101] [Anon.], 'Notes', *Concord*, 36.3 (Sept. 1887), 106; Martin Ceadel, *Semi-Detached Idealists: The British Peace Movement and International Relations, 1854–1945* (Oxford and New York: Oxford University Press, 2000), 146.

[102] Felix Moscheles, *Patriotism as an Incentive to Warfare* (London: Hodder & Stoughton, [n.d.]), 2.

selfishness' inasmuch as it generated conflicting national interests, 'practically disuniting the citizens of the world.'[103] Like Perris, Moscheles believed that the ongoing evolution of human civilization naturally pointed towards the ideal of world citizenship. The challenge for the present was to find ways in which Kant's philosophical ideas of universal law and world peace could be built into practical ethics, fostering positive forms of identity that counteracted the spread of chauvinistic nationalism.

It was natural that Esperantists and supporters of peace and international arbitration should converge, as both groups believed that conflicts between nations could be avoided by increased and more efficient communication. Thus Moscheles and Stead attended together the first Hague Conference in 1899, and published their impressions in another pamphlet of the International Arbitration Association, edited by Perris.[104] Moscheles, Stead, and Crane all contributed to the *Concord*—the journal of the International Arbitration Association, which aimed to promote peace through enlightened international dialogue. And the close relationship between *The Concord*, *The Esperantist*, and the *Review of Reviews* can be gauged by the fact that each of these three journals regularly advertised the other two. In fact, in 1902 Moscheles even sent a copy of *The Concord* to Zamenhof, hoping to cement the links between international Esperanto networks and the International Arbitration Association.[105] Esperanto also opened a channel of communication between British and French pacifism: in his interview with Zamenhof in the *Review of Reviews*, Stead quoted the French Esperantist Gaston Moch as declaring: 'I am a citizen of the world. [ . . . ] I speak Esperanto, which is the language of my country.'[106] Moch, a former military officer and, like Moscheles, an assimilated Jew, was an active dreyfussard and in 1905 he founded the Internacia Societo Esperantista por la Paco (International Esperanto Society for Peace), which issued the monthly journal *Espero pacifista*. Like Moscheles, he used Esperanto to criticize patriotism.

These connections reveal the extent to which the British Esperanto movement overlapped with the networks of other groups that fought an explicitly political, as well as cultural, struggle against nationalism. When interest in Esperanto reached different sectors of the periodical press, it cross-pollinated with other social and political causes. From 1904, for instance, the New Woman magazine *Womanhood*, edited by Ada Ballin, included regular features about Esperanto and

[103] Ibid. 3.
[104] *A History of the Peace Conference at The Hague*, ed. G. H. Perris (London: International Arbitration Association, 1899).
[105] See *Zamenhof Leteroj*, 83.
[106] [W. T. Stead], 'Character Sketches: Dr. Zamenhof', 259. Moch was the author of *La Question de la langue internationale et sa solution par l'esperanto* (Paris: Giard & Brière, 1897). On Moch's activism, see Paul-Henri Bourrellier, 'Portrait d'un dreyfussard: Gaston Moch, combattant de la paix', *Bulletin de la SABIX*, 42 (2008), 75–91; and Garvía, *Esperanto and its Rivals*, 107–108 and *passim*.

language instruction, provided by the Esperantist doctor Martyn Westcott.[107] This collaboration showed a dialogue at work between Esperanto, feminism, and women's health—a special focus of interest for this magazine—that was not restricted to the British press alone.[108] Encouraged by this growing interest in various sectors of the specialized press, the liberal newspaper *Daily News* started publishing regular items on and in Esperanto in 1905, including a pacifist intervention by Moch that vigorously promoted Esperanto as laying the foundations for 'an international nation'.[109] Such visible connections between Esperanto and pacifism, socialism, Russian émigré circles, feminism, and other internationalist radical movements fuelled fears that the universal language, being so easy to learn, might be used by revolutionaries to improve communication between cells in different countries. The *British Esperantist* reported on a story according to which Paris police found illegal correspondence written in Esperanto in the course of an investigation into anarchist milieus.[110] And, in the interview with Stead, Zamenhof himself quoted an Austrian ambassador's fears that Esperanto may play into the hands of 'scoundrelly anarchists [who], with a grammar and a dictionary, could in half a dozen lessons acquire quite sufficient Esperanto to be able to communicate with each other all over the world'.[111] Despite Zamenhof's continued warnings that Esperanto should stay out of the political sphere, such rumours about its connections with the subversive politics of 'the cosmopolitan revolution' proved hard to contain.[112]

## From Cambridge to the East End

The high point of the early years of the English Esperanto movement came undoubtedly in the summer of 1907, with the third World Esperanto Congress, which took place in Cambridge. The congress sealed, in the words of Louis de Beaufront, 'the adhesion of the English-speaking people to the Esperanto cause'.[113] The year 1907 had a special importance because it marked the twentieth anniversary of the publication of the First Book. In order to prepare for this symbolic event, the *British Esperantist* told its readers that their first duty should be 'to learn to speak as perfectly in Esperanto as we do in our mother tongue', and then to

[107] Martyn Westcott, 'Esperanto: The Auxiliary International Language', *Womanhood: The Magazine of Woman's Progress and Interests, Political, Legal, Social, and Intellectual, and of Health and Beauty Culture*, 12.72 (1904), 356–360.
[108] On Esperanto as offering practical advantages for international women's rights movements, see Espalion, 'L'Esperanto', *La Ligue: Organe belge du droit des femmes*, 15 (1907), 31–38 (31).
[109] Gaston Moch, 'Esperanto and the Peace Movement', *Daily News*, 23 Sept. 1905, 4.
[110] A. E. W., 'Ĉu la lingvo esperanto estas lingvo anarhista?', *British Esperantist*, 2.18 (June 1906), 51.
[111] [Stead], 'Character Sketches: Dr. Zamenhof', 256.    [112] Ibid.
[113] Louis de Beaufront, 'Impressions of the Esperanto Congress at Cambridge', *North American Review*, 186 (Sept. 1907), 273–275 (274). Ironically Beaufront was, together with Louis Couturat, one of the minds behind the Ido schism that was to take place shortly afterwards.

spread the word about Esperanto as widely as possible.[114] Their success was measured by the fact that, as reported in the *Daily Telegraph* on the eve of the congress, the British Esperanto Association managed to double its number of affiliated societies in the course of the year, so that the extent of England's Esperantists was now second only to France.[115] World congresses were important for practical reasons, as they offered precious opportunities for practising the spoken language and building international social networks. At the same time, they were intended to increase public awareness about Esperanto and its cosmopolitan cause. Cambridge was no exception. The congress was organized by a team that soon became known by the nickname of the 'trio por la tria' ('the three for the third'), consisting of John Pollen, Harold Bolingbroke Mudie, and the medical doctor George Cunningham. The busy programme, which stretched over a whole week, included talks, concerts, official and private receptions, banquets, balls, visits to local sights and excursions, Esperanto church services, and official photographs.[116] An organized excursion to the newly built Letchworth Garden City acquainted the international Esperanto community with the utopian social ideals of the British garden city movement, whose founder, Ebezener Howard, addressed them in Esperanto on the principles behind his vision.[117] Both the city of Cambridge and several of the female and male colleges hosted receptions for the international delegates. Commemorative postcards show Cambridge decked out in Esperanto flags, with shops sporting Esperanto signs on their fronts; reports spoke of shop assistants and policemen who had made the effort to learn some of the rudiments of the new language in order to assist delegates.

Consisting of an estimated 1,400 delegates from thirty countries, attendance in Cambridge was larger than ever before, and testified to the steady international growth of the movement.[118] The Cambridge congress also showcased the diversity of the Esperanto community, which gathered into a number of sub-groups that catered for, among others, Catholics, socialists, freemasons, doctors, dentists, jurists, mathematicians, chess players, and the blind, as well as members of the Red Cross Society, the Peace Society, the International Teachers' Union, and associations for the Prevention of Cruelty to Animals and the Protection of Women and Children. The proliferation of specialized groups reflects the fact that Esperanto functioned simultaneously as a network for the international

---

[114] E. A. Lawrence, 'To the English-Speaking Esperantists Everywhere', *British Esperantist*, 2.22 (Oct. 1906), 115.

[115] [Anon.], 'Esperanto Congress', *Daily Telegraph*, 12 Aug. 1907, 4.

[116] George Cunningham, John Pollen, and Harold Bolingbroke Mudie, *Kongresa Libro* (London: Arundel St., 1907).

[117] Ian Wilson, *The Third Esperanto Congress* (London: British Esperanto Association [1908?]), 24–29; see also Alfred E. Wackrill, 'Gardenurbo—Garden City', *British Esperantist*, 3.4 (Apr. 1907), 74–75.

[118] Wilson, *Third Esperanto Congress*, 8, 18; Ziko Marcus Sikosek, *Sed homoj kun homoj: Universalaj kongresoj de Esperanto, 1905–2005* (Rotterdam: Universala Esperanto-Asocio, 2005), 42–45.

circulation of knowledge but also, equally importantly, as a social movement supporting tolerance, diversity, and generally progressive causes. Indeed, the diversity agenda took a somewhat carnivalesque form as many delegates attended events in their national costumes—including a much noted 'Tyrolese gentleman in the simple life costume, showing as much of his manly form as was desirable'[119]—in order to make the point that Esperantists did not forsake their national identity; rather, if anything, the Esperanto movement celebrated cosmopolitan diversity even to the point of eccentricity.

Literature was represented in the form of a dedicated exhibition and, following a tradition inaugurated at Boulogne two years previously, by the performance of an Esperanto translation of a literary classic from the host country. In Boulogne, the French Esperantists had staged Molière's *Le Mariage forcé* (1664). The British organizers chose Dickens's 'Bardell contra Pickwick', which was, again as in previous congresses, played by a cast of amateur actors of different nationalities. These included the 'trio', the well-known Cambridge don Oscar Browning (who played Pickwick), and the 14-year-old Venezuelan Esperantist Nestor Volcan, who became the mascot of the congress because of his young age. The purpose of these dramatic performances was to provide a practical demonstration of the adaptability of Esperanto and its ability to convey emotions immediately to an international audience—including, in the case of Dickens, idiomatically complex humour. A report in the *Cambridge Daily News*—which followed the proceedings closely, and included news items and advertisements in Esperanto during the duration of the congress—sympathetically explained how Esperanto translation turned national literature into world literature by making it understandable to a mixed international audience:

> Here is a plain, incontrovertible fact—that a play, and not one of the easiest, can be made intelligible by and to a collection of varying nationalities in a common tongue. Nothing more need be said. What was furthest from Charles Dickens' thoughts than such a circumstance when he conceived the immortal Pickwick? He wrote for his own people, and his own people alone, little dreaming that upon a certain historic occasion his bust, crowned with laurel, would be set up in the midst of a cosmopolitan gathering, and his incomparable humour communicated through a tongue understood of all. Literature owes a heavy debt to Dr Zamenhof.[120]

Despite the success of the social events, however, expectations that the congress would raise the cultural capital of Esperanto were only partly fulfilled. The choice

---

[119] Robin Goodfellow, 'Table Talk', *Cambridge Daily News*, 17 Aug. 1907, 3.
[120] [Anon.], 'The Esperanto Congress. Dickens Esperantised. "O. B." as Pickwick at the Theatre', *Cambridge Daily News*, 15 Aug. 1907, 3.

La malfermo de la
**TRIA UNIVERSALA KONGRESO**
*Kembriĝo. Aŭgusto 12 1907*

**Illustration 5.5**  Postcard commemorating the opening of the third World Esperanto Congress ('La malfermo de la Tria Universala Kongreso'). Österreichische Nationalbibliothek, Sammlung für Plansprachen

of Cambridge was undoubtedly intended to give Esperanto an academic blessing by bringing its community into one of Europe's oldest and most prestigious universities. Interactions with the university were, however, limited. A postcard commemorating the opening of the congress shows an international group of men thick in conversation, presided over by a little winged Esperanto fairy who, reversing the Babel myth, magically bestows on them the gift of mutual comprehension (illustration 5.5). Curiously observing them from a distance are two lone dons, in full academic dress. These figures probably hinted at the only two Cambridge academics who took an active part in the proceedings: Oscar Browning, who was a notoriously larger-than-life character always on the look-out for opportunities for self-display, and the aged classicist John E. B. Mayor, a vegetarian activist who addressed the congress in Esperanto. Other than these somewhat eccentric figures, there was little participation from the university and no public endorsement of Esperanto. Pollen seems to have hoped that Cambridge would award Zamenhof an honorary degree, following the example of Oxford, which had recently granted that honour to William Booth, founder of the Salvation Army.[121] Not only was there no such award but newspapers commented ironically on the fact that a city that was associated with rigorous philological learning should have become home to the most simplified

---

[121]  Goodfellow, 'Table Talk', 3.

language, which prided itself on having got rid of the grammatical complexities that were the domain of classical scholarship.[122]

The reactions of the British press split along predictable lines. Positive reports emphasized the feeling of international camaraderie among Esperantists and attempted to explain their utopian aims; while negative ones tended to set Esperanto in competition with English, defending the latter's claim to being the only practical world language. Thus, on the one hand, the *Daily News* soberly portrayed Esperanto as 'a reaction against unbalanced nationalism' and as a sign of the cosmopolitan Zeitgeist of the present;[123] on the other, the *Observer* lampooned it as 'a hotch-potch of cosmopolitan dialect' that threatened to extinguish the feeling of 'national pride' that was the legacy of great writers. For this newspaper, the problem of international communication had only one possible 'solution'—to make English compulsory all over the world: 'It is a noble tongue, worthy of the study of all mankind'.[124] While not always positive, the British papers' coverage of the congress certainly helped to spread knowledge of Esperanto among the general public and to enlarge the circle of culturally influential sympathizers, which was now said to include Israel Zangwill, Edward Carpenter, and Robert Baden-Powell among others.[125] Some journalists noted that the Cambridge Esperanto Congress ran simultaneously with the Second Hague Peace Conference—Stead, for instance, could not make it to Cambridge because he was in attendance in the Netherlands. In an enthusiastic report, the associate editor of the *North American Review*, Henry James Forman, compared the two events, speculating whether Cambridge had been, in fact, 'the true peace congress': while delegates in The Hague spent months in earnest, but also sombre, abstract, and endless conversations about warfare and arbitration, the Cambridge Esperantists gave a practical demonstration of how to lay the foundations for 'the federation of man', providing the very embodiment of 'the spirit of peace'.[126] Esperantists, in other words, practised a sort of hands-on diplomacy that brought people together, promoting a broad humanism that was the most effective antidote to violent nationalism.

As in the previous international congresses, much of the attention was focused on Zamenhof himself. Zamenhof was initially reluctant to accept the invitation to Britain, writing to Moscheles that he feared that his presence put too personal a stamp on Esperanto gatherings, skewing the proceedings and potentially doing

---

[122] [Anon.], 'The Outlook: International Language', *Daily Mail*, 12 Aug. 1907, 4.

[123] [Anon.], 'Esperanto', *Daily News*, 12 Aug. 1907, 6.

[124] [Anon.], 'Babel or Esperanto!', *The Observer*, 11 Aug. 1907, 6.

[125] See, for instance, [anon.], 'Esperanto Congress', *Daily Telegraph*, 12 Aug. 1907, 4; *La Londona Gazeto* 9 (July–Aug. 1909), n.p.

[126] Henry James Forman, 'The Progress of Esperanto', *North American Review*, 186 (Sept. 1907), 276–280 (276). This Boston-based periodical ran frequent reports on Esperanto, including an article by Zamenhof (May 1907) about Esperanto in America and items on language instruction.

harm to the cause.[127] It was undeniable that there was a Zamenhof cult among Esperantists and that congresses tended to magnify that. But he was persuaded in the end and, in his plenary address, he explained that the English-speaking countries held a special strategic importance for the Esperanto cause because Esperanto might reasonably be perceived as being in conflict with the progress of English as a world language.[128] Cambridge therefore gave him hope that the international language would eventually be embraced not only by small nations, but also by big and powerful ones. Zamenhof also called on Esperantists to take a more active role in the fight against belligerent nationalisms. He urged listeners to hasten the realization of what he called 'esperantujo' or 'Esperanto-land'—the utopian transnational nation of Esperanto speakers that was eventually to put an end to global inequalities and conflict.[129] In other words, Zamenhof stressed the importance of holding on to Esperanto's idealistic commitment to cosmopolitanism and humanism.

After the close of the Cambridge proceedings, Zamenhof went on to London, where he was Moscheles's guest. In London, his official engagements included a visit to the House of Commons and a public lecture in the Guildhall, where the anti-nationalist agenda was again paramount. Echoing Moscheles in his writings for the Arbitration Association, Zamenhof attacked those who conflated and confused patriotism with nationalism, perverting the essentially positive emotions of the former into a form of hatred that manifested itself as chauvinism and xenophobia. Instead, he presented Esperanto as a true, ethical patriotism, 'part of that great worldwide love, which constructs, preserves, and brings happiness everywhere'.[130] True patriotism and Esperantism, far from excluding one another, were therefore mutually supporting ethical positions. In order to make this argument as vivid as possible, Zamenhof included a highly emotional address to his native 'Lithuania', as he said, referring to the border region of Białystok, which was torn by nationalistic tensions, calling it 'my unhappy fatherland [...] who cannot ever be replaced in my heart by any other piece of land'.[131] He wanted to stress the point that the most idealistic of Esperantists was, at the same time, the most fervent patriot, because the love of his country was not polluted by feelings of hatred and exclusion:

Oh, patriotism, patriotism, when will people finally understand your true meaning! When will your holy name cease to be a weapon in the hands of various liars!

[127] Zamenhof to Moscheles, 11 Feb. 1907, in *Zamenhof Leteroj*, 136.
[128] Künzli, *Zamenhof*, 277–278.    [129] Forman, 'Progress of Esperanto', 278.
[130] Zamenhof, 'Parolado en la Guildhall de Londono, 21. Aŭg. 1907', in *Originala Verkaro*, ed. Johannes Dietterle (Leipzig: Hirt & Sohn, 1929), 381–383 (383) ('la vera patriotismo estas parto de tiu granda tutmonda amo, kiu ĉion konstruas, konservas kaj feliĉigas').
[131] Ibid. ('mia malfeliĉa patruio...kiun nenia alia parto de la tero iam povos anstataŭi en mia koro').

When will every person finally have the right and ability to be attached with their whole heart to that piece of land that bore them![132]

The most emotionally charged image of Zamenhof's visit to Britain appeared in an interview for the *Jewish Chronicle*, also conducted during his stay in London. Unlike the mainstream and Esperanto presses, which tended not to draw too much attention to Zamenhof's Jewishness, the *Jewish Chronicle* presented Esperanto as a direct benefit to the Jewish people and as a product of a distinctly Jewish form of cosmopolitanism. For this paper, Zamenhof was first and foremost a successful Jewish man who rose from 'the heart of the Ghetto' to international acclaim.[133] The interview, conducted in Moscheles's London studio, provided detailed coverage of Zamenhof's relation to Hebrew and Yiddish, and his idea of Hillelism.

After the official part of the interview was over, Zamenhof asked to be taken on a visit of Whitechapel and the Leman Street Shelter, which housed Jewish refugees from the Russian Empire who had fled the horrors of the pogroms. This request introduced a highly politicized edge, as that very Jewish community had been at the centre of widespread fears and public debates about limiting foreign migrants' access to Britain, which had recently resulted in the Aliens Act of 1905.[134] In the East End, Zamenhof met Hermann Landau, a wealthy philanthropist who had emigrated from Poland and now took a leading role in organizing care for Jewish migrants. Zamenhof's exchanges with the refugees and with Landau were sadly left unreported, except for a brief comment that the two men 'engaged in the same kind of work, and eagerly compar[ed] notes about their experiences'.[135] However, the image of Dr Esperanto 'painfully [making] his way through the Jewish quarter of the East End' makes a stark contrast to the many written and visual testimonies of the Cambridge congress, where Esperanto was associated with optimism, leisure, and social privilege.[136] It speaks of Zamenhof's desire to break across barriers of class no less than nationality but, at the same time, it reveals the limits of the liberal humanism of the Esperanto movement, when faced with the terrible reality of ethnic violence. Most importantly, Zamenhof's visit to the Jewish East End brought face to face two types of cosmopolitan experience, respectively linked to cultural authority and forced displacement, that seldom shared the same space.

---

[132] Ibid. ('Ho patriotismo, patriotismo, kiam fine la homoj lernos kompreni ĝuste vian sencon! Kiam via sankta nomo ĉesos esti armilo en la manoj de diversaj malhonestuloj! Kiam fine ĉiu homo ricevos la rajton kaj la eblon algluiĝi per sia tuta koro al tiu peco da tero, kiu lin naskis!').

[133] [Anon.], 'Esperanto and Jewish Ideals: Interview for the *Jewish Chronicle* with Dr. Zamenhof', *Jewish Chronicle*, 6 Sept. 1907, 16–18 (16).

[134] A full transcript of the Aliens Act, 1905 can be found at <https://www.legislation.gov.uk/ukpga/1905/13/pdfs/ukpga_19050013_en.pdf> [accessed 30 June 2020]. For an analysis of the inflated rhetoric of 'invasion' that accompanied these debates, see Bernard Gainer, *The Alien Invasion: The Origins of the Aliens Act of 1905* (London: Heinemann, 1972).

[135] [Anon.], 'Esperanto and Jewish Ideals', 18.     [136] Ibid. 16.

Just as Zamenhof's identities as 'King of Esperanto-land' and 'Ghetto Jew' were inseparable and, in an important sense, complementary,[137] the Cambridge Esperantists and the migrants of the East End were part of the extended and uneven continuum of world citizenship that this book has attempted to trace—a continuum that is marked by conflicting impulses of belonging and alienation, connection and distance, positive identification and estrangement, strength and vulnerability, hope and melancholia, and that constitutes a vital source of cultural critique and innovation in the literature of the *fin de siècle*.

---

[137] Ibid.

# Conclusion

## Citizens of Nowhere: One Last Ghost

A map of the world that does not include Utopia is not worth even glancing at, for it leaves out the one country at which Humanity is always landing.

(Oscar Wilde, 'The Soul of Man under Socialism')

Perhaps the man who never wanders away from the place of his birth may pass all his life without knowing ghosts; but the nomad is more than likely to make their acquaintance. I refer to the civilized nomad, whose wanderings are not prompted by hope of gain, nor determined by pleasure, but simply compelled by certain necessities of his being,—the man whose inner secret nature is totally at variance with the stable conditions of a society to which he belongs only by accident.

(Lafcadio Hearn, 'A Ghost')

This book started with Max Müller lecturing on world literature in 1886 and it has ended with a glimpse of Ludwik Zamenhof, alias Dr Esperanto, meeting East European migrants in London's East End, just over twenty years later. These events frame a period in English literature in which the liberal humanism of the nineteenth century came to terms with the need to confront the reality, and embrace the potential, of an increasingly globalized world. Müller and Zamenhof exemplify both the continuity within the turn-of-the-century culture of cosmopolitanism— its fundamental commitment to tolerance and intercultural dialogue, and its fight against nationalism—and the different modes of engagement that make it such a dynamic phenomenon. The foregoing chapters have attempted to convey some of that dynamism by charting the progressive influence that cosmopolitanism had on English literary culture. At the same time, I have also drawn attention to problematic instances in which cosmopolitan ideology intersected with free-trade capitalism and imperialism, or overlapped with forms of materialism and social privilege associated with ideas of worldliness. The figure of the citizen of the world as citizen of nowhere, originally formulated within the discourse of anti-cosmopolitanism in order to stigmatize the perceived rootlessness of cosmopolitan subjects as a lack of loyalty and moral principles, has enabled me to delineate the paradox of world citizenship as involving simultaneously privilege and marginalization, authority and dispossession, connectivity and extreme individualism.

What eventually became *Citizens of Nowhere* started its life with a different working subtitle: 'The Love of Strangers'. This earlier formula captured the utopianism of the cosmopolitan ideal in a more straightforwardly positive key: the emphasis, there, was on the foreign other as a figure of curiosity and desire, and on the ethical drive behind the ideal of world citizenship. Unselfconsciously at first, the change to *Citizens of Nowhere* shifted the weight towards identity politics, but it also introduced a note of self-questioning—an anxious note, no doubt, that reflects the geo-political changes that have taken place during the period of gestation and writing of this book. The public debate around questions of national identity, international relations, and free movement has moved on very quickly from the turn of the twenty-first century, when the humanities and social sciences first turned their attention to cosmopolitanism. At that point, critics such as Nussbaum, Robbins, and Appiah—to name some of the most influential— interrogated philosophical and political models of world citizenship with the explicit or implicit belief that they could be reactivated in the present, albeit in self-critical and modified forms, to address the problems and opportunities presented by globalization. In the space of a few years, the cosmopolitan ideal may have come to seem more remote, fragile, and beleaguered, yet it has lost none of its relevance to our own social and political crises. If anything, as cosmopolitan idealism becomes further removed from the centres of gravity of realpolitik, it becomes even more urgent to understand its history and cultural representations. The greatest similarity, in this respect, between the *fin de siècle* and our present moment is that they are both starkly polarized cultures: in Britain (as in other countries in the West), we see an ever widening gulf between, on the one hand, progressive, internationally oriented writers, critics, and activists who campaign for inclusivity and diversity, and, on the other, a vocal and politically empowered resurgence of cultural chauvinism that reinforces national boundaries and struc- tures of exclusion. As at the turn of the twentieth century, there is today a growing disquiet about the rise of xenophobic nationalism, the populism of the media, and the instrumentalization of patriotism for the oppression of minorities.

Understanding the fragility, paradoxes, and internal fractures of cosmopolit- anism does not entail a lessening in its power to change the way we look at the world and understand our place in it. On the contrary, my study of the literature of the *fin de siècle* has sought to redeem that 'nowhere' that nationalists then and now have vilified as the dark heart of world citizenship: I have argued that cosmopolitan writers and readers did not see it as a place of emptiness and fear, but rather as a fecund space of insight, resistance, and cultural critique. As Wilde provocatively asserts in 'The Soul of Man under Socialism', the non-places that are excluded from official cartographies are not, for that reason, less real. Utopia is 'the one country at which Humanity is always landing', writes Wilde, appropriating the imagery of colonialism and turning it into an aphoristic motto of his cosmopolitan socialism.[1] Wilde himself shows that the cosmopolitan subject's forever self-questioning relationship to place and identity is a strategy of defamiliarization: it is motivated by a desire to push beyond engrained perspectives of nationality and language in order to stretch one's imaginative sympathy. In terms of critical practice, this means, above all, developing a critical understanding of how the concept of the nation and its ideology have shaped the way we produce, read, and assign value to literature.

In other words, that space outside national paradigms—the nowhere that haunts ideas of world citizenship—is a place to ask why certain works—Wilde's *Salomé*, Egerton's translations of Scandinavian authors, Hearn's Japanese sketches, the multilingual *Cosmopolis*, Esperanto magazines—do not quite fit the category of English literature as we know it. It is the threshold to recovering encounters that took place beyond familiar landscapes and to recognizing the contribution made to English literature by silenced agents such as the inhabitants of rural Japan who told Hearn their legends and ghost stories, or the Scandinavian migrants in New Zealand who found in Egerton echoes of the home they had left behind on the other side of the world. Studying the literature of the *fin de siècle* from a cosmopolitan perspective, however, involves much more than trawling through the margins of history to look for exceptions to the national norm. It means drawing a revised map of literary culture as a ground of transcultural dialogue, focusing on encounters, transitions, and proximities that cut across boundaries. It means rehabilitating translation as a constituent part of the literary landscape. By so doing, criticism not only throws a new light on individual works and larger international patterns for the circulation of literature; but it also furthers our understanding of the culture of mobility and migration, of social identities, and of the aesthetics and politics of national feeling.

In an essay published shortly before he left America for Japan, Hearn describes the cosmopolitan subject as a haunted being. With evident autobiographical reference, he explores the unique psychology of the modern 'nomad', caught between the conflicting desires to belong and to be 'still a stranger' everywhere.[2] The need to lay down roots in one place and to assimilate into one community is constantly overcome by a deep-seated impulse to keep moving on, and abandon the familiar in order to explore new worlds, forge new connections, and embrace new opportunities of self-creation. According to Hearn, such beings are haunted by a special type of ghost that grows more powerful every time they part from familiar cities or friends. He calls this ghost a 'Composite'—a combined image of the people and places that his 'civilized' or modern nomads have left behind in the course of their lives, 'the sum of all lost sympathies' brought into being by the

---

[1] Oscar Wilde, 'The Soul of Man', 247.

[2] Lafcadio Hearn, 'A Ghost', *Harper's New Monthly Magazine*, 80 (Dec. 1889), 116–119 (117).

impossible desire to encompass the whole world.[3] This is Hearn's meditation on what it means to be a citizen of nowhere. Collapsing the melancholy affect of unsettlement into the uncanny, his ghost is a way of redeeming the negative imagery of loss and absence attached to 'nowhere' as a place of fear. In Japan, as we have seen, Hearn would come to understand ghosts as the manifestations of human diversity, associating the state of being haunted with tolerance, curiosity, and power of perception. Here too the ghost that haunts the cosmopolitan subject is a benign and stimulating presence, a way of claiming a special type of knowledge and a cultural sensitivity that are not granted to those who identify unquestion- ingly with the native, the rooted, and the settled. The literature of the English *fin de siècle* opened itself to the world with the mixture of desire and self- consciousness encapsulated by Hearn. Its experiments in cosmopolitanism have proved durable and so has its message that criticism should continue to reach beyond the limits of the nation.

[3] Ibid. 118.

# Bibliography

## Manuscripts

Harry Ransom Center, The University of Texas at Austin, John Lane Company Records
Harry Ransom Center, The University of Texas at Austin, Lafcadio Hearn Collection
Howard-Tilton Memorial Library, Tulane University, New Orleans, Lafcadio Hearn Papers
National Library of Ireland, Dublin, George Egerton MSS
New York Public Library, Astor, Lenox and Tilden Foundations, The Henry W. and Albert
    A. Berg Collection of English and American Literature, Lafcadio Hearn Papers
Princeton University Library, Manuscript Division, Special Collections, Selected Papers of
    Mary Chavelita Bright
Toyama University Library, Lafcadio Hearn Library
William Andrews Clark Memorial Library, University of California, Los Angeles, Oscar
    Wilde papers, in Oscar Wilde & *le fin de siècle* MSS
William Andrews Clark Memorial Library, University of California, Los Angeles, George
    Egerton's correspondence, in Oscar Wilde & *le fin de siècle* MSS

## Printed Sources

Abberley, Will, *English Fiction and the Evolution of Language, 1850–1914* (Cambridge and
    New York: Cambridge University Press, 2015).
A. E. W., 'Ĉu la lingvo esperanto estas lingvo anarhista?', *British Esperantist*, 2.18 (June
    1906), 51.
Agathocleous, Tanya, *Urban Realism and the Cosmopolitan Imagination in the Nineteenth
    Century: Visible City, Invisible World* (Cambridge and New York: Cambridge University
    Press, 2011).
Agathocleous, Tanya, and Jason R. Rudy, 'Victorian Cosmopolitanisms: An Introduction',
    *Victorian Literature and Culture*, 38.2 (2010), 389–397.
Albert, Henri, 'Les Letters Scandinaves: Knut Hamsun', *Revue blanche*, 8 (1895), 188–190.
Allen, Grant, 'The New Hedonism', *Fortnightly Review*, 327 ns (March 1894), 377–392.
Anderson, Amanda, *The Powers of Distance: Cosmopolitanism and the Cultivation of
    Detachment* (Princeton and Oxford: Princeton University Press, 2001).
Anderson, Benedict, *Imagined Communities: Reflections on the Origin and Spread of
    Nationalism* (London and New York: Verso, 1991).
[Anon.], 'A Literary Adventurer: Lew Vanderpoole and the George Sand Manuscripts', *The
    Sun*, 21 September 1887, 1.
[Anon.], 'An Alexandrian Age', *Macmillan's Magazine*, 55 (November 1886), 27–35.
[Anon.], 'A New University', *Cosmopolitan*, 23.5 (September 1897), 463–464.
[Anon.], 'An International Review and its Editor', *The Sketch*, 1 January 1896, 6.
[Anon.], 'A Universal Language', *Review of Reviews*, 28 (December 1903), 633.
[Anon.], 'Babel or Esperanto!', *The Observer*, 11 August 1907, 6.
[Anon.], 'Blind Alley-gories. By Dunno Währiar', *Punch*, 108 (20 April 1895), 184.

[Anon.], 'British Esperanto Association', *British Esperantist*, 1.7 (July 1905), 99.

[Anon.], 'Discontinuance of Count Tolstoy's Novel', *Cosmopolitan*, 27.4 (1899), 447–449.

[Anon.], [Double review of *Discords* and *Young Ofeg's Ditties*], *Saturday Review*, 30 March 1895, 416–417.

[Anon.], 'Editorial Notice', *The Cosmopolitan/Kosmopolan*, 1 (February 1891), 1–3.

[Anon.], 'Esperanto', *Daily News*, 12 August 1907, 6.

[Anon.], 'Esperanto', *Review of Reviews*, 27 (February 1903), 168.

[Anon.], 'Esperanto', *Review of Reviews*, 27 (May 1903), 504.

[Anon.], 'Esperanto and Jewish Ideals: Interview for the *Jewish Chronicle* with Dr. Zamenhof', *Jewish Chronicle*, 6 September 1907, 16–18.

[Anon.], 'Esperanto Congress', *Daily Telegraph*, 12 August 1907, 4.

[Anon.], 'Esperanto: The Next Step', *Review of Reviews*, 30 (September 1904), 310.

[Anon.], 'Impressions and Opinions', *Anglo-Saxon Review*, 1 (June 1899), 243–254.

[Anon.], 'In the World of Art and Letters', *Cosmopolitan*, 15.3 (July 1893), 378–381.

[Anon.], 'Lecture by Colonel Pollen. "To India with the Flag"', *Cambridge Daily News*, 15 August 1907, 3.

[Anon.], 'Making a Magazine', *Cosmopolitan*, 23.5 (September 1897), 465–482.

[Anon.], 'More Universal Language', *Fun*, 7 April 1886, 151.

[Anon.], 'Notes', *Concord*, 36.3 (September 1887), 106.

[Anon.], 'Our President's Movements', *British Esperantist*, 3.5 (May 1907), 83.

[Anon.], 'Oscar Wilde: A Visit to the Apostle of Modern Art', *Daily Picayune*, 16 June 1882, afternoon edition, 1.

[Anon.], 'Oscar Wilde. Lecture at Spanish Fort on Home Decorations. Practical Talk from an Apparently Unpractical Man', *Daily Picayune*, 27 June 1882, 3.

[Anon.], 'President's Speech at Annual Meeting, Dr. Zamenhof's Greetings by Phonograph', *The Esperantist*, 1.4 (February 1904), 49–52.

[Anon.], 'Programme', *Review of Reviews*, 1.1 (January 1890), 14.

[Anon.], [Review of Knut Hamsun, *Hunger*], *Black and White*, 19 August 1899, 242.

[Anon.], [Review of Knut Hamsun, *Hunger*], *Literature*, 5 (15 July 1899), 54.

[Anon.], [Review of Knut Hamsun, *Hunger*], *The Academy*, 56 (24 June 1899), 682–683.

[Anon.], '*Salomé* par Oscar Wilde', *Mercure de France*, 8 (July 1893), 279–280.

[Anon.], 'Sounding Brass and Tinkling Symbols', *Daily Chronicle*, 6 May 1895, 3.

[Anon.], '"The Case Against Goethe": A Severe Indictment', *Review of Reviews*, 13 (June 1896), 523.

[Anon.], 'The Censure and *Salome*: An Interview with Mr. Oscar Wilde', *Pall Mall Gazette*, 29 June 1892, 1–2.

[Anon.], 'The Esperanto Congress. Dickens Esperantised. "O. B." as Pickwick at the Theatre', *Cambridge Daily News*, 15 August 1907, 3.

[Anon.], 'The Outlook: International Language', *Daily Mail*, 12 August 1907, 4.

[Anon.], *The Unity of Man* (London: [privately printed for the International Arbitration Association], 1886).

[Anon.], 'To All English-Speaking Folk', *Review of Reviews*, 1.1 (January 1890), 15–20.

[Anon.], 'Translations', *The Athenæum*, 3596 (26 September 1896), 415–416.

[Anon.], 'Volapük as a Universal Language', *The Academy*, 850 (18 August 1888), 107.

[Anon.], 'Young Ofeg's Ditties', *Bookman*, 48 (September 1895), 172.

Andreas Salomé, Lou, 'Skandinavische Dichter', *Cosmopolis*, 11 (November 1896), 552–569.

Appiah, Kwame Anthony, 'Boundaries of Culture', *PMLA*, 123.3 (2017), 513–525.

Appiah, Kwame Anthony, 'Cosmopolitan Patriots', *Critical Inquiry*, 23.3 (1997), 617–639.

Appiah, Kwame Anthony, *Cosmopolitanism: Ethics in a World of Strangers* (London: Allen Lane, 2006).

Appiah, Kwame Anthony, *The Ethics of Identity* (Princeton and Oxford: Princeton University Press, 2005).

Apter, Emily, *Against World Literature: On the Politics of Untranslatability* (London and New York: Verso, 2013).

Apter, Emily, *The Translation Zone: A New Comparative Literature* (Princeton and Oxford: Princeton University Press, 2006).

Archer, William, 'A Pessimist Playwright', *Fortnightly Review*, 50 (September 1891), 346–354.

Archer, William, 'Norway Today', *Fortnightly Review*, 38 (September 1885), 413–425.

Arnold, Matthew, *Culture and Anarchy*, ed. R. H. Super (Ann Arbor: University of Michigan Press, 1965).

Arnold, Matthew, *Lectures and Essays in Criticism*, ed. R. H. Super (Ann Arbor: University of Michigan Press, 1962).

Arnold, Matthew, 'Up to Easter', *Nineteenth Century*, 21 (May 1887), 629–643.

Ashby, Charlotte, Grace Brockington, Daniel Laqua, and Sarah Victoria Turner, eds, *Imagined Cosmopolis: Internationalism and Cultural Exchange, 1870s–1920s* (Oxford and Bern: Peter Lang, 2019).

Atkinson, Juliette, 'Continental Currents: Paris and London', in Joanne Shattock, ed., *Journalism and the Periodical Press in Nineteenth-Century Britain* (Cambridge: Cambridge University Press, 2017), 224–244.

Auld, William, ed., *Esperanta antologio: poemoj 1887–1981* (Rotterdam: Universala Esperanto-Asocio, 1984).

Auld, William, *The Development of Poetic Language in Esperanto* (Rotterdam: Universala Esperanto-Asocio, 1976).

Bain, Robert Nisbet, 'Contemporary Scandinavian Belles Lettres', *Cosmopolis*, 11 (November 1896), 355–369.

Bain, Robert Nisbet, 'Scandinavian Current Belles-Lettres', *Cosmopolis*, 33 (September 1898), 673–683.

Balakian, Anna, ed., *The Symbolist Movement in the Literatures of the European Languages* (Budapest: Akadémiai Kiadó, 1982).

Balibar, Etienne, 'The Nation Form: History and Ideology', in Etienne Balibar and Immanuel Maurice Wallerstein, *Race, Nation, Class: Ambiguous Identities* (London and New York: Verso, 1991), 86–106.

Barrès, Maurice, 'La Querelle des nationalistes et des cosmopolites', *Le Figaro*, 4 July 1892, 1.

Basch, Victor, 'Ibsen et George Sand', *Cosmopolis*, 26 (February 1898), 466–492.

Bashford, Bruce, *Oscar Wilde: The Critic as Humanist* (Madison, NJ: Fairleigh Dickinson University Press, 1999).

Baudelaire, 'Le Peintre de la vie moderne', in *Critique d'art, suivi de Critique musicale*, ed. Claude Pichois (Paris: Gallimard, 1992), 343–384.

Baudelaire, Charles, 'The Painter of Modern Life', in *The Painter of Modern Life and Other Essays*, tr. Jonathan Mayne (New York: Da Capo, 1986), 1–40.

Baxter, Sylvester, 'The First Woman of Spain', *Cosmopolitan*, 15.2 (June 1893), 228–234.

Baylen, J. O., 'W. T. Stead as Publisher and Editor of the *Review of Reviews*', *Victorian Periodicals Review*, 12.2 (1979), 70–84.

Bazalgette, Léon, 'Nouvelles Scandinaves, traduites par Jean de Néthy', *L'Ermitage*, 8 (August 1894), 136–137.

Beasley, Rebecca, *Russomania: Russian Culture and the Creation of British Modernism 1881–1922* (Oxford and New York: Oxford University Press, 2020).

Beckson, Karl, ed., *Oscar Wilde: The Critical Heritage* (London: Routledge & Kegan Paul, 1970).

Bell, Alexander Melville, 'Volapük', *Science*, 11 (27 January 1888), 39–40.

Bell, Alexander Melville, *World-English: The Universal Language* (London: Trübner & Co., 1888).

Benjamin, Walter, *Gesammelte Schriften*, ed. Rolf Tiedemann et al., 7 vols (Frankfurt a. M.: Suhrkamp, 1991), v: *Das Passagen-Werk*, ed. Rolf Tiedemann.

Benjamin, Walter, *The Arcades Project*, tr. Howard Eiland and Kevin McLaughlin (Cambridge, MA, and London: Harvard University Press, 2002).

Berman, Jessica, *Modernist Fiction, Cosmopolitanism, and the Politics of Community* (Cambridge and New York: Cambridge University Press, 2001).

Bhabha, Homi K., 'The Vernacular Cosmopolitan', in Ferdinand Dennis and Naseem Khan, eds, *Voices of the Crossing: The Impact of Britain on Writers from Asia, the Caribbean, and Africa* (London: Serpent's Tail, 2000), 133–142.

Bhabha, Homi K., 'Unsatisfied: Notes on Vernacular Cosmopolitanism', in Laura García-Moreno and Peter C. Pfeiffer, eds, *Text and Nation: Cross-Disciplinary Essays on Cultural and National Identities* (Columbia, SC: Camden House, 1996), 191–207.

Bhambra, Gurminder K., and John Narayan, eds, *European Cosmopolitanism: Colonial Histories and Postcolonial Societies* (London: Routledge, 2016).

Billiani, Francesca, and Stefano Evangelista, 'Carlo Placci and Vernon Lee: The Aesthetics and Ethics of Cosmopolitanism in Florence', *Comparative Critical Studies*, 10.2 (2013), 141–161.

Biltcliffe, Pippa, 'Walter Crane and the *Imperial Federation Map showing the Extent of the British Empire* (1886)', *Imago Mundi*, 57.1 (2005), 63–69.

Bird, Isabella L., *Unbeaten Tracks in Japan: An Account of the Interior, Including Visits to the Aborigines of Yezo and the Shrines of Nikkō and Isé*, 2 vols (London: John Murray, 1880).

Bisland, Elizabeth, 'A Flying Trip around the World', *Cosmopolitan*, 9.6 (October 1890), 666–677.

Bisland, Elizabeth, *A Flying Trip around the World* (London: Osgood, McIlvaine, & Co., 1891).

Bisland, Elizabeth, 'A Nineteenth-Century Arcady', *Cosmopolitan*, 7.5 (September 1889), 512–519.

Bisland, Elizabeth, *At the Sign of the Hobby Horse* (Boston and New York: Houghton Mifflin, 1910).

Bisland, Elizabeth, 'Introduction', in Gustave Flaubert, *The Temptation of Saint Anthony*, tr. Lafcadio Hearn (New York and Seattle: Alice Harriman, 1910), n. p.

Bisland, Elizabeth, *Life and Letters of Lafcadio Hearn*, 2 vols (Boston and New York: Houghton Mifflin, 1911).

Bisland, Elizabeth, *The Secret Life: Being the Book of a Heretic* (New York and London: John Lane and Bodley Head, 1906).

Bisland, Elizabeth, 'The Studios of New York', *Cosmopolitan*, 7.1 (May 1889), 3–22.

Bizzotto, Elisa, and Stefano Evangelista, eds, *Arthur Symons: Poet, Critic, Vagabond* (Cambridge: Legenda, 2018).

Bjørhovde, Gerd, *Rebellious Structures: Women Writers and the Crisis of the Novel 1880–1900* (Oslo: Norwegian University Press, 1987).

Bjork, Robert E., 'A Bibliography of Modern Scandinavian Literature (Excluding H. C. Andersen) in English Translation, 1533–1900, and listed by Translator', *Scandinavian Studies*, 77.1 (2005), 105–42.

Bly, Nellie, *Around the World in 72 Days* (New York: Pictorial Weeklies, 1890).

Boehmer, Elleke, *Indian Arrivals, 1870–1915: Networks of British Empire* (Oxford and New York: Oxford University Press, 2015).

Borland, Harold H., *Nietzsche's Influence on Swedish Literature, with Special Reference to Strindberg, Ola Hansson, Heidestam, and Fröding* (Gotheborg: Wettergren & Kerbers, 1956).

Boulton, Marjorie, *Zamenhof, Creator of Esperanto* (London: Routledge & Kegan Paul, 1960).

Bourget, Paul, *Cosmopolis*, [tr. anon.] (New York: Tait, Sons, & Co., 1893).

Bourget, Paul, *Cosmopolis* (Paris: Lemerre, 1894).

Bourrellier, Paul-Henri, 'Portrait d'un dreyfussard: Gaston Moch, combattant de la paix', *Bulletin de la SABIX*, 42 (2008), 75–91.

Brake, Laurel, 'Stead Alone: Journalist, Proprietor, and Publisher, 1890–1903', in Roger Luckhurst, Laurel Brake, James Mussell, and Ed King, eds, *W. T. Stead: Newspaper Revolutionary* (London: British Library, 2012), 77–97.

Brake, Laurel, *Subjugated Knowledges: Journalism, Gender, and Literature in the Nineteenth Century* (Basingstoke: Macmillan, 1994).

Brandes, Georg, 'Henrik Ibsen en France', *Cosmopolis*, 13 (January 1897), 112–124.

Brandes, Georg, 'Othello', *Cosmopolis*, 1 (January 1896), 154–170.

Brandes, Georg, *Samlede Skrifter*, 18 vols (Copenhagen: Gyldendal, 1899–1910).

Brandes, Georg, 'World Literature', in Theo D'haen, César Domínguez, and Mads Rosendhal Thomsen, eds, *World Literature: A Reader* (London and New York: Routledge, 2013), 24–27.

Breckenridge, Carol A., Sheldon Pollock, Homi K. Bhabha, and Dipesh Chakrabarty, *Cosmopolitanism* (Durham, NC, and London: Duke University Press, 2002).

Brennan, Timothy, *At Home in the World: Cosmopolitanism Now* (Cambridge, MA: Harvard University Press, 1997).

Bristow, Joseph, ed., *Oscar Wilde and Modern Culture: The Making of a Legend* (Athens, OH: Ohio University Press, 2008).

Bristow, Joseph, ed., *Wilde Discoveries: Traditions, Histories, Archives* (Toronto: Toronto University Press, 2013).

Bristow, Joseph, and Rebecca N. Mitchell, *Oscar Wilde's Chatterton: Literary History, Romanticism, and the Art of Forgery* (New Haven: Yale University Press, 2015).

Brockington, Grace, 'Introduction: The Expanded Universal Language Movement', in Charlotte Ashby et al., eds, *Imagined Cosmopolis: Internationalism and Cultural Exchange, 1870s–1920s* (Oxford and Bern: Peter Lang, 2019), 351–378.

Brockington, Grace, 'Rhyming Pictures: Walter Crane and the Universal Language of Art', *Journal of Verbal/Visual Enquiry*, 28.4 (2012), 359–373.

Brocky, Sister Mary Damascene, 'A Study of Cosmopolitan Magazine, 1890–1900: Its Relation to the Literature of the Decade' (unpublished doctoral thesis, Notre Dame University, 1958).

Bronner, Simon J., ed., *Lafcadio Hearn's America: Ethnographic Sketches and Editorials* (Lexington: University Press of Kentucky, 2002).

Brooker, Peter, Andrew Thacker, Sascha Bru, and Christian Weikop, eds, *Oxford Critical and Cultural History of Modernist Magazines*, 3 vols (Oxford and New York: Oxford University Press, 2009–13).

Brown, Daniel, 'George Egerton's *Keynotes*: Nietzschean Feminism and *fin-de-siècle* Fetishism', *Victorian Literature and Culture*, 39.1 (2011), 143–166.

Bruford, W. H., *Germany in the Eighteenth Century: The Social Background of the Literary Revival* (Cambridge: Cambridge University Press, 1935).

Bullock, Philip Ross, 'Ibsen on the London Stage: Independent Theatre as Transnational Space', *Forum for Modern Language Studies*, 53.3 (2017), 360–370.

Burchardt, C. B., *Norwegian Life and Literature: English Accounts and Views Especially in the Nineteenth Century* (London and Edinburgh: Oxford University Press, 1920).

Casanova, Pascale, 'The Ibsen Battle: A Comparative Analysis of the Introduction of Henrik Ibsen in France, England and Ireland', in Christophe Charle, Julien Vincent, and Jay Winter, eds, *Anglo-French Attitudes: Comparisons and Transfers between English and French Intellectuals since the Eighteenth Century* (Manchester: Manchester University Press, 2007), 214–232.

Casanova, Pascale, *The World Republic of Letters*, tr. M. B. DeBevoise (Cambridge, MA, and London: Harvard University Press, 2004).

Cassin, Barbara, ed., *Dictionary of Untranslatables: A Philosophical Lexicon*, tr. Steven Rendall et al. (Princeton: Princeton University Press, 2013).

Ceadel, Martin, *Semi-Detached Idealists: The British Peace Movement and International Relations, 1854–1945* (Oxford and New York: Oxford University Press, 2000).

Challaye, Félicien, 'Lafcadio Hearn: Un philosophe japonisant', *Revue de métaphysique et de morale*, 11 (1903), 338–351.

Chamberlain, Basil Hall, *More Letters from Basil Hall Chamberlain to Lafcadio Hearn*, ed. Kazuo Koizumi (Tokyo: Hokuseido Press, 1937).

Chan, Gerald, 'China and the Esperanto Movement', *Australian Journal of Chinese Affairs*, 15 (January 1986), 1–18.

Cheah, Pheng, 'Grounds of Comparison', *Diacritics*, 29.4 (1999), 2–18.

Cheah, Pheng, *Inhuman Conditions: On Cosmopolitanism and Human Rights* (Cambridge, MA: Harvard University Press, 2006).

Claes, Koenraad, *The Late-Victorian Little Magazine* (Edinburgh: Edinburgh University Press, 2018).

Clark, Daniel A., and Paul S. Boyer, *Creating the College Man: American Mass Magazines and Middle-Class Manhood, 1890–1915* (Madison, WI: University of Wisconsin Press, 2010).

Coakley, Davis, *Oscar Wilde: The Importance of Being Irish* (Dublin: Town House, 1994).

Cohen, Joshua, ed., *For Love of Country: Debating the Limits of Patriotism* (Boston: Beacon Press, 1996).

Cohen, William A., 'Wilde's French', in Joseph Bristow, ed., *Wilde Discoveries: Traditions, Histories, Archives* (Toronto: Toronto University Press, 2013), 233–259.

Collini, Stefan, *Public Moralists: Political Thought and Intellectual Life in Britain 1850–1930* (Oxford and New York: Clarendon Press, 1991).

Conrad, Joseph, 'An Outpost of Progress', *Cosmopolis*, 19 (July 1897), 1–15.

Conrad, Joseph, *The Collected Letters of Joseph Conrad*, ed. Frederick R. Karl, 9 vols (Cambridge and London: Cambridge University Press, 1983–2008).

Conrad, Joseph, *The Secret Agent*, ed. Tanya Aghathocleous (Peterborough, Ont.: Broadview, 2009).

Cotterell, George, 'New Novels', *The Academy*, 1196 (6 April 1895), 293–294.

Couturat, Louis, and Léopold Leau, *Histoire de la langue universelle* (Paris: Hachette, 1903).

Crane, Walter, *An Artist's Reminiscences* (London: Methuen, 1907).

Culler, Jonathan, 'Anderson and the Novel', *Diacritics*, 29.4 (1999), 19–39.

Cunningham, George, John Pollen, and Harold Bolingbroke Mudie, *Kongresa Libro* (London: Arundel St., 1907).

Damrosch, David, *What is World Literature?* (Princeton and Oxford: Princeton University Press, 2003).

Danson, Lawrence, *Wilde's Intentions: The Artist in his Criticism* (Oxford: Clarendon, 1997).

Davies, Laurence, '"Don't you Think I am a Lost Soul?" Conrad's Early Stories and the Magazines', *Conradiana*, 41.1 (2009), 7–28.

Davis, John R., and Angus Nicholls, 'Friedrich Max Müller: The Career and Intellectual Trajectory of a German Philologist in Victorian Britain', *Publications of the English Goethe Society*, 85.2 and 3 (2016), 67–97.

Dawson, Carl, *Lafcadio Hearn and the Vision of Japan* (Baltimore and London: Johns Hopkins University Press, 1992).

De Beaufront, Louis, 'Impressions of the Esperanto Congress at Cambridge', *North American Review*, 186 (September 1907), 273–275.

De Beaufront, Louis, 'L'Esperanto peut-il être littéraire?', *L'Esperantiste*, 1.4 (April 1898), 54–56.

De la Sizeranne, Robert, 'Volapükistes et anti- Volapükistes', *Le Volapük*, 12, supplement (November/December 1887), 1.

Dellamora, Richard, 'Productive Decadence: "The Queer Comradeship of Outlawed Thought": Vernon Lee, Max Nordau, and Oscar Wilde', *New Literary History*, 35.4 (2004), 529–546.

Demoor, Marysa, ed., *Friends over the Ocean: Andrew Lang's American Correspondents* (Ghent: Universa, 1989).

Derrida, Jacques, *Of Hospitality*, tr. Rachel Bowlby (Stanford, CA: Stanford University Press, 2000).

Derrida, Jacques, *On Cosmopolitanism and Forgiveness*, tr. Mark Dooley and Michael Hughes (London: Routledge, 2001).

De Saint Victor, Carol, 'Cosmopolis', in Alvin Ed Sullivan, ed., *British Literary Magazines: The Victorian and Edwardian Age, 1837–1913* (Westport, CT: Greenwood Press, 1984), 85–92.

Dierkes-Thrun, Petra, *Salome's Modernity: Oscar Wilde and the Aesthetics of Transgression* (Ann Arbor: University of Michigan Press, 2011).

Diogenes Laertius, *Diogenis Laertii Vitae Philosophorum*, ed. Miroslav Marcovich, 3 vols (Stuttgart and Leipzig: Teubner, 1999–2002).

Dohm, Hedwig, *Die Antifeministen: Ein Buch der Verteidigung* (Berlin: Dümmlers, 1902).

Dowden, Edward, 'The Case Against Goethe', *Cosmopolis*, 6 (June 1896), 624–642.

Dowling, Linda, *Hellenism and Homosexuality in Victorian Oxford* (Ithaca, NY: Cornell University Press, 1994).

Dowling, Linda, *Language and Decadence in the Victorian* Fin de Siècle (Princeton, NJ and Oxford: Princeton University Press, 1986).

Downs, Brian W., 'Anglo-Norwegian Literary Relations 1867–1900', *Modern Language Review*, 47.4 (1952), 449–494.

Dunckley, Henry, 'The Jubilee of Free Trade', *Cosmopolis*, 6 (June 1896), 643–659.

Eco, Umberto, *The Search for the Perfect Language* [1993], tr. James Fentress (London: Fontana, 1997).

Editorial Committee, 'Nia Alparolo/Our Message', *British Esperantist*, 1.1 (January 1905), 6–7.

Eells, Emily, 'Naturalizing Oscar Wilde as an *homme de lettres*: The French Reception of *Dorian Gray* and *Salomé* (1895–1922)', in Stefano Evangelista, ed., *The Reception of Oscar Wilde in Europe* (London and New York: Continuum, 2010), 80–95.

Eells, Emily, 'Wilde's French *Salomé*', *Cahiers victoriens et édouardiens*, 72 (Autumn 2020) <https://journals.openedition.org/cve/2729> [accessed 10 January 2019].

Egerton, George, 'A Christmas Idyl', *Universal Magazine*, 2 (1900), 213–221.

Egerton, George, 'A Keynote to *Keynotes*', in John Gawsworthy, *Ten Contemporaries* (London: Ernest Benn, 1932), 57–60.

Egerton, George, *A Leaf from the Yellow Book: The Correspondence of George Egerton*, ed. Terence de Vere White (London: Richard Press, 1958).

Egerton, George, 'Arne Garborg', *Outlook*, 2.34 (24 September 1898), 240–241.

Egerton, George, *Fantasias* (London and New York: John Lane, 1898).

Egerton, George, 'Introductory Note', in Ola Hansson, *Young Ofeg's Ditties*, tr. George Egerton (London: John Lane; and Boston: Roberts Bros, 1895), 5–13.

Egerton, George, *Keynotes and Discords* (London: Virago, 1983).

Egerton, George, 'Prefatory Note', in Knut Hamsun, *Hunger*, tr. George Egerton (London: Smithers, 1899), pp. v–x.

Egerton, George, 'Translator's Note', in Knut Hamsun, *Hunger*, tr. George Egerton (London: Duckworth, 1921), pp. v–x.

Ellis, Alexander J., 'On the Conditions of a Universal Language, in Reference to the Invitation of the American Philosophical Society of Philadelphia, U.S., to Send Delegates to a Congress for Perfecting a Universal Language in an Aryan Basis, and its Report on Volapük', *Transactions of the Philological Society*, 21.1 (November 1890), 59–98.

Ellis, Havelock, 'Introduction', in Johann Wolfgang von Goethe, *Conversations of Goethe with Eckermann*, tr. John Oxenford (London and Toronto: Dent & Sons, 1930), pp. vii–xix.

Ellis, Havelock, *My Life* (Boston: Houghton Mifflin, 1939).

Ellis, Havelock, 'Preface', in Henrik Ibsen, *The Pillars of Society and Other Plays*, tr. William Archer, Henrietta Frances Lord, and Eleanor Marx-Aveling (London: Walter Scott; and New York: Whittaker, 1888), pp. vi–xxx.

Erber, Nancy, 'The French Trials of Oscar Wilde', *Journal of the History of Sexuality*, 6.4 (1996), 549–588.

Escott, T. H. S., 'The Press as an International Agency', *Cosmopolis*, 3 (March 1896), 664–677.

Espalion, 'L'Esperanto', *La Ligue: Organe belge du droit des femmes*, 15 (1907), 31–38.

Esperanto, Dr [Ludwik L. Zamenhof], *An Attempt towards an International Language*, tr. Henry Phillips Jr (New York: Henry Holt & Co., 1889).

Esperanto, Dr [Ludwik L. Zamenhof], *Dr Esperanto's International Tongue*, tr. J. St. [Julius Steinhaus] (Warsaw: Kelter, 1888).

Esty, Jed, *A Shrinking Island: Modernism and National Culture in England* (Princeton and Oxford: Princeton University Press, 2004).

Evangelista, Stefano, *British Aestheticism and Ancient Greece: Hellenism, Reception, Gods in Exile* (Basingstoke and New York: Palgrave Macmillan, 2009).

Evangelista, Stefano, ' "Life in the Whole": Goethe and English Aestheticism', *Publications of the English Goethe Society*, 82.3 (2013), 180–192.

Evangelista, Stefano, 'Symphonies in Haze and Blue: Lafcadio Hearn and the Colours of Japan', in Charlotte Ribeyrol, ed., *The Colours of the Past in Victorian England* (Oxford and Bern: Peter Lang, 2016), 71–94.

Evangelista, Stefano, ed., *The Reception of Oscar Wilde in Europe* (London and New York: Continuum, 2010).

Evangelista, Stefano, 'The Time of Ola Hansson: Translating Scandinavian Decadence in *Fin de Siècle* France and England', in Pirjo Lyytikäinen, Riikka Rossi, Viola Parente-Čapková, and Mirjam Hinrikus, eds, *Nordic Literature of Decadence* (New York and Oxford: Routledge, 2020), 205–222.

Faguet, Emile, 'Cronique littéraire', *Cosmopolis*, 1 (January 1896), 184–195.

Fiske, A. K., 'Profligacy in Fiction', *North American Review*, 131 (July 1880), 79–88.

Fjågesund, Peter, 'Knut Hamsun and George Egerton: Factual and Fictional Encounters', in Bjørn Tysdahl, Mats Jansson, Jakob Lothe, and Steen Klitgård Povlsen, eds, *English and Nordic Modernisms* (Norwich: Norvik Press, 2002), 41–59.

Fletcher, Ian, 'Decadence and the Little Magazines', in Ian Fletcher, ed., *Decadence and the 1890s* (London: Edward Arnold, 1979), 173–202.

Forman, Henry James, 'The Progress of Esperanto', *North American Review*, 186 (September 1907), 276–280.

Forster, Peter G., *The Esperanto Movement* (The Hague and Paris: Mouton, 1982).

Fraser, Hilary, 'Vernon Lee: England, Italy and Identity Politics', in Carol M. Richardson and Graham Smith, eds, *Britannia, Italia, Germania: Taste and Travel in the Nineteenth Century* (Edinburgh: VARIE, 2001), 175–191.

Freedman, Jonathan, *The Temple of Culture: Assimilation and Anti-Semitism in Literary Anglo-America* (Oxford and New York: Oxford University Press, 2000).

Fryer, Jonathan, *André and Oscar: Gide, Wilde and the Gay Art of Living* (London: Constable, 1997).

Fulsås, Narve, and Tore Rem, *Ibsen, Scandinavia, and the Making of a World Drama* (Cambridge and New York: Cambridge University Press, 2018).

Gagnier, Regenia, *Individualism, Decadence, Globalization: On the Relationship of Part to Whole, 1859–1920* (Basingstoke and New York: Palgrave Macmillan, 2010).

Gagnier, Regenia, *Literatures of Liberalization: Global Circulation and the Long Nineteenth Century* (Basingstoke and New York: Palgrave Macmillan, 2018).

Gainer, Bernard, *The Alien Invasion: The Origins of the Aliens Act of 1905* (London: Heinemann, 1972).

Gallagher, Mary, 'Lafcadio Hearn's American Writings and the Creole Continuum', in Martin Munro and Celia Britton, eds, *American Creoles: The Francophone Caribbean and the American South* (Liverpool: Liverpool University Press, 2012), 19–39.

Gandhi, Leela, *Affective Communities: Anticolonial Thought, Fin-de-Siècle Radicalism, and the Politics of Friendship* (Durham, NC, and London: Duke University Press, 2006).

Garvía, Roberto, *Esperanto and its Rivals: The Struggle for an International Language* (Philadelphia: University of Pennsylvania Press, 2015).

Gautier, Théophile, *Contes fantastiques* (Paris: Corti, 1986).

Gautier, Théophile, *One of Cleopatra's Nights and Other Fantastic Tales*, tr. Lafcadio Hearn (New York: Worthington, 1882).

Gide, André, 'In Memoriam', in *Oscar Wilde*, tr. Bernard Frechtman (London: Kimber, 1951), 11–45.

Gide, André, *Les Nourritures terrestres* (Paris: Gallimard, 1921).

Gide, André, 'Oscar Wilde', *L'Ermitage*, 13.6 (June 1902), 401–429.

Giles, Paul, *Transnationalism in Practice: Essays on American Studies, Literature and Religion* (Edinburgh: Edinburgh University Press, 2010).

Gilroy, Paul, *Postcolonial Melancholia* (New York: Columbia University Press, 2005).

Goedhals, Antony, *The Neo-Buddhist Writings of Lafcadio Hearn: Light from the East* (Leiden and Boston: Brill, 2020).

Goethe, Johann Wolfgang von, *Conversations of Goethe with Eckermann and Soret*, tr. John Oxenford, 2 vols (London: Smith, Elder, & Co., 1850).

Goodfellow, Robin, 'Table Talk', *Cambridge Daily News*, 17 August 1907, 3.

Goodlad, Lauren M. E., 'Cosmopolitanism's Actually Existing Beyond; Toward a Victorian Geopolitical Aesthetic', *Victorian Literature and Culture*, 38 (2010), 399–411.

Goodlad, Lauren M. E., *The Victorian Geopolitical Aesthetic: Realism, Sovereignty, and Transnational Experience* (Oxford and New York: Oxford University Press, 2015).

Goodman, Jonathan, *The Oscar Wilde File* (London: Allen & Co., 1988).

Goodman, Matthew, *Eighty Days: Nellie Bly and Elizabeth Bisland's History-Making Race around the World* (New York: Ballantine, 2013).

Gosse, Edmund, 'Current French Literature', *Cosmopolis*, 6 (June 1896), 660–677.

Gosse, Edmund, 'Editor's Note', in Bjørnsterne Bjørnson, *In God's Way*, tr. Elizabeth Carmichael (London: Heinemann, 1890), n. p.

Gosse, Edmund, 'Norway Revisited', *North American Review*, 167 (November 1898), 534–542.

Gosse, Edmund, *Studies in the Literature of Northern Europe* (London: Kegan Paul, 1879).

Gould, George M., *Concerning Lafcadio Hearn* (London: Fisher Unwin, 1908).

Greenwood, Frederick, 'Sentiment in Politics', *Cosmopolis*, 10 (October 1896), 340–354.

Greenwood, Frederick, 'The Safeguards of Peace Considered', *Cosmopolis*, 5 (May 1896), 346–360.

Guy, Josephine M., and Ian Small, *Oscar Wilde's Profession: Writing and the Culture Industry in the Late Nineteenth Century* (Oxford: Oxford University Press, 2000).

Hading, Jane, 'The Story of my Career', *Cosmopolitan*, 6.3 (January 1889), 220–224.

Hagler, Margaret, 'The Esperanto Language as a Literary Medium: A Historical Discussion of Esperanto Literature, 1887–1970, and a Stylistic Analysis of Translated and Original Esperanto Poetry' (unpublished doctoral thesis, Indiana University, 1970).

Halim, Hala, *Alexandrian Cosmopolitanism: An Archive* (New York: Fordham University Press, 2013).

Hamsun, Knut, *Fra det moderne Amerikas Aandsliv* (Copenhagen: Philipsen, 1899).

Hamsun, Knut, *Hunger*, tr. George Egerton (London: Smithers, 1899).

Hamsun, Knut, *La Faim*, tr. Edmond Bayle (Paris: Langen, 1895).

Hamsun, Knut, *Paa Turné: Tre foredrag om litteratur*, ed. Tore Hamsun (Oslo: Gyldendal, 1960).

Hansson, Ola, 'Hans Thoma', *Cosmopolis*, 7 (July 1896), 249–270.

Hansson, Ola, 'La maladie dans la littérature actuelle', *Revue des revues*, 5 (June 1894), 353–358.

Hansson, Ola, 'Les Chants d'Ofeg', tr. Jean de Néthy, *Mercure de France*, 30 (June 1892), 103–113.

Hansson, Ola, 'Mouvement littéraire en Suède', tr. Jean de Néthy, *Revue des revues*, 4 (July 1893), 481–489.

Hansson, Ola, *Young Ofeg's Ditties*, tr. George Egerton (London: John Lane; and Boston: Roberts Bros, 1895).

Harley, J. Brian, 'Maps, Knowledge and Power', in Denis Cosgrove and Stephen Daniels, eds, *The Iconography of Landscape* (Cambridge: Cambridge University Press, 1988), 277–312.

Harris, Frank, *Oscar Wilde: His Life and Confessions* (London: Constable: 1938).

Harrison, Frederic, 'The True Cosmopolis', *Cosmopolis*, 8 (August 1896), 325–340.

Hearn, Lafcadio, 'A Ghost', *Harper's New Monthly Magazine*, 80 (December 1889), 116–119.

Hearn, Lafcadio, 'A Society of Many Colorings', *Cosmopolitan*, 9.3 (July 1890), 337–341.

Hearn, Lafcadio, 'A Study of Half-Breed Races in the West Indies', *Cosmopolitan*, 9.2 (June 1890), 167–172.

Hearn, Lafcadio, 'A Winter Journey to Japan', *Harper's New Monthly Magazine*, 81 (June 1890), 860–868.

Hearn, Lafcadio, *American Writings*, ed. Christopher Benfey (New York: Library of America, 2009).

Hearn, Lafcadio, *Appreciations of Poetry*, ed. John Erskine (London: Heinemann, 1916).

Hearn, Lafcadio, *Books and Habits*, ed. John Erskine (London: Heinemann, 1922).

Hearn, Lafcadio, *Editorials*, ed. Charles Woodward Hutson (Boston and New York: Houghton Mifflin, 1926).

Hearn, Lafcadio, *Essays in European and Oriental Literature*, ed. Albert Mordell (London: Heinemann, 1923).

Hearn, Lafcadio, *Glimpses of Unfamiliar Japan* (Rutland, VT, and Tokyo: Tuttle, 1997).

Hearn, Lafcadio, *Gombo Zhèbes: Little Dictionary of Creole Proverbs* (New York: Coleman, 1885).

Hearn, Lafcadio, *Interpretations of Literature*, ed. John Erskine, 2 vols (London: Heinemann, 1916).

Hearn, Lafcadio, *Japan: An Attempt at Interpretation* (New York and London: Macmillan, 1904).

Hearn, Lafcadio, *La Cuisine Créole: A Collection of Culinary Recipes* (New Orleans: Hansell & Bro., 1885).

Hearn, Lafcadio, *Life and Literature*, ed. John Erskine (London: Heinemann, 1917).

[Hearn, Lafcadio], 'Oscar Wilde as Fashion Designer', *Times-Democrat*, 14 May 1882, 4.

Hearn, Lafcadio, *Out of the East: Reveries and Studies of New Japan* (Rutland, VT, and Tokyo: Tuttle, 1972).

Hearn, Lafcadio, *Period of the Gruesome: Selected Cincinnati Journalism of Lafcadio Hearn*, ed. Jon Christopher Hughes (Lanham, MD, and New York: University Press of America, 1990).

Hearn, Lafcadio, *Pre-Raphaelite and Other Poets*, ed. John Erskine (London: Heinemann, 1923).

[Hearn, Lafcadio], 'The Apostle of Aestheticism', *Times-Democrat*, 16 April 1882, 4.

Hearn, Lafcadio, *The Japanese Letters of Lafcadio Hearn*, ed. Elizabeth Bisland (London and Boston: Constable and Houghton Mifflin, 1910).

Hearn, Lafcadio, 'To the Reader', in Théophile Gautier, *One of Cleopatra's Nights and Other Fantastic Romances*, tr. Lafcadio Hearn (New York: Worthington, 1882), pp. v–ix.

Herder, Johann Gottfried, *Philosophical Writings*, tr. and ed. Michael N. Forster (Cambridge and New York: Cambridge University Press, 2002).

Herder, Johann Gottfried, *Werke in zehn Bänden*, ed. Martin Bollacher et al. (Frankfurt a. M.: Suhrkampf, 1985–2000).

Herford, C. H., 'An English Goethe Society', *The Academy*, 26 (1884), 324.

Herold, Katharina, '"Against Civilisation": Symons, the Gypsy Lore, and Politicised Aestheticism', in Elisa Bizzotto and Stefano Evangelista, eds, *Arthur Symons: Poet, Critic, Vagabond* (Cambridge: Legenda, 2018), 145–159.

Hibbitt, Richard, 'The Artist as Aesthete: The French Creation of Wilde', in Stefano Evangelista, ed., *The Reception of Oscar Wilde in Europe* (London and New York: Continuum, 2010), 65–79.

Higginson, Thomas Wentworth, *Concerning All of Us* (New York: Harper & Bros, 1893).

Hirakawa, Sukehiro, ed., *Rediscovering Lafcadio Hearn: Japanese Legends, Life and Culture* (Folkestone: Global Oriental, 1997).

Hobsbawm, E. J., *Nations and Nationalism since 1870: Programme, Myth, Reality* (Cambridge and New York: Cambridge University Press, 1990).

Hollenberg, Günter, 'Die English Goethe Society und die deutsch-englischen kulturellen Beziehungen im 19. Jahrhundert', *Zeitschrift für Religions- und Geistesgeschichte*, 30 (1978), 36–45.

Hollinger, David A., 'Not Universalists, Not Pluralists: The New Cosmopolitans Find their own Way', *Constellations*, 8.2 (2001), 236–248.

Holton, Robert J., *Cosmopolitanisms: New Thinking and New Directions* (Basingstoke and New York: Palgrave Macmillan, 2009).

Horne, Philip, 'Henry James and the Economy of the Short Story', in Warren Chernaik, Warwick Gould, and Ian Willison, eds, *Modernist Writers and the Marketplace* (Basingstoke: Palgrave Macmillan, 1996), 1–35.

Horne, Philip, 'Henry James: The Master and the "Queer Affair" of "The Pupil"', *Critical Quarterly*, 37.3 (1995), 75–92.

Horne, Philip, '"Reinstated": James in Roosevelt's Washington', *Cambridge Quarterly*, 37.1 (2008), 47–63.

Hoy, Helen, 'Homotextual Duplicity in Henry James's "The Pupil"', *Henry James Review*, 14.1 (1993), 34–42.

Hsu, Hsuan L., 'A Connecticut Yankee in the Court of Wu Chih Tien: Mark Twain and Wong Chin Foo', *Common-Place*, 2.1 (2010) <www.common-place-archives.org/vol-11/no-01/hsu> [accessed 17 May 2019].

Hume, David R., *The German Literary Achievements of Ola Hansson* (Bern and Frankfurt a. M.: Peter Lang, 1979).

Hunt, Leigh, 'Abou Ben Adhem', tr. John F. Davis, *Cosmopolitan/Kosmopolan*, 6 (July 1892), 84.

Hunt, Leigh, *The Poetical Works of Leigh Hunt*, ed. H. S. Milford (London and New York: Oxford University Press, 1923).

Huysmans, Joris-Karl, *Against Nature*, tr. Robert Baldick (London and New York: Penguin, 1959).

Ignotus, 'Politisches in deutscher Beleuchtung', *Cosmopolis*, 9 (September 1896), 909–924.

Ingalls, John J., 'Lessons of the Fair', *Cosmopolitan*, 16.2 (December 1893), 141–149.

Ingleheart, Jennifer, *Ancient Rome and the Construction of Modern Homosexual Identities* (Oxford and New York: Oxford University Press, 2015).

Ishikawa, Daichi, 'For Curiosity's Sake: British Aestheticism and Cosmopolitan Notions of Curiosity in Walter Pater, John Addington Symonds, and Lafcadio Hearn, 1864–1904' (unpublished doctoral thesis, Queen Mary, University of London, 2018).

Jackson, Holbrook, 'Introduction', in Oscar Wilde, *Salome* (London: Limited Editions Club, 1938), 11–27.

James, Henry, *Literary Criticism: French Writers, Other European Writers, The Prefaces to the New York Edition* (New York and Cambridge: Literary Classics of the United States and Press Syndicate of the University of Cambridge, 1984).

James, Henry, *The Ambassadors* (London and New York: Penguin, 2008).

James, Henry, *The Princess Casamassima* (London and New York: Penguin, 1987).

James, Henry, 'The Pupil', *Longman's Magazine*, 17 (March 1891), 512–531; and (April 1891), 611–632.

James, Henry, 'Wolcott Balestier', *Cosmopolitan*, 13.1 (May 1892), 43–47.

Janton, Pierre, *Esperanto: Language, Literature, and Community*, tr. Humphrey Tonkin, Jane Edwards, and Karen Johnson-Weiner (Albany, NY: State University of New York Press, 1993).

Kant, Immanuel, *Kant's Political Writings*, ed. Hans Reiss, tr. H. B. Nisbet, 2nd edn (Cambridge: Cambridge University Press, 1990).

Keary, C. F., *Norway and the Norwegians* (London: Percival, 1892).

Kendle, John, *Federal Britain: A History* (London: Routledge, 1997).

Kennard, Nina H., *Lafcadio Hearn: Containing Some Letters from Lafcadio Hearn to his Half-Sister, Mrs Atkinson* (New York: Appleton & Co., 1912).

Kiberd, Declan, 'Oscar Wilde: The Resurgence of Lying', in Peter Raby, ed., *The Cambridge Companion to Oscar Wilde* (Cambridge: Cambridge University Press, 1997), 276–294.

Kohn, Hans, *The Age of Nationalism: The First Era of Global History* (New York and Evanston, IL: Harper, 1968).

Koizumi, Kazuo, *Father and I: Memories of Lafcadio Hearn* (Boston and New York: Houghton Mifflin, 1935).

Krajewski, Markus, 'Organizing a Global Idiom: *Esperanto, Ido* and the World Auxiliary Language Movement Before the First World War', in W. Boyd Rayward, ed., *Information beyond Borders: International Cultural and Intellectual Exchange in the Belle Époque* (Farnham and Burlington, VT: Ashgate, 2014), 97–108.

Kristeva, Julia, *Strangers to Ourselves*, tr. Leon S. Roudiez (New York: Columbia University Press, 1991).

Kundera, Milan, 'Die Weltliteratur', in Theo D'haen, César Domínguez, and Mads Rosendahl Thomsen, eds, *World Literature: A Reader* (London and New York: Routledge, 2013), 290–300.

Künzli, Andreas, *L. L. Zamenhof (1859–1817): Esperanto, Hillelismus (Homaranismus), und die 'jüdische Frage' in Ost- und Westeuropa* (Wiesbaden: Harrassowitz, 2010).

Laachir, Karima, Sara Marzagora, and Francesca Orsini, 'Significant Geographies: In Lieu of World Literature', *Journal of World Literature*, 3 (2018), 290–310.

Labruyère, 'Le Volapuk', *Le Figaro*, 17 September 1886, 1.

Laity, Paul, *The British Peace Movement, 1870–1914* (Oxford: Clarendon, 2001).

Lambourne, Lionel, *Japonisme: Cultural Crossings between Japan and the West* (London: Phaidon, 2005).

Landers, James, *The Improbable First Century of Cosmopolitan Magazine* (Columbia, MO, and London: University of Missouri Press, 2010).

Lang, Andrew, 'Literary Chronicle', *Cosmopolis*, 1 (January 1896), 70–87.

Laqua, Daniel, and Christophe Verbruggen, 'Beyond the Metropolis: French and Belgian Symbolists between the Region and the Republic of Letters', *Comparative Critical Studies*, 10.2 (2013), 241–258.

Larsen, Svend Eric, 'Georg Brandes: The Telescope of Comparative Literature', in Theo D'haen, David Damrosch, and Djelal Kadir, eds, *The Routledge Companion to World Literature* (London and New York: Routledge, 2012), 21–31.

Latham, R. G., *Norway and the Norwegians*, 2 vols (London: Bentley, 1840).

Lavelle, Isabelle, '*Anywhere Out of the World*: Translating *Décadence* in Japanese Literature, 1885–1925' (PhD thesis, Waseda University, 2018).

Lavery, Grace E., *Quaint, Exquisite: Victorian Aesthetics and the Idea of Japan* (Princeton: Princeton University Press, 2019).

Lawrence, E. A., 'To the English-Speaking Esperantists Everywhere', *British Esperantist*, 2.22 (October 1906), 115.

Lawrence, Paul, *Nationalism: History and Theory* (Harlow and London: Longman, 2005).

Lazare, Bernard, '*Salomé* par Oscar Wilde', *Entretiens politiques et littéraires*, 41 (25 April 1893), 382–384.

Lederer, Siegfried, 'Volapük im Dienste der Weltliteratur', *Rund um die Welt: Zeitschrift für Volapükisten und solche, die es werden wollen*, 4.9-10 (August 1891), 146.

Ledger, Sally, 'Introduction', in George Egerton, *Keynotes and Discords* (London: Continuum, 2003), pp. ix–xxvi.

Lee, Vernon, 'A Worldly Woman', *Contemporary Review*, 58 (October 1890), 520–541; and (November 1890), 693–711.

Lee, Vernon, 'Bismarck Towers', *New Statesman*, 20 February 1915, 481–483.

Lee, Vernon, *Hauntings and Other Fantastic Tales*, ed. Catherine Maxwell and Patricia Pulham (Peterborough, Ont.: Broadview, 2006).

Leerssen, Joep, 'Englishness, Ethnicity, and Matthew Arnold', *European Journal of English Studies*, 10.1 (2006), 63–79.

Lemaître, Jules, *Les Contemporains: Études et portraits littéraires*, 6th ser. (Paris: Lecène, Oudin, et Cie, 1896).

Lemoine, Bernadette, 'Lafcadio Hearn as an Ambassador for French Literature in the United States and Japan', *Revue de littérature comparée*, 319 (2006), 299–317.

Levine, Caroline, *Forms: Whole, Rhythm, Hierarchy, Network* (Princeton: Princeton University Press, 2015).

Levine, Caroline, 'From Nation to Network', *Victorian Studies*, 55.4 (2013), 647–666.

Lewes, George Henry, *The Life and Works of Goethe* (London: Smith, Elder, & Co., 1864).

Lewis, Pericles, *Modernism, Nationalism, and the Novel* (Cambridge and New York: Cambridge University Press, 2000).

Lloyd, R. J., 'On the Economic Value of an International Business Language', *Westminster Review*, 160 (December 1903), 673–683.

Lyngstad, Sverre, 'Translator's Trap: Knut Hamsun's *Hunger* in English', in Knut Hamsun, *Hunger*, tr. Sverre Lyngstad (Edinburgh and London: Canongate, 2001), 223–241.

McCormack, Jerusha, ed., *Wilde the Irishman* (New Haven and London: Yale University Press, 1998).

McGuinness, Patrick, *Maurice Maeterlinck and the Making of Modern Theatre* (Oxford and New York: Oxford University Press, 2000).

McGuinness, Patrick, *Poetry and Radical Politics in* Fin-de-Siècle *France: From Anarchism to the Action française* (Oxford and New York: Oxford University Press, 2015).

MacLeod, Kirsten, *Fictions of British Decadence: High Art, Popular Writing, and the Fin de Siècle* (Basingstoke and New York: Palgrave Macmillan, 2006).

Madsen, Peter, 'World Literature and World Thoughts: Brandes/Auerbach', in Christopher Prendergast, ed., *Debating World Literature* (London and New York: Verso, 2004), 54–75.

Maeterlinck, Maurice, *Le Cahier bleu*, ed. Joanne Wieland-Burston, *Annales de la Fondation Maurice Maeterlinck*, 22 (1976), 7–184.

Maguire, Robert, 'Oscar Wilde and the Dreyfus Affair', *Victorian Studies*, 41.1 (1997), 1–29.

Mahoney, Kristin, 'On the *Ceylon National Review*, 1906–1911', *BRANCH: Britain, Representation, and Nineteenth-Century History* (2018) < http://www.branchcollective. org/?ps_articles=kristin-mahoney-on-the-ceylon-national-review-1906-1911#_ftn1.end> [accessed 28 July 2020].

Makino, Yoko, 'Lafcadio Hearn and Yanagita Kunio: Who Initiated Folklore Studies in Japan?', in Sukehiro Hirakawa, ed., *Lafcadio Hearn in International Perspectives* (Folkestone: Global Oriental, 2007), 129–138.

Malcomson, Scott L., 'The Varieties of Cosmopolitan Experience', in Bruce Robbins and Pheng Cheah, eds, *Cosmopolitics: Thinking and Feeling beyond the Nation* (Minneapolis and London: University of Minnesota Press, 1998), 233–245.

Mallarmé, Stéphane, 'Un coup de dés jamais n'abolira le hasard', *Cosmopolis*, 17 (May 1897), 417–427.

Marcus, Sharon, 'Same Difference? Transnationalism, Comparative Literature, and Victorian Studies', *Victorian Studies*, 45.4 (2003), 677–686.

Marholm, Laura, *Modern Women*, tr. Hermione Ramsden (London: Bodley Head; and Boston: Roberts Brothers, 1896).

Marholm, Laura, *The Psychology of Woman*, tr. Georgia A. Etchison (London: Grant Richards, 1899).

Marks, Jason, *Around the World in 72 Days: The Race between Pulitzer's Nellie Bly and Cosmopolitan's Elizabeth Bisland* (New York: Gemittarius, 1993).

Marx, Karl, *The Communist Manifesto*, ed. Frederic L. Bender (New York and London: Norton, 1988).

Marx, Karl, and Friedrich Engels, *Critique of the Gotha Programme* (London: Electric Book Co., 2001).

Matsumura, Hisashi, 'Bin Ueda and Lafcadio Hearn on William Collins', *Otsuma Journal of Comparative Culture*, 5 (2004), 109–135.

Matthews, Brander, 'Concerning Certain American Essayists', *Cosmopolitan*, 13.1 (May 1892), 86–90.

Matthews, Brander, 'More American Stories', *Cosmopolitan*, 13.5 (September 1892), 626–630.

Matthews, Brander, *The American of the Future and Other Essays* (New York: Charles Scribner's Sons, 1910).

Maxwell, Catherine, *Scents and Sensibility: Perfume in Victorian Literary Culture* (Oxford and New York: Oxford University Press, 2017).

Millan, Gordon, 'La Publication d'*Un coup de dés* dans *Cosmopolis*', *Études Stéphane Mallarmé*, 1 (2003), 21–28.

Millaud, Albert, 'Carnet d'un interviewer: Sur le volapuk', *Le Figaro*, 15 February 1888, 2.

Miller, Elizabeth Carolyn, 'William Morris, Print Culture, and the Politics of Aestheticism', *Modernism/Modernity*, 15.3 (September 2008), 477–502.

Mitchell, Rebecca N., 'Oscar Wilde and the French Press, 1880–91', *Victorian Periodicals Review*, 49.1 (2016), 123–148.

Mitford, A. B., *Tales of Old Japan*, 2 vols (London: Macmillan, 1871).

Moch, Gaston, 'Esperanto and the Peace Movement', *Daily News*, 23 September 1905, 4.

Moch, Gaston, *La Question de la langue internationale et sa solution par l'esperanto* (Paris: Giard & Brière, 1897).

Moi, Toril, *Henrik Ibsen and the Birth of Modernism: Art, Theatre, Philosophy* (Oxford: Oxford University Press, 2006).

Monod, Gabriel, 'Le Jubilé des Nibelungen', *Cosmopolis*, 2 (February 1896), 471–493.

Mordell, Albert, 'Introduction', in *Stories from Pierre Loti*, tr. Lafcadio Hearn (Tokyo: Hokuseido Press, 1933), pp. v–xi.

Moréas, Jean, [Letter to the editor], *Le Figaro*, 14 September 1891, 1.

Moretti, Franco, 'Conjectures on World Literature', *New Left Review*, 1 (January–February 2000), 54–68.

Moretti, Franco, 'Evolution, World-Systems, *Weltliteratur*', in Gunilla Lindberg-Wada, ed., *Studying Transcultural Literary Theory* (Berlin: de Gruyter, 2006), 113–121.

Morgan, Peter, 'Literary Transnationalism: A Europeanist's Perspective', *Journal of European Studies*, 47.1 (2017), 3–20.

Moscheles, Felix, *Fragments of an Autobiography* (London: James Nisbet & Co., 1899).

Moscheles, Felix, *In Bohemia with Du Maurier* (London: Fisher Unwin, 1896).

Moscheles, Felix, 'Kion Max Müller diris / What Max Müller said', *The Esperantist*, 1.2 (December 1903), 19–20.

Moscheles, Felix, *Patriotism as an Incentive to Warfare* (London: Hodder & Stoughton, [n.d.]).

Mukherjee, Pablo, 'Introduction: Victorian World Literatures', *Yearbook of English Studies*, 41.2 (2011), 1–19.

Müller, Max, 'Goethe and Carlyle', *Contemporary Review*, 49 (1886), 772–793.

Müller, Max, *Lectures on the Science of Language, Delivered at the Royal Institution of Great Britain, Second Series* (London: Longman, Green, Longman, & Roberts, 1864).

Müller, Max, *The German Classics from the Fourth to the Nineteenth Century: A German Reading-Book* (London: Longman, 1858).

Murray, Paul, *A Fantastic Journey: The Life and Literature of Lafcadio Hearn* (London and New York: Routledge Curzon, 1993).

Mussel, James, '*Review of Reviews* (1890–1936)', in Laurel Brake and Marysa Demoor, eds, *Dictionary of Nineteenth-Century Journalism* (Ghent: Academic Press; London: British Library, 2009), 537–538.

Myers, Rollo, *Richard Strauss and Romain Rolland: Correspondence, Together with Fragments from the Diary of Romain Rolland and Other Essays* (London: Calder & Boyars, 1968).

Nicholls, Angus, 'Max Müller and the Comparative Method', *Comparative Critical Studies*, 12.2 (2015), 213–234.

Niemirowski, Wieńczysław A., *Der Schriftsteller Ola Hansson in Berlin 1890–1893* (Lublin: Wydawnictwo Uniwersytetu Marii Curie-Skłodowskiej, 2000).

Nogai, Kaori, 'The New Bilingualism: Cosmopolitanism in the Era of Esperanto', in Janet Wilson, Cristina Şandru, and Sarah Lawson Welsh, eds, *Rerouting the Postcolonial: New Directions for the Millennium* (London and New York: Routledge, 2010), 48–59.

Noguchi, Yone, *Lafcadio Hearn in Japan* (New York: Mitchell Kennerley; London: Elkin Mathews; and Yokohama: Kelly & Walsh, 1911).

Nordau, Max, *Degeneration* [tr. anon.] (London: Heinemann, 1895).

Nordau, Max, *Paradoxes* [tr. anon.] (Chicago: Schick, 1886).

Norton, Charles Eliot, ed., *Correspondence between Goethe and Carlyle* (London: Macmillan, 1887).

Nussbaum, Martha, 'Patriotism and Cosmopolitanism', *Boston Review*, 19.5 (1994), 1–6.

O'Neill, Morna, *Walter Crane: The Arts and Crafts, Painting, and Politics, 1875–1890* (New Haven and London: Yale University Press, 2010).

Ono, Ayako, *Japonisme in Britain: Whistler, Menpes, Henry, Hornel, and Nineteenth-Century Japan* (London and New York: Routledge, 2003).

Orrells, Daniel, *Classical Culture and Modern Masculinity* (Oxford and New York: Oxford University Press, 2011).

O'Toole, Tina, *The Irish New Woman* (Basingstoke and New York: Palgrave Macmillan, 2013).

Ouida, 'The Genius of D'Annunzio', *Fortnightly Review*, 61 (March 1897), 349–373.

Ouida, 'Unwritten Literary Laws', in *Critical Studies* (London: Fisher Unwin, 1900), 180–200.

Pater, Walter, *Appreciations* (London: Macmillan, 1889).

Pater, Walter, 'Introduction', in *The Purgatory of Dante Alighieri: An Experiment in Literal Verse Translation*, tr. C. L. Shadwell (London and New York: Macmillan, 1892), pp. xiii–xxviii.

Peaker, Carol, 'We are Not Barbarians: Literature and the Russian Émigré Press in England, 1890–1905', *19: Interdisciplinary Studies in the Long Nineteenth Century*, 3 (2006), 1–18 <https://19.bbk.ac.uk/issue/115/info/> [accessed 31 July 2020].

Perkins, P. D., and Ione Perkins, *Lafcadio Hearn: A Bibliography of his Writings* (Boston and New York: Houghton Mifflin, 1934).

Perris, George H., ed., *A History of the Peace Conference at The Hague* (London: International Arbitration Association, 1899).

Perris, George H., *The New Internationalism* (London: International Arbitration Association, [1900]).

Petöfy [sic.], Alexander, 'This Thought Ever Troubles me / Tik at obi egelo vexadom', tr. Madrassy Pál/[George Walters], *Cosmopolitan/Kosmopolan*, 1 (February 1891), 6.

Poliakov, Léon, *The Aryan Myth: A History of Racist and Nationalist Ideas in Europe*, tr. Edmund Howard (London: Chatto, Heinemann, 1974).

Pollen, John, *Rhymes from the Russian, Being Faithful Translations of Selections from the Best Russian Poets: Pushkin, Lermontof, Nadson, Nekrasof, Count A. Tolstoi, Tyoutchef, Maikof, Lebedef, Fet, K. R., etc.* (London: Kegan Paul, Trench, & Trübner, 1891).

Pollock, Sheldon, et al., 'Cosmopolitanisms', *Public Culture*, 12.3 (2000), 577–589.

Posnett, H. M., *Comparative Literature* (London: Kegan Paul, Trench, & Co., 1886).

Posnett, H. M., 'The Science of Comparative Literature', *Contemporary Review*, 79 (January 1901), 855–872.

Potolsky, Matthew, *The Decadent Republic of Letters: Taste, Politics, and Cosmopolitan Community from Baudelaire to Beardsley* (Philadelphia: University of Pennsylvania Press, 2013).

Potter, Simon J., 'Journalism and Empire in an English-Reading World: The *Review of Reviews*', in Joanne Shattock, ed., *Journalism and the Periodical Press in Nineteenth-Century Britain* (Cambridge: Cambridge University Press, 2017), 281–298.

Praz, Mario, *The Romantic Agony*, tr. Angus Davidson (Oxford and London: Oxford University Press, 1970).

Prendergast, Christopher, 'Negotiating World Literature', *New Left Review*, 8 (2001), 100–121.

Prewitt-Brown, Julia, *Cosmopolitan Criticism: Oscar Wilde's Philosophy of Art* (Charlottesville, VA, and London: University Press of Virginia, 1997).

Puchner, Martin, 'Goethe, Marx, Ibsen, and the Creation of a World Literature', *Ibsen Studies*, 13.1 (2013), 28–46.

Ramsden, Hermione, 'The New Mysticism in Scandinavia', *Nineteenth Century*, 47 (February 1900), 279–296.

Ransome, Arthur, 'Introductory Essay', in Théophile Gautier, *Stories by Théophile Gautier*, tr. Lafcadio Hearn (New York: Dutton & Co., 1908), pp. xiii–xxii.

Reed, Christopher, *Bachelor Japanists: Japanese Aesthetics and Western Masculinities* (New York: Columbia University Press, 2016).

Reid, Victoria, 'André Gide's "Hommage à Oscar Wilde" or "The Tale of Judas"', in Stefano Evangelista, ed., *The Reception of Oscar Wilde in Europe* (London and New York: Continuum, 2010), 96–107.

Rein, D. M., 'Howells and the *Cosmopolitan*', *American Literature*, 21.1 (1949), 49–55.

Rem, Tore, *Knut Hamsun: Rejsen til Hitler* (Oslo: Cappelen Damm, 2014).

Rem, Tore, 'The Englishing of *Hunger*: Knut Hamsun, George Egerton and Leonard Smithers', in Bjørn Tysdahl et al., eds, *English and Nordic Modernisms* (Norwich: Norvik Press, 2002), 61–76.

Rhodes, Joseph, 'Progress and Prospects of Esperanto', *North American Review*, 184 (February 1907), 282–291.

Ribeyrol, Charlotte, ed., *The Colours of the Past in Victorian England* (Oxford and Bern: Peter Lang, 2016).

Robbins, Bruce, 'Comparative Cosmopolitanism', *Social Text*, 31/32 (1992), 169–186.

Robbins, Bruce, and Pheng Cheah, eds, *Cosmopolitics: Thinking and Feeling beyond the Nation* (Minneapolis and London: University of Minnesota Press, 1998).

Robbins, Bruce, and Paulo Lemos Horta, eds, *Cosmopolitanisms* (New York: New York University Press, 2017).

Rod, Edouard, 'Le Mouvement des idées en France: l'esprit littéraire', *Cosmopolis*, 2 (February 1896), 447–456.

Rodenbach, Georges, 'The Story of a Portrait in Bruges', *Cosmopolitan*, 18.5 (March 1895), 620–628.
Roggenkamp, Karen, 'Dignified Sensationalism: *Cosmopolitan*, Elizabeth Bisland, and Trips around the World', *American Periodicals*, 17.1 (2007), 26–40.
Roosevelt, Theodore, 'A Colonial Survival', *Cosmopolitan*, 14.2 (December 1892), 229–236.
Rose, David Charles, *Oscar Wilde's Elegant Republic: Transformation, Dislocation, and Fantasy in* fin-de-siècle *Paris* (Newcastle upon Tyne: Cambridge Scholars Publishing, 2015).
Roylance-Kent, C. B., 'The Growth of National Sentiment', *Macmillan's Magazine*, 69 (November 1893), 340–347.
Said, Edward W., *Orientalism* (London and Henley: Routledge & Kegan Paul, 1978).
Sainte-Beuve, Charles Augustin, 'Introduction', in Johann Wolfgang von Goethe, *Conversations de Goethe pendant les dernières annés de sa vie*, tr. Émile Délerot (Paris: Charpentier, 1863), pp. i–xxii.
Sapiro, Gisèle, 'Field Theory from a Transnational Perspective', in Thomas Medvetz and Jeffrey J. Sallaz, eds, *The Oxford Handbook of Pierre Bourdieu* (New York: Oxford University Press, 2018), 161–182.
Sarcey, Francisque, 'Alexandre Dumas', *Cosmopolis*, 1 (January 1896), 171–183.
Sarcey, Francisque, 'Henrick Ibsen', *Cosmopolis*, 6 (June 1896), 738–752.
Sarcey, Francisque, 'In the World of Art and Letters', *Cosmopolitan*, 17.4 (August 1894), 500–502.
Schiller, Friedrich, 'On Naïve and Sentimental Poetry', tr. Julius A. Elias, in H. B. Nisbet, ed., *German Aesthetic and Literary Criticism: Winckelmann, Lessing, Hamann, Herder, Schiller, Goethe* (Cambridge: Cambridge University Press, 1985), 180–232.
Schoolfield, George C., *A Baedeker of Decadence: Charting a Literary Fashion, 1884–1927* (New Haven and London: Yale University Press, 2003).
Schor, Hesther, *Bridge of Words: Esperanto and the Dream of a Universal Language* (New York: Holt & Co., 2016).
Schroda, Julia, '*Cosmopolis*—drei Jahre *Internationale Revue* im Dienst der europäischen Verständigung (1896–98)', in Michel Grunewald and Uwe Puschner, eds, *Krisenwahrnehmungen in Deutschland um 1900: Zeitschriften als Foren der Umbruchszeit im wilhelminischen Reich/Receptions de la Crise en Allemagne au début du XX^e siècle: Les Périodiques et la mutation de la societé allemande à l'époque wilhelmienne* (Bern and Berlin: Peter Lang, 2010), 419–437.
Secor, Robert, 'Henry James and Violet Hunt, the "Improper Person of Babylon"', *Journal of Modern Literature*, 13.1 (1986), 3–36.
Seeley, J. R., *Goethe, Reviewed After Sixty Years* (London: Seeley & Co., 1894).
Shaffer, Elinor, 'Series Editor's Preface', in Stefano Evangelista, ed., *The Reception of Oscar Wilde in Europe* (London and New York: Continuum, 2010), pp. vii–xii.
Sharp, William, '*Keynotes*. By George Egerton', *The Academy*, 1137 (17 February 1894), 143–144.
Shattock, Joanne, ed., *Journalism and the Periodical Press in Nineteenth-Century Britain* (Cambridge: Cambridge University Press, 2017).
Shaw, George Bernard, 'Preface', in Frank Harris, *Oscar Wilde: His Life and Confessions* (London: Constable: 1938), pp. ix–lii.
Shaw, George Bernard, *Shaw's Music: The Complete Musical Criticism*, ed. Dan H. Laurence, 3 vols (London: Max Reinhardt, Bodley Head, 1981).
Shaw, George Bernard, *The Quintessence of Ibsenism* (London: Walter Scott, 1891).
Shepherd-Barr, Kirsten, *Ibsen and Early Modernist Theatre, 1890-1900* (Westport, CT: Greenwood Press, 1997).

Sherard, Robert H., *Oscar Wilde: The Story of an Unhappy Friendship* (London: Privately Printed at the Hermes Press, 1902).

Sikosek, Ziko Marcus, *Sed homoj kun homoj: Universalaj kongresoj de Esperanto, 1905–2005* (Rotterdam: Universala Esperanto-Asocio, 2005).

Simmel, Georg, *Gesamtausgabe*, 27 vols (Frankfurt a. M.: Suhrkamp, 1989–2015).

Simmel, Georg, 'The Metropolis and Mental Life', in Richard Sennett, ed., *Classic Essays on the Culture of Cities* (Englewood Cliffs, NJ: Prentice-Hall, 1969), 47–60.

Sisley, Maurice, 'La *Salomé* de M. Oscar Wilde', *Le Gaulois*, 29 June 1892, 1.

Sjølyst-Jackson, Peter, *Troubling Legacies: Migration, Modernism, and Fascism in the Case of Knut Hamsun* (London and New York: Continuum, 2010).

Sletten Kolloen, Ingar, *Knut Hamsun: Dreamer and Dissenter*, tr. Deborah Dawkin and Erik Skuggevik (New Haven and London: Yale University Press, 2009).

Sluga, Glenda, *Internationalism in the Age of Nationalism* (Philadelphia: University of Pennsylvania Press, 2013).

Spencer, Herbert, *First Principles*, ed. Michael Taylor (London: Routledge/Thoemmes, 1996).

Starr, S. Frederick, 'Introduction', in Lafcadio Hearn, *Inventing New Orleans: Writings of Lafcadio Hearn* (Jackson, MS: University Press of Mississippi, 2001), pp. xi–xxvii.

Starrs, Roy, 'Lafcadio Hearn as Japanese Nationalist', *Japan Review*, 18 (2006), 181–213.

St.-Cère, Jacques, 'A l'Étranger, Scandales partout!', *Le Figaro*, 6 April 1895, 2.

Stead, Estelle W., *My Father* (London: Heinemann, 1913).

[Stead, W. T.], 'Character Sketches: Dr. Zamenhof, the Author of Esperanto', *Review of Reviews*, 32 (September 1905), 255–263.

Stead, W. T., 'Esperanto', *The Esperantist*, 1.1 (November 1903), 1–2.

Stead, W. T., 'The Paris Exposition', *Cosmopolitan*, 29.4 (August 1900), 339–360.

Stetz, Margaret Diane, ' "George Egerton": Woman and Writer of the Eighteen-Nineties' (unpublished doctoral thesis, Harvard University, 1982).

Stetz, Margaret D., '*Keynotes*: A New Woman, her Publisher, and her Material', *Studies in the Literary Imagination*, 30.1 (1997), 90–106.

Stetz, Margaret D., 'New Women Writing beyond the Novel: Short Stories', in H. A. Laird, ed., *The History of British Women's Writing, 1880–1920* (Basingstoke and New York: Palgrave Macmillan, 2016), 215–231.

Stetz, Margaret D., 'Publishing Industries and Practices', in Gail Marshall, ed., *The Cambridge Companion to the Fin de Siècle* (Cambridge and New York: Cambridge University Press, 2007), 113–130.

Stetz, Margaret D., and Mark Samuels Lasner, *The Yellow Book: A Centenary Exhibition* (Cambridge, MA: Houghton Library, 1994).

Stevenson, Elizabeth, *Lafcadio Hearn* (New York: Macmillan, 1961).

Stilling, Robert, *Beginning at the End: Decadence, Modernism, and Postcolonial Poetry* (Cambridge, MA: Harvard University Press, 2018).

Strich, Fritz, *Goethe and World Literature*, tr. C. A. Sym (London: Routledge & Kegan Paul, 1949).

Strich, Fritz, *Goethe und die Weltliteratur* (Bern: Francke, 1946).

Sturgis, Matthew, *Oscar: A Life* (London: Head of Zeus, 2018).

Sturmer, K. R. C., *Esperanto in Literature: Notes and Impressions* (London: Esperanto Publishing, 1930).

Stutfield, Hugh E. M., 'Tommyrotics', *Blackwood's Edinburgh Magazine*, 157 (June 1895), 833–845.

Sutton, Geoffrey, *Concise Encyclopedia of the Original Literature of Esperanto 1888–2007* (New York: Mondial, 2008).

Symonds, John Addington, *Studies of the Greek Poets* (London: Smith, Elder, & Co., 1873).

Symons, Arthur, *The Symbolist Movement in Literature*, ed. Matthew Creasy (Manchester: Carcanet, 2014).

Tagore, Rabindranath, *Nationalism* (New York: Macmillan, 1917).

Thomas, Edward, *Lafcadio Hearn* (London: Constable; Boston and New York: Houghton Mifflin, 1912).

Tintner, Adeline R., 'Rudyard Kipling and Wolcott Balestier's Literary Collaboration: A Possible Source for James's "Collaboration"', *Henry James Review*, 4.2 (1983), 140–143.

Tolstoï, Léon, 'Zola et Dumas', *Cosmopolis*, 3 (March 1896), 761–774.

Tran, Ben, 'Queer Internationalism and Modern Vietnamese Aesthetics', in Mark Wollaeger and Matt Eatough, eds, *The Oxford Handbook of Global Modernisms* (Oxford and New York: Oxford University Press, 2012), 367–387.

Turner, Mark W., '*Cosmopolis: An International Review* (1896–98)', in Laurel Brake and Marysa Demoor, eds, *Dictionary of Nineteenth-Century Journalism in Great Britain and Ireland* (Ghent and London: Academia Press and British Library, 2009), 145–146.

Tydeman, William, and Steven Price, *Wilde: Salome* (Cambridge and New York: Cambridge University Press, 1996).

Vadillo, Ana Parejo, 'Cosmopolitan Aestheticism: The Affective Italian Ethics of A. Mary F. Robinson', *Comparative Critical Studies*, 10.2 (2013), 163–182.

Vadillo, Ana Parejo, 'Cosmopolitan Disturbances: Amy Levy in Dresden', *Forum for Modern Language Studies*, 53.3 (2017), 325–337.

Van Dam, Frederik, 'Resonant with a Whole World of Meaning: The Diplomatic Aesthetic of *Cosmopolis*', *Victoriographies*, 8.2 (2018), 170–186.

Van Puymbroeck, Birgit, '"The Age of Mistaken Nationalism": *Histoire Croisée*, Cross-National Exchange, and an Anglo-French Network of Periodicals', *Modern Language Review*, 107.3 (2012), 681–698.

Venuti, Lawrence, 'Local Contingencies: Translation and National Identities', in Sandra Bermann and Michael Wood, eds, *Nation, Language, and the Ethics of Translation* (Princeton and Oxford: Princeton University Press, 2005), 177–202.

Venuti, Lawrence, *The Translator's Invisibility: A History of Translation* (London and New York: Routledge, 2002).

Vicinus, Martha, 'Rediscovering the "New Woman" of the 1890s: The Stories of "George Egerton"', in Vivian Patraka and Louise A. Tilly, eds, *Feminist Re-Visions: What has been and might be* (Ann Arbor: University of Michigan Press, 1983), 12–25.

Wackrill, Alfred E., 'Gardenurbo—Garden City', *British Esperantist*, 3.4 (April 1907), 74–75.

Walker, John Brisben, 'Introduction: The World's College of Democracy', *Cosmopolitan*, 15.5 (September 1893), 517–527.

Walker, John Brisben, 'The Making of an Illustrated Magazine', *Cosmopolitan*, 14.3 (January 1893), 259–272.

Walkowitz, Rebecca L., *Cosmopolitan Style: Modernism beyond the Nation* (New York: Columbia University Press, 2006).

Walsh, Wm S., 'In the Library', *Cosmopolitan*, 8.3 (January 1890), 380–383.

Walters, George, 'All's Well that Ends Well / Whither?', *Cosmopolitan/Kosmopolan*, 1 (February 1891), 4.

Warren, Arthur, *London Days: A Book of Reminiscences* (Boston: Little, Brown, & Co., 1920).

Wawn, Andrew, 'Early Literature of the North', in *The Oxford History of Literary Translation in English*, 5 vols (Oxford and New York: Oxford University Press, 2005–), iv: *1790–1900*, ed. Peter France and Kenneth Haynes (2006), 274–285.

Westcott, Martyn, 'Esperanto: The Auxiliary International Language', *Womanhood: The Magazine of Woman's Progress and Interests, Political, Legal, Social, and Intellectual, and of Health and Beauty Culture*, 12.72 (1904), 356–360.

Whibley, Charles, 'Spain at the New Gallery', *Cosmopolis*, 3 (March 1896), 678–683.

Whistler, James McNeill, *The Gentle Art of Making Enemies* (London: Heinemann, 1890).

White, Horatio S., 'The Meeting of the Weimar Goethe Society and the New "Faust" MS.', *The Academy*, 31 (1887), 395.

Whiteley, Giles, *Oscar Wilde and the Simulacrum: The Truth of Masks* (Oxford: Legenda, 2015).

Whyte, Frederic, *The Life of W. T. Stead*, 2 vols (London: Jonathan Cape; and New York: Houghton Mifflin, 1925).

Wilde, Oscar, *Essays and Lectures*, ed. Robert Ross (London: Methuen & Co., 1909).

Wilde, Oscar, *Oscar Wilde's Oxford Notebooks: A Portrait of Mind in the Making*, ed. Michael S. Helfand and Philip E. Smith (New York and Oxford: Oxford University Press, 1989).

Wilde, Oscar, *Salome* (London: Limited Editions Club, 1938).

Wilde, Oscar, *Salomé*, ed. Pascal Aquien (Paris: Flammarion, 1993).

Wilde, Oscar, *The Complete Letters of Oscar Wilde*, ed. Merlin Holland and Rupert Hart-Davis (London: Fourth Estate, 2000).

Wilde, Oscar, *The Complete Works of Oscar Wilde*, ed. Ian Small (Oxford and New York: Oxford University Press, 2000–).

Wilfert, Blaise, 'Cosmopolis et l'homme invisible: Les Importateurs de literature étrangère en France, 1885–1914', *Actes de la recherche en sciences sociales*, 144 (2002), 33–46.

Wilfert, Blaise, 'La place de la littérature étrangère dans le champ littéraire français autour de 1900', *Histoire et Mesure*, 23.2 (2008), 69–101.

Williams, Raymond, *Keywords: A Vocabulary of Culture and Society*, rev. edn (New York: Oxford University Press, 1983).

Williams Hyman, Erin, '*Salomé* as Bombshell, or How Oscar Wilde Became an Anarchist', in Joseph Bristow, ed., *Oscar Wilde and Modern Culture: The Making of a Legend* (Athens, OH: Ohio University Press, 2008), 96–109.

Wilson, Ian, *The Third Esperanto Congress* (London: British Esperanto Association, [1908?]).

Wilson, W. Daniel, *Goethe, Männer, Knaben: Ansichten zur 'Homosexualität'* (Berlin: Insel, 2012).

Witt-Brattström, Ebba, *Dekadensens kön: Ola Hansson och Laura Marholm* (Stockholm: Norstedts, 2007).

Wohlgemut, Esther, *Romantic Cosmopolitanism* (Basingstoke: Palgrave Macmillan, 2009).

Wolff, Janet, 'The Feminine in Modern Art: Benjamin, Simmel, and the Gender of Modernity', *Theory, Culture, and Society*, 17.6 (2000), 33–53.

Wollstonecraft, Mary, *Letters written in Sweden, Norway, and Denmark*, ed. Tone Brekke and Jon Mee (Oxford and New York: Oxford University Press, 2009).

Wong, Chin Foo, 'The Chinese in New York', *Cosmopolitan*, 5.4 (August 1888), 297–311.

Wong, Chin Foo, 'Why I am a Heathen', *North American Review*, 145 (August 1887), 169–179.

WReC [Warwick Research Collective], *Combined and Uneven Development: Towards a New Theory of World-Literature* (Liverpool: Liverpool University Press, 2015).

Wyzewa, Téodor de, 'M. Oscar Wilde et les jeunes littérateurs anglais', *La Revue bleue*, 49 (2 April 1892), 423–429.

Yeats, William Butler, 'The Celtic Element in Literature', *Cosmopolis*, 30 (June 1898), 675–686.

Yeats, William Butler, *The Collected Letters of W. B. Yeats*, ed. John Kelly (Oxford: Clarendon Press, 1986–).

Yildiz, Yasemin, *Beyond the Mother Tongue: The Postmonolingual Condition* (New York: Fordham University Press, 2012).

Yung, Judy, Gordon H. Chang, and Him Mark Lai, eds, *Chinese American Voices: From the Gold Rush to the Present* (Berkeley and Los Angeles: University of California Press, 2006).

Zamenhof, Ludwik L., *A Few Words on the International Language 'Esperanto'*, tr. Richard Henry Geoghegan (Uppsala: Nya Tidning, 1898).

[Zamenhof, Ludwik L.] Dr Esperanto, *An Attempt towards an international Language*, tr. Henry Phillips Jr (New York: Henry Holt and Co., 1889).

[Zamenhof, Ludwik L.] Dr Esperanto, *Dr Esperanto's International Tongue*, tr. J. St. [Julius Steinhaus] (Warsaw: Kelter, 1888).

Zamenhof, Ludwik L., *Fundamenta krestomatio de la lingvo Esperanto* (Paris: Hachette, 1903).

Zamenhof, Ludwik L., *Leteroj*, ed. Adolf Holzhaus (Helsinki: privately printed, 1975).

Zamenhof, Ludwik L., *Leteroj de L. L. Zamenhof*, ed. Gaston Waringhien, 2 vols (Paris: Sennacieca Associo Tutmonda, 1948).

Zamenhof, Ludwik L., *Originala Verkaro*, ed. Johannes Dietterle (Leipzig: Hirt & Sohn, 1929).

Zamenhof, Ludwik L., 'The Birth of Esperanto (Freely Translated, from an Esperanto Version of a Private Letter of Dr. Zamenhof Written in Russian, by John Ellis) / Eltiro el privata letero de D-ro Zamenhof al S-ro B., Presita kun permeso de ambaŭ korespondantoj, en jaro 1896. Tradukis el lingvo rusa V. G.', *The Esperantist*, 1.5 (March 1904), 76–78; and 1.6 (April 1904), 87–90.

Zamenhof, Ludwik L., *The International Language 'Esperanto': Complete Instruction-Book with Two Vocabularies*, tr. R. H. Geoghegan (Uppsala: Nya Tidning, 1898).

Zamenhof, Ludwik L., 'What is Esperanto?', *North American Review*, 184 (4 January 1907), 15–21.

Zangwill, Israel, 'Chad Gadya', *Cosmopolis*, 7 (July 1896), 1–17.

Zangwill, Israel, 'Minorities in Literature and Art', *Cosmopolitan*, 21.2 (June 1896), 213.

Zangwill, Israel, *Without Prejudice* (London: Fisher Unwin, 1896).

Zatlin, Linda Gertner, *Beardsley, Japonisme, and the Perversion of the Victorian Ideal* (Cambridge and New York: Cambridge University Press, 1997).

Zhang, Qingsong, 'The Origins of the Chinese Americanization Movement: Wong Chin Foo and the Chinese Equal Rights League', in K. Scott Wong and Sucheng Chan, eds, *Claiming America: Constructing Chinese American Identities during the Exclusion Era* (Philadelphia: Temple University Press, 1998), 41–63.

Zorn, Christa, 'Cosmopolitan Shaw and the Transformation of the Public Sphere', *Shaw*, 28 (2008), 188–208.

Zweig, Stefan, *Die Welt von Gestern: Erinnerungen eines Europäers* (Frankfurt a. M.: Fischer, 2010).

Zweig, Stefan, 'Lafcadio Hearn', in Lafcadio Hearn, *Das Japanbuch: Eine Auswhal aus den Werken von Lafcadio Hearn* (Frankfurt a. M.: Rütten & Loening, 1919), 1–12.

Zweig, Stefan, *The World of Yesterday: Memoirs of a European*, tr. Anthea Bell (London: Pushkin Press, 2011).

# Online Sources

http://www.1890s.ca
http://www.goethe-gesellschaft.de/netzwerk.html

# Index

For the benefit of digital users, indexed terms that span two pages (e.g., 52–53) may, on occasion, appear on only one of those pages.